SPONSORED BY

Katie Shu Sui Pui Charitable Trust

（本系列丛书由舒小佩慈善基金赞助）

| 酒店及旅游业管理系列教材 |

主编 邱汉琴

THE HONG KONG
POLYTECHNIC UNIVERSITY
香港理工大學

Hospitality and Tourism Human Resource Management

酒店及旅游业
人力资源管理

韩晓莹（Alice Hon）/著

ZHEJIANG UNIVERSITY PRESS
浙江大学出版社

图书在版编目(CIP)数据

酒店及旅游业人力资源管理 = Hospitality and Tourism Human Resource Management：英汉对照/ 韩晓莹著.—杭州：浙江大学出版社，2019.5

ISBN 978-7-308-16287-6

Ⅰ.①酒… Ⅱ.①韩… Ⅲ.①饭店—企业管理—双语教学—高等学校—教材—英、汉②旅游业—人力资源管理—双语教学—高等学校—教材—英、汉 Ⅳ.①F719.2②F590.652

中国版本图书馆 CIP 数据核字（2016）第 240898 号

酒店及旅游业人力资源管理

Hospitality and Tourism Human Resource Management

韩晓莹（Alice Hon）　著

责任编辑	樊晓燕
责任校对	袁菁鸿
封面设计	春天书装
出版发行	浙江大学出版社
	（杭州市天目山路 148 号　邮政编码 310007）
	（网址：http://www.zjupress.com）
排　　版	杭州林智广告有限公司
印　　刷	杭州杭新印务有限公司
开　　本	787mm×1092mm　1/16
印　　张	21
字　　数	403 千
版 印 次	2019 年 5 月第 1 版　2019 年 5 月第 1 次印刷
书　　号	ISBN 978-7-308-16287-6
定　　价	72.00 元

总　序

　　香港理工大学酒店及旅游业管理学院已经有 40 多年的历史。学院致力于引领全球酒店及旅游教育的发展，无论在科研还是教学等方面，都在全球享有较高知名度，尤其是在发表学术研究文献方面，在全球位列第二，在教与学方面，亦处于国际领先地位。学院 65 位教职人员来自 22 个国家和地区，着重教学创新与研究。学员能够在多元文化环境下追随国际知名的学者学习有着良好职业前景的学科。2011 年，香港理工大学的教学及研究酒店——唯港荟正式启用，强化了学院的人才培育工作，以满足香港地区内以至全球酒店及旅游业界对专业人才的殷切需求。

　　"酒店及旅游业管理硕士学位课程"是引进了国际、国内最前沿的教育理念，为从事旅游业研究与实践的业界人士而开设的学历教育课程。该课程自 2000 年与浙江大学合办以来，依托世界一流的香港理工大学和浙江大学的教学资源，已经培养了 600 多位政府各级官员、业界管理人才以及学术界科研精英。课程通过综合的、先进的知识为学生提供了宏观的视野，让学生在具有扎实的工作经验的基础上，提高经营管理的深度，建立超前的意识，发展系统地解决问题的能力。

　　虽然香港理工大学酒店及旅游业管理学院的酒店及旅游业管理硕士学位课程取得了一定的成功，为业界培养了优秀人才，但是在办学的过程中，我们深刻地意识到教材资源的缺乏。因此，香港理工大学具有优秀双语能力的教授等师资人员专门为"酒店及旅游业管理硕士学位课程"设计

Prelude

With more than 40 years' history, the School of Hotel and Tourism Management (SHTM) at The Hong Kong Polytechnic University (PolyU) is positioned to lead the world's hospitality and tourism education in the years to come. It has high reputation in both academic research and teaching. Especially, the School is ranked No. 2 in the world among academic institutions in hospitality and tourism based on research and scholarly activities. In terms of teaching and learning, it is also in a leading position. With a faculty of 65 academic staff members from 22 countries and regions, the School offers innovative teaching and research in a creative learning environment. Students are able to study in a multicultural context and to learn from an internationally renowned faculty whose programmes provide outstanding career opportunities. The official opening of the teaching and research hotel—Hotel ICON in 2011 has further strengthened the School's efforts in nurturing hospitality graduates to address the growing demands of the hospitality and tourism industry in Hong Kong, the region, and around the world.

The MSc in Hotel and Tourism Management is a programme designed for hotel and tourism practitioners, with the aim of introducing latest education concept in Hong Kong and internationally. Since 2000, the programme has been offered collaboratively by the Hong Kong Polytechnic University and Zhejiang University, which has cultivated more than 600 government officials, industry managers, and academic talents. The programme provides students with a macro perspective from the comprehensive and advanced knowledge, improves the ability of management, and establishes advanced awareness, as well as develops systematic problem-solving skills based on solid work experience.

了一套中英文对照双语教材——"酒店及旅游业管理系列教材"。本系列教材包括《中国内地酒店及旅游业》《酒店及旅游业人力资源管理》《酒店及旅游业财务管理》《酒店及旅游业研究方法》以及《酒店及旅游业市场营销》。这种双语式的硕士学位课程教材在酒店及旅游业管理专业的研究生教育历史上是具有开创性的,充分体现了我们开办该课程的特色与进一步构建更好的教学交流平台的愿望。该系列教材的开发和推出,将有力地促进香港理工大学与浙江大学的双语课程的持续发展。同时,我们也期待该系列教材可以有助于中国内地日益成熟的旅游管理学硕士(MTA)市场的发展。中国的各行各业已逐渐趋向于国际化,旅游教育更是如此,我们希望这套双语教材的问世将会对内地的旅游教育起到促进作用。

最后,作者要特别感谢舒小佩慈善基金的全力资助,该基金的慷慨资助使得本系列教材得以面世。舒小佩女士寄语并祝福每位读者都能在书中找到自己的"黄金屋",并为响应国家的"一带一路"倡议做出最好的准备。

丛书总编

邱汉琴教授

香港理工大学酒店及旅游业管理学院

Although the programme of MSc in Hotel and Tourism Management offered by SHTM-PolyU has been highly successful and has cultivated many talents for the industry, we are fully aware of the lack of bilingual teaching and learning resources during the process of delivering these courses. Therefore, professors, who have excellent bilingual competencies from The Hong Kong Polytechnic University, have designed and developed this bilingual book series for this programme, including *Hospitality and Tourism in Chinese Mainland*, *Hospitality and Tourism Human Resource Management*, *Hospitality and Tourism Financial Management*, *Hospitality and Tourism Research Methods*, and *Hospitality and Tourism Marketing Management*. The uniqueness of this bilingual book series is that it is the first time that such book series were created for a bilingual master degree in hotel and tourism education history, which fully represents the characteristics of this programme and also acts as an interaction platform for students and teachers to interact in order to enhance the teaching and learning experiences. The development and introduction of the bilingual book series is not only to promote the sustainable development of bilingual programme offered by The Hong Kong Polytechnic University and Zhejiang University, but also to look forward to facilitating the development of the increasingly mature market of Master of Tourism Administration (MTA) in Chinese Mainland. Nowadays, various industries in China have been gradually internationalized and we hope that the introduction of the bilingual book series will play a significant role in enhancing tourism education in the Mainland.

Last but not least, the authors wish to express their sincere gratitude to the Katie Shu Sui Pui Charitable Trust for its financial support in making the project of publishing of the Bilingual Hotel and Tourism Management Book Series a reality. They also hereby acknowledge Ms. Shu's wish for each reader to find his/her own dream career by making the best use of the material in the book series in preparation for China's Belt and Road Initiative as a result.

Managing Editor

Hanqin Qiu

Professor

School of Hotel and Tourism Management

The Hong Kong Polytechnic University

C ONTENTS
目 录

C ONTENTS
目 录

第 1 章　酒店业的人力资源管理

学习目标

- 了解什么是酒店业的战略人力资源
- 了解酒店业员工聘用的特点和挑战
- 通过研究成果和案例了解酒店业的战略如何制定

人力资源管理在影响企业竞争力和效能方面扮演了至关重要的角色。这里指的是企业的实践、政策方针和系统，都影响着员工的行为举止、态度和表现(Tracey,2014)。在过去的几十年里，学科本位的关于人力资源管理的研究已经有相当显著的发展。这段时期，研究学者们越来越多地去关注人力资源的主体功能，从而更深入地了解何种特定类型的政策、实践活动和过程方式，才可能会对员工个人、团队以及企业层面的成果产生一系列的影响(Hon、Bloom、Crant,2014;Hon 和 Leung,2011)。除此之外，对战略维度应用的关注度也越来越高，由此去深入了解如何利用人力资源系统达成关键商业目标。现已有更新、更全面的人力资源实践出现。基于独立实证研究的结果，学者们提出了大量独特见解，涉及人力资源系统的本质，以及如何设计并将其应用于企业，进而帮助企业提升竞争地位。

将人力资源应用在酒店业相关研究的做法显露出日益上升趋势，并已有成果发表。许多专注于酒店人力资源管理的研究都从直接和间接两方面展开进行，目的是将调查范围由广义整体转向酒店环境中。然而，尽管此类研究的贡献比较有限，但这些成果在评估更多基础研究的适用性方面很有帮助。不过，酒店人力资源管理研究相关的学者们将更多的兴趣点放在检测变量及变量之间的关系方面，这和劳动密集型企业及作为服务业的酒店业的设置具有独特相关性(Hon,2013;Hon 和 Chan,2013)。诸如此类的研究的确

Chapter 1　Human Resource（HR）Management in the Hospitality Context

The objectives of this chapter

- Understand what is hospitality strategic human resources
- Investigate the characteristics and challenges of hospitality staffing
- Understand strategic hospitality setting through research findings and case studies

Human resource management（HRM）plays a key role in determining the competitiveness and effectiveness of a firm. HRM refers to the practices, policies and systems that influence employees' behaviour, attitudes and performance (Tracey, 2014). The discipline-based research on HRM has developed considerably over the past decades. Scholars have become increasingly interested in learning more about the ways in which specific types of HR policies, practices and procedures influence an array of individual, team and firm-level outcomes (Hon, Bloom & Crant, 2014; Hon & Leung, 2011). In addition, there has been growing interest in the use of strategic lenses to learn how HR systems may be leveraged to achieve key business objectives. New and more comprehensive HR practices have been presented, and empirical research findings have generated numerous insights into the nature of HR systems and how they can be designed and implemented to help companies improve their competitive position.

These trends can be seen in the HR research in hospitality-specific sectors. Many of the hospitality-specific HR studies have been conducted—either explicitly or implicitly—to determine the extent to which findings from the general domain apply to hospitality contexts. Although the contributions of this type of study are generally quite modest, the results have been helpful in assessing the applicability of the more general frameworks. However, there appears to be a growing interest among hospitality HR scholars to examine the factors and relationships that may be particularly relevant to the labour-intensive, service-focused settings that characterise the hospitality industry (Hon, 2013; Hon & Chan, 2013; Tracey, 2014). These studies not only provide a basis for examining the extent to which the findings from the general HR domain may extend to hospitality settings, they also offer a foundation for developing new models that account for the distinctive nature of hospitality contexts (Hon, 2012a; 2012b; Hon & Lu, 2016).

引人注目,因为其不仅为将检测范围从综合角度延伸到酒店情景设置中提供了依据,而且为建立新模型打下了基础,这些模型能为酒店人力资源管理提供解释说明(Hon,2012a;2012b;Hon 和 Lu,2016)。

酒店战略人力资源

近期战略人力资源研究呈现的两大主要趋势都在酒店业中明确显现出来。首先,酒店业研究的学者们调查并证实了植入人力资源公司和绩效之间的各类作用关系,且发表的研究结果已扩展到一般的人力资源领域。举例来说,Tsai 等(2009)的近期研究检测了一系列高绩效工作运行政策、企业级别人员流动和生产力(被当作个人销售业绩)之间的关联。实验样本数据来源于 161 家台湾餐厅及酒店,结果表明,高绩效工作运行政策和企业级别绩效中的两个关键指标之间具有显著相关性。同时,在企业级别雇佣模式运作下全职员工和兼职员工之间的比例显示,其似乎可以调整人力资源与绩效间的关系。具体地说,Tsai 等(2009)指出,"承诺性"政策(例如关注奖赏和赞誉)和提高全职员工利用率有显著相关性;"控制性"政策(例如关注技能培训)和提高兼职员工、外部员工利用率呈显著相关。Tsai 等(2009)也发现,雇用模式和单元级绩效措施呈正相关。这些成果和其他有关战略人力资源行业的研究成果(例如,Chand,2010;Chang 等,2011)都提供了对"复杂型"人力资源绩效关系的额外见解,特别是对人力资源实务进行了剖析,从而为跨行业设置和分段的关键绩效指标的显著差异性做出了解析。

酒店的人员配置

在酒店环境中,对人力资源的注意力大多集中在个人技能和竞争力上(Brownell,2008;Gursoy 等,2008)。学者们的研究焦点并不是在人员数量的挑战上,而是愈来愈多地关注人员的发展技能和竞争力,这可能对广大酒店的人员配置有所帮助(Bharwani 和 Jauhari,2013;Brownell,2008;Gursoy 等,2008;Testa 和 Sipe,2012),同时可能和特定行业部门(DiPietro 等,2007;Fjelstul 和 Tesone,2008)及其选址(Chan 和 Coleman,2004;Haven-Tang 和 Jones,2008)有关联。除此之外,从相关但更广泛的意义来说,酒店研究方向的学者们也观察了其他方面,即个人竞争力可能会影响员工的工作态度、行为举止以及绩效,这将贯穿其职业生涯的不同阶段(Newman 等,2014;Walsh 和 Taylor,2007)。这些研究结果突出强调进一步观察对特定产业的竞争力有相关影响的需求。特别是,有证据显示,个人性格特征分析,例

Strategic Human Resources in Hospitality

Two key trends have emerged from recent strategic HR studies that are specific to the hospitality industry. First, hospitality scholars who have examined various links embedded in the HR-firm and performance have not only confirmed, but also extended the findings that have been published in the general HR domain. For example, a recent study by Tsai, *et al*. (2009) examined the links between a set of high-performance work practices and employee turnover and productivity (operationalised as sales per employee). Using data from a sample of 161 Taiwanese restaurants and hotels, the results showed that high-performance work practices were significantly related to firm perfomance, and that the unit's firm's employment mode, operationalised as the ratio of full-time to part-time employees, appears to mediate the focal HR-performance relationship. Especially, Tsai *et al*. (2009) found that "commitment-based" practices (e. g. focus on rewards and recognition) were significantly related to the use of more full-time staff, and that "control-based" practices (e.g. focus on technical training) were significantly related to the use of more part-time, external staff. Tsai *et al*. (2009) also found that employment mode was positively correlated with measures of unit performance. These results, and those presented in several other industry-specific strategic HR studies (e.g. Chand, 2010; Chang, *et al*., 2011), provide additional insights into the "complex" nature of the HR-performance relationship, particularly the profiles of HR practices that account for significant variance in the key performance indicators across industry settings and segments.

Staffing in Hospitality

In hospitality settings, a great deal of attention is given to individual skills and competencies. However, rather than focusing on headcount challenges, hospitality scholars have focused on developing skill and competency profiles that may be useful in a wide range of hospitality staffing (Bharwani & Jauhari, 2013; Brownell, 2008; Gursoy, *et al*., 2008; Testa & Sipe, 2012), and those that may be relevant to specific industry segments (DiPietro, *et al*., 2007; Fjelstul & Tesone, 2008) and locations (Chan & Coleman, 2004; Haven-Tang & Jones, 2008). In a related but slightly broader manner, hospitality scholars have also examined the ways in which individual competencies may influence their job attitudes, behaviour and performance throughout various stages in one's career (Newman, *et al*., 2014; Walsh & Taylor, 2007). These findings highlight the need to further examine the relative influence of industry-specific competencies, especially in light of the evidence showing that characteristics such as general mental ability and conscientiousness are among the best predictors of employee performance across a wide range of contexts. Another trend in hospitality staffing research that is consistent with trends in the general staffing literature is the growing attention to online

如判断其一般心理（智力）能力和责任心，是预估员工绩效的最佳工具，这适用于诸多不同领域。与其他一般性人员配置的文献著作的研究方向相似，酒店员工配置研究的另一个趋势则是越来越多地关注于线上招聘，尤其是利用社交媒体及其时效性（Chang 和 Madera，2012；Madera，2012；Millar，2010；Zelenskaya 和 Singh，2011）。此外，众多学者使人们对通过何种招募政策方式和手段去吸引某些特定类别的申请者有更好的认识（Dermody 等，2004），并且也加深了人们对采取怎样的招募政策可提升申请者对品牌及公司形象的认知力的了解（Hurrell 和 Scholarios，2014；Yen 等，2011）。这些研究成果皆格外引人注目，同时强调了我们对多学科框架的需求，以此来阐述酒店招聘体系的作用和影响。

从现有的科研选题可以看出，酒店研究方向的学者们关注的焦点话题与学科化学者们相近，其专注于各类个体特征带来的影响，包括一般心理能力和性格特征（Tracey 等，2007；Tews 等，2011）、诚信（Sturman 和 Sherwyn，2009）以及外貌体态（Tews 等，2009）。此外，学者们尝试去观察与服务密集型环境显著相关的因素，如客户服务能力（Costen 和 Barrash，2006）。另外，与上述成果相符，酒店研究方向的学者们已经开始探索新的各类招聘及选拔人才的渠道，其也许可以通用于全球，尤其是在亚洲（Chan 和 Kuok，2011；Sun 等，2013）。

最后，学者们将相当多的精力放在与招聘相关的各类挑战上，从而在日趋多样化和竞争"白热化"的劳动力市场中选拔出优秀个体（Gröschl，2007；Houtenville 和 Kalargyrou，2012；Jasper 和 Waldhart，2013）。诸多调查结果显得尤为重要，其表明了在特定人力资源管理实践中核算外部因素的重要性。举例来说，当经济景况良好时，市场对劳动力的需求就会逐步增长。在此状况下，酒店企业会需要将更多资源投入招聘及采取留用措施中，来寻找能帮助企业实现增长目标的个体。然而，当劳动力市场状况松散、需求量下降时，人员培训和发展的措施就可能会与达到关键商业目标的关系更紧密，其将会为达到提升员工个人能力和技巧这一目的提供一些新机会。该措施对取得大量经营业务上的以及与客户相关的成果至关重要。因此，了解关于人力资源管理灵活性的最新研究，有助于我们洞察对适应性人力资源实践的需求，以及这类政策对具体的酒店行业人员聘用情况的影响。

酒店人员战略布局

文献研究表明，整体市场和单一酒店市场培训之间有些相似之处，值得

recruiting, particularly the use of social media and its timeliness (Chang & Madera, 2012; Madera, 2012; Millar, 2010; Zelenskaya & Singh, 2011). Hospitality scholars have extended our understanding of the ways in which recruiting practices may attract specific types of job applicants (Dermody, et al., 2004), and have enhanced our understanding of the ways in which recruitment practices may affect broader perceptions about the brand and image of the firm (Hurrell & Scholarios, 2014; Yen, et al., 2011). These findings are particularly noteworthy and reinforce the need for multi-disciplinary frameworks to explain the roles and effects of hospitality recruiting systems.

In terms of selection research, hospitality scholars have focused on many of the same topics as discipline-oriented scholars. Substantial attention has been given to the effect of various individual characteristics, including general mental ability and personality (Tracey, et al., 2007; Tews, et al., 2011), integrity (Sturman & Sherwyn, 2009) and physical appearance (Tews, et al., 2009). Efforts have been made to examine the factors that may be especially relevant in service-intensive settings, such as customer service capabilities (Costen & Barrash, 2006). In addition, and consistent with the efforts noted above, hospitality scholars have explored the ways in which various recruitment and selection methods may be used in various cultural contexts, particularly Asia (Chan & Kuok, 2011; Sun, et al., 2013).

Finally, considerable attention has been given to the challenges associated with recruiting and selecting individuals from increasingly diverse and more competitive labour markets (Gröschl, 2007; Houtenville & Kalargyrou, 2012; Jasper & Waldhart, 2013). These findings are particularly important in that they demonstrate the importance of accounting for the external factors of specific HR practices. For example, when economic conditions are positive, the demand for labour generally increases. Under these conditions, hospitality firms may need to dedicate more resources to recruitment and retention practices to find individuals who can help the organisation achieve its growth objectives. However, when labour market conditions loosen and demand goes down, training and development practices may be more important for achieving key business objectives. This type of situation provides an opportunity for employers to upgrade or enhance the employee skills that are critical for achieving a number of important performance and customer-related outcomes. Thus, it may be beneficial to consider some of the emerging research on HR flexibility (Way, et al., 2013) to gain insights into the need for adaptive HR systems and the implications of such systems for specific HR practices, particularly staffing.

The Strategic Setting in Hospitality

There are several noticeable similarities in the topics that have been examined in the general training research literature and those that have been published in hospitality-specific outlets. First, several studies have examined the nature and effect of specific

我们注意。首先,部分研究针对特定类别培训的实质和影响进行调查,也正如我们所料,调查内容反映的主题与酒店布局显著相关。除多样性外(Madera 等,2011),研究调查包括食品安全(Murphy 等,2011)、客户服务(Butcher 等,2009)以及环保知识和人脸识别能力(Magnini 和 Honeycutt,2005)。这些课题为个人能力研究提供了重要信息,这些能力对部分类型的酒店职位和工作安排来说可能至关重要,因此值得深入探究。同时,可以将其纳入培训项目来辅助关键职位的工作。同样地,站在设计的立场上,酒店研究方向的学者们研究了若干教学方法和教学过程(Chen 和 Tseng,2012;Magnini,2009;Sobaih,2011;Torres 和 Adler,2010),包括利用技术辅助解决方案(Kim 等,2011b;Lema 和 Agrusa,2009;Singh 等,2011;Zakrzewski 等,2005)。这些研究提供了若干重要且互补的关于各类实现效果和设计特色的见解,同时,与之前调查得到的启示很相似,其论证了将个体在态度、能力、学习行为以及其他培训效果上的差异纳入整体考量的必要性。

在酒店培训的相关文献中,另一引人注目的话题就是员工个体以及情境因素对关键培训成果的影响。举例来说,Roberts 和 Barrett(2011)针对为餐饮服务领域的培训提供管理支持的因素进行了研究。研究结果显示,员工个人对食品安全培训的态度很可能会对日后的训练行为产生重大影响(例如必要项目的执行)。连同相关领域已发表的诸多研究成果(Ellis 等,2010;Frash 等,2010;Kalargyrou 和 Woods,2011;Tews 和 Tracey,2009;Chew 和 Wong,2008;Zhao 和 Namasivayam,2009),这些研究提出了一些对影响因素更全面、深刻的理解,即这些影响因素可能会左右个体在培训的筹备过程、学习过程中的表现,以及是否能将已获得的知识和技能应用到工作中去。再者,与先前得到的启示相一致的是,一部分影响因素与酒店组织(例如"服务质量文化")有关,由此而言,日后研究应予以考虑。

从关于不同个体培训的效果和组织产出结果的研究成果中,我们可以得出相似的结论(Chiang 等,2005;Choi 和 Dickson,2010;Costen 和 Salazar,2011;Ubeda-Garcia 等,2013)。这些研究成果强调了利用更广泛、多样化途径去开展设计并植入有效的学习系统的必要性,同时说明了在未来的研究中,调查研究特定行业情景因素的必要性,其可能减缓或加速预期结果的实现。

酒店绩效评估

与其他实用性课题相比,关于酒店绩效评估的研究较少。在该研究领域

types of training, and, as would be expected, the content reflects topics that are particularly relevant to hospitality settings. In addition to diversity (Madera, *et al.*, 2011), studies have examined food safety (Murphy, *et al.*, 2011) and customer service (Butcher, *et al.*, 2009) as well as environmental knowledge and face recognition abilities (Magnini & Honeycutt, 2005). These studies provide important details about the individual qualities that may be essential for some types of hospitality jobs and work settings, and thus should be accounted for and incorporated into training programmes that support the focal positions. Similarly, from a design standpoint, hospitality scholars have examined the utility of a number of instructional methods and procedures (Chen & Tseng, 2012; Magnini, 2009; Sobaih, 2011; Torres and Adler, 2010), including the use of technology-enabled solutions (Kim, *et al.*, 2011b; Lema & Agrusa, 2009; Singh, *et al.*, 2011; Zakrzewski, *et al.*, 2005). These studies provide several important and complementary insights into the efficacy of various implementation and design features, and, similar to the implications noted above, demonstrate the need to account for individual differences in attitudes, abilities and behaviour associated with learning and other important training outcomes.

Another topic that has received considerable attention in the hospitality training literature is the effect of individual and contextual factors on key training outcomes. For example, Roberts and Barrett (2011) conducted a study on the antecedents of managerial support for training in food service settings. The results suggested that an individual's attitude toward food safety training may have a significant effect on future training behaviour (e.g. implementing needed programmes). These findings, along with those of several related studies (Ellis, *et al.*, 2010; Frash, *et al.*, 2010; Kalargyrou & Woods, 2011; Tews & Tracey, 2009; Chew & Wong, 2008; Zhao & Namasivayam, 2009), provide a more comprehensive understanding of the factors that may influence an individual's preparation for training, performance during the learning experience and the transfer of acquired knowledge and skills back to the job. Moreover, and consistent with the implications noted above, some of these factors may be particularly relevant to hospitality organisations (e.g. climate for service quality), and thus should be considered in future research.

Similar conclusions can be drawn from studies that have examined the effect of training on various individual and organisational outcomes (Chiang, *et al.*, 2005; Choi & Dickson, 2010; Costen & Salazar, 2011; Ubeda-Garcia, *et al.*, 2013). These results reinforce the need to use a broad, multi-faceted approach to designing and implementing effective learning systems, and demonstrate the need for future research that examines industry-specific situational factors that may mitigate or enhance the desired results.

Performance Appraisal in Hospitality

In comparison to the other functional topics, the research on hospitality

现在有两个主要趋势。

第一个趋势,与一般绩效评估类的研究相似,学者们持续调查来自多种渠道反馈结果的用途和效用(Law 和 Tam,2008;Patiar 和 Mia,2008;Sharma 和 Christie,2010),包括"核心自我评估"、这些评估结果与其他绩效指标是如何关联的以及个人工作业绩(Karatepe,2011;Karatepe 和 Demir,2014;Karatepe 等,2010)。

第二个趋势,着重关注影响整体反馈过程的因素。尽管很有限,但这些研究已找出若干因素,例如社会强化作用(Weisman,2006)、非言语行为表现(Hinkin 和 Schriesheim,2004)和酒店设置的类型(Noone,2008),这些都可能影响绩效评定的过程和结果。此外,很多因素可能与各类行业都显著相关,因此在日后研究中这些应成为主要课题。

酒店薪酬及福利

与绩效评估和鉴定相关研究的情形很相似,酒店薪酬及福利的研究受到的关注相对有限。少数该领域的研究集中在以下两方面。第一,着重在薪酬制度的多面性与员工个人特征(比如动机)(Wu 等,2013)、组织公平(McQuilken 等,2013;Wu 和 Wang,2008)、性格特征(Aziz 等,2007)和相关特性(Hon,2012b)之间的关系。第二,着重在薪酬政策的组织影响力(Moncraz 等,2009;Namasivayam 等,2007)、行业分布(Torres 和 Adler,2012)以及侧重饭店方面(Barber 等,2006;Guillet 等,2012;Miller,2010;Murphy 和 DiPietro,2005)。最后,学者们尝试对外部影响力在薪酬制度上的作用进行调查并做出解释(Croes 和 Tesone,2007;Kline 和 Hsieh,2007;Sturman 和 McCabe,2008)。这些研究特别说明需要进行额外的研究,研究要将特殊环境因素的挑战考虑进去(例如技能要求、员工流动率、人工成本等),它可能会影响关于各类薪酬和福利政策的策略及运作。

显而易见的是,"一个适合所有人"的策略在人力资源管理中并不适用。近期关于人力资源管理的研究对业界的第一个启发是调查检测意外突发事件和变化,这可以指出怎样执行人力资源职能才可以全力辅助公司经营战略,并且这些经营理念将会进一步强化概念基础。例如,在人力资源战略领域,一些类型的人力资源政策(比如集中式与分散式、重创新与重成本等)很有可能更适合某些类型的酒店,但对其他类型而言似乎并不适合(例如全方位服务与限定服务、多元化企业与独立运营企业、国际性的与本土的,等等)。相似的是,一些用在选择决策中(例如一般心智能力和个人性格特征)的个人

performance appraisal has been rather limited. There are two primary trends in this research domain.

First, and consistent with the general performance appraisal research, scholars have continued to examine the use and utility of feedback from multiple sources (Law & Tam, 2008; Patiar & Mia, 2008; Sharma & Christie, 2010), including "core self-evaluations" and how these assessments relate to other indices of performance and individual work outcomes (Karatepe, 2011; Karatepe & Demir, 2014; Karatepe, et al., 2010).

The second stream of research in this area has focused on factors that affect the overall feedback process. Although limited, these studies have identified several factors, such as social reinforcement (Weisman, 2006), non-verbal behaviour (Hinkin & Schriesheim, 2004) and the type of hospitality setting (Noone, 2008), that may influence the procedure and outcomes of performance assessment. Again, many of these factors may be relevant across a variety of industry contexts, and thus should be the subject of future research.

Compensation and Benefits in Hospitality

Similar to the research on performance appraisal and evaluation, the research on hospitality compensation and benefits has received comparatively limited attention. The few studies in this domain have addressed only two areas of inquiry. The first area focuses on the links between various facets of compensation systems and individual characteristics, such as motivation (Wu, et al., 2013), organisational justice (McQuilken, et al., 2013; Wu and Wang, 2008), personality (Aziz, et al., 2007) and related characteristics (Hon, 2012b). The second area focuses on the organisational effect of compensation practices (Moncraz, et al., 2009; Namasivayam, et al., 2007) and industry segment (Torres & Adler, 2012) with particular emphasis on restaurants (Barber, et al., 2006; Guillet, et al., 2012; Miller, 2010; Murphy & DiPietro, 2005). Finally, there have been a couple of attempts to examine and account for external influences on pay systems (Croes & Tesone, 2007; Kline & Hsieh, 2007; Sturman & McCabe, 2008). These findings clearly demonstrate the need for additional research that considers the particular contextual challenges in the hospitality setting (e. g. skill requirements, employee turnover rates, costs of labour etc.) that may influence the strategic and operational effect of various compensation and benefits practices.

It is clear that a "one-size-fits-all" approach in human resource management is not appropriate. The first implication of recent HRM research is that existing conceptual foundations would be enhanced by the examination of additional contingencies and situational variables that may indicate how an HR function can be implemented to fully support a firm's strategic and operational objectives. For example, within the strategic HR domain, it is likely that some types of, or profiles of, HR practices (e.g. centralised versus decentralised; innovation-focused versus cost-focused, etc.) are better suited to certain types of hospitality settings than others (e.g. full-service versus limited service

因素,相比其他类型(例如低复杂性职位与高复杂性职位)而言,对部分类型的工作来说更高效。在培训及绩效评估范畴,越来越多的证据表明,多元化个体和相关职能的因素都可能调节或缓和焦点性人力资源政策与相关成果之间的关系。

第二个重要的启示是,可以改变人力资源体系和政策,以应对酒店产业的动态性。事实上,研究人力资源灵活性的报告表明,大量竞争的作用力可能直接或间接影响人力资源体系及政策的效能。举例来说,使用临时工或合同工对高变动性和季节性的企业来说可能更有效;反之,其他类型的企业更需要高比例的全职员工,来确保理想的客户服务目标能以一个持续且高效的方式实现。

与此同时,学者们应深入思考各色人力资源方针政策之间关系的本质,以采取应对酒店业的不可预见性及多变性的政策。例如,针对新员工培训的数量和种类将依赖于严格的人事程序。除此之外,新近招聘绩效反馈的频率和类型将取决于初级培训的类别及质量。因此,日后的研究须基于近期成果之上,即阐明如何量化人力资源灵活性及其意义(Way 等,2013),还有如何将人力资源系统设计及应用在酒店业中,从而在不同的组织层级中实现效能最大化。

结　论

在过去几十年里,人力资源领域的研究有着相当显著的发展。以上论述表明了学科本位的人力资源研究与专一酒店方向的人力资源研究两者之间具有众多相似之处。两个领域中已发表的研究成果为人力资源功能性的战略及运营提供了强有力的支持,研究发现拓展了我们对企业人力资源系统的理解,系统可能用来提高个体、部门和组织机构的整体绩效。此外,人们越来越了解各类情境因素的本质及影响力——机构组织内部及外部环境,这些都将可能影响企业人力资源政策和实践的效力。这些成果对建立起更广泛、更具行动力的社会角色有很大帮助。

然而,尽管人力资源在所有类型工种中都占据重要地位,但和其他性质

settings; multi-unit versus independent operations; international versus local; etc.). Similarly, it is likely that some individual factors used in selection decisions (e.g. general mental ability and personality characteristics) may be more effective for some types of jobs than others (e.g. lower complexity versus higher complexity positions). In the training and performance appraisal fields, there is growing evidence that various individual and work-related factors may mediate or potentially moderate the relationships between the focal HR practices and relevant outcomes.

The second major implication is that HR systems and practices can be adapted in response to the dynamic nature of hospitality settings. Indeed, research on the HR flexibility construct has shown that a wide array of competitive influences may have direct and/or indirect influence on the effectiveness of any HR system or practice. For example, the use of contract or contingent workers may be very effective for companies that operate in highly unstable or seasonal settings, whereas some settings may require a higher percentage of full-time employees to ensure that desired customer service objectives are met in a consistent and high-quality manner.

Similarly, consideration should be given to the nature of the relationships among the various HR practices that are implemented in response to the unpredictable and changing nature of hospitality settings. For example, the amount and type of training that is needed for new employees will depend on the rigor of the staffing procedures that attract and hire individuals for open positions. In addition, the frequency and type of performance feedback that is most relevant for new hires may depend on the type and quality of the initial training. Therefore, future research can build on the recent work that has clarified the meaning and measurement of the HR flexibility construct (Way, et al., 2013), and examine the ways in which HR systems may be designed and used in hospitality settings to maximise performance at different organisational levels.

Conclusion

The HR field has evolved considerably over the past decades. The above review shows that there is a great deal of similarities in the HR research in discipline-based and hospitality-specific fields. Studies in both domains provide strong and compelling support for the strategic and operational relevance of the HR function, and the findings have expanded our understanding of the ways in which a firm's HR system may be leveraged to enhance individual, departmental and organisational performance. In addition, there is growing understanding of the nature and influence of various situational factors-within and outside the organisational context-that may influence the effect and utility of a firm's HR policies and practices. These results have been instrumental in developing more comprehensive and actionable explanations of the roles that the HR function can play.

However, although HR is clearly an important function in all types of work settings,

的企业相比,企业人力资源系统的某些方面对酒店业来说意义更重大。服务的无形性和季节性、需求波动、依赖低薪和低技能工人、高固定成本以及相关行业特点,这些因素都对酒店业人力资源管理提出了诸多独特的挑战。正因为如此,酒店业人力资源学者们才需要更进一步观察劳动密集型、服务密集型产业的显著特点,由此推断怎样的政策方针、实践及系统最实用,影响最显著。这样做,将加深我们对高效的酒店人力资源系统的概念性理解,并且将为制定更具可行性的管理指导方针打下基础。

案例研究 1-1[①] ▶▶▶▶▶▶

银座酒店(Silver Hotel)是一家联合经营的旅游酒店,坐落于广东珠海市。酒店内员工基本来自当地的旅游学校。酒店近期聘请了 20 位新员工承担一系列不同的职责。大约 20 位已雇员工在酒店管理、行政、餐饮、接待、维修及其他部门任职。

案例讨论 ▶▶▶▶▶▶

银座酒店于 2007 年正式投入运营,为四星级酒店,拥有 130 间客房,包括标准间、小套房及豪华套房。根据一年中不同时段,酒店大约拥有 50%～80% 的入住率。酒店内配有若干餐厅、会议室、会议大厅,以及美容美发沙龙、小型艺术廊。虽然该酒店更倾向于接待商务人士,但是也愿意接待度假游客。当然,酒店也提供多样化的娱乐设施及观光指南。所有房间都有互联网接入,这点对招徕商务人士显得十分重要。

这里着重讨论五个在中国服务行业中普遍存在的典型问题。首当其冲的是员工薪资问题,该酒店薪资水平低于其他行业以及更高评价的酒店,尽管和其他同等大小的酒店相比是相差不多的。许多酒店的利润率偏低,在如此激烈的市场竞争中,成本竞争力是必须被考虑的因素。薪资是个问题,但若能有保障地维持固定收入,其就可作为留住员工的相当有效的工具。其二,是在行业内留住人才的问题,这与薪水紧密相关,要考虑到其他行业中存

---

① 资料来源:Davies, D., & Wei, L.(Eds).(2011). *Human Resources Management in China: Cases in HR Practice*, 120-126. Oxford England: Chandos Pub.

emerging evidence suggests that some aspects of a firm's HR system may be more relevant to hospitality companies than to other types of firms. The intangible nature of services, seasonality and demand fluctuations, reliance on low-wage, low-skill workers, high fixed costs and related industry characteristics present the hospitality industry with several industry-specific HR challenges. Therefore, hospitality HR scholars need to take a closer look at the characteristics that are particularly salient in labour-intensive, service-focused settings and determine which HR polices, practices and systems may have the most utility and effect. Doing so will enhance our conceptual understanding of effective hospitality HR systems and provide a basis for developing more actionable guidelines for management.

Case Study 1 – 1[①] ▶▶▶▶▶▶

Silver Hotel is a combined business and tourist hotel, located in Zhuhai, Guangdong. The normal source of employees for the hotel is the local Hotel School. The hotel recently hired 20 new employees to work in a range of functions. About 20 of the existing employees work in management roles and in the areas of administration, catering, reception and maintenance, among others.

Disussions ▶▶▶▶▶▶

The hotel commenced operations in 2007. It is a four-star hotel with 130 rooms, ranging from standard to deluxe rooms to small suites. Depending on the time of year, the hotel has an occupancy rate of 50% to 80% of its capacity. It has a number of restaurants, meeting rooms and conference rooms, a beauty salon and a small art gallery. Although it tends to cater more to business people, it is quite happy, obviously, to take holidaymakers. Various recreational facilities are available and local tourist advice is provided. All of the rooms have Internet access, which is viewed as an important incentive for business travellers.

Silver Hotel has five problems that are characteristic of China's service industry in general. The first is staff salaries; they are low compared to what is offered in many other industries and in higher rated hotels, although they are equivalent to other similar-sized hotels in the area. Many hotels work on a low profit margin, and as competition may be fierce, cost competitiveness is a factor that must be examined. Salary is an issue, but it may also be used as an effective tool in retaining staff if the employees can maintain a guaranteed regular income. The second problem, which is strongly related to salary, is staff retention, as there are higher-paid opportunities in many other industries. The third issue is

---

① Source: Davies, D., & Wei, L.(Eds).(2011). *Human Resources Management in China: Cases in HR Practice*, 120 – 126.Oxford Egland: Chandos Pub.

在更高报酬的机会。其三,则是企业文化,员工应协助公司实现其经营目标,跟随其发展方向,同时实现个人职业目标。其四,是员工在酒店内晋升机会有限。类似酒店这类较小型的企业很难为员工提供一条明确的职业道路,同时,管理层面的机会也很受限,升职空间较小。最后一个问题是就业保障,这依赖于产业的稳定性,其受整体经济波动的影响,以及一年中的不同时段,与职位空缺率也有关联。以上每个问题在下文都会进行详细的讨论研究,接下来首先要研究的是员工薪酬与激励。

1. 薪酬与激励

银座酒店倾向于将本企业员工的薪水与同等级别酒店、同级别城市或区域的酒店相比较。这个过程建立在一个基准体系上,以确保该酒店在同级别酒店中具有竞争力。尽管该酒店员工薪水相对丰厚,但员工依旧觉得所付出的劳动与取得的收入不成正比,或者说没有得到足够的奖励。尽管存在晋升机会和职业道路受限的问题,但考虑到提供给员工的其他福利,酒店认为自己给出了合理且具诱惑力的薪酬方案。这些福利包括就业保障、员工餐厅、奖励杰出员工的免费旅行。当然,员工培训也包含在内,下文会在关注职业发展的部分进行详细讨论。举办种类繁多的社会活动也会使员工对酒店产生归属感,以此来实现对出色员工承诺的奖励。酒店正在考虑实施一个员工争夺赛的月计划项目,从而鼓励员工间友好竞争。尽管奖品并不贵重,但这能让员工们为自己取得的商业成绩感到自豪。

酒店提供给员工的各类培训方案包括职业道德、人力资源管理和领导技能等领域,还有各类与自身职位相关的专业技能培训。内容涵盖许多方面,例如,如何准确服务客户、应用于酒店的新型计算机系统、酒店区域和场地的维护。当员工表现出可以晋升到管理层的潜质时,类似管理和发展类的相关培训就会陆续提供给他们。虽然岗位空缺并不会一直存在,但重点在日后机遇。一旦员工经过了适当的培训,他将有更出色的表现,这也是一种激励方式。

2. 酒店内部文化

酒店文化承担着在组织中规划共同愿景和建立行为规范的角色。该酒店的目标就是成为珠海最佳的商业酒店,这样的理念在员工间传播开来,促

that of corporate culture; employees are expected to follow the direction of the company and assist it in achieving its goals and objectives. The fourth issue is the limited availability of opportunities for promotion for hotel employees. A small company, such as a hotel, cannot provide a distinct career path for all of its employees, and as management opportunities are limited, there is minimal scope for promotion. The final issue is that of employment security. This tends to be dependent on the stability of the industry, which is susceptible to fluctuations in the economy and the time of year. These five problems are the major areas of concern for this hotel and its employees. Each of these problems is examined in more detail below.

Remuneration and Motivation

Silver Hotel tends to compare the salaries paid to its employees with those paid to equivalent staff in hotels of a similar standard within the city and the region or province. This process is done through a benchmarking system, which ensures that the company is competitive with hotels of a similar ranking. Although the employees are comparatively well paid, they would probably say that for the work they do, they do not get sufficient money or other incentives. The hotel, however, believes that the other employee benefits it provides, despite the lack of promotion opportunities and career paths, comprise a very reasonable and attractive package. These benefits include job security, a staff canteen and free trips for excellent employees. Training, discussed below, is also provided, with a focus on employees' career development. Various social activities are provided to make employees feel part of the hotel's extended family. These allow the hotel to reward the commitment of its better employees. A hotel employee of the month programme is being considered for future implementation in an attempt to encourage some friendly competition. Although the award will not be an expensive one, it will allow employees to be proud of their achievements in the business.

Various training packages are provided to staff, including training in such areas as ethics, human resources management, leadership skills and various technical skills directly related to the employee's position within the organisation. These cover topics such as how to serve customers correctly, new computer systems that are applicable to the hotel and maintenance of the hotel areas and grounds. If an employee shows potential to move into management, training in areas related to future managerial positions is provided. Although a vacancy may not exist, the opportunity to fit into a position in the future is emphasised. Acting in a higher grade role can also be an incentive for an employee once appropriate training has been provided to that person.

Culture within the Hotel

The role of culture within the hotel is to establish a shared vision within the organisation and to create some behavioural norms within the hotel environment. The mission of the hotel

使他们与时俱进。这将使持续改善的整体进程融入酒店内部文化中,当然这也意味着提高了对全体员工的要求。管理层人员借助绩效管理系统,认可和表彰努力工作以提高顾客服务质量和顾客体验的员工。

对顾客体验的关注要求员工成为细节导向型人才。换句话说,酒店管理层要求员工关注在细微却十分重要的细节上,从而提升客户服务质量以及改善客户体验。客户服务包括客房清洁、客房服务满意度的电话回访,如果有需要的话,甚至包含协助客户解决问题、重新预订机票等。提倡员工对客户的问题持有主人翁意识,待人如待己。

这样的主人翁理念将延伸至酒店的各个层级,从管理层至设施提供部门。每位员工各持有一个信箱,酒店鼓励他们发表促进酒店发展的意见和观点,同时,让他们也参与到经营和管理中去。若某位员工的想法被管理层采纳,则该员工将得到奖金作为嘉奖。奖金额度由该建议的价值及其效果决定,当然奖励也不一定全是经济上的。

管理层试图让每位员工对酒店都有家的归属感。举例来说,若某员工生病且需要照顾的话,酒店将安排人员专门照料;若是住院治疗的话,将安排人员前往探病。尽管可能只是一个问候的电话,但却让员工们深深感到自己是大家庭的一分子,并且企业是真切关心他们的。如此方法,可以营造并保持关切员工安危的良好氛围,进一步增强酒店的"家庭氛围"。同时,也可以帮助员工减少孤独感,让他们感到自身是受到重视的。

3. 员工晋升与保留

由于酒店本身是相对小型的组织,很多员工的职业道路可能会受限。因此酒店需要考虑的事情之一就是扩张发展,即开发或接管本区域甚至全国的其他酒店。为了进一步实现这个目标,酒店希望所有员工能提升核心竞争力。紧接着,学习掌握核心竞争力又可以让员工在更广阔的环境下工作,同时,促使企业提供更多的晋升机会。管理层人员相信,如此做法可以让企业在竞争激烈的市场中占有不败之地。这些核心竞争力包括建立团队的能力、专业技术能力、市场营销能力、沟通技巧和人员管理能力。虽然他们意识到

is to become the best business hotel in Zhuhai. The message sent to the staff is to improve a little bit every day. This is expressed through continually incorporating improvements into the hotel culture, and continually raising the targets to be achieved by all of the hotels' employees. A performance management system is used to recognise the efforts of staff to provide better customer service or a better experience in the hotel.

This focus on customer experience requires employees to be detail-oriented. In other words, the management of the hotel asks the staff to focus on the little but important details that improve customer service and customers' perception of the hotel. These can be the cleanliness of the room, a follow-up call to determine if room service has been satisfactory or even assistance in resolving a problem or re-booking a flight if needed. The employees are given a sense of ownership of the guest's problems, and treat them as if they were their own.

This sense of ownership extends to other areas within the hotel, even those related to the management and facilities. Employees have a mailbox in which they are encouraged to give their views and ideas about improvements that can be made to the hotel. They are also invited to give ideas to management about the running of the hotel. If any of employee suggestions are adopted, the employee who makes the suggestion is given a bonus. The size of the bonus varies depending on the value and result of the suggestion, and it may not necessarily be a monetary award.

Management tries to make employees feel as if they are part of an extended family within the hotel. As an example, if an employee is sick, the hotel will send another member of staff to assist in looking after the sick person if this is needed, or to visit them if they are hospitalised. Although generally only a social call, it makes the employees feel as if they are a valued member of the hotel community and that the company does care about their welfare. This approach helps to create and maintain a system of caring for the individual employees, which further enhances the family-focused atmosphere of the hotel. This can also work to make employees feel less alone and like a valued employee as well as a part of the larger hotel family.

Promotion and Retention

As the hotel is only a small organisation, career paths for many of the employees may be limited. One thing that the hotel is looking at is expansion, to open up or take over other hotels in the area even throughout China. To further this goal, the hotel wishes all of its staff to promote certain core competencies. It is hoped that learning these core competencies will allow the employees to operate in a larger environment, and enable the company to create more opportunities for promotion. Management also believes that this would enable the business to gain a competitive advantage over its competition. Examples of the core competencies that the hotel would like all of its employees to have include team-building skills, technical skills, marketing skills, communication skills and people management skills. Although they realise that not all employees can attain all of these skills, they believe that a

并不是所有人都能掌握这些技能,但考虑到企业扩张的需要,使更多人具有竞争力是必要的。因此,他们选择着重培训选定出来的优秀员工。

为了协助员工获得某些技能,以及识别出员工知识水平的合理区间,同时也为了避免员工在同一职位持续工作而产生厌烦感,岗位轮换是必要的。这并不是强制性的,如果他们希望的话,员工享有拒绝职位调动的权利,因此部分员工可能更倾向于留在某一岗位,但若接受的话,该规定可以允许他们拓展酒店及经营方面的知识储备,成为更具价值的员工。对员工离职这一情况来说该政策显得尤为重要,因为其很有可能导致酒店内某些特殊且必要的技能人才的缺乏。该政策也可以让复合型人才依据需要安排进适合的岗位,与此同时着力建立起自动的新老接替计划。

为了辅助激励员工,良好的领导才能与沟通能力是酒店管理中相当重要的能力。奖金附加对员工的称赞是最常用来激励员工的手段,尽管管理层早已意识到其局限性。同时,晋升或者培训可以让员工有机会进入管理层,这也是激励员工高效能开展工作的有效途径。另一有效手段是带领员工参加外部活动,员工还可携带家属,参加与商业经营无关的活动,包括烧烤、野餐、其他社会活动或体育运动等。这能让员工们更感激企业本身,日积月累,也更珍惜这份工作。

4. 员工流动率

即使酒店尽其所能地使用上述诸多方法去挽留员工,员工流动率依旧居高不下。其中占很大比例的是一线员工,即处于初级阶段的新进员工。例如,酒店某些部门的员工,如清扫房间的员工,一年里流动率高达百分之百。如此高的流动率对酒店业或是其他相似的服务行业来说,尽管并非很不寻常,但始终让人难以接受。

造成较高的员工流失率的原因并非是单一的,其中部分可能来自酒店文化,因为该酒店相对年轻,而且雇用了很多新员工。尽管一个年轻的酒店不具备成熟的文化,但是,发展一种新的酒店文化可能比改变已存在多年的文化容易些。

再来看管理层,部分基层部门经理获得的薪资虽然和其他同级别酒店的薪资相差很小,但很可能由于长期待在同一个部门而产生疲倦感,进而想要寻求新的开始。该现象可能是因为他们在工作中缺乏挑战,缺少职能变换。另一个原因是企业刚刚起步,需要大量新进员工。这类员工大都缺乏相关工作经验,他们可能不具备适合的或是正式的任职资格,且如果他们认为自己的能力不符合工作要求,就会在岗位上缺乏自信。这些都会导致他们去寻求其他企业、其他层级的岗位,找到与他们的技能更相符的职位。

widespread competence in these areas is needed for the proposed expansion. As a result, they are training selected staff members.

To assist employees to obtain some of these skills and to identify possible gaps in employees' knowledge, job rotations with appropriate training is also provided. This prevents staff from becoming bored with performing the same role on a continual basis. This is optional, and staff have the right to decline any new placement, as some staff may prefer to remain doing the same job. However, if accepted, such rotations allow them to extend their knowledge of the hotel and the business and to become more valuable to the organisation. This is especially important in instances of employee departure, which could result in a shortage of a particular necessary skill for the hotel. A multi-skilled employee can be slotted into other positions as required, while the hotel works to build an automatic succession plan.

Good leadership skills and communication are important in motivating staff. Bonuses plus praise are the most commonly used tool to motivate staff, although the hotel managers realise that these tools have limitations. Promotion and training that can lead to promotion can also be effective tools to motivate high performers.

Another motivational tool is to take employees and their families on external activities that are not related to the business. These may include barbeques or picnics, or other social and sporting activities. Such activities can make employees appreciate the organisation and value the work that they do on a daily basis.

Staff Turnover

Although the hotel tries its best to retain staff using a number of the initiatives mentioned above, staff turnover is still reasonably high. The majority of staff turnover tends to be in the first line of employment, which is the entry phase for most of the new staff. For example, in some departments within the hotel, such as those staff who prepare the rooms, staff turnover can be as high as 100% over a twelve-month period. This rate of turnover is not that unusual for hotels and similar service industries, but it is still an unacceptable rate.

There appears to be no single reason for this high turnover of staff. One reason could be the culture of the hotel, as it is relatively new and is hiring many new employees to work for it.Although a new hotel does not have a very mature culture, developing a new culture is possibly easier than changing an old culture that has been in place for many years.

At the management level, some line managers, who are paid a rate similar to that offered for a similar position in other hotels, may look for a fresh establishment to work for because they lack challenge and variety in their position. Another reason for the high turnover may be that, as the company is newly established, it has a large number of new and relatively inexperienced employees. They may not have the proper or formal qualifications, and if they consider themselves under-qualified, they may lack confidence in their jobs. This may make them look for a position in another company at a level that they feel matches their skills, despite the training that they were given when commencing at the hotel.

5. 其他奖赏制度

除去薪水和病假工资,酒店额外提供给员工其他的奖励。这包括员工若完成任务会获得月奖金,任务是借助员工评估程序且在员工与管理层之间达成一致的情况下设定的。与此同时,也要设定年终目标,若达到,将获得额外的年终奖励。若月任务和年终目标都达到了,则将在年底获得更为丰厚的年终奖。这是持续性的绩效评估及测评方式,以月或年为基准单位。

总　结

本次研究调查了一定数量存在于中国的诸多酒店及其他服务行业的问题。许多员工认为服务业只是一份兼职工作,并会寻找其他领域的职位。这同样也适用于许多其他国家。

本次案例研究着重讨论了造成上述问题的某些原因。许多人认为是因为薪资不足,也有部分人认为是缺乏职业生涯管理的规划。尽管都配以相应的员工培训,此类看法始终存在。组织机构试图建立起企业文化并促进其发展,若这些措施能有所成效,不仅员工流动率将降低,管理层人员流动率也会随之下降。

问　题

(1) 请评价案例研究 1-1 中该酒店政策上的优劣势。

(2) 你将如何解决案例研究 1-1 中该酒店的这些问题?请给出详细说明。

Other Incentives

In addition to salary and sick pay, the hotel provides other incentives to its employees, including a monthly bonus if the employee reaches a target that is mutually set between the employee and the management through a staff appraisal process. There is also a yearly target set for the employees and if this target is achieved, they are then provided with an additional bonus for the year. The realization of combined monthly and yearly targets can provide a substantial end-of-year bonus. This programme provides a form of continuous performance appraisal or assessment that is carried out on a monthly and yearly basis.

Conclusion

This study examines a number of problems that exist in many hotels and related service industries in China. Many staff members believe that the service industry offers only part-time jobs, and they will therefore look for positions in other areas. In China, as in other countries, this is becoming a problem in this industry, as a stronger focus is being placed on service and hospitality in China's developing economy.

The reasons for some of these problems have been highlighted in the case study. Many employees view the remuneration as insufficient, while others think that the industry lacks sufficient career paths. Although training is given, this perception still remains. The organisation is attempting to build a culture that will lead to growth, but it remains to be seen if these efforts succeed and whether staff turnover, not only in the lower ranks in the organisation but also at the higher management level, can be reduced.

Questions

(1) Evaluate the pros and cons of the policies in this hotel.

(2) How would you solve the problems of this company? Please provide detailed explanations.

第 2 章　战略人力资源管理中的领导力

学习目标

- 了解各种领导理论的原则
- 了解不同类型的领导风格
- 通过研究成果和案例探究领导风格的效用

领导力是能够影响、支配他人想法及行为的个人能力(Hon、Bloom 和 Grant,2014)。从心理学上讲,领导者的能力通常体现在他所领导的团队中,领导者能引导及推动整个团队完成既定目标。领导者的角色就是激励、管理下属尽可能地朝着目标前进(Dessler,2017)。在组织内部,领导者可以称作主管或经理,掌握一定权力,凭借个人出色的能力,由企业所有人任命。领导者借助对下属的奖惩、资源配置、专业知识、处理人际关系等途径来实现其功能(Dessler,2017)。将这些诸多因素整合在一起就是所谓的管理风格,即采取有效措施实现下属效能最大化(Dessler,2017)。

早期领导力方法的观点认为性格占有重要地位。此方法论认为领导力是与生俱来的,而非经过后天培养。性格理论指出具有某些特征才是成功的领导者——智力过人、正直不阿、顽强毅力等。后来的研究从行为方式角度展开,在实际工作环境中观察领导与下属的行为活动,以此来发掘怎样的领导行为才是更高效的。该方法论将领导分为两类。

(1)员工中心理论——强调重视人员内部关系、个人偏好、需求、下属个人能力。领导者认为需要帮助下级提升能力,且给予他们更宽松的、而不是严密的监管。

Chapter 2   Leadership in Strategic Human Resources Management

The objectives of this chapter

■ Understand the principles of various leadership theories

■ Understand the types of leadership styles

■ Examine the effectiveness of different leadership through research findings and case studies

Leadership is the ability of a person to influence the thoughts and behaviour of others (Hon，Bloom & Grant，2014). In psychological studies，a leader is usually defined in terms of the group he or she leads; the leader is the person who directs and controls the group so that the purposes of the group can be achieved. An official leader is a person who motivates and directs subordinates to work towards goals that are regarded by the organisation as desirable and possible. In an organisation，the official leader may be called a supervisor or manager，and possesses authority because he or she has been appointed by the owners of the company and because of his or her competence to hold the post. Official leaders have power over subordinates through their right to punish or reward，control of resources，knowledge of the job，skills in handling people etc. The way these factors are combined creates a management style; a manager should adopt a consistent management style to achieve the best results from subordinates (Dessler，2017).

Early approaches to leadership took the view that the personality of the leader was all-important: leaders were born，not made. This approach compiled lists of the personal qualities (e.g. intelligence，mindedness，sympathetic) that were expected in a successful leader. More recent work on leadership has been conducted from a behavioural point of view; leaders and their subordinates are studied in actual work situations to discover whether certain kinds of leadership behaviour are more effective than others. This research has identified two types of leaders.

(1) Employee-centred supervisors emphasise interpersonal relationships，and the preferences，needs and capabilities of individual subordinates. The supervisor believes in helping subordinates to get promotions and in giving them relaxed rather than close supervision.

（2）工作中心理论——强调严格监管及控制，包括任务进行的节奏和方法。依照规定，按时完成任务是该理论的典型特征。

倾向工作中心的领导者视下级为工作的一部分，由他们解决或执行一定任务（Dessler，2017）。而领导者将对他们进行严格、精确的指导和掌控，并采用金钱方式来给予奖励。而倾向员工中心的领导者则一视同仁，并不向员工施加过多的权威。他们鼓励下级表达个人想法，而制定主要决策则是上级主管的职责。另一种假设是在没有过多严密的监管下，下级的表现会更为出色，例如任务本身就具有激励作用，下级会因为能实现更高的自我需求而感到满意。

判断哪种管理风格最高效的重要因素是任务结构——工作任务界定或规划的明确程度。大部分案例依赖于领导技巧，将其分为两个具有代表性的任务结构来阐述最为恰当。

（1）高结构性任务，例如批量生产工厂的流水线作业，其工作部署的时间和方法都有严格的规定。每位员工都有明确、详细的分工，且必须严格按规定执行才能恰当配合其复杂的工厂作业系统，员工只有少量决策权。

（2）开放性、松散式任务，则是相对广义的概念，该风格给予员工大量决策权及任务执行的灵活性。有些时候任务本身并不明确，可以用多种手段完成既定目标。下级有较大的空间，可根据个人偏好进行选择。

费德勒的"领导效能"理论

费德勒认为尽管一般情况下"任务结构"模式对结构性工作十分有效，但对于开放式任务、在主管与下属之间关系较差、领导者权力薄弱的情况下，则"领导效能"模式将更有效果（Dessler，2017）。接下来他的理论肯定了在一般情况下"员工导向"模式对开放式任务更适宜，但若工作任务更结构化、领导权力更强，则"领导效能"模式效果将更显著，不过该模式似乎并不受欢迎。

费德勒的理论分析使用了四个变量因素：（1）强调任务本身或员工个体；（2）任务结构；（3）领导者与成员之间的相互关系；（4）领导者的职位权力。其理论认为管理风格要想更高效，需要考虑到领导技巧、社会关系以及领导者职位高低等因素。

在此之后，他的领导权变理论方法表明，不存在某单一管理风格适用于所有情境。更准确地说，领导风格须根据特定情境按需要进行变化，因此，领

(2) Production-centred supervisors closely supervise and control subordinates, both as to the pace and method of work. The need to get the work done on time is continually emphasised.

Managers who emphasise production regard subordinates as factors of production at his or her disposal for performing a certain task (Dessler, 2017). Such managers will direct and control subordinates in precise terms, and their reward for accepting this supervision is monetary payment. Managers who emphasise people regard subordinates almost at equals and do not exercise strict authority over them. The manager assumes that they have ideas to contribute and that it is part of the leadership function to draw out these ideas. Another assumption is that they will produce good work without close or detailed supervision, i.e. that the job itself provides part of the motivation, perhaps by satisfying higher needs.

An important factor determining which particular management style is effective is the task structure—the extent to which the work is defined or programmed. Task structure in most cases depends on the technology, and is best illustrated by describing its two extremes.

(1) Structured or highly programmed work, e.g. assembly-line work in a mass-production factory, is strictly defined as to method and time. Each individual job is specialised and must be carried out as defined so that it may fit into a complex production system. There are few work decisions the subordinates can make.

(2) Unstructured or loosely programmed work is defined in very broad terms and gives subordinates a large number of decisions regarding methods and sequence. Sometimes the task itself is rather vague, and there may be many possible ways of accomplishing it. The subordinate is often given the freedom to choose the methods he or she prefers.

Fiedler's Theory of Leadership Effectiveness

Fiedler suggests that although in general the task-centred approach is best for structured work, it may also be effective when the work is unstructured, relations between the manager and subordinates are poorer when the manager's formal powers are weak (Dessler, 2017). The theory goes on to confirm that in general, the people-centred approach is best for unstructured work, but this approach may also be effective when the work is structured and the manager is powerful but not well-liked.

Fiedler's analysis use four variables: (1) emphasis on task or people; (2) task structure; (3) manager-subordinate relationships; and (4) the power of the manager. The analysis shows that to be effective, management style should take account of technology, social relationships and the manager's place in the organisation.

Subsequently, the contingency approach to leadership asserts that there is no single management style that can be relied on to be completely effective in all situations.

导者要根据具体情况调节其领导行为。

自我领导与自我管理型团队

现代职场多关注团队协作。在此情况下,无论面对是否具有吸引力的工作任务时,员工大多都能够自我激励,并能够判断哪些团队成员更能胜任这项任务。自我管理型团队的优势包括更低的监管成本、对整体工作更高的热情。在某些工作情境中,企业降低了对领导力的需求,这包括以下诸多因素:

(1)组织机构特点,即具有凝聚力的团队省去了对领导力的依赖,以及形式化的工作流程(其带来的效果就是团队成员无须就如何履行职责向上级请示)。

(2)工作特点,例如常规工作、对任务的意见反馈,或是对工作的兴趣度和满意度。

(3)员工特点,具有丰富经验的、被培训过的及具有主观能动性的员工大都不需要他人指导。既专业又有能力的员工通常能够管理好自身。

X-Y 理论

道格拉斯·麦格雷戈(Douglas McGregor)提出了关于员工行为的两种截然相反的观点,称为 X-Y 理论(Dessler,2017)。

(1)X 理论,即人们基本上都厌恶工作,会试图逃避责任,并且必须用严格的控制或是威逼利诱才能使人们工作。

(2)Y 理论,即工作是一种天性,是受欢迎的行为,只要员工得到足够的激励,就不需要使用极端控制的手段,且员工会主动寻求责任感,在解决问题时提供有价值的帮助。

X 理论认为较低层次的需要支配着个人的行为,而 Y 理论的管理态度则能够满足个人较高层次的需求,特别是自我意识和自我价值实现的需求。一个人的工作应该建立在完整自我发展的基础之上。

交易型与变革型领导

近期关于领导力的研究总结了交易型领导和变革型领导之间的关系。交易型领导通过高效的组织尽可能提供给下属足够的技术和资源支援,去帮助他们完成既定目标,但并不会为了提高员工的忠诚度而试图改变其工作态

Rather, a leader's style should be varied to meet the needs of the particular situation. Thus, leaders must be prepared to adjust their behaviours as situation change.

Self-leadership and Self-managed Teams

Modern workplaces are focusing more on work teams. According to this view, employees are quite capable of motivating themselves to perform unappealing as well as appealing tasks and to determine which group members are best qualified to complete particular duties. The advantages of self-managed teams include lower supervision costs and higher levels of employee interest in the work of the organisation as a whole. The need for leadership can be mitigated in many workplace situations by a number of factors.

(1) Organisational characteristics such as cohesive work groups that remove the need for supportive leadership, and the formalisation of work procedures (which results in group members not needing to ask a leader how to perform duties).

(2) Job characteristics e. g. routine duties, feedback within a task and/or interestingness and satisfaction of the work.

(3) Employee characteristics. It is unlikely that workers who are experienced, trained, willing and able will need to be led. Professionally qualified employees are normally capable of looking after themselves.

Theory X and Y

Douglas McGregor describes two contrasting assumptions about the behaviour of employees, called theory X and theory Y (Dessler, 2017).

(1) Theory X takes the view that the average employee dislikes work, will try to avoid responsibility and will only be made to work by a mixture of close control and threats.

(2) Theory Y assumes that work is a natural and welcome activity that need not be externally controlled if the employee is adequately motivated, that employees will seek responsibility and that they can give valuable help in solving work problems.

Theory X gave employees the opportunity to satisfy only basic and security needs at work, but a theory Y management attitude enables them to satisfy higher needs, in particular ego and self-actualisation needs. A person's job should be based on complete self-development.

Transactional and Transformation Leaders

Recent research into leadership has drawn a distinction between transactional and transformational leaders. Transactional leaders organise work efficiently and provide subordinates with the assistance and resources necessary for them to complete their duties, but do not attempt to transform employees' attitudes to increase their

度。相反地,变革型领导大都魅力非凡,具有远见卓识,能激励、鼓舞下属为超越目标而加倍努力。

参与、赋能授权与工作生活质量

参与度是提高公司员工工作生活质量的重要组成部分。管理中的"工作生活质量"大体包括改善工作条件、增强公司内部人际互动、增强员工工作自主性、确定工作任务、介绍员工职业生涯发展、由员工自主解决问题、更好的领导风格和人际关系、减压项目以及整体提升企业文化。提高工作生活质量的作用就是使员工的工作更有效率,使他们能主动地去享受工作过程。

赋能授权就是授予员工独立完成任务和目标的权力,消除了不断向上级请求指示的过程,信任员工能做出合情合理的决定(Hon 和 Rensvold,2006)。例如,赋予销售人员额外的权力,允许他们为潜在客户提供特殊折扣优惠;团队拥有决定使用公司资源的程度与强度的权力。此手段就是释放给员工更多的权力,让他们能更高效地解决问题,排除上级监管的干扰,提升企业管理能力。

赋能授权不仅是将权力按等级由上而下释放,而且能推动员工个体有更出色的表现。其效果表现在(Hon 和 Rensvold,2006):

- 鼓励激发个体创造力和主动性,对企业及团队充满使命感;
- 适当程度地采纳决策;
- 对客户的要求能更快、更灵活地反应;
- 员工自信程度更强、积极性更高;
- 促进管理层与一线员工之间的人际关系;
- 从一线员工那里获得更有价值的想法;
- 对客户投诉建议有所准备;
- 及时修正错误。

执行赋能授权时需要注意的是,选拔招募员工的时候要比在常规情境时投入更多的培训指导。员工可能会做出错误的决定,顾客可能会被区别对待等,这些将导致未接受额外恩惠的员工心生怨念,甚至整个企业管理方案都要重新制定,才能保证系统高效运转。

commitment to the firm. Transformational leaders, conversely, possess charisma, vision and the ability to inspire subordinates to transcend their self-directed goals.

Participation, Empowerment and the Quality of Working Life

Participation is an important ingredient of any program intended to improve employees' quality of working life (QWL). Other elements of a QWL scheme might include the improvement of environmental conditions, increasing the flow of communication within the organisation, employee involvement in target setting, job design, introduction of staff development systems, having employees solve workplace problems, better leadership styles and interpersonal relationships, stress-reduction programmes and generally enhancing the culture of the workplace. The aim for improving the quality of working life is that employees normally become more productive; rather than just tolerating their lives at work, they actively enjoy the work experience.

Empowerment is achieved when an employee feels he or she can complete tasks and attain targets independently, without constantly having to refer back to management for permission to take certain actions (Hon & Rensvold, 2006). The employee is trusted to make sensible decisions. For example, salespeople might be empowered to offer special discounts to prospective customers, and work teams may be empowered to determine the extent and intensity of the use of resources within a section of a firm. The aim is to enable employees who actually have to deal with problems to implement solutions quickly and without involving supervisors and higher levels of management.

Empowerment is not just passing down power and responsibility through a hierarchy; it allows the individual worker to actively contribute to improving the performance of tasks. Benefits to empowerment (Hon & Rensvold, 2006) include the following:

- encouragement of individual creativity and initiative, commitment to the enterprise and team spirit;
- decision-taking at the most suitable levels;
- faster and more flexible responses to customer requirements;
- higher levels of self-confidence and motivation among employees;
- better relations between management and front-line employees;
- receipt of valuable ideas for new products from front-line employees;
- provision of any early warning system regarding customer dissatisfaction; and
- immediate correction of mistakes.

The problems with empowerment are that greater care has to be exercised when hiring employees, who then need more training than in conventional circumstances. Staff might take bad decisions, and customers may be treated differently, leading to resentment among those not receiving favours. The entire organisation might need to be redesigned to make empowerment operationally effective.

研究表明,领导可以让人性的善恶两面都展现出来。领导者可以启发、激励他人完成难以完成的任务,同时也可以使其走上一条自毁之路。企业每个级别的领导者的能力和才华将对激励与保留优质员工产生相当大的影响。毫无疑问,领导力包括对权力的利用,并运用它去影响他人思想和行为。管理专家们提出了领导力涵盖的五个方面。

(1) 合法权力,指凭借个人品德、公司职位或是法律规定来行使的权力。

(2) 参照权力,指的是因个人魅力、无形的特质等而形成的权力。

(3) 专家权力,指的是领导者在某些领域具有专长,例如特定的技术或专业能力。

(4) 强制权力,即由于未按指令完成工作的、惩罚他人的权力。

(5) 奖赏权力,即奖赏他人认为有价值的东西的权力。

要想评估领导者的才能,可以经常去观察他是如何履行职责的(Stoner、Freeman 和 Gilbert,1995)。其主要职能如下。

(1) 制定方案:负责其管辖职能内整体方案计划的设计和制订,并给出方案实施方向。

(2) 设置任务优先级:每个组织机构都会面临各个工作需求间的矛盾冲突,领导者的职能之一就是设定优先级别给那些需要被解决的问题、需要制作的方案或是产生冲突时推迟的事项。

(3) 沟通交流:负责在整个企业大环境下沟通协商其计划与优先任务。

(4) 评判:常常需要评估员工个人绩效及分配奖赏。

(5) 供给:确保员工能够获得他所需要的资源。

(6) 处理问题:负责为他人扫清障碍。

(7) 调节矛盾:通过建设性的手段解决矛盾冲突。

(8) 分配数据资料:掌管分配数据及资料。

(9) 预计未来问题:具有前瞻性视野,提前预测未来可能发生的问题。为此,领导者需要持续监控内外部环境,才能在危机升级前采取有效措施。

Research has shown that effective leaders can bring out both the best and the worst that human nature has to offer. Leaders can inspire and motivate people to make seemingly impossible achievements, or lead people to go to a wrong direction. The quality of a firm's leadership at every level greatly affects its ability to motivate and retain high-quality staff. Clearly, leadership involves the use of power—the ability of one person to influence the thinking or behaviour of another. Leadership experts claim that there are five sources of power available to a leader:

(1) legitimate power is the power bestowed on someone by virtue of his or her position in the organisation, or by law;

(2) referent power refers to the charismatic or intangible quality that gives some leaders power over other people;

(3) expert power is the power that a leader has by virtue of his or her knowledge of a particular subject area, such as a technical specialisation;

(4) coercive power is the power to punish someone for not doing what the leader wants; and

(5) reward power is the power a leader has to grant rewards or other things that people want.

To evaluate leaders, we often look to how well they fulfil their responsibilities (Stoner, Freeman, & Gilbert, 1995). Leaders have nine key responsibilities.

(1) Planning: Leaders are responsible for developing the overall plan for their area of responsibility, whatever that may be. They are also the ones who set the direction for the efforts of whatever group they are leading.

(2) Setting priorities: In every organisation, individuals face many conflicting demands for their jobs. The leader's responsibility is to establish the priorities for what problems need to be solved, what needs to be produced or what has to be delayed in the face of conflicting demands.

(3) Communicating: Leaders are responsible for communicating their plan and priorities in the context of the overall goals of the firm.

(4) Judging: Leaders are often responsible for evaluating individuals' performance as well as distributing rewards.

(5) Providing: Leaders secure whatever resources their staff need to meet their objectives.

(6) Solving problems: Leaders are responsible for clearing roadblocks out of the way for their people.

(7) Resolving conflict: Leaders are responsible for resolving conflicts constructively.

(8) Dispensing performance data: Leaders are responsible for dispensing performance data.

(9) Anticipating future problems: Leaders are responsible for looking to the future and anticipating problems before they occur. To fulfil this goal, leaders need to

　　成功的领导者是否具有相似特质？哈佛心理学教授 David McClelland 将人的高层次需求分为三类——成就需求、权力需求、亲和需求（寻求与他人之间的密切接触），这三种需求在管理人才和专业人才中有着不同程度的表现（Hon & Leung，2011）。他的研究结果表明，成功的领导者倾向高权力需求以及低亲和力需求。

　　通过对成百上千位经验丰富的管理人才和专业人士长达一定时间的观察和研究，我们发现出色的领导者具有以下相似特质（Stoner、Freeman 和 Gilbert，1995）。

　　（1）敢于承担风险——不是草率粗心的，而是经过计算的风险，某种程度上说领导并不将之视为风险。

　　（2）勇于直面问题和冲突——出色的领导者并不太在意他人对自己的看法，以避免让它影响到自己执行或是表达必要观点的能力。

　　（3）拥有坚定信念，坚信自己选择的方向是正确的，并且与他人能进行有效沟通。

　　（4）坚决维护组内成员，除非被证明是错误的，否则他们会始终坚信其成员的决定是正确的。

　　（5）不会因组员表现不佳而严厉批评，相反却会主动承担后果。

　　（6）促进成员团结一心实现共同目标。他们并不担心引起组内冲突或竞争，只要最终结果能证明该决策的正当性。

　　（7）树立待人如待己的模范，都是非常努力工作的人。

　　（8）树立正直、诚实的典范，无论哪种形式的谎言、欺骗或是剽窃，他们都不会做。

　　（9）具有感召力，并借此特质来激发下属。增强成员的自尊心而不是一味地控制他们。

　　（10）积极向上，坚信"我能行"，不认为自己的失败是时运不济。他们会思考这件事会成功的所有原因，相信事在人为。高效的领导者会去控制周围的环境，而非完全为环境所制。

　　（11）具有紧迫感，清楚明白在竞争激烈的市场环境里，需要尽可能迅速地完成任务。

　　（12）敢于承认错误，懂得谦虚可以树立威信。

continuously monitor both internal and external environments so that action can be taken before crises develop.

Do good leaders share certain characteristics? Harvard psychology professor David McClelland studied individuals' need for achievement, need for power and need for affiliation (the need for close relations with others). These three needs are present in varying degrees in all managerial or professional people (Hon & Leung, 2011). His research concluded that the most successful leaders had a high need for power and a low need for affiliation.

Observations of the leadership performance of hundreds of managerial and professionals over an extended time period show that the best leaders share many of the following characteristics (Stoner, Freeman, & Gilbert, 1995).

(1) They are willing to take risks—not careless risks, but calculated risks, which the leader may not even perceive as risky.

(2) They confront problems and conflict head-on. Good leaders are not so concerned with how others perceive them that it affects their ability to do and say what is necessary.

(3) They have a deep inner conviction that their direction is true, that they can effectively communicate to others.

(4) They defend group members to those outside of the group. They assume that one of their own is right until proved otherwise.

(5) They do not blame their own group members for poor performance, and instead accept responsibility for results.

(6) They have the ability to bring people together to focus on a common goal; they are not afraid to promote intergroup conflict (competition) if the final results justify the tactic.

(7) They act as a role model by not having a double standard for themselves and the rest of the group. They are hard workers.

(8) They exemplify the characteristics of integrity and honesty. They do not lie, cheat or steal in any form.

(9) They are inspirational, and they bring out the best in people through this intangible quality. They bolster the self-esteem of others rather than merely manipulating them.

(10) They are positive thinkers; "can do" people who do not see themselves as victims of circumstance. They think of all of the reasons why something will work, instead of otherwise, and they believe one person's efforts can make a difference. Effective leaders control the environment instead of it controlling them.

(11) They have a sense of urgency, and know that in the competitive business marketplace, anything that needs to be accomplished must be done as quickly as possible.

(12) They are able to admit when they have been wrong or have made a mistake. They know humility builds credibility.

在中国背景下的研究发现[①]

在团队合作中,领导力的地位日益提升(Hon 和 Chan,2013a)。随着团队合作这种形式流行开来,领导者的核心地位变得更加显著。愈来愈多的酒店经理人开始意识到,以团队为基础的架构与工作设计可以迎合科技的快速变革和经济全球化,最终大大有助于企业创新变革、提高生产力及生存能力。因此,众多研究课题对此展开讨论,关注领导者风格与员工创造力、工作绩效表现之间的关联(Kim、Hon 和 Lee,2010)。从内在动机角度来讲,支持型领导管理风格将促进员工内在动机的提升,而操控型的领导方式将会降低员工内在动机,阻碍员工的创造性绩效的建立(Deci 和 Ryan,1985;Hon 和 Chan,2013a)。支持型的领导者会表达对员工情绪的关心,给出非主观性的建议和工作上的信息反馈,鼓励他们表达自己的顾虑。相反地,操纵型领导者则密切监管员工的行为表现,做决定时并不参考员工意见,要求员工严格按规章制度办事。

在酒店业工作,团队协作是必不可少的,无论你是在前台、后勤,还是餐饮服务部门工作,团队精神是不可或缺的,不管是对个人团队还是整个酒店而言(Chen 等,2007)。在众多不同的领导风格之中,授权领导一直被认定是服务行业中强有力的领导行为(Hon,2011;Srivastava、Bartol 和 Locke,2006),这是因为其将权力下放,来提升员工动机,以及增加对员工的投入(Seibert、Wang 和 Courtright,2011),当然这也顺应了提高工作自主权及团队创造力的趋势。在近期由 Hon 和 Chan(2013)带领展开的研究中,作者融合了 Amabile(1996)的成分模式以及 Deci 和 Ryan(2000)的自我决定理论,研究两种创造力相关联的动机的影响力(团队自我协调与团队创造力效能)在授权领导力和团队创造力两者关系中的体现。

授权领导与创造力

大量研究成果一致表明,支持型领导力、授权型领导力和愿景型领导力与员工绩效和创造力之间呈显著正相关,反之,控制型和强制型领导力与创造力表现之间呈负相关(Hon,2012a)。当员工掌握一定量的自主权和决定

---

①　资料来源:Hon,A.H.Y.(2012).When competency-based pay relates to creative performance:The role of employee psychological need. *International Journal of Hospitality Management*,31(1):130 – 138.

Research Findings in Chinese Context [①]

Leadership is increasingly taking place within a team context (Hon & Chan, 2013a). As teams grow in popularity, the role of the leader in guiding team members takes on heightened importance. More and more hotel managers are coming to realise that team-based structures and work designs can cope with rapid technological change and a fierce global economy, which ultimately can contribute to organisational innovation, productivity and survival. Hence, numerous studies have examined relations between a supervisor's leadership style and employee creativity and job performance (Hon, 2012a; Kim, Hon, & Lee, 2010). According to the intrinsic motivation perspective, supportive leadership styles are expected to boost intrinsic motivation, whereas those that are controlling in nature are expected to diminish intrinsic motivation and creative performance (Deci & Ryan, 1985; Hon & Chan, 2013a). When supervisors are supportive they show concern for employees' feelings, provide non-judgmental, informational feedback about their work and encourage them to voice their own concerns. In contrast, controlling supervisors closely monitor employees' behaviour, make decisions without involving employees and generally demand that employees follow strict rules and guidelines.

Working in the hospitality industry means working in a team; whether one works in the front or back office, housekeeping or food and beverage services, becoming an effective team player is essential for the success not only of the individual team but also of the business as a whole (Chen *et al.*, 2007). Of the different leadership styles, empowering leadership is considered a suitable leader behaviour for service organisations (Hon, 2011; Srivastava, Bartol, & Locke, 2006), as it involves sharing power with a view toward enhancing the motivation and investment of employees in their work (Seibert, Wang, & Courtright, 2011), and is consistent with the trend toward increasing both employee autonomy and team creativity. In a recent study conducted by Hon and Chan (2013), the authors integrated Amabile's (1996) componential model and Deci and Ryan's (2000) self-determination theory to examine the effects of two creativity-related motivations (team self-concordance and team creative efficacy) on the relationship between empowering leadership and team creativity.

Empowering Leadership and Creativity

A growing body of research has consistently found that supportive, empowering, visionary leadership is positively related to employee performance and creativity, whereas controlling or coercive leadership is negatively related to creative performance

---

[①] Source: Hon, A. H. Y. (2012). When competency-based pay relates to creative performance: The role of employee psychological need. *International Journal of Hospitality Management*, 31(1): 130–138.

权时,团队创造力的成果才能实现最大化。授权型领导行为包括以下五个方面:(1) 以身作则——对自身工作恪守承诺,推动团队成员更好地表现;(2) 指导——培训员工,帮助他们变得更高效、更独立;(3) 参与决策——鼓励成员间分享各自的想法,为决策贡献己见;(4) 信息传递——推动整个公司范围内的宣传信息的传播,目的是让团队成员尽可能地了解公司的使命和愿景;(5) 表示关切——表现出对下属的支持与平等对待(Arnold、Arad、Rhoades 和 Drasgow,2000;Srivastava 等,2006)。以上这些授权领导行为在概念上与团队创造力显著相关。

借助政策方针、发表声明、行为活动等手段,授权领导者们可以正式地将一定的自主权授权给下属(Aherne、Mathieu 和 Rapp,2005;Arnold 等,2000)。除此之外,如此举措也是为了推动和建立起员工的自主、竞争意识,领导者希望用切实的行动来表明他们给员工自主权、不直接干预员工的强烈愿望。授权领导者们也表现出了对工作强烈的忠诚度,这同时也向其下属们传达着自我价值和重要地位(Aherne 等,2005;Arnold 等,2000)。如此“以身作则”的方式是为了鼓励员工效仿楷模,接受并认同工作目标,反过来说,这也将使团队的创造力达到新的高度。此外,他们还为员工提供大量培训指导以及相关资讯,从而使员工获得自信,在自己的工作领域更游刃有余(Amabile 等,1996;Shalley 等,2004)。这种将培训指导与信息资源分享结合在一起的方式会带来社会性、工具性两方面的效用。它会帮助建立起良好的团队关系,培养成员间的相互信任,并且通过向团队输出重要信息来提高成员的绩效表现(Mesmer-Mangus 和 DeChurch,2009)。最后,授权领导者们能够与下属成员建立起良好的合作关系,从而给日后的工作需要提供支持(Arnold 等,2000;Zhang 和 Bartol,2010)。

内在激励原则:团体自我协调

Sheldon 和 Elliot(1998)的自我协调模型深入探索研究了基于价值的内在激励。团队自我协调就是内在激励,是因为它是来自于团队成员自我选择的结果,其反映出成员的个体信念以及自我认知的结果(Bono 和 Judge,2003;Sheldon 和 Elliot,1999;Sheldon 和 Houser-Marko,2001)。当团队成员认同企业追寻的目标(认同性动机)或他们对企业目标产生浓厚兴趣和乐趣时,团队的自我协调度就会提高(Sheldon 和 Houser-Marko,2001;Sheldon 等,2003)。但当他们认为追求目标只是为了获得外在报酬,或是为了避免受到惩罚(外在激励),抑或是受到来自社会的高压,例如社会义务(内摄动机)时,团队的自我协调度将降低。

(Hon，2012a). Creative teams work best when they have considerable autonomy and decision-making ability. Empowering leader behaviour consists of five dimensions: (1) leading by example，which reflects a leader's commitment to his or her own work and the work of team members to achieve better performance; (2) coaching，which refers to actions that educate team members and help them become more efficient and self-reliant; (3) participative decision making，which encourages the sharing among team members of ideas and opinions on group decision making; (4) informing，which promotes the company-wide dissemination of information，resulting in team members who are more likely to understand the compelling mission and expectations of their leader; and (5) showing concern，which indicates the support and fair treatment of subordinates by a team leader (Arnold，Arad，Rhoades，& Drasgow，2000; Srivastava *et al.*，2006). Such empowering behaviour is conceptually highly relevant to team-level creativity.

Through their policies，statements and actions，empowering leaders formally delegate significant freedom and autonomy to their employees (Aherne，Mathieu，& Rapp，2005; Arnold *et al.*，2000). In addition to granting formal autonomy，these acts of delegation are likely to promote a strong sense of autonomy and competence among subordinates because leaders are demonstrating，in tangible ways，their desire to give employees autonomy without their own direct intervention. Empowering leaders also show strong personal commitment to their work，which conveys its value and importance to their employees (Aherne *et al.*，2005; Arnold *et al.*，2000). This leading-by-example style is likely to encourage subordinates to follow their leaders' model by embracing and identifying with work goals，which in turn will likely lead to higher levels of team creativity. Empowering leaders also provide a great deal of coaching and information to employees designed to help them become more confident and proficient in their work (Amabile *et al.*，1996; Shalley *et al.*，2004). This combination of coaching and information sharing has both social and instrumental effects: it helps to build high-quality relationships，fostering trust among team members，and it bolsters performance by providing important informational inputs necessary for team creativity (Mesmer-Mangus & DeChurch，2009). Lastly，empowering leaders develop positive relationships with their subordinates that support meeting the latter's relatedness needs (Arnold *et al.*，2000; Zhang & Bartol，2010).

Intrinsic Motivation Principle: Team Self-Concordance

Sheldon and Elliot's (1998) self-concordance model more fully explores this value-based intrinsic motivation. Team self-concordance is intrinsically motivating because team members feel that it emanates from their self-choices that reflect both their personal convictions and their true sense of self within the team (Bono & Judge，2003; Sheldon & Elliot，1999; Sheldon & Houser-Marko，2001). Team self-concordance is high when team members identify with the work goals they are pursuing (identified

　　领导者必须激励员工去解决创造性的问题,且给予他们充分的自由。授权领导力包括下放权力,通过向员工阐述工作的意义来提高工作积极性;放宽决策自主权;对员工个人能力给予充分的信任,以及保证其在工作中有随机应变的空间(Arnold 等,2000)。这些行为表现理论上与创造力有很大关联。举例来说,调查研究表明,这些具有说服力的愿景是由授权领导者精心设计的,它给员工带来活力和热情,反过来提升了员工的内在动力(Bono 和Judge,2003)。如此愿景也会提升员工的自我协调程度,促使目标导向朝着有意义、十分重要的方向发展,反过来可以推动团队创造力的进步。同时,授权领导者们将充分表现出对员工的愿景、工作目标的强烈认同感(Arnold等,2000)。员工们效仿领导者对于工作目标的接受和认同,这是团队自我协调的核心(Ahearne 等,2005;Sheldon 和 Houser-Marko,2001;Sheldon 等,2003)。因此,推动员工树立自主、自立意识的重心在于促进提升下属的自主权意识,从而使其反过来提高团队创造力。

内在激励原则:团队创造力效能

　　讨论创造力的文献研究一致认为,团队创造力效能通过激励员工个体,最终达到提升团队创造力的效果(Shin 和 Zhou,2007)。这是因为团队成员心中对创造力效能的信赖将激励他们积极与他人合作,进而挑战现状,竭尽全力地给出新颖、有效的想法,面对困难绝不退缩,最后促使团队取得更高的成就(Tierney 和 Farmer,2011)。通过互动和社交活动,团队成员间将建立起一个共同的信念,那就是集体创造新主意,这将大大有助于团队合作。当一个团队拥有关于创造性成果的强大的集体效能信念时,成员们会更愿意承担尝试新方法解决问题的风险,遇到困难时坚持不懈,并提出更多、更新、更有效的办法。如此一来,自然会达到团队创造力的新高度(Shin 和 Zhou,2007)。

motivation) or when they find the goals highly interesting and enjoyable (Sheldon & Houser-Marko, 2001; Sheldon *et al.*, 2003). It is low when members believe they are pursuing goals only to obtain extrinsic rewards or avoid punishment (external motivation) or because of coercive social pressure such as a sense of obligation (introjected motivation).

Leaders must encourage employees' motivation to solve problems associated with creativity, and to do this they must allow employees considerable latitude. Empowering leadership involves sharing power, which enhances employee motivation by delineating the significance of the employee's job; providing greater decision-making autonomy; demonstrating trust in the employee's capabilities and providing him or her with the freedom to act as flexibly as circumstances warrant (Arnold, *et al.*, 2000). This behaviour is conceptually highly relevant to creativity. For example, research has indicated that the compelling visions crafted by empowering leaders create energy and excitement about the work among their employees, which in turn increases the latter's intrinsic motivation (Bono & Judge, 2003). This vision is also likely to enhance employees' sense of self-concordance by promoting and endorsing the goals they are pursuing as meaningful and important, which in turn contributes to team creativity. Empowering leaders also show their own commitment to, and identification with, their vision and the work goals and objectives derived from it (Arnold, *et al.*, 2000). This leading-by-example may compel subordinates to follow the model of their leaders by embracing and identifying with work goals, which is the essence of team self-concordance (Ahearne, *et al.*, 2005; Sheldon & Houser-Marko, 2001; Sheldon, *et al.*, 2003). Thus, the emphasis that empowering leaders place on employee self-determination and self-reliance is likely to promote a strong sense of autonomy among their subordinates, which in turn promotes team creativity.

Intrinsic Motivation Principle: Team Creative Efficacy

The creativity literature has converged in suggesting that "team creative efficacy contributes to team creativity by boosting team members' motivation" (Shin & Zhou, 2007). The efficacy beliefs of team members about creativity will motivate them to cooperate with one another to challenge the status quo, generate novel and useful ideas and persevere when dealing with obstacles, thus facilitating their achievement of higher levels of creative performance (Tierney & Farmer, 2011). Through interaction and socialisation, team members develop a shared belief in the team's collective ability to produce novel and creative ideas, which contributes to the team's collective action. When a team has a strong collective efficacy belief regarding creative outcomes, its members are more likely to take risks in trying different ways to solve difficult problems, to persevere in the face of challenges inherent in creative work and to generate a greater number of new and useful ideas. In this way, a high level of team creativity is achieved (Shin & Zhou, 2007).

授权领导力在增强团队创造效能中扮演着关键角色,因为它很有可能对以下四种效能信念的来源产生影响:观察学习、言语劝说、生理激发、过去经验(Bandura,1986)。首先,通过对工作和团队展示责任感,授权领导者为下属团队树立模范榜样。也就是说,团队成员通过观察学习,学会将自身致力于工作之中。这能建立他们的自信,坚信团队有能力挑战现状并想出更新颖的点子。然后,借助在公司内传播信息、阐明未来期望的方式,授权领导者能够用言语劝说的方法让个体成员共同努力,实现集体目标,例如提升团队创造力。其次,授权领导者通过向员工表示关心和爱护的方法,鼓舞他们毫无畏惧和担忧地去完成任务,这将大大提高集体效能,且能激发员工尝试新事物。如此这般对下属的关爱会让他们更了解领导者的价值所在,更感激团队的努力,反过来,这将引起他们的生理激发,强化集体创造效能的信念。最后,凭借培训指导和委任授权两个途径,领导者们可以使成员执行任务时更高效、更自立,同时也能培养团队的独立性。由此,成员们将会拥有成功的经验,进而将团队效能提升到新高度(Tierney 和 Farmer,2011)。如此一来,授权领导力对团队创造力效能有正面积极的作用,反过来也作用于团队的创造力。

另外,其他研究学者(Zhang 和 Bartol,2010)也强调了授权领导力在培养员工创造力方面的重要作用。授权领导力从理论上讲适合于促进创新能力的发展,因为领导者凭借诸多方式着眼于激发员工创造力相关的潜能,如树立正面典范形象、与下属建立良好关系、培训指导和提供大量信息来培养他们强烈的创造意识、与员工共商决策等(Arnold 等,2000;Zhang 和 Bartole,2010)。因此,我们断定授权领导者可以激发员工更高层次的自主性动机。例如,根据指令、声明以及行动,授权领导者们正式将一定的自主权和自由度授予员工(Aherne、Mathieu 和 Rapp,2005;Arnold 等,2000;Zhang 和 Bartol,2010)。此做法将推动员工树立强烈的独立、自主、竞争意识,因为领导者们用实际行动表明了他们对给予员工自主权、坚信他们能有效利用自主权的迫切愿望。

授权领导者展现出对工作强烈的使命感——如此做法传递出该工作的价值与重要性。他们同时也为员工们提供大量工作指导和相关资讯,来帮助员工建立更强的自信心,培养更娴熟的技能。如此培训与分享资讯相结合,

Empowering leadership plays a key role in enhancing team creative efficacy because it is likely to influence the four sources of efficacy beliefs: observational learning, verbal persuasion, physiological arousal and enactive mastery (Bandura, 1986). First, by showing commitment to the work and to the team itself, empowering leaders act as role models for subordinate team members; that is, team members learn to commit to their work through observational learning. This makes team members more confident in their team's ability to challenge the existing situation and develop new ideas. Second, by disseminating information throughout the company and clarifying expectations, empowering leaders can verbally persuade team members to coordinate their efforts to achieve collective goals such as team creativity. Third, by showing care and consideration for team members, empowering leaders encourage them to perform tasks without fear or anxiety, which increases the level of collective efficacy and can inspire team members to try different things. Such consideration and care helps team members understand that their leader values and appreciates the team's efforts to achieve collective goals; this in turn causes physiological arousal among team members and strengthens their shared creative-efficacy belief. Lastly, through coaching and the delegation of authority, empowering leaders help team members to become more efficient and self-dependent in accomplishing tasks while helping the team to act autonomously. Team members are then likely to have successful enactive mastery experiences, thereby increasing the level of team efficacy related to creative outcomes (Tierney & Farmer, 2011). Thus, empowering leadership positively contributes to team creative efficacy, which in turn, contributes to team creativity.

Other research scholars (Zhang & Bartol, 2010) has highlighted the importance of empowering leadership in fostering employees' creativity. Empowering leadership seems ideally suited to promoting creativity because empowering leaders focus on enhancing employees' creativity-relevant motivation by being positive role models, creating positive relationships with their subordinates, coaching and providing information to employees to foster strong creative beliefs and involving employees in work decisions (Arnold, *et al.*, 2000; Zhang & Bartole, 2010). We therefore posit that empowering leaders will foster higher levels of autonomous motivation among their subordinates. For instance, through their instructions, statements and actions, empowering leaders formally delegate significant freedom and autonomy to their employees (Aherne, Mathieu & Rapp, 2005; Arnold, *et al.*, 2000; Zhang & Bartol, 2010). These acts of delegation are also likely to promote a strong sense of autonomy and competence because leaders are demonstrating, in tangible ways, their desire to give employees autonomy and their confidence in employees' ability to use that autonomy productively.

Empowering leaders show strong personal commitment to their work—an act that conveys the value and importance of that work. Empowering leaders also provide a great deal of coaching and information to employees to help them become more confident and

会带来社会性和工具性效应：它帮助建立起高质量的人际关系，培养互相信赖的团队，通过提供重要资讯来增强员工表现力。最后，授权领导者能与下属间建立良好的合作关系，从而帮助员工实现相关需求。综合以上效果我们可以发现，与授权领导者一同工作的员工感到更自主、更能干，与工作保持更良好的关系，从而获得更高层次的激励。

综上所述，领导力在了解团队行为中占有核心地位，因为领导者通常需要给出员工执行任务的方向。因此，在提升团队表现、创造力和效率时，更准确的预测能力显得格外宝贵。当我们对员工所认为的授权领导者该具有的个人和环境特征以及如何产生这些特征有更多的认识时，我们就能更好地预测能使下属建立对领导和团队的目标深切的使命感和忠诚度的条件。

案例研究 2 - 1[①] ▶▶▶▶▶▶

Delmar 酒店诞生于世纪之交，坐落在美国东北部中型城市的中心地带。该酒店经过了精心修复，对酒店餐厅进行了升级，桃花心木厅（The Mahogany Room）近期被美国享有威望的 AAA 协会授予"五钻奖"（five-diamond），使其成为美国唯一一家五钻餐厅。Joe Huang 在桃花心木厅做服务生已经达三年之久，与酒店餐饮部总监 Adam 常常有密切的合作，是他使酒店焕然一新。首先，酒店聘请了一位新主厨，其在高级西餐餐饮界享有盛誉。Adam 主管服务方面，培训所有高级西餐餐饮的服务生。他投资成千上万美元于餐厅的酒单，以提升酒水品质、扩大酒品范围。现在，有传言说"桃花心木厅"在《葡萄酒观赏家》杂志颁发的享有盛誉的奖项的备选名单之中。更重要的是，餐厅主厨已受纽约知名餐厅 James Beard House 之邀准备一顿特餐。Joe 认为："我们真的获得了巨大的成功，在这么好的宣传氛围下，生意一定会兴隆很久。"

在 Joe 刚到岗的一个下午，Adam 请他来自己的办公室。他说："Joe，你是我见过的最棒的服务生，你的小费也一直是所有人中最高的，你管理和组织工作的能力十分让人敬佩。"随后 Adam 夸奖了他对酒单十分熟悉，以及

---

① 资料来源：Sommerville，K. L.（2007）. *Hospitality Employee Management and Supervision：Concepts and Practical Applications*：334 - 335. Hoboken NJ：John Wiley & Sons.

proficient in their work. This combination of coaching and information sharing has both social and instrumental effects; it helps build high-quality relationships, fosters trust between co-workers and it bolsters performance by providing the information necessary for employee performance. Lastly, empowering leaders develop positive relationships with their subordinates that help meet employees' relatedness needs. As a result of these combined effects, employees who work for empowering leaders are more likely to feel autonomous, competent and positively connected to their work, and consequently they will experience higher levels of autonomous motivation.

To summarise, leadership plays a central part in understanding team behaviour, for it is the leader who usually directs employees toward goal attainment. Therefore, a more accurate predictive capability should be valuable in improving team performance, creativity and effectiveness. As we learn more about the personal and situational characteristics that employees act on empowering leaders, and about the conditions that facilitate their emergence, we should be better able to predict the conditions under which employees exhibit extraordinary commitment and loyalty to their leaders and to those leaders' goals.

Case Study 2 – 1[①] ▶▶▶▶▶▶

The Delmar Hotel is a turn-of-the-century property located in the heart of a mid-sized, north-eastern city in USA. The hotel has been meticulously restored, and its upscale restaurant, The Mahogany Room, has recently been awarded five-diamond status by the prestigious AAA organisation, making it the only five-diamond restaurant in the state. Joe Huang has been a waiter at The Mahogany Room for more than three years, and he has cooperated closely with Adam, the hotel's food and beverage director, who has turned the restaurant around. First, the hotel hired a new chef with an excellent reputation in fine dining. Then, Adam went to work on the service aspect, training all of the waiting staff in the finer points of fine-dining service. Thousands and thousands of dollars were invested in improving the depth and breadth of the restaurant's wine list, and now rumour has it that the magazine *Wine Spectator* is considering The Mahogany Room for a prestigious award. To top it off, the restaurant's chef has been invited to prepare a special meal at New York's famed James Beard House. "We've really hit the big time," thought Joe. "Business will be booming for months with all this great publicity."

One afternoon as Joe is arriving at work, Adam calls him into his office. "Joe," Adam begins, "you're one of the best waiters I've ever seen. Your tips are consistently among the highest of the waiting staff, and your ability to manage and organise your work station is impressive." Adam goes on to praise Joe's knowledge of the menu as well as the quick

---

① Source: Sommerville, K.L.(2007).*Hospitelity Employee Management and Supervision: Concepts and Practival Applications*: 334 – 335.Hoboken NJ: John Wiley & Sons.

他熟记新酒单的快速记忆法。在大加称赞 Joe 的才能之后,Adam 随后说:"我想给你一个晋升的机会,我们需要一个服务生领班,我觉得你是这个位置的不二人选。"

起初,Joe 有些吃惊,他是所有服务生中最年轻、阅历最浅的一个。虽然他很开心 Adam 对自己能力的赏识,但他不确定自己就是最佳人选。他问道:"这个职位需要做什么呢?"

紧接着 Adam 跟他详细解释了该职位需要负责培训其他新雇员,建立周工作日程,每晚夜班结束工作时处理一些常规的文件工作。Adam 补充说道:"这是公司的决定,我可能没有太多的时间培训你,但我会带你走上正轨,当然你有需要尽管来找我。"Adam 告诉 Joe 利用周末考虑一下,下周一给他答复。

问 题

(1) Joe 应该接受这次晋升机会吗?为什么?或为什么不接受?在决定接受或拒绝这个机会之前,Joe 会有哪些补充问题?

(2) 哪些能力会让他觉得自己可以胜任这份工作?未来他还需要培养哪些才能?为什么?

(3) 若 Joe 接受了此次晋升,鉴于自己是员工中最年轻、阅历最浅的一个,他会面临怎样的挑战?Adam 要怎样帮助他解决这些问题?

(4) 若他拒绝了这次机会,会不会影响到他在公司日后的发展?为什么会?或为什么不会?Joe 该如何向 Adam 陈述拒绝的理由呢?

案例研究 2-2[①] ▶▶▶▶▶▶

Amy 在一家大型酒店的咖啡厅做午班餐厅主管。她来自一家小得多的酒店,并在那里有相似的职位,但她有自信可以适应更广阔的环境和更多的员工。因为她渴望有一个良好的开端,她要求每班结束后留 10 分钟时间,和每个人讲几句话。她从自己的背景和经历开始讲起,然后是自己的经管理念。"我对每个人都有很高的期望。我要看到你们最佳的状态,希望这也是

---

① 资料来源:Walker, J., & Miller, J.(2009).*Supervision in the Hospitality Industry:Leading Human Resources*,31.Hoboken, NJ:John Wiley & Sons.

manner in which he memorised the new wine menu. After a few more minutes of heaping praise on Joel, Adam says, "I'd like to offer you a promotion. We are creating a new position of head waiter, and I think you would be perfect for the job."

At first, Joe is shocked; he is one of the youngest and least experienced of the entire waiting staff. While he is pleased that Adam is impressed with his abilities, he is not sure that he would be the best choice for the position. "What exactly would this position entail, Adam?" asks Joe.

Adam explains that Joe would be responsible for training all of the new hires, developing the weekly work schedule and handling some routine paperwork that he would have to complete at the end of each evening's shift. Adam adds, "This is something that corporate wants to happen. I won't be able to spend a lot of time training you, but I will get you started on the right foot, and then, of course, make myself available to you as the need arises." Adam tells Joe to think about the offer over the weekend and to come in Monday to let him know what decision he has made.

Questions

(1) Should Joe accept this promotion? Why or why not? What additional questions might Joe want to ask Adam before deciding to accept or decline Adam's offer?

(2) What skills does Joe possess that would assist him should he decide to accept the promotion? What skills would he need to further develop and why?

(3) If Joe does accept the promotion, what challenges is he likely to face considering that he is among the youngest and least experienced of the current waiting staff? How could Adam better prepare Joe to face such challenges?

(4) Does Joe risk his future with this organisation should he decide not to accept Adam's offer? Why or why not? How might Joe present his reasoning to Adam should he decline the offer?

Case Study 2 – 2① ▶▶▶▶▶

Amy has just been hired as the dining room supervisor on the noon shift in the coffee shop of a large hotel. She came from a similar job in a much smaller hotel, but she feels confident that she can handle the larger setting and the larger staff. Because she is eager to start things off right, she asks all of the servers to stay for 10 minutes at the end of the shift so that she can say a few words to everyone. She begins by describing her background and experience and then proceeds to explain her philosophy of management. "I expect a lot of my people," she says. "I want your best work, and I hope you want it, too, for your own sake. You will not find me easy, but you will find

---

① Source: Walker, J., & Miller, J. (2009). *Supervision in the Hospitality Industry: Leading Human Resources*, 31. Hoboken, NJ: John Wiley & Sons.

你们想看到的,为了你们自己。你们会觉得我不容易敷衍,但会看到我的公平、开放,同时我希望你们可以自由地跟我讨论问题或是建议。我无法处理所有的难题,但我会尽力而为。"她微笑着环顾每个人。

她接着说:"现在,首要任务是介绍一下轮岗制度,因此每个人都会轮到最忙碌的餐桌、得到最多的小费、离厨房最近等。我已经将任务张贴在公告栏里了,从明天开始实施,保持一周时间。我也会标出一些新的变动,然后一步一步进行。请问大家有什么问题或是想法吗?"Amy 停顿了 3 秒钟,然后接着说,"我尤其在意工作准时、统一着装、仪容仪表,以及快速敏捷、谦虚有礼地服务这几方面。我建议大家从明天开始就步入正轨,合作愉快。明天10 点 25 分见!"

问　题

(1) 你认为 Amy 留给员工怎样的印象呢?她的陈述中有哪些好想法?你觉得她犯了什么错误?

(2) 从第一印象来看,你认为她的管理风格是怎样的?

(3) 你认为大家会自由地跟她讨论建议或是问题吗?

(4) 你认为她树立了好的榜样吗?她的要求合理吗?

案例研究 2-3① ▶▶▶▶▶

Erica Ho 曾经很热爱她的工作——Third Street Bar & Grill 的流水线厨师。薪水不错,主厨围绕着她的时刻表工作也感觉很愉快,同样她也很享受和同事们一起共事。对 Erica 来说这一切再好不过了,可是,在一个下午主厨召集所有人开了次非常重要的会之后,一切突然都变了。

主厨 Chen 说,"兄弟们,我们虽然只开业了一年,但生意日新月异、蓬勃发展。老板们都特别开心。因此,他们决定在市中心开一家分店。"

"哇哦!太棒了!"几个员工说道。

"那我们怎么办?我的意思是以后要向谁汇报工作呢?"Erica 问道。

"因此我们决定提拔 Kevin Tse 做副厨师长,以后大家向他汇报工作,再由他转达给我。"主厨 Chen 说道。

---

① 资料来源:Sommerville,K. L.(2007). *Hospitality Employee Management and Supervision:Concepts and Practical Applications*,281-283.Hoboken,NJ:John Wiley & Sons.

me fair and open with you, and I hope you will feel free to come to me with suggestions or problems. I can't solve them all, but I will do my best for you." She smiles and looks at each one in turn.

"Now, the first thing I want to do," she continues, "is to introduce a system of rotating your stations so that everyone gets a turn at the busiest tables and the best tips and the shortest distance to the kitchen. I've posted the assignments on the bulletin board, and you will start off that way tomorrow and keep these stations for a week. I will be making some other changes, too, but let's take things one at a time. Are there any questions or comments?" Amy pauses for three seconds and then says, "I am very particular about being on time, about uniforms and grooming, and about prompt and courteous customer service. I advise you all to start off tomorrow on the right foot and we'll all be much happier during these hours we work together. See you tomorrow at 10:25."

Questions

(1) What kind of impression do you think Amy is making on the workers? What are the good points in her presentation? What mistakes do you think she is making?

(2) From this first impression, what would you say is her management style?

(3) Do you think that people will feel free to come to her with suggestions and problems?

(4) Do you think that she will set a good example? Is she reasonable in her demands?

Case Study 2 – 3[①] ▷▷▷▷ ▶▶▶

Erica Ho used to love her job as a line cook at the Third Street Bar & Grill. The money was good, the chef was great about working around Erica's school schedule and she had a lot of fun working with the other employees at the restaurant. Things could not have been better for Erica, but all that changed when the chef called everyone together early one afternoon for a very important meeting.

"Guys," said Chef Chen, "you know we've only been open a year, and business is already booming. The owners are so pleased," he continues, "that they've decided to open another location downtown." Chef Chen explains that the restaurant's owners have requested that he immediately transfer to the new location so that he can take charge of all of the preopening activities.

"Wow, that's great," respond a few of the kitchen employees.

"But what about us?" asks Erica. "I mean, who will we report to later?"

"Well, that's one of the reasons I called all of you in," says Chef Chen. "We have decided to promote Kevin Tse to the position of sous chef, so you guys will now report to

---

① Source: Sommerville, K.L.(2007). Hospitality Employee Management and Supervision: Concepts and Practical Applications, 281 – 283. Hoboken, NJ: John Wiley & Sons.

厨房里突然鸦雀无声,大家看着彼此都不说话,一脸吃惊的表情。Kevin Tse 是个出色的流水线厨师,但这才是问题所在。大部分同事都觉得他显得太过自命不凡,因为在来到现在的餐厅之前,他和主厨在其他的餐厅一起搭档工作。主厨 Chen 说:"我希望无论什么时候大家都听从 Kevin 的领导。我知道他会是个出色的领导者。我不会离开大家的,只是不能像以前一样天天在你们身边。"

尽管对提拔 Kevin 这个决定有些顾虑,但 Erica 依然脸上挂着微笑,走向他,跟他握手表示祝贺,"恭喜你,Kevin。我想我会从您身上学到很多东西。"陆陆续续地,其他同事们也上前跟他道喜。

随后主厨 Chen 拎起公文包离开了厨房。这时,Kevin 大声宣布:"大家听好了,我们会做一些调整,从日程表开始。明早你们会看到新的日程表贴在我办公室的公布栏上。我不想听到关于日托问题、学校课程表或是周六晚上的约会等问题的抱怨。我们在经营一家餐厅。"说完这些,他走进主厨办公室,关上门,把脚跷在桌子上自言自语道:"终于是我的了。"

"这简直就是噩梦。"Jason 说道,他是另一位流水线厨师,"如果新的日程打乱了我的日托安排,我会因此失去我孩子们的监护权的。"

"谁说不是呢!"Jennifer 补充道,她是餐厅两位糕点厨师之一,"我男朋友和我只有一辆车,他挣钱比我多很多,所以通勤上我得依赖他。"

Erica 在深思后补充说道,"我根本不能修改学校课程时间,这是我最后一个学期了,并且我也不能辞职。"她说,"因为这是最后一个实习工作,如果这关过不了我就得退学了。"

随着夜幕降临,餐厅开始忙碌起来了,但 Kevin 却还待在主厨办公室里,只是偶尔出来一两次,在菜被端出去前检查一下。很晚了,他才又出来,从盛菜盘中随手抓起一盘沙拉,然后递给 Erica,她那天晚上做冷房厨师长。"喂,烹饪学生",他对着 Erica 大声说道,大到厨房里的每个人都听得到,"你的学校没有教你什么叫控制份量吗?这盘沙拉太大了。"他把沙拉盘递给 Erica 然后说,"重新制作它,下次不要错。现实生活中,我们叫它控制材料成本。" Erica 一脸尴尬地站在那里,他转身回到自己的办公室,狠狠地摔了下房门。

厨房里的每个人看着 Erica 有条不紊地重做了那份沙拉。"我简直不敢相信他竟然这么混蛋,"Jason 说道,"我觉得这沙拉看起来正好。""不开玩笑

him，and he'll continue to report to me."

The kitchen suddenly becomes very quiet as each of the employees look at one other，somewhat astonished. Kevin Tse was a decent line cook，but that was about it. Most of the employees felt that he had a holier-than-thou attitude，as he and Chef Chen had worked together at a couple of other restaurants before coming to the Third Street Bar & Grill. "I'll expect each of you to follow Kevin's lead in all matters，" says Chef Chen. "I know he'll make a good boss，and besides，I'm not leaving; I just won't be around every day like before."

Although she had concerns about the decision to promote Kevin，Erica puts on her best smile，walks up to Kevin，extends her hand and says，"Congratulations，Kevin. I know I'll learn a lot by working for you." Slowly，the other employees come up too and offer Kevin their congratulations.

As Chef Chen gathers his briefcase and leaves the kitchen，Kevin announces，"Listen up，everybody. We're going to make a few changes around here，starting with the schedule. In the morning，" he says，"you'll find your new work schedules posted on my office bulletin board. And I don't want to hear any whining about day care issues，school schedules，or hot Saturday night dates. We've got a restaurant to run." With that，Kevin goes into the chef's office，closes the door，pros his feet on the desk，and thinks to himself，"I've finally arrived."

"This is terrible，" says Jason，one of the other line cooks. "If his new scheduling system messes up my day care arrangements，I could lose custody of my kids."

"Tell me about it，" adds Jennifer，one of the restaurant's two pastry chefs. "My boyfriend and I only have one car，and he makes a lot more money than I do，so I have to rely on him for transport."

Erica has already thought about these things when she adds，"I can't adjust my school schedule at all，and this is my last semester. I can't even quit，" she says，"because this job is my final internship，and I would flunk out of school if I don't get through this."

As the evening wears on，the restaurant gets busier and busier，but Kevin remains in the chef's office，only coming out once or twice for a few moments to scrutinise the plates being picked up by the servers. Near the end of the evening，he comes out again，grabs a salad plate off of a server's tray，and takes it to Erica who is at the garde manager station that evening. "Hey，culinary student，" he says to Erica，loudly enough for everyone else to hear. "Don't they teach you anything about portion control at that school of yours? This salad is way too big." He slides the salad plate toward Erica and says，"Remake it，and do it right this time. In the real world，we call this controlling food cost." As Erica stands with an embarrassed look on her face，he wheels around，goes back into the chef's office and slams the door behind him.

Everyone in the kitchen watches as Erica methodically remakes the salad. "I can't believe what a jerk he's being，Erica，" says Jason. "That salad looked perfect to me."

地说，"Jennifer 补充说。"他早就知道这次会提拔他了，我可以预见到未来我们都会身在水深火热之中啊。"Erica 笑笑说，"哦，他这是在施行'海鸥管理'模式。""你说什么？"Jason 问她，他是另一位流水线厨师。"就是上周课上教授告诉我们的，你知道的，像海鸥一样，主管进来，发出各种声音，对每个人指指点点，然后就离开。"

问　题

（1）主厨 Chen 是否可以用一种更好的、更有条理的方式对待厨房的员工们？ 在他向其他人宣布餐厅新消息的方法上，有什么问题吗？

（2）Kevin 在自己担任副厨师长的第一天犯了哪些反馈性的错误，或是沟通上的问题？ 他怎样做可以改正这些错误，重树领导榜样？

（3）厨房的员工们需要向主厨 Chen 反映他们的顾虑吗？ 如果他们这么做了，会有什么后果？ 如果你是主厨 Chen，你将如何知道新提拔的副厨的表现？

（4）若 Erica 的情况继续糟糕下去，她应该选择离开，因此会结束实习工作，最终导致推迟毕业，还是应该选择继续坚持？ 请解释你这么选择的原因。

"No kidding," adds Jennifer. "This promotion has already gone to his head; I can see we're all in for some real hell".

Erica, laughing, says, "Oh, he's just practicing 'seagull management,' that's all."

"What?" asks Jason, as the other line cook looks at Erica.

"Just something one of my professors told us in class last week," she says. "You know, like a seagull, the manager flies in, makes a lot of noise, dumps on everybody, then flies off again."

Questions

(1) Could Chef Chen approach this meeting with his kitchen staff in a better, more organised fashion? What were some problems with the way he chose to communicate the restaurant's news to the employees?

(2) What feedback errors and communication blunders has Kevin made during his first evening as sous chef of the restaurant? How can he overcome these errors and re-establish good employee morale?

(3) Should the rest of the kitchen staff go to Chef Chen with their concerns? What might be the result if they did? If you were in Chef Chen's shoes, how might you counsel the newly promoted sous chef?

(4) If things get worse for Erica, should she quit and thus terminate her internship, which may delay her graduation, or should she stick it out? Explain the reasons for your response.

第3章　组织文化与其对人力资本的影响

学习目标

- 了解组织文化的重要性和其职能
- 介绍文化对人力资源管理的影响
- 通过研究成果和案例分析中国酒店业的具体文化,与其对人力资源的影响

人们越来越意识到组织文化在国际化管理和跨国管理中的核心地位(Hofstede,1980)。组织文化指的是全体成员共同接受的组织的行为准则、价值观念与预期目标,其由对组织的实践活动的诠释而得。大量学者指出,组织文化能促进或是抑制个体的创造力与工作表现,通过组织文化与组织气氛所产生的价值观念和行为方式(Amabile 等,1996;Shalley 等,2004)。

什么才是文化[①]?

从根本上讲,组织文化就是企业的个性特征。它由组织内部成员和行为的设想、价值观、规范和有形的标志(人工制品)组成。组织成员可以很快地感受到一个企业文化的特别之处。企业文化这一特定词语很难清晰地表达出来,但当每个人感受到它的时候就明白了。举例来说,一家大型营利性企业与医院之间差别显著,同样,和大学相比也是一样。你只需要观察企业的家具设备的摆放、员工们都在吹嘘些什么、着装如何,等等,就能判定它的企业文化。

可以把企业文化看作是一个系统。系统投入包括反馈,例如来自社会的、专家的、法律的、新闻故事、名人、关于竞争或是服务的价值观念等。整个

---

① 资料来源:http://www.mapnp.org/library/org_thry/culture/culture.htm

Chapter 3 Organisational Culture and Its Impact on Human Capital

The objectives of this chapter

- Understand the importance of organizational culture and its functions
- Introoluce the influence of culture on human resource management
- Investigate how specific Chinese culture and its impact on human capital through research findings and case studies

There is a growing awareness of the importance of understanding organisational culture in cross-border settings (Hofstede, 1980). Organisational culture refers to members' shared perceptions and interpretations of what organisational policies, practices and procedures signal about the organisation's norms, value system and desired objectives. A number of scholars have proposed that organisational culture can either promote or inhibit individual creativity and job performance through the values and behaviour that the culture or climate engender (Amabile *et al.*, 1996; Shalley *et al.*, 2004).

What Is Culture?[①]

Basically, organisational culture is the personality of an organisation. Culture is comprised of the assumptions, values, norms and tangible signs (artefact) of organisation members and their behaviour. Members of an organisation soon come to sense the particular culture of an organisation. Culture is one of those terms that is difficult to express distinctly, but everyone knows it when they encounter it. For example, the culture of a large, for-profit corporation is quite different than that of a hospital, which in turn is quite different from that of a university. You can determine the culture of an organisation by looking at the arrangement of furniture, what the members brag about, what members wear etc.—just as you can use similar signals to get a feeling about someone's personality.

Organizational culture can be looked at as a system. Inputs include feedback from various places such as society, professions, laws, stories, heroes, values related to

---

① Source: http://www.mapnp.org/library/org_thry/culture/culture.htm

过程建立在我们的设想、价值观、规范准则之上，例如我们对金钱、时间、设施、空间、人本身等的观念。组织文化的输出或影响包括组织行为、技术、策略、形象、产品、服务、外形等（Stoner、Freeman 和 Gilbert，1995）。

文化理念在组织级别的变革管理中显得尤为重要。从业者开始意识到除了拥有完美的计划之外，组织管理变革不仅要包括结构和过程的改变，同时还要改变企业文化。

过去几十年的大量研究形成了组织文化的理念，特别是关于如何改变组织文化（Hon、Bloom 和 Crant，2014）。有传言说组织级别的变革大都以失败告终，而通常失败的原因是缺乏对文化核心地位的理解，以及对文化在组织中扮演怎样的角色的理解。因此，许多组织的政策制定者把确立组织策略和价值观念摆在与建立组织使命和愿景同等重要的位置上。

组织文化

和个体本身一样，组织文化也有其个性特征，它具有持久稳定的特性，可以帮助我们预测其态度及行为表现。一个组织的文化可能很难去界定，但它对组织中个体的行为表现有很大的影响。去了解组织中个体的行为可以帮助我们深入理解组织机构中突出的文化特征，并且能够弄清楚个体如何学习企业文化以及企业文化是如何反过来影响个体的。

近期研究表明，组织文化的核心部分有七个主要特征（Hofsted，1980）。

（1）创新与冒险，指的是鼓励员工开拓创新和敢于冒险的程度。

（2）注重细节，指期待员工展现出对细节的准确把握、分析和注意力。

（3）结果导向，指管理更侧重结果或成果，而不是为实现目标所使用的技术和经历的过程。

（4）以人为本，指管理决策考虑结果对组织内成员的影响。

（5）团队导向，指工作活动围绕团队展开而不是单一个体。

（6）进取性，指成员更具进取心、竞争性，而不是懒散随便。

（7）稳定性，指组织将重心放在保持现状上，而不是扩大发展。

competition or service etc. The process is based on our assumptions, values and norms, e. g. our values related to money, time, facilities, space and people. Outputs, or the effects of organisational culture, are things such as organisational behaviour, technologies, strategies, image, products, services, appearance etc (Stoner, Freeman, & Gilbert, 1995).

The concept of culture is particularly important when attempting to manage organisation-wide change. Practitioners are coming to realise that despite the best-laid plans, organisational change must include not only changing structures and processes, but also changing the corporate culture.

There has been a great deal of research over the past decades about the concept of organisational culture—particularly in regard to learning how to change organisational culture (Hon, Bloom, & Crant, 2014). Organisational change efforts are rumoured to fail in the vast majority of cases. Usually, this failure is credited to a lack of understanding of the strong role that culture plays in organisations. Therefore, many strategic planners now place as much emphasis on identifying strategic values as they do on mission and vision.

Organisational Culture

Organisations have personalities like individuals, they have enduring and stable traits that help us predict their attitudes and behaviour. An organisation's culture may be hard to define, but it has a major effect on the behaviour of individuals in the organisation. To understand behaviour in an organisational culture will help us to understand the organisation's dominant culture and to understand how individuals adopt a culture.

Recent research has shown that there are seven primary characteristics that capture the essence of an organisation's culture (Hofstede, 1980).

(1) Innovation and risk taking. That's the degree to which employees are encouraged to be innovative and take risks.

(2) Attention to detail. That's the degree to which employees are expected to exhibit precision, analysis and attention to detail.

(3) Outcome orientation. That's the degree to which management focuses on results or outcomes rather than on the techniques and processes used to achieve these outcomes.

(4) People orientation. That's the degree to which management decisions take into consideration the effect of outcomes on people within the organisation.

(5) Team orientation. That's the degree to which work activities are organised around teams rather than individuals.

(6) Aggressiveness. That's the degree to which people are aggressive and competitive rather than easy-going.

(7) Stability. That's the degree to which an organisation focuses on maintaining the status quo in contrast to growth.

以上每种文化特征存在从低到高连续的等级。详估组织机构的这七类特征,能够给出组织文化的综合状况。组织文化成了成员们对机构达成共识的重要基础,包括对机构的想法感触、组织内事务是怎样完成的以及成员应该要怎样表现。我们认为,组织内部个体成员有着不同背景、在不同层级工作,他们就会倾向以不同的措辞来描述组织文化。举例说明,中国经理人在做决策时比美国人更以群体为导向,那是由于中国的文化价值更具有一致性与合作性。因此,中国的总裁在做出重要决策之前,都会收集大量信息,在团体决策时用来达成共识。

文化一词属于描述性术语

组织文化与员工如何接受或感知这七类特征有很大关系,而不在于他们是否喜欢。也就是说,它是一个描述性的说法。这点如此重要是因为它将组织文化的概念和工作满意度区别开来。

关于组织文化的研究旨在评估员工是如何看待组织机构本身的:是否具有清晰的目标和业绩预期? 组织是否鼓励创新? 是否鼓励竞争? 与此相反,关于工作满意度的研究试图去评估对工作环境的有效反应,其更多关注的是,员工对组织预期、薪酬实践、处理冲突的方式等此类问题有怎样的感受。尽管两个术语在特性上有重叠的地方,但需要记住的是,组织文化一词属于描述性的,工作满意度属于评估性的。

强势文化与弱势文化

区别强势文化与弱势文化变得日益流行起来,强势文化对员工行为具有更大的影响力,与离职率更具有相关性。

在有着强势文化的组织中,组织的核心价值理念被广泛的大众深刻地接受着(Stoner、Freeman 和 Gilbert,1995)。越多成员接受核心价值,对价值观的信赖越多,文化自然就越强势。与该定义一致,强势文化对成员的行为具有巨大的影响力,因为高共识度和凝聚力可以建立高强度行为控制的内部氛围。例如,Giordano Ltd. 建立了零售业中最强大的服务文化之一。该企业的员工们十分清楚地知道企业对自己有什么样的期待,并且这些期待在

Each of these cultural characteristics exists on a continuum from low to high. Appraisingan organisation on these seven characteristics gives a composite picture of the organisation's culture. This culture becomes the basis for feelings of shared understanding that members have about the organisation, how things are done in this organisation and the way members are supposed to behave. We should expect that individuals with different backgrounds or at different levels in an organisation will tend to describe the organisation's culture in different ways. For example, decision making by Chinese managers is much more group oriented than in the United States because of the Chinese value conformity and cooperation. So before Chinese CEOs make an important decision, they collect a large amount of information, which is then used in consensus-forming group decisions.

Culture Is a Descriptive Term

Organisational culture is concerned with how employees perceive the seven characteristics, not whether they like them. That is, it is a descriptive term. This point is important because it differentiates the concept of organisational culture from that of job satisfaction.

Research onorganisational culture has sought to measure how employees see their organisation. Are there clear objectives and performance expectations? Does the organisation reward innovation? Does it encourage competitiveness?

In contrast, research on job satisfaction seeks to measure affective responses to the work environment. It is concerned with how employees feel about the organisation's expectations, reward practices, methods for handling conflict and the like. Although the two terms undoubtedly have characteristics that overlap, keep in mind that the term *organisational culture* is descriptive, whereas *job satisfaction* is evaluative (Stoner, Freeman, & Gilbert, 1995).

Strong vs. Weak Cultures

It has become increasingly popular to differentiate between strong and weak cultures. The argument is that strong cultures have a greater effect on employee behaviour and are more directly related to turnover rates.

In an organisation with a strong culture, the organisation's core values are both intensely held and widely shared (Stoner, Freeman, & Gilbert, 1995). The more members who accept the core values and the greater their commitment to those values, the stronger the culture is. Consistent with this definition, a strong culture will have a greater influence on the behaviour of its members because the high degree of sharedness and intensity creates an internal climate of high behavioural control. For example, Giordano Ltd. has developed one of the strongest service cultures in the retailing industry. In the company, employees know in no uncertain terms what is expected of

很大程度上会影响个人行为。

强势文化带来的具体结果之一就是降低员工流失率。强势文化表明员工们对企业代表着什么达成了共识。目标一致可以建立起内部凝聚力、忠诚度和组织认同感(Hon、Bloom 和 Crant,2014;Hon 和 Leung,2011)。这些品质反过来会减少员工离职的倾向。

文化有什么作用

我们前面已经提到了组织文化对个体行为的影响作用,也明确提出了观点——强势文化与降低员工流失率之间有关联。在这个部分,我们将全面仔细地回顾组织文化的功能,并分析文化是否会为组织制造麻烦。

文化的功能

组织文化表现出以下几种功能(Stoner、Freeman 和 Gilbert,1995),其中最重要的是"制定游戏规则"。

(1)划定界限:它将该组织机构与其他组织机构区别开来。

(2)使组织成员产生认同感。

(3)促使形成对大于个人利益的事情的认同,而非限于个人私利。

(4)增强社会体系的稳定性,类似于一种社会黏合剂。

(5)建立责任意识以及控制组织机制,它可以引导、塑造员工的态度和行为。

企业文化的定义其实是很难摸透的,是模糊的、含蓄的并常被认为是理所当然的(Hofstede,1980)。但每个组织机构都会建立起一组核心的构想、协议和隐含规则,从而管理日常工作行为。新成员们在了解并掌握了这些规则后,才被认为是组织的一员。部分高层主管或是一线员工的违规行为会引起全体员工的谴责,并受到严厉的处罚。遵守规则成为得到奖赏和向上晋升的基本要求。

本章后面会陆续提到,谁会得到工作机会,谁被认定为是高效员工,以及选择提拔哪位员工与个人和组织的契合度有很大关系。在迪士尼乐园和迪士尼世界工作的员工通常看起来很有魅力、很整洁,有着健康的体魄,面带灿烂的微笑,这些都不是巧合。这就是迪士尼始终追求的形象,公司选拔出来的员工也将保持这一形象。因此无论是不成文的规定、正式规则还是管理条例,都确保了其员工一旦在岗,就会表现得整齐划一,符合组织的要求。

them，and these expectations go a long way in shaping their behaviour.

One specific result of a strong culture should be low employee turnover. A strong culture demonstrates high agreement among members about what the organisation stands for（Hon，Bloom，& Crant，2014；Hon & Leung，2011）. Such unanimity of purpose builds cohesiveness，loyalty and organisational commitment. These qualities，in turn，lessen employees' propensity to leave the organisation.

What Does Culture Do?

We have discussed to the effect of organisational culture on behaviour. We have also explicitly argued that a strong culture should be associated with reduced turnover. In this section，we more carefully review the functions that culture performs and assess whether a culture should be called a liability for an organisation.

Culture's Functions

Culture performs several functions（Stoner，Freeman，& Gilbert，1995）；most importantly it"defines the rules of the game". Specifically，culture

（1）defines boundaries by distinguishing an organisation from other organisations；

（2）provides a sense of identity for organisation members；

（3）facilitates the generation of commitment to something larger than one's individual self-interest；

（4）enhances social system stability which is similar to a kind of social glue；and

（5）operates as a sense making and control mechanism that guides and shapes the attitudes and behaviour of employees.

Culture by definition is elusive，intangible，implicit and taken for granted by everyone（Hofstede，1980）. However，every organisation develops a core set of assumptions，understandings and implicit rules that govern day-to-day behaviour in the workplace. Until newcomers learn the rules，they are not accepted as full-fledged incumbents of the organisation. Transgressions of the rules by high-level executives or front-line employees result in universal disapproval and powerful penalties. Conformity to the rules becomes the primary basis for reward and upward mobility.

As we show later in this chapter，job offers，high performance appraisals and promotions are strongly influenced by the individual-organisation fit，that is，whether the applicant or employee's attitudes and behaviour are compatible with the organisation's culture. It is not a coincidence that employees at Disneyland's strong culture seem to be attractive，clean and wholesome with bright smiles. That is the image that Disneyland seeks，and the company selects employees who will maintain that image. Both the informal norms and formal rules and regulations ensure that Disneyland employees，once on the job，will act in a relatively uniform and predictable way.

文化作为一种负担[①]

我们始终用客观的方式看待文化。我们并不说它是好还是坏，只讨论它的存在。如上文所述，文化的诸多功能对组织机构和员工来说都是有价值的。文化可以强化组织成员的承诺精神，增加员工行为的一致性，这些很明显有利于组织发展。从员工的角度来看，企业文化有价值是因为它能降低职业的模糊性。它可以明确指出怎样完成任务、哪些是重要的。但我们不能忽略的是文化具有潜在的功能障碍，特别是在强势文化中。

当共同价值观与推动组织效能不相符的时候，文化就成为一种负担。这常常出现在组织环境多变的情况下，因为当环境正在快速变化时，根深蒂固的文化就会显得不合时宜（Stoner、Freeman 和 Gilbert，1995）。在稳定的环境下行为一致性对机构来说是一项财富。然而，它也有可能给企业造成负担，使组织应对多变环境的能力降低。

近些年，众多人力资源相关的研究在中国内地展开，这是因为中国内地已经成为最热门的外商直接投资地点（Leung、Wang 和 Hon，2011；Luo，2001）。许多跨国集团开始出现在中国内地市场，与中国合伙人经营国际联合投资，或是组建子公司。但这些公司很难将处于核心层级的中国员工留在公司内。然而，为了发展合作文化，保持这些员工的稳定性是很有必要的，并且要使他们的能力和素养更适应公司的发展。因此，经理人需要审视他们的工作态度，考核其工作行为，与不同类型公司的员工相比较（跨国合资公司、国有企业、私营公司）。人力资源经理人尤其对文化差异在中外合作中所扮演的角色感兴趣。

在中国背景下的研究成果[②]

文化是一种社会认知结构，它反映的是特定群体中成员的意识形态，Zohar 和 Luria（2004）把它描述为"群体搜寻线索，随后去检验，得到证实后趋向于协商达成一致（例如社会性解释推断），从而建立起一个更易让人理解和接受的环境"。在工作环境中，我们关注的是团队成员拥有同样的工作价

[①]　资料来源：http://web.cba.neu.edu/~ewertheim/macro/culture.htm

[②]　资料来源：Leang, K., Wang, Z. M., & Hon, A. H. Y. (2011). Moderating effects on the compensation gap between locals and expatriates in China: A multilever analysis. *Journal of International Management*, 17(1): 54-67.

Culture as a Liability [1]

We have been treating culture in a non-judgmental manner. We have not said that it is good or bad, only that it exists. Many of its functions, as outlined, are valuable for both organisations and employees. Culture enhances organisational commitment and increases the consistency of employee behaviour. These clearly are benefits to an organisation. From an employee's standpoint, culture is valuable because it reduces ambiguity. It tells employees how things are done and what is important, but we should not ignore the potentially dysfunctional aspects of culture, especially a strong culture.

Culture becomes a problem when the shared values do not agree with those that will facilitate organisation's effectiveness. This situation is most likely to occur when an organisation's environment is dynamic (Stoner, Freeman, & Gilbert, 1995). When the environment is undergoing rapid change, an organisation's entrenched culture may no longer be appropriate. Consistency of behaviour is an asset to an organisation in a stable environment. It may, however, burden the organisation and hinder its ability to respond to changes in the environment.

In recent years, numerous HR-related studies have been conducted in Chinese Mainland, because it has become the most popular destination for foreign direct investments (Leung, Wang, & Hon, 2011; Luo, 2001). Many multinational corporations (MNCs) are present in Chinese Mainlend, operating either international joint ventures with their Chinese partners or wholly owned subsidiaries. These companies have problems keeping Chinese employees in core positions. A stable staff is absolutely required to develop a corporate culture in which employees can adapt their competency and ability to the company. Managers need to consider work-related attitudes and behaviour and to compare them across different types of companies (international joint ventures, state-owned, private). HR managers are particular interested in the role of cultural differences in expatriate Chinese collaborations.

Research Findings in Chinese Context [2]

Culture is a social-cognitive construct that reflects sense-making among a particular group of individuals; Zohar and Luria (2004) describe it as "a collaborative search for cues, and subsequent testing and validation leading to negotiated (i. e., socially construed) agreements that make an environment more understandable". In the workplace context, we are interested in the degree to which a group of people share

---

[1] Source: http://web.cba.neu.edu/~ewertheim/macro/culture.htm

[2] Source: Leang, K., Wang, Z.M., &. Hon, A.H.Y.(2011).Moderating effects on the compensation gap between locals and expatriates in China: A multilever analysis.*Journal of International Management*, 17(1): 54－67.

值和准则的程度。通过不断的社会互动和群体意识交流，员工能够将组织和管理的实践、政策、过程和行为表现解析为一种标志，内容是组织期望看到、支持鼓励、奖赏员工什么样的行为活动和决策。这些共享的意识形态可以创造文化，反过来，它能指出制定规范法则和社会价值的正确途径，从而实现既定目标。

在中国有两个重要的文化价值特点——现代性与传统性，这两者与员工的创造力和绩效表现有着极大的关联。在过去的几十年里，中国经历了巨大的现代化发展，Yang(1998)称之为"一段持续抗争与变革的进程"。一部分组织机构和个体拥护传统儒家伦理价值观和五伦关系准则中的遵从权威，重点强调和谐共处，以及形式主义的人际关系(Farh 等 1997；Yang 1998)。另一部分组织机构和个人则远离传统价值，倾向于现代化价值观(Hon、Bloom和 Crant，2014；Yang，1998)，包括开放思维、自由平等以及自信自主。越来越多的文献表明，在中式工作环境中，选择遵循传统或是现代价值观对多变的工作环境起着重要作用，影响的方面包括领导力、组织公平、组织公民行为和组织支持感。有一种文化强调的是传统、遵循规则、等级森严的人际关系、严格的上下级关系以及稳固性，从而阻碍了员工创造力的发展，因为这些都向员工传达了一个强烈的信号——组织不欢迎改变，鼓励员工维持固有的趋势，拒绝变革(Hon、Bloom 和 Crant，2014；West，等，2004)。另一种文化强调创新和发现新鲜事物，拒绝传统权威，提倡平等和人员自由流动，接收合理的、富有野心的工作指示，这些都指向一个方向——欢迎变化。对于后一种文化来说，其中一种推动创新的方式是，通过发送强烈的信号向员工表明，为了实现高创造性，冒风险进行探索性的、可能失败的活动是受到鼓励和保护的(Amabile 等，1996；George，2007；Shalley 等，2004)。由于现代化观念的影响，对于创新的新态度开始在中国的环境中显现出来，并被认为是中国文化中一项重要的社会价值。

与传统相反的是，现代化主要反映了开放、前卫的思维模式，以及追求进步、不断改进的精神(Triandis，1989；Earley 和 Erez，1997)。在现代化的组织中，每个个体成员都有自由选择权和自我表达权(Fahr 等，1997；Zhang等，2003)。现代化以求进步、求发展为先，主动参与强有力的，甚至革命性的变革，从而确保不断前进发展(Zhang 等，2003)。因此，我们断定更注重现代化文化的工作环境更富有创造力。尽管我们知道还没有研究表明，现代化文

common perceptions of work values and norms. Through on-going social interaction and collective construal, employees interpret the organisational and management practices, policies, procedures and behaviour as signals about what kinds of actions and decisions are expected, supported and rewarded. These shared interpretations create a culture that, in turn, indicates the correct ways of enacting norms and values, and achieving desired objectives.

In China, two important cultural values—modernity and tradition—are of particular relevance to employee creativity and work performance. Over the past several decades, China has undergone significant modernisation, what Yang (1998) calls "a continuous process of protest and change". Some organisations and individuals have responded by adhering to traditional Confucian values and the Five Cardinal Relations system of deference to authority, and by emphasising harmony and formalistic interpersonal relationships (Farh, *et al.*, 1997; Yang, 1998). Other organisations and individuals have responded by shifting away from traditional values and toward modernity (Hon, Bloom, & Crant, 2014; Yang, 1998) and values of open-mindedness, egalitarianism and assertiveness. A growing body of research suggests that in Chinese work contexts, these differences in adherence to tradition versus modernity may have important implications for a variety of work phenomena including leadership, organisational justice, organisational citizenship behaviour and perceived organisational support. Cultures that emphasise such things as tradition, adherence to rules, hierarchical interpersonal relationships, strict lines-of-authority and stability are thought to inhibit creativity because they send a strong signal to employees that organisations do not welcome change, and thus encourage employees' inherent tendency to resist change (Hon, Bloom, & Crant, 2014; West, *et al.*, 2004). In contrast, cultures that emphasise openness to new experiences, novelty, rejecting traditional authority, equality of members, freedom to move and taking a rational, ambitious approach to work signal that change is welcome. One way this latter kind of culture is thought to promote creativity is through the powerful signals it sends that it is safe for employees to undertake the risky, exploratory failure-prone activities that are integral to creative performance (Amabile, *et al.*, 1996; George, 2007; Shalley, *et al.*, 2004). This different attitude to creativity is manifest in Chinese contexts through the concept of modernity, which has been identified as an important social value in Chinese culture.

In contrast to tradition, modernity promotes open, forward-thinking mindsets and progressive, improvement-oriented actions (Triandis, 1989; Earley & Erez, 1997). In organisations expressing modernity, each individual is assumed to have freedom of choice and the right to self-expression (Fahr, *et al.*, 1997; Zhang, *et al.*, 2003). Modernity manifests itself in a preference for progress and a willingness to engage in strong, even revolutionary change to ensure progress (Zhang, *et al.*, 2003). As a consequence, we posit that work environments that emphasise modernity are likely to be more creative.

化与拒绝改变之间有怎样程度的关联,但先前的一些理论和研究为该观点提供了间接的理论支持(例如,Fahr 等,1997;George,2007;Yang,1998)。注重现代化文化的工作环境会鼓励员工进行创造性思考,公开讨论问题和机会,探索处理事情的新方法,挑战传统思维和现状。如此开放性、革新性的思维模式或许传达出一个强有力的信号,即变化是件好事,同时可以预料和接受的是创新会带来风险,个人的努力应该更具有创造力,还应该鼓励和支持诚信。未来前进的方向是为员工建立更积极的期待值,包括创造力带来的成果以及变革。在此环境下,员工的工作会更具积极性,并尝试新颖、独特的方式去解决问题。

文化及人力资源策略

促进推广文化的进程、提升企业生产力和人文发展是指导制定人力资源策略的关键所在。其中有两个因素需要考虑:其一是外部文化或企业环境;其二则是内部或个人应对新环境的优缺点。在定义人力资源策略时这两个因素都必须考虑进去(Dessler,2017)。

在现有的经济改革环境下,中国企业的管理策略受诸多快速变化的因素影响(社会经济因素、科技进步因素、商业环境因素)。根据这些方面对中国人力资源发展的影响,有四项主要变化正在发生(Zhang 和 Wu,2004):国有企业的结构性变革和市场经济导向分散化、市场化;社会价值观导向从集体主义到个人主义;组织变革中人力管理政策从单向分配工作到在人才市场上双向选择;管理模式中的文化变革从国内导向到跨国集团(MNCs)和国际化管理导向(Luo,2001)。合资企业的迅速发展对强化中国管理策略的跨文化性和战略职能提出了要求。

近些年中国酒店业人力资源管理的飞速发展对企业的成功起着至关重要的作用,人们更倾向于考虑自主性决策者,而不是被动、听话的服从者(Hon,2012)。同时也出现了许多新的、更综合全面的人力资源管理政策。各个实证研究结果提出了众多学术观点,关于人力资源体系的本质,如何设计并植入企业,从而帮助企业提升核心竞争力。跨国企业(MNCs)在诸如中国等发展中国家建立运营中心,利用它们的廉价劳动力和市场潜力的优势。

Although we are aware of no research that has examined the degree to which modernity is associated with resistance to change, prior theory and research have provided indirect support for this idea (e.g. Fahr, *et al.*, 1997; George, 2007; Yang, 1998). When work environments emphasise modernity, they encourage progressive thinking, open discussions of problems and opportunities, exploring new ways of doing things and challenging conventional thinking and the status quo. This openness and progressive thinking may send powerful signals that change is good, that the risks of creativity are expected and accepted and that an individual's efforts to be creative, including integrity, will be supported and encouraged. The progressive orientation toward the future is likely to create positive expectations among employees about the outcomes of creativity and change. Employees in these work environments are likely to be encouraged to take the initiative and to try new and different approaches to work.

Culture and Human Resource Strategy

Facilitating the process of cultural and corporate productivity as well as human development are the key concerns of a human resource strategy. Two factors have to be taken into account to reach these goals. One is the external culture or corporate environment, and the other is the internal or personal strengths and non-strengths that allow an employee to cope with the new environment. Both factors must be considered when defining a human resource strategy (Dessler, 2017).

Under the present economic reforms, management practices in Chinese companies are being greatly affected by rapid changes (socio-economic, technological and business). In terms of their effect on HR development in China, four main changes have been observed (Zhang & Wu, 2004): structural changes in the state-owned enterprises and market economy toward decentralisation and market orientation; social changes in value orientation from collectivist values to individualistic ones; organisational changes in personnel management practice from one-way assigned jobs to the two-way-choice labour market; and cultural changes in management patterns from domestic orientations to multinational corporations (MNCs) and international management orientations (Luo, 2001). The rapid development of international joint ventures has created a need for the strengthening of the cross-cultural and strategic functions in Chinese management.

HRM is crucial to organisational success in the hospitality industry, and recent changes in China have moved towards considering people as autonomous decision-makers rather than passive, compliant followers (Hon, 2012). New and more comprehensive HRM practices have been presented, and the respective empirical research findings have generated numerous insights about the nature of HR systems and how they can be designed and implemented to help companies improve their competitive position. Multinational corporations (MNCs) have set up operations in many developing countries such as China to take advantage of their low labour costs and high market potential.

　　然而,前来中国的美国企业中有一半都以失败告终,原因是国外专家和商务人士对派遣员工赴海外工作并没有充分准备,这在中国也有相似的情况。尽管预料中的中国经理人短缺状况正在改变,企业家精神正在被培养,但未来的冲突依旧无可避免。其中最典型的冲突就是外籍员工和本地员工之间的薪酬差异。考虑到合作的巨大潜力,管理者理解并接受文化差异带来的结果便显得尤为重要。

　　外籍员工常被安置在企业核心职位,以此来确保企业高效运营。由此带来的主要问题是外籍员工薪酬是依据其原籍人力市场标准来制定的,然而本地员工薪酬是依照当地人力市场发放的,这造成了两个群体间薪酬的巨大鸿沟(Black、Gregersen、Mendenhall 和 Stroh,1998;Harvey,1993)。关于双重工资体系的研究调查发现,新员工得到的薪资比老员工低很多,表明其中弱势群体通常视其薪酬待遇为不公平的(Lee 和 Martin,1991;Martin 和 Peterson,1987)。在跨国集团的双重工资体系中,薪资差距比本土企业大很多,且通常给跨国集团带来更极端的负面影响。

　　外籍员工与本地员工间巨大的薪酬差距确实引起了两个群体间不小的冲突(例如,Gladwin 和 Walter,1980;Hon 和 Lu,2015),也是本地员工不公平待遇的来源之一(例如,Chen、Choi 和 Chi,2002)。由于大部分的冲突都会产生反效果,如此巨大的薪酬差距正在威胁着跨国集团在境外的正常运营(De Dreu 和 Weingart,2003),不公平现象也引起了大范围的负面反馈,从士气萎靡、不合作、表现不佳到退缩行为、高流失率和员工工作场所偏离行为(Colquitt、Conlon、Wesson、Porter 和 Ng,2001)。鉴于薪酬差距极具破坏力的潜能,对人力资源经理人来说,制定正确的人力资源管理政策来减少薪酬差距带来的负面影响,十分重要。

　　研究发现,参与决策和信任的氛围能够降低由外籍员工和本地员工的薪酬差距带来的负面影响。除此之外,外籍员工的其他积极的自主决断的行为也可能减少该负面影响。Shen 和 Cho(2005)提出了一个有关管理决断自主权的理论框架,它建立在对目标自由和行动自由考量的基础上。尽管企业的目标任务通常是由总部来制定的,跨国集团下属子公司有少数变更的权力,但在外籍人士的控制下,行动更为直接。例如,Zhang、George 和 Chan(2006)报道称,在中国跨国集团内,若本地高级主管与集团总部间保有高质

However，half of the assignments of American companies in China fail because the foreign experts and business people are unprepared for their work in an international context. The situation on the Chinese side is similar. Although the supposed "inadequacy" of Chinese managers is changing and their entrepreneurial spirit has been fostered，nonetheless，future conflicts seem inevitable. Given the growing potential for cooperation，it is important for managers to understand and accept the effects of cultural differences. One of the typical conflicts is the compensation difference between expatriates and local employees.

This difference in compensation occurs because expatriates are placed in key posts to ensure the effectiveness of these multinational operations. A major problem with this arrangement is that expatriates are paid according to their home labour market，whereas locals are paid according to the local labour market，resulting in a large compensation gap between these two groups (Black，Gregersen，Mendenhall，& Stroh，1998；Harvey，1993). Research on two-tier wage systems，in which new employees are paid substantially less than existing employees，has shown that，the disadvantaged group typically regards its compensation as unfair (Lee & Martin，1991；Martin & Peterson，1987). The compensation gap is much larger in MNCs than in domestic two-tier wage systems，and its negative consequences are likely to be more extreme in an MNC context than in a domestic context.

The compensation gap between expatriates and locals is indeed a cause of conflict between these two groups (e.g. Gladwin & Walter，1980；Hon & Lu，2015) and an example of injustice to local employees (e.g. Chen，Choi，& Chi，2002). This compensation gap threatens the viability of the foreign operations of MNCs，as conflict is mostly counterproductive (De Dreu & Weingart，2003)，and injustice breeds a wide range of negative reactions，ranging from low morale，uncooperativeness and poor performance to withdrawal behaviour，turnover and workplace deviance (Colquitt，Conlon，Wesson，Porter，& Ng，2001). Given the destructive potential of the compensation gap，it is important for HR managers to identify HRM practices that minimise the negative effects associated with the compensation gap.

Previous studies have found that participation in decision making and a climate of trust reduce the negative effect of the compensation gap between expatriates and locals. Other positive discretional acts on the part of the expatriates may also reduce the negative consequences associated with the compensation gap. Shen and Cho (2005) have developed a framework for conceptualising management discretion based on latitude in objectives and latitude in actions. Although objectives may be prescribed by headquarters and less alterable in MNC subsidiaries，actions are more directly under the control of expatriates. For instance，Zhang，George and Chan (2006) reported that in China，MNC senior local executives were less likely to quit in reaction to low perceived local staff competence if they

量的交流沟通,并互相信任,则大多不可能因为意识到本地员工薪资较低而选择离职。这些研究成果表明若外籍员工在建立信任氛围、培养员工间高质量的沟通氛围方面有所贡献,则这些行为可以传达给本地员工集团非剥削的意图,并能有效减少两群体间薪资差距造成的消极影响。与该观点相一致,Chen、Tjosvold 和 Fang(2005)调查发现,在中国,若本地员工与外籍经理人之间达成一致的合作目标,他们更有可能参与建设性争论,从而得到更高的工作满意度以及组织认同感。本地与外籍员工间合作氛围的存在将标志着集团对外籍员工并没有利用、剥削的初衷。而其他一些积极的人力资源管理政策则由外籍员工共同发起,例如赋权、上级支持、训练和指导,这些也都将起到同样的作用。综上所述,中国人力资源管理的问题为该领域的研究指出了新方向,即外籍与本土人力资源经理人共同进行管理实践,从而降低两个群体薪资差距造成的损失。

中国人力资源经理人在跨国集团中始终面临诸多挑战。与上述例子相似,本地员工强烈反对薪资差距的存在,这与消极对待外籍员工和机构有关。显然,为了促使跨国集团良好运营,这些消极作用是阻碍发展的,且需要被控制住。外籍员工将本地员工纳入决策制定之中,目的是缓冲薪酬差距的负面作用力,他们应当付出真心实意、明确的努力,齐心协力地为本地人才营造一个协作、包容的氛围。外籍经理人作为一个群体,需要学习如何更高效地将本地员工纳入决策行列,从而受益于包容、信任、合作的文化氛围。

理解文化所含的价值观,能最小化跨文化的冲突;明白"关系"的本质所在以及当地的人际交往的核心,能最小化人与人之间的矛盾冲突。当做出决定时,二者是识别家庭、工作及人际关系的基本途径,同时二者具有共同特征。这需要员工自发性地进行自我了解。除此之外,成功的跨文化管理不是一蹴而就的。如果目标是真正理解和接受其他文化和企业形象,那么这将是一个持续自省的过程。

融入新的文化或组织环境可以借助诸多途径,其中包括灵活性、开放性、主动接受一个问题的多个解决方案、抗压性、应对孤立与陌生情境的自我激励,对未知的好奇。意识训练以及培养沟通技巧可以提高透明度,降低(不切实际的)互相的期望,从而使跨文化与组织环境更富有成效、更和谐。

had high-quality communication with the headquarters and regarded the headquarters as trustworthy. These findings suggest that if expatriates make an effort to establish a climate of trust and develop a climate of high-quality communication, they are likely to convey to local employees a non-exploitative intent on their part and cushion the negative effect of the compensation gap between the two groups. Consistent with this argument, Chen, Tjosvold and Fang (2005) found that if local employees in China identified a cooperative goal with expatriate managers, they were more likely to engage in constructive controversy with expatriates, resulting in high job satisfaction and organisational commitment. The existence of a cooperative climate between locals and expatriates should signal the absence of an exploitative intent on the part of expatriates. Other positive HR management practices that may be collectively initiated by expatriates, such as empowerment, supervisory support, and coaching and mentoring, may work as well. In a nutshell, HRM issues in China open up a new line of research on management practices that may be collectively initiated by HR expatriate managers and local managers to reduce the damages of the compensation gap between locals and expatriates.

HR managers in China constantly face challenges specific to MNCs. Consistent with the above example, local employees strongly disapprove of the compensation gap, which is related to negative reactions toward expatriates and their organisations. Obviously, these negative reactions are counterproductive and need to be contained. Including local employees in decision making buffers the negative effect of the compensation gap, and expatriates should make genuine, visible and concerted efforts to build a collaborative and inclusive climate for local employees. Expatriate managers as a group need to learn how to effectively engage locals in decision-making to benefit from the effects of an inclusive, trusting and collaborative cultural climate.

Intercultural conflicts can be minimised by knowing the underlying values; interpersonal conflicts can be minimised by knowing the underlying "guanxi" and personal relationships in the local country. Both are basic approaches to family, work and relationships that are part of decision making, and have a common denominator. They require a person to be willing to become more aware of him or herself. Moreover, successful intercultural management is not a one-time-event; if true understanding and acceptance of the other cultural or corporate identity is the goal, it is a process of constant self-examination.

Incorporation into the new cultural or organisational environment will be made easier through flexibility, openness, the readiness to accept more than one solution to every question, stress tolerance, ability to deal with isolation and estrangement, and curiosity about the unknown. Awareness training and the development of communication skills can bring clarity and reduce (unrealistic) mutual expectations, making an intercultural and organisational environment more productive and harmonious.

案例研究 3 - 1　▷▷▷▷▷▷

Happy Electronics 和它的组织文化

李先生,30 岁毕业于香港理工大学管理学专业,得到了一个绝佳的机遇,去经营管理一个香港的家族企业(Happy Electronics),现企业由他父亲的好友王先生管理,而他有退休的打算。

该电子公司生产十分专业的半导体零件,但近期受到了来自中国内地的企业的巨大压力,这些企业能力日益提升,逐渐占领了该市场。该公司已经损失了一些市场份额,且只能维持成本,并没有盈利。

Happy Electronics 占据葵涌某工业大厦的仓库用地。8 位高素质工程师和 6 名销售人员都拥有各自的办公室,却只有一间小会议室,远离工作车间,车间内有 15 名技术人员。每位工人有各自明确的任务,并直接向王先生汇报工作。

王先生人很友善,是一个传统的人,对待员工像对待家人一样,给予员工十分慷慨的奖励,并与年度总利润挂钩。这里并没有正式的绩效考核,但王先生每天和每个员工交谈,这样王先生对公司内发生的事情就非常了解。

王先生利用他个人的关系网络来制定公司决策,并且他也负责与公司主要客户和供应商沟通协商。他建立了一套严格的规章制度,期望每个员工出勤早、下班晚,且勤奋工作。他奖励对公司忠诚的员工。每年整个公司会组织出国旅行作为奖励。

问　题

(1) 请使用书中的基本理论来描述 Happy Electronics 的企业文化。

(2) 请使用至少两种正式的方法去描述组织文化,并用最恰当的方式简述该公司的文化。

(3) 请指出最适合该企业现状的文化,以及适合未来竞争环境的文化。

(4) 请给李先生提出战略性建议和用于改变组织文化的建议。若李先生采用这些策略,他将遇到怎样潜在的问题?

案例研究 3 - 2① ▷▷▷▷▷▷

在当下这个时代,企业正在逐渐接受全球化趋势,在这种情况下,领导者

---

① 资料来源:Grainger, S.(2003).Organizational guanxi in China's hotel sector.In *Chinese Culture, Organizational Behavior, and International Business Management*, edited by Alon, I., 57 - 72.Westport, CT:Praeger.

Case Study 3 – 1 ▶▶▶▶▶▶

Happy Electronics and Organisational Culture

Mr Li，a 30 year-old management graduate from PolyU，has been given a great opportunity to manage a family Hong Kong business（Happy Electronics）currently run by his father's close friend（Mr Wang），who wants to retire.

The electronics company makes rather specialised semiconductor parts，but recently has been under pressure from mainland firms of Chinese Mainland that increasingly have the ability to chase this niche market. The company has been losing market share and is just breaking even.

Happy Electronics occupies warehouse premises in an industrial building in Kwai Chung，Hong Kong. The well-qualified teams of eight engineers and six sales people each have their own office，but there is only one small meeting room apart from the shop floor，where there are 15 technicians. Each worker has a clearly defined task and reports directly to Mr Wong.

Mr Wang is a very friendly but traditional person and treats his employees like family，with generous reward schemes tied to annual overall profit. There are no formal performance appraisals，but Mr Wang makes a point of socialising with every employee every day，and seems to know what is happening inside his company quite well.

Mr Wang uses his personal network to decide company strategy，and is the one who negotiates with major clients and suppliers. He has established a strict set of rules and expects everyone to come in early，leave late and work diligently. He rewards loyalty from employees. Every year the whole company goes on a foreign tour as a type of "bonus" reward.

Questions

（1）Using the above information describe the culture of Happy Electronics.

（2）Research at least two formal ways to describe an organisational culture，and briefly use the most appropriate of these to describe the culture of Happy Electronics.

（3）Identify the fit of this culture with the likely current and future competitive environment of Happy Electronics.

（4）Advise Mr Li on some strategies that he might use to change the organisational culture. What potential problems might Mr Li experience in implementing these strategies?

Case Study 3 – 2[①] ▶▶▶▶▶▶

In an age in which corporations are globalising，it is important that leaders embrace

---

① Source：Grainger，S.（2003）.Organizational guanxi in China's hotel sector. In *Chinese Culture*，*Organizational Behavior*，*and International Business Management*，edited by Alon，I.，57–72.Westport，CT：Praeger；Grainger，S.（2010）.*Organizational Guanxi and State Owned Enterprises in South West China：The Roaring Dragon.Ho*，VDM：Saarbrucken.

拥有文化智能是十分重要的,为的是使他们能够建立新视角、培养新技能,带来高效领导力。文化智能是个体在不同文化间能有效履行个人职责的一种能力(Dyne、Ang 和 Livermore,2009)。文化知识与适应性对任何一位领导者来说都至关重要,尤其是在各类不同文化环境中工作的领导者。处在不同文化环境中,领导者很重要的一点就是要熟悉和理解文化基本的规范习俗和行为,目的是加以利用,适应它,最终实现高效领导力。领导者也应当知晓自己的文化背景与工作环境文化背景间的异同,以及这些基本文化将如何推动企业发展。

在中国"关系"是一种文化特征,指的是个人与组织间的互相关系,可以用来获得支持、推动相关贸易或个人的发展。"关系"不仅仅涉及中国人对社会和人际关系的态度,关系网络还让人们互相了解、给予人们责任义务和基本保障(Park 和 Luo,2001)。在中国,无论是本地企业还是跨国公司,若想挤进竞争激烈的市场环境并占有一席之地,都一定要尝试理解这些盘根错节的人际关系,及其对实现经营目标的影响。在商界,"关系"能够影响公司的财务表现、资金或资源流动、市场效益、竞争优势,并且依赖于公司的战略能力、经营方向、规模大小和历史(Park 和 Luo,2001)。"关系"代表了一种文化,一种深入企业内部且错综复杂的文化,它是企业做生意、招聘员工、签约合同的方式方法。为了避免经营失败,任何一位经理人或是领导者在不熟悉的文化环境下工作,都应该要试图理解这些文化是如何影响商业经营的,以及在此情景下如何应对各色问题。

案例研究 3-3① ▶▶▶▶▶▶

在 20 世纪 60 年代的中国,Roaring Dragon 酒店是一家远近闻名的四星级国有制酒店。由于其自身与国家政府的关联,酒店的业务从来访政要、高官贵人,到国宾。该酒店员工都是从其他国有酒店派遣过来的,他们认为自己是在享有盛誉的酒店里工作。酒店拥有两部分,旧的和新的部分。1993年一家跨国公司 KYZ 由省级行政单位接手经营来给该酒店提供管理策略,但与中国经理人的情况并不相适应,这使其丧失了在酒店的权利。这一做法导致酒店业绩下滑。合约结束后该酒店又回到了松散悠闲的环境氛围里。1998 年这一情境随着 Nothill 担任新总经理一职再次重演。Harvey 是Nothill 方的一名代表,他指出了该酒店文化里有代表性的几个问题,例如根深蒂固的关系、客户服务质量低,以及无竞争的工作环境。然而这一切并未

---

① 资料来源:Grainger,S.(2010).*Organizational Guanxi and State Owned Enterprises in South West China:The Roaring Dragon*.Ho,VDM:Saarbrucken.

cultural intelligence so that they are able to develop effective leadership. Cultural intelligence is the ability of an individual to effectively function across different cultures （Dyne，Ang，& Livermore，2009）. Cultural knowledge and adaptability are crucial skills of any leader working in a cultural environment different than his or her own. When working in different cultures，effective leaders must understand the norms，habits and behaviour of the underlying culture so that they can use them as strengths. A leader should also understand the differences between his or her culture and that of his or her working environment and how the underlying culture drives business.

"Guanxi"，a feature of Chinese culture，refers to a web of relationships both personal and organisational that is used to derive business or personal favours. "Guanxi" not only governs the attitude of the Chinese to social and personal relationship，the network also bestows mutual understanding，obligations and assurances（Park & Luo，2001）. Business people in China，whether local or international，have to understand these intricate relationships and their effect on business objectives if they are to achieve any competitive advantage over their competitors. In business，"guanxi" affects the financial performance of businesses，flow of resources，market benefits and competitive advantage and is dependent on a firm's strategic capabilities，orientation，size and history（Park & Luo，2001）. "Guanxi" is so entwined in Chinese culture that it is found in organisations and has become a way of doing business，recruitment and awarding contracts. To avoid failure，any manager or leader working in an unfamiliar cultural environment should seek to understand how that culture affects the business and how various issues are handled in that culture.

Case Study 3 – 3[①] ▶▶▶ ▶▶▶

The Roaring Dragon Hotel is a state-owned enterprise（SOE）and was the most famous four-star hotel in China in the 1960s. Due to its state connections，the hotel has enjoyed business from visiting government officials，dignitaries and state guests. The hotel has traditionally been staffed with employees who transferred from other SOEs and who considered working in the hotel prestigious. The hotel has two wings，an older one and more modern one. In 1993，KYZ，an international company，was contracted by the provincial administration to manage the hotel，a move that did not auger well for the Chinese managers who lost the privileges bestowed by their positions in the hotel. This move led to a decline in the returns made by the hotel. The contract was ended and the hotel went back to its relaxed environment. In 1998，Nothill became the new managers of the hotel. Harvey，a Nothill representative，identified problems in the hotel's culture such as entrenched "guanxi" practices，poor quality customer service and a non-competitive work environment. However，

---

① Source：Grainger，S.(2010).*Organizational Guanxi and State Owned Enterprises in South West China：The Roaring Dragon.Ho*，VDM：Saarbrucken.

取得显著成果（Graniger，2003）。

　　该酒店由 T. Erhi 接手掌管，Nothill 任命 Fortune 为酒店总经理，他使酒店在诸多其他四星酒店如雨后春笋般迅速发展的市场中，依旧保持快速增长。旧的部门被砍掉，在原处建起了新的五星级酒店。在进行大规模裁员后，酒店为剩余员工提供了相关培训。由于新职员的离职金比起老员工来说相对低廉，大部分新员工因此都被解雇了。因为缺乏对市场的敏感度，以及 Nothill 主管 Chef Thomason 坚持维持高价，酒店与 NuFu 旅行社之间的不合愈演愈烈。导致许多重要的员工们不是辞职，就是被调去 Roaring Dragon 公司，或是与酒店有重要业务往来的相关企业。员工与管理层之间的沟通存在障碍是一个很严重的问题。酒店市场部团队消极怠工，加上报酬不公，因此，员工们认为没必要额外努力工作去开拓酒店市场或业务范围。受到了财务方面的约束，五星酒店业务的发展十分缓慢。这些原因又夹杂了来自其他方面的挑战，共同导致了最后合约解除，酒店又恢复到以前的经营模式，甚至一部分被解雇的员工再次回到了中国管理者的手下（Grainger，2003）。

案例讨论 ▶▶▶▶▶▶

　　该案例的问题所在：文化不敏感、缺乏紧密的工作伙伴关系以及充分的沟通、管理变更不足、规划与发展策略不周密。

　　由于中外管理层人员和员工间文化背景的差异，在外国管理人员做事的方式与中国文化的行为规范间，势必会产生文化冲突和碰撞。这些都会带来不必要的问题或是挑战，特别是在裁去多余员工、沟通交流、战略发展布局和规划，甚至是管理变革方面。外籍管理层人员缺乏对中国文化的敏感度，这也可能导致管理失败。中国是从计划经济发展起来的，依旧烙着"关系网"的印记。外籍管理者常常没有意识到这些关系网对推动商业发展是必不可少的，这么做将损失很多利益，不仅是员工间的，甚至包括潜在客户。在礼仪方面也是如此，解聘员工时务必考虑文化因素，不让他们觉得十分丢脸。在该案例中，裁员本身是正确的，但是展开裁员的方式和角度并不正确。经理人针对年轻员工进行大量裁员是为了节省不必要的开支，但也减少了酒店的活力。

　　外籍经理人在沟通上的障碍、缺少和员工相处的时间，这都使员工和管理者之间缺少牢固的工作关系。并且他们也完全忽视了市场竞争力。这也说明了他们拒绝接受和 NuFu 预售合作，是基于他们认为 NuFu 价格低廉且拒绝提供折扣优惠的态度很强硬。同时外籍经理人管理变革的过程效果不佳。循序渐进地引入变革，与员工建立牢固的工作伙伴关系，这对任何一方都是再好不过的了。酒店管理者严格把控价格，导致缺少价格活动空间，这

no changes were achieved（Grainger，2003）.

The hotel was taken over by Erhi T，and Nothill appointed Fortune as the manager of the hotel amidst increased competition from new four-star hotels. The old section was to be demolished and a five-star wing put up in its place. Employees were provided with training after massive downsizing took place. Most young employees were laid off as their severance pay was cheaper than that of older employees. Crucial connections were severed，especially between the hotel and the NuFu travel agency due to competition insensitivity and insistence on high prices by Nothill head Chef Thomason. Important employees either resigned or transferred to the Roaring Dragon Limited or other associate companies with important contacts. Poor communication was also an issue between the employees and the new management. The marketing team was demotivated and poorly remunerated and thus saw no need to work extra hard to market the hotel or its services. The development of the five-star wing was slow due to financial constraints. These and other challenges led to the cancellation of the contract and hotel reverted to the old way of doing business with even some of the laid off employees coming back to work under the Chinese management（Grainger，2003）.

Discussions ▶▶▷▶▶▷

This case illustrates challenges related to cultural insensitivity，poor communication and lack of strong working relationships，poor change management and poor planning development.

Cultural collision between the ways things are done in foreign managers' cultures and the norms of Chinese culture can lead to problems and challenges especially in the downsizing and redundancy of employees，communication，strategy development and planning，and even change management. The case of the Roaring Dragon Hotel shows that foreign managers' lack of cultural sensitivity towards the Chinese culture can lead to business failure. China，while emerging from a planned economy，is still characterised by "guanxi" connections in its business network. If foreign managers fail to appreciate the value of these connections as business drivers，they will lose the good will of not only their employees but also potential clients. Furthermore，the manner in which employees are laid off must be culturally sensitive，so that employees do not feel they have lost face. In the case of the Roaring Dragon，downsizing was the right move，but it was carried out poorly. The managers made many young people redundant as they wanted to save costs，but as a result，they reduced the vibrancy of the hotel.

Communication barriers and a small amount of time spent by expatriate mangers with employees can lead to a lack of strong working relationships between the managers and the employees. In the Roaring Dragon case，the Nothill managers were oblivious to the competition they were facing，as indicated by their refusal to accept NuFu bookings on the basis that they were cheap，and they were adamant about not providing discounts. The expatriate managers also managed the change process poorly. A gradual introduction of the changes while generating strong working relationships with the employees would have worked best for all parties. The hotel management insisted on stringent prices and this lack of price

都使得酒店失去和其他新型酒店的竞争力。酒店的市场团队消极且缺乏动力，因此未能寻求到新客户。

1. 挑战：跨文化环境下的管理

将视角转向组织全球化的前景，经理人必须学会如何适应跨文化的环境，并协同工作。在本土国家成功经营企业并不能保证在其他国家背景下也能如此。因此，经理人应该了解并熟悉他国文化常识，包括与其他国家文化有何差异，赏识文化的差异性，必须保持对来自其他文化背景个体的兴趣度，在理解差异的前提下建立良好关系。缺乏对文化差异的了解和熟悉，只会导致管理上的功能障碍。了解跨文化差异性可以从诸多角度展开，如从人与环境的关系角度去分析问题，分析人与人之间的关系、行为活动模式、人性本身、时间还有空间（IMD International，2003）。这些方方面面不仅影响企业目标的实现，在特定文化下还会影响企业项目计划的实施。该企业文化倾向于个人主义还是集体主义会影响到不同的人际关系与交往模式。从 Roaring Dragon 酒店案例中我们可以发现，中国人倾向于较强的集体主义文化，而不是个人主义，这从对"关系"的描述中也可以看出。集体主义文化要求领导者关心、在乎与下属及团队的人际关系。为了建立和培养人际关系，外籍管理者必须找到在跨文化环境下与其员工交流的模式。

2. 集体主义与个人主义的特征

集体主义领导者表现出对下属个体的关心，团队拥有一致的目标，倾向集体奖励。个人主义领导者授予个人决策权，团队认可个人角色、贡献和奖励。

Nothill 经理人对这些诸多问题理解不当，和下属员工也缺少人际往来。他们对中国文化内涵理解不够，因此缺乏应对该环境的管理方法。即使在相近的文化背景下实施管理变革，同样也是一项挑战。变革需要逐步推进，鼓励员工积极参与到变革之中，以便于让他们理解变革的必要性。换句话说，裁员始终是管理层与员工之间存在的棘手问题，常常引起情绪波动。有时裁员是必要的，但整个过程需要公平进行。组织策略应该要经过清晰的深思熟虑，详细计划如何开展行动。

问 题

（1）请评价 Roaring Dragon 酒店面临的问题。

（2）如果是你，要如何解决该公司的问题？请给出详细说明及建议。

flexibility made them loose customers to other up and coming hotels. The hotel's marketing team was demotivated and thus failed to look for clients.

1. Challenge: Managing in a Cross Cultural Context

With the shift to a more globalised organisational outlook, managers must learn to cooperate and work together across borders. Success in the home country does not necessarily ensure success in a foreign country. Managers should therefore understand their culture and how it differs from those of others and appreciate these differences. They must take an interest in individuals from other cultures and understand and build good relationships on their differences. Failure to understand cultural differences leads to dysfunctional conflicts. Understanding cross-cultural differences can be done by analysing issues such as people's relationship to the environment, relations among people, mode of activity, human nature, time and space (IMD International, 2003). Highly individualistic and highly collective cultures promote different relationships between humans. The Roaring Dragon Hotel example shows that Chinese culture is highly collective rather than individualistic, as depicted by the "guanxi". A collective culture requires leaders who develop personal relationships with subordinates and engage in teamwork. To forge personal relationships, expatriate managers must learn how to communicate with their employees in a cross-cultural environment.

2. Characteristics of Collectivism and Individualism

Collectivism Leaders show personal care and concern for subordinates. Teams have joint goals, and members prefer joint rewards. Individualism Leaders empower subordinates to make own decisions. Teams identify individual roles and contributions and prefer individual rewards.

The Nothill managers failed to understand these issues and they had no personal relationships with their employees. They did not understand Chinese culture, and as a result they did not adapt their management methods so to their environment. Change management can be challenging even in familiar grounds. Change should be introduced gradually and the employees actively involved in the change process so that they understand the need for the changes. Downsizing is always a thorny issue between the management and employees and is always emotional. Downsizing is at times necessary, but the process should be carried out in a fair manner. Strategies should always be clearly thought out and carefully implemented.

Questions

(1) Evaluate the problems of the Roaring Dragon Hotel.

(2) How would you solve the problems of this company? Please provide detailed explanations and recommendations.

第4章 企业伦理、公平和企业社会责任

学习目标

- 了解什么是商业道德和专业道德准则
- 了解什么是企业社会责任（CSR）和酒店业员工对环保规划的看法
- 通过研究成果和案例，了解不同类型的公平及其对员工工作的影响

商业伦理渗透于人力资源管理的各个方面，包括选拔人才、员工安置、绩效评估、薪酬、人才保留决策。因此，商业从业者们应该建立一种伦理的企业文化，并把人力资源系统建设作为争取企业竞争优势的重要步骤。在本章中，正义、公平以及企业社会责任都被划归在企业伦理的范畴中，它们是影响一个组织策略构建的根本的、核心的道理理念（Dessler，2017）。

什么是商业组织伦理？

大多描述伦理的定义都涉及道德判断与行为准则。伦理就是关于好坏、对错、道德责任和义务的规章制度（Ferrel、Fraedrich 和 Ferrell，2017）。现在大多数大型跨国企业都拥有道德准则，内容包括书面行为标准、内部教育；还有行业标准的正式协议、伦理部门、社会会计、社会项目（Brewster 等，2008）。尽管如此，至今商业丑闻仍然是头条新闻。很不幸的是，各类商业丑闻几乎每天都在上演，如在简历上撒谎、妨碍司法公正、销毁记录、操纵股价、商业诈骗、资源浪费、滥用（职权）等。这意味着组织需要有能力且愿意将企业伦理渗透进组织文化之中的领导者。

诸多组织正在研究找出可以强化企业文化基础的方法。通过建立起强大的企业伦理文化，公司能够更好地赢得员工和股东们对它的信心与忠诚，这也能降低企业财务上、法律上、名誉上的风险，同时提高企业绩效表现。事

Chapter 4　Business Ethics, Justice and Corporate Social Responsibility

The objectives of this chapter

- Understand what are business ethics and professional codes of ethics
- Understand what is corporate social responsibility（CSR）and hospitality employees' perceptions of environmental programmes
- Understand different types of justices and its impact on employee work outcomes through research findings and case studies

Business ethics pervade human resources（HR）practices through selection and staffing, performance appraisal, compensation and retention decisions. Thus, an organisation's HR system and ethical corporate culture should be considered partners in the process of creating a competitive advantage for the organisation（Dessler, 2017）.

What Are Business Ethics?

Ethics are the basis of moral judgments and standards of conduct. As a discipline, ethics is concerned with what is good and bad, right and wrong, or with moral duty and obligation（Ferrell, Fraedrich, & Ferrell, 2017）. Most large and international corporations now have a code of ethics, which can encompass written conduct standards, internal education, formal agreement of industry standards, ethics offices, social accounting and social projects（Brewster, et al., 2008）. Even so, business ethics scandals continue to be headline news. Lying on resumes, obstruction of justice, destruction of records, stock price manipulation, fraud, waste and abuse are, unfortunately, all too common examples of the lack of business ethics. Organisations need leaders who are able and willing to instil ethics into the culture of the organisation.

Many organisations are examining ways to strengthen their cultural underpinnings. By fostering a strong ethical culture, firms can gain the confidence and loyalty of their employees and other stakeholders, which can result in reduced financial, legal and reputation risks, and improvements in organisational performance. In fact, evidence exists that ethical companies perform better financially（Velasquez, 2002）. To build and sustain an ethical culture, organisations need a comprehensive framework that

实上,诸多证据表明,一个有道德的企业在金融财务上会有更好的表现(Velasquez,2002)。为了建立并保持企业伦理文化,组织需要一个全面的综合框架,其内容包括对行为预期的交流、针对伦理及遵守准则相关事项的培训、股东投入、针对报告问题的解决方案以及对整个伦理文化项目的分析。为了使其能真正发挥功效,高层管理职能的介入是必不可少的。

人力资源专业伦理准则

伦理或行为准则建立起组织赖以生存的规范法则,并且成为组织企业文化的一部分(Brewster 等,2008)。一旦这些规则公开发布,企业内外的每个人都会明白了解,公司员工都应依照此规定工作。该准则是公司、员工及主管一致通过的价值观陈述,它是针对高层管理职能关于行为预期所设定的官方基调。许多行业协会接受这些准则,然后将其推荐给其他成员。现存在许多不同类型的伦理准则,在香港由人力资源管理协会(SHRM)建立和发展起来的伦理准则就是个很好的例子。人力资源管理协会的伦理准则的主要条款包括职业责任、职业发展、领导伦理、公平公正、利益冲突以及资讯利用(Brewster 等,2008)。

企业社会责任

企业社会责任(corporate social responsibility,CSR)是一种对企业经理人隐含的、强制性的责任,表现出官方领导者风范,来服务或保护除自身外的员工的利益(Chan 等,2017)。CSR 要顾及的是企业对整个社会的影响作用,不仅仅局限于持股者的利益。这就是公司作为一个整体如何面对社会的行为表现。

在酒店业,伴随着环境保护法律数量的不断上升以及来自市场的压力,组织企业和经理人们的环保意识逐渐提升。由于酒店昼夜不断地服务客人、员工和顾客,频繁大量地消耗能源、水资源和易耗品,酒店经理人们将面对逐步增长的社会压力,要求他们给予环境问题适当的关注(Chan 等,2017)。现在他们要解决的是企业利益与环保效能、稀缺资源、公共法则、烦冗的诉讼与盈利之间如何保持平衡的问题。因此,植入环境保护项目来管理能源、水资源消耗、资源浪费的问题,可以提升企业的稳定性,从而节省开支,保持企业竞争力(Bowe,2005;Chen 等,2005;Dodd 等,2001)。大多数国际连锁酒店都拥有公司层面的环境保护政策,且他们都会提供给旗下各个酒店物业及员工指导方针,来促进环保措施的开展。举例来说,可以规定办公室职员使用

encompasses the communication of behaviour expectations, training in ethics and compliance issues, stakeholder input, resolution of reported matters and analysis of the entire ethics programme. To make it really work, involvement by top management is necessary.

HR Professional Codes of Ethics

A code of ethics or conduct establishes the rules by which an organisation operates and should become part of the organisation's corporate culture (Brewster, *et al.*, 2008). Once these rules are published, everyone within and outside the firm knows the rules that company employees should live by. The code is a statement of the values adopted by the company, its employees and its directors, and it sets the official tone of top management regarding expected behaviour. Many industry associations adopt such codes, which are then recommended to members. There are many kinds of ethical codes. A good example of a code of ethics was developed by the Society for Human Resource Management (SHRM) in Hong kong. Major provisions in the SHRM code of ethics include professional responsibility, professional development, ethical leadership, fairness and justice, conflicts of interest and use of information (Brewster, *et al.*, 2008).

Corporate Social Responsibility (CSR)

CSR is an implied, felt or enforced obligation of managers, acting in their official capacity, to serve or protect the interests of groups other than themselves (Chan, *et al.*, 2017). CSR considers the overall influence of corporations on society and goes beyond the interests of shareholders. It is a reflection of how a company as a whole behaves toward society.

In the hotel industry, the escalating number of environmental laws and increasing market pressure have raised organisations' and managers' awareness of environmental practices. As hotels operate around the clock, customers and employees can consume substantial quantities of energy, water and non-durable products, hotel managers face increasing pressure to pay attention to environmental issues (Chan, *et al.*, 2017). Managers must balance concerns about environmental performance, scarce resources, public legitimacy, burdensome litigation and profitability. Thus, environmental programmes to manage energy and water consumption and waste are increasingly common in the industry, as a way to lower costs and maintain corporate competitiveness (Bowe, 2005; Chen, *et al.*, 2005; Dodd, *et al.*, 2001). Most international hotel chains have corporate-level environmental policies and they provide individual hotel properties and employees with guidelines on how to promote environmental initiatives. For example, office staff may be asked to use double-sided printing or photocopying; room attendants may need to adjust guest room temperatures and sort rubbish for recyclable items such as plastic bottles; kitchen staff are required to turn on cooking equipment only

双面打印还是扫描;客房服务员需要调节客房温度,对可回收垃圾进行分类,例如塑料瓶等;要求后厨员工有需要时才打开烹饪设备,下班前关掉设备;规定洗衣房员工在清洗衣物时满载运转,将废弃的亚麻布切成小块作其他用途;要求宴会厅服务员调节室内温度和风扇转速;采购人员需要尽力搜寻环保产品及设备。同样的一个设计优良的环境管理系统(EMS)也要保持更多、更完善的记录,这能促使经理人和工作人员寻找到准备文档文件更好的方法(Chan 等,2017)。

员工对于环保项目的看法

个体的生态行为可以促进有利的酒店环保措施的实施。当该行为演变成一种习惯,每个个体将用不同的方式方法,带有主观能动性地重复该行为。充分理解环境管理的含义及政策能带给"绿色酒店经营者"新的启发,当他们在选拔和招聘员工时,会将个人生态行为视为标准条件之一。事实上,许多公司正试图寻找更具环保资质的专业人士,使他们的经营更环保。

如果绿色酒店经营者希望员工能够以遵从酒店的环保政策并保证实施必要的措施,选拔和聘用具有环保意识的员工就显得尤为重要。组织机构需要为员工提供环保方面的培训,提高他们对环保和环保实践的系统性认识。除此之外,Perron 等(2006)也指出,环保方面的培训,尤其是对环保意识的培训,不仅可以帮助企业克服一些与组织文化和变革管理相关的问题(这些问题对正在转型为更具环保意识的组织来说很常见),而且使员工更了解他们的职能和决策将如何影响环境。因此,良好的环保知识训练会有助于提高酒店业工作人员的就业率及市场性。

培训及教育可以提升员工技能并加强对环保知识的了解。因此,对环境友好的公司而言,选拔具有正确环保意识的人才是十分重要的。个人对于环境问题的态度将影响酒店环境绩效表现,以及环保项目的成功,这是因为他们才是真正实施环保措施的执行者。选取具有良好环保知识背景、环保意识、关注环保事业的人才,并为酒店业员工提供持续性的环保培训,这是改善酒店环保绩效和形象的可能的解决方案之一。

另一个与 CSR 以及商业公平相关的例子来自国际企业为降低劳动力成本而将公司运作转移至海外的背景。诸多发展中国家,如中国,欢迎海外企业的加入,欢迎它们带来更多的就业机会,以及承诺的管理与技术层面的转

as needed, and not to leave it on until the end of a shift; laundry staff are required to run full loads when washing and cut condemned linens into smaller pieces for other purposes; banquet staff are asked to adjust air-conditioning temperatures and fan speeds; and purchasing staff may need to make extra efforts to search for eco-products and equipment. A well-designed EMS also requires more and better record keeping, which forces managers and workers to find better ways to prepare documentation (Chan, *et al.*, 2017).

Employees' Views of Environmental Programmes

The ecological behaviour of individuals can lead to the implementation of favourable green measures in hotels. When ecological behaviour becomes a habit, an individual is likely to take the initiative to repeat his/her ecological behaviour in different ways. Understanding environmental management and practices helps green hoteliers who may consider an individual's ecological behaviour as one of the criteria for selecting and hiring employees. In fact, many companies are looking to hire professionals and people with green credentials to make their businesses more environmentally friendly.

Organisations need to provide employees with environmental training, from which better environmental knowledge and environmental awareness can be cultivated. Selecting employees with the right environmental attitude is also of utmost importance if a green hotelier really wants his or her subordinates to follow the hotel's green policies and to implement the required measures. Additionally, Perron *et al.* (2006) noted that environmental training, particularly awareness training, can help to overcome issues related to organisational culture and change management, which are common during a transformation to an environmentally conscious organisation, and can also teach employees how their duties and decisions will affect the environment. Thus, good environmental training is likely to improve the employability and marketability of individuals working in the hotel industry.

Training and education can upgrade employees' skills and their environmental knowledge. Thus, it is important for environmentally friendly companies to select people with the right environmental attitudes; employees' attitudes towards environmental issues will affect a hotel's environmental performance and the success of any environmental programme, because they are the ones who perform the environmental duties. Selecting people with good environmental knowledge, awareness and concerns, and providing continuous environmental training to hotel staff are ways to improve a hotel's environmental performance and image.

Another example relating to CSR and business justice occurs when, to reduce labour costs, Western enterprises decide to take their operations offshore. Many developing countries such as mainland China welcome foreign enterprises for the employment opportunities they provide and the managerial and technological transfers they promise.

移。然而,许多欠发达国家缺乏约束雇用童工的法律制度、最低生活工资、工作场所、消费群体和环境安全标准。

随着酒店业全球化和跨国企业(MNCs)趋势的蔓延,越来越多的外籍高级主管被派遣到当地监管本地员工(Magnini,2009)。这种管理方式的成功依赖于完成工作任务和领导层与本地员工关系的建立,因为这些能使组织获得更高水平的表现(Harrison 和 Shaffer,2005;Hon 和 Lu,2013)。

跨国企业(MNCs)在中国开展业务,并派遣外籍管理者到华,充分利用本地的廉价劳动力以及较大的市场潜力。通常来说外籍管理者被安置在核心职位,以确保运营的高效性。由此带来的主要问题为,通常情况下外籍管理者依据当地劳动力市场来制定薪资,本地员工则依据本地的市场情况,这会导致两者间巨大的薪酬差距以及不公平现象的产生。

什么是正义

公平,指的是个人对于公平性的一种感知,或是组织机构内过程或是结果的正当性,它涉及分配上的、程序性的、互动性的层面。这些分类通过预测各种各样的组织态度和行为丰富了人力资源的研究(Colquitte 等,2001;Hon 和 Lu,2013)。特别是互动公平,反映出领导者对下属员工自尊的尊重程度(Bies 和 Shapiro,1987),它把对公平的注意力转移到了工作环境中的日常人际互动过程中。在预测工作态度和行为方面,互动公平比其他两方面(分配上和程序上)更强有力,因为在每天的日常生活和资源分配进程中,它出现的次数更频繁,更易感知(Bies 和 Moag,1986)。

互动公平包括态度和行为两个方面,其对象指的是具有公平品质的个体。它与分配公正和程序公正刚好相反,两者导致结果指向组织本身(Masterson 等,2000)。一些研究成果证明,互动公平在预测工作态度和结果上具有积极作用,例如工作和主管满意度、组织公民行为(OCB)、绩效(Cropanzano 等,2002)。与此同时,实证研究始终未能将互动公平与工作绩效联结在一起,这表明互动关系中的公平对于工作和任务表现来说只具有相对弱的心理学上的预测力。

现代对公平的研究调查起源于西方国家。结果显示,大多数有影响力的研究成果都是在西方文化背景下提出假设,并进行试验的,特别是在北美地区(Li 和 Cropanzano,2009)。和东亚地区相比,分配公平和程序公正在北美

However, many less developed countries have few, if any, laws governing child labour, a living wage, or workplace, consumer and environmental safety standards.

With the trend towards globalisation and multinational corporations (MNCs) in the hotel industry, an increasing number of expatriate supervisors are now being assigned to oversee local employees (Magnini, 2009). The success of such expatriate supervision is believed to depend on task completion and relationship building with local employees, as these enable organisations to achieve high levels of overall performance (Harrison & Shaffer, 2005; Hon & Lu, 2013).

Multinational corporations (MNCs) have set up operations in China to take advantage of the country's low labour costs and high market potential. Typically, expatriates are placed in key posts to ensure the effectiveness of these operations. A major problem of this arrangement is that expatriates are paid according to their home labour market, whereas locals are paid according to the local labour market, resulting in a large compensation difference or injustice between these two groups.

Justice

Justice, which is defined as an individual's perception of the fairness or appropriateness of processes and outcomes in an organisation, has distributive, procedural and interactional dimensions; these classifications have enriched HR research by predicting a variety of organisational attitudes and behaviour (Colquitte, *et al.*, 2001; Hon & Lu, 2013). Specifically, interactional justice, which reflects the degree to which a leader respects the dignity of his or her subordinates (Bies & Shapiro, 1987), draws the attention of people from the organisational and informational aspect of justice to the daily interpersonal social exchange process in the workplace. Interactional justice is a stronger predictor of work attitude and behaviour than the other two dimensions (distributive and procedural), as it is experienced more often and more sensitively in daily encounters and resource allocation processes (Bies & Moag, 1986).

Interactional justice involves attitudes and behaviour directed at the person to whom fairness is attributed, whereas distributive and procedural justice lead to outcomes directed towards the organisation (Masterson, *et al.*, 2000). Several studies have provided evidence of the positive role of interactional justice in predicting job attitudes and outcomes such as job and supervisory satisfaction, organisational citizenship behaviour (OCB) and performance (Cropanzano, *et al.*, 2002). In contrast, empirical studies have repeated failed to link interactional justice to job performance, suggesting that fairness in the interactive treatment is a psychologically distant predictor of job or task performance.

Modern justice studies originated in Western countries. As a result, most influential justice findings were posited and tested in Western cultures, especially in North America (Li & Cropanzano, 2009). The effect of distributive justice and procedural justice is more

地区的效果格外突出(Li 和 Cropanzano,2009)。然而,关于公平的概念,特别是在互动公平方面,也已在东方文化环境下广泛应用,并起到了效果,其中也包括中国(例如,Farh 等,1997;Leung 等,2011;Wu 等,2011)。

公平与工作绩效结果

将公平分为分配、程序、互动三个层面是有文献可依的(Cohen-Charash 和 Spector,2001)。在这些文献证据中,互动公平指的是员工从上级主管身上感受到的关系公平性(Bies 和 Moag,1986)。换句话说,当人们觉得上级主管用尊重的态度对待自己时,他们就感知到了高层次的互动公平。

根据社会交换理论(Blau,1964),若员工将互动公平归为上级领导的功劳,他们就会用对企业的承诺作为报答,然后转化为人际交往的态度和行为表现(Masterson 等,2000;Moorman,1991)。事实上,诸多证据表明,感知到互动公平可以提升对上级的忠诚度与信任度、促进领导—成员交换以及提升领导满意度(Cohen-Charash 和 Spector,2001;DeConinck,2010)。例如,DeConinck(2010)提出下属员工感知到的互动公平能正向预测其对上级提供的支持的感知程度。Hon 和 Lu(2010) 的报告提出,若外籍管理者向本地员工表现出程序公正,比如看到他们向本地员工表达认知信任和情感信任(affective trust),那么本地员工会更愿意帮助并支持其外籍上级领导。

下属感知到的互动公平扎根于领导处理个人人际关系的技巧之中。在该关系中,积极的人际交换关系催生员工的安全感受以及对来自上级的支持的感知(DeConinck,2010;Rupp 和 Cropanzano,2002)。上级主管展现出的人际关系公平可以建立下属的义务感(Toh 和 DeNisi,2007)。根据社会交换原则,下属会用其积极的态度和行为表现回馈给直接向他表现公平态度的那个人(Blau,1964)。在他们之中,组织公民行为是最典型的表现互惠关系的方式。获得公平对待的下属员工更容易将公平归因于特定的主管。他们直觉的反应就是更愿意向上级伸出援助之手去帮助其解决一些问题(Fassina 等,2008)。鉴于受到公平对待的员工并不总是有机会发生即时行为,他们愿意给出帮助的主观态度,而不一定是帮助行为本身,可以成为测量互动公平效果的更好的指标。

在竞争压力日渐增加的时代,对公平公正的人力资源策略和战略优势的追求,不可避免地会陷入众多道德困境,时常会引起复杂的职责冲突。这些伦理上进退两难的问题很少能够自我消化,并且未经检验的个人价值体系缺乏必要的严谨性。

salient in North America than in East Asia (Li & Cropanzano, 2009). However, the construct of justice, especially interactional justice, has been widely applied and validated in Eastern culture, including China (e.g. Farh *et al.*, 1997; Leung *et al.*, 2011; Wu *et al.*, 2011).

Justice and Work Performance Outcomes

The categorisation of justice into distributive, procedural and interactional dimensions is well documented (Cohen-Charash & Spector, 2001). Interactional justice refers to the relational fairness that employees perceive in their immediate superiors' actions (Bies & Moag, 1986). In other words, when people think they are treated with respect and dignity by authorities, they perceive a high level of interactional justice.

According to the social exchange theory (Blau, 1964), if employees attribute interactional justice to a supervisor, they repay the fairness received with commitment that turns into interpersonal attitudes and behaviour (Masterson, *et al.*, 2000; Moorman, 1991). In fact, studies have shown that the perception of interactional justice is positively related to commitment and trust in the supervisor, leader-member exchange and supervisory satisfaction (Cohen-Charash & Spector, 2001; DeConinck, 2010). For example, DeConinck (2010) claimed that subordinates' perceptions of interactional justice positively predict their perceived supervisory support. Hon and Lu (2010) reported that if expatriate supervisors displayed procedural fairness toward locals, i.e. if they were seen as having cognitive and affective trust in locals, then the locals were more willing to help and support their expatriate supervisors.

Interactional justice perceived by subordinates is rooted in the personal relationship-handling skills of the supervisors. In this relationship, positive interpersonal exchanges induce in employees' feelings of security and perceived support from the upper authority (DeConinck, 2010; Rupp & Cropanzano, 2002). Interpersonal fairness displayed by a supervisor creates a feeling of obligation in subordinates (Toh & DeNisi, 2007). According to the social exchange principle, the subordinates repay this fair treatment with positive attitudes and behaviour directed at the person who initiated the fairness (Blau, 1964). OCB is a typical expression of reciprocity. The subordinates receiving fair treatment can easily attribute the fairness to a specific supervisor. Thus, their immediate reaction is a willingness to assist that supervisor (Fassina *et al.*, 2008). As justice receivers may not always find chances to express their feelings in a particular behaviour, their willingness to help, rather than helping behaviour, is a better indicator of the interactional justice effect.

In an era of increasing competitive pressures, the pursuit of strategic and fair HR practices inevitable raises myriad ethical dilemmas and conflicts of duties that are often complex. Ethical dilemmas rarely resolve themselves and unexamined personal value systems lack the necessary rigour.

由此而言,对人力资源实践者来说很重要的是,逐步发展识别伦理问题的能力,并参与道德推理,从而使他们可以代表组织内利益相关者的既得利益,包括员工、管理层、社区和整个社会。

案例研究 4-1[①] ▶▶▶▶▶▶

香港沃特·迪士尼公司

沃特·迪士尼公司是世界最大的媒体与娱乐集团之一。总部设在加利福尼亚州伯班克,其主要运营业务包括影视娱乐、主题公园和度假村、媒体网络和消费产品。公司在 2004 年的年收入达 308 亿美元。该企业承担企业社会责任(CSR)的方法包括以下六项主要内容:

(1) 商业标准和伦理——包括职场制度、招聘、培训、平等机遇、防止性骚扰和性别歧视、商业行为准则、伦理和法律标准。

(2) 企业管理——包括董事会构成、针对总监的商业行为和伦理守则、商业运营标准、股东及其他利害关系人与董事会沟通交流的流程规则。

(3) 社会——包括服务大众的主动性、社区服务带头性、慈善捐款、员工志愿参与本地社区项目。

(4) 环境——包括环保理念,公司声称建立起基本伦理准则,将其融入商业目的与环境保护之中。在环保浪潮下迪士尼将环保工作融入日常运营中。公司声称其全球员工通过其业务的各个方面积极支持环保举措,并且承诺在全球努力平衡环保工作与实现集团商业目标的关系。

(5) 国际劳工标准——迪士尼设立了国际劳工标准(ILS)项目,内容包括用来保护参与迪士尼商品制造业员工的个人利益的政策、协议和方针,无论是持牌者或是企业直接销售商。这也包括与迪士尼相关商品制造商的行为准则(涵盖工作条件、健康和安全、遵守法律条款等)。

(6) 安全与治安——包括主题公园项目的安全守则和政策、网络安全、

---

① 资料来源:Hills, J. & Welford, R.(2006).Dilemmas or debacles? A case study of Dishey in Hong Kong. *Corporate Social Responsibility and Enviroment Management*, 13(1):47-54.

It is therefore important that HR practitioners take steps to develop their competence in identifying ethical issues and engaging in sound moral reasoning so that they can represent the interests of all of the organisational stakeholders, including employees, management, the community and society.

Case Study 4 – 1[①] ▶▶▶ ▶▶

Walt Disney in Hong Kong

The Walt Disney Company is one of the largest media and entertainment corporations in the world. Headquartered in Burbank, California, Disney's main operating units are studio entertainment, theme parks and resorts, media networks and consumer products. Disney had revenues of US $ 30.8 billion in 2004. Disney's approach to undertake social responsibility (CSR) has six main components.

(1) Business standards and ethics—includes workplace policies, hiring, training, equal opportunities, the prevention of harassment and discrimination, business conduct guidelines and ethical and legal standards.

(2) Corporate governance—includes guidelines on the composition of the board of directors, codes of business conduct and ethics for directors, standards of business conduct, bylaws and processes for shareholders and other parties to communicate with the board.

(3) Community—includes public service initiatives, community outreach initiatives, philanthropic donations and employee volunteer programmes within local communities.

(4) The environment—includes the concept of environmentality, which the company says it established as a fundamental ethic to blend its business needs with conservation. Under this environmentality umbrella, Disney has integrated conservation efforts into its daily operations. The company states that its employees around the world proactively support environmental initiatives through every aspect of its business and states that it is "committed to balancing environmental stewardship with our corporate goals throughout the world".

(5) International labour standards—Disney has implemented an International Labour Standards (ILS) programme that includes policies, practices and protocols designed to protect the interests of workers engaged in the manufacture of Disney merchandise, whether for licensees or for direct sale at company properties. This includes a code of conduct (covering working conditions, health and safety, compliance with the law etc.) for manufacturers of Disney-related merchandise.

(6) Safety and security—includes theme part safety programmes and policies, Internet

---

① Source: Hills, J. & Welford, R. (2006). Dilemmas or debacles? A case study of Dishey in Hong Kong. *Corporate Social Responsibility and Enviroment Management*, 13(1): 47 – 54.

工作场所安全项目和培训项目、治安、产品安全以及关于荧幕吸烟镜头的规定。

　　香港迪士尼度假村由迪士尼公司与香港特区政府合作建立,1999 年正式对外宣布计划,于 2005 年 9 月 12 日正式对外营业。它包括香港迪士尼主题乐园、两家酒店、零售店、餐厅和娱乐设施等,在大屿山占地面积 1.3 平方公里(310 英亩)。

　　迪士尼公司在该项目投资 3.16 亿美元并持有 43% 的股权,香港政府投资 29 亿美元持有 57% 的股权。尽管迪士尼公司在香港国际主题乐园有限公司 HKITP(一家由迪士尼公司和香港政府拥有的公司)持有 43% 的股份,但对土地并无所有权。经过数月的协商沟通,政府正式宣布该项目,香港政府预计该项目将对香港未来 40 年增加约合 192 亿美元的经济效益,相当于 6% 的香港地区生产总值。度假村的建筑施工提供了超过 11000 个岗位和未来约 18400 个岗位。这一数字在未来 20 年里预计会增长到 35800 个。

　　第一部分:在 2005 年 5 月 18 日这个特殊的日子,香港《英文虎报》报道称鱼翅羹与烤乳猪、切片鲍鱼将引入迪士尼婚宴餐桌,迪士尼将在主题乐园和度假村的两家酒店大力推行这些菜肴。

　　享用鱼翅具有很重要的文化意蕴,鱼翅被视为一种奢侈品,象征着富裕与慷慨。然而,获取该美食食材的过程和方式一直受到各类指责,因其需要捕捉并猎取鲨鱼才能获得。世界自然保护联盟(IUCN)2004 年的一项调查发现,全球 262 种鲨鱼中有 56 种濒临灭绝。

　　随后《英文虎报》于 5 月 23 日陆续报道称,迪士尼公司提供鱼翅羹这一行为激怒了当地的环保人士。Brian Darvell,一名香港大学教授兼香港海洋动物保护协会前主席,向迪士尼首席执行官 Michael Eisner 致信,其中说道:"我认为这一行为是最高等级的错误。尽管鱼翅羹是否被部分消费者视为享有盛誉的美食,但你们只是想牟利而已,太可耻了。"

　　迪士尼公关部经理 Esther Wong 发表声明回应:"香港迪士尼乐园非常重视自身在环保中的职责,我们同样也十分关注本地文化。餐厅和五星级酒店提供鱼翅羹服务是香港本地区的习俗,这也是中式宴会的重要组成部分。"

　　两天后也就是 5 月 25 日,《英文虎报》发表报道称,环保人士对迪士尼供应鱼翅羹给出的"文化敏感"借口表示十分愤慨。Victor Wu,一名新加坡本土的保护动物权益野生救援协会 Wild Aid 的积极分子,对此回应道:"这是

safety, workplace safety programmes and training, part security, product safety and a policy on the depiction of smoking in movies.

The Hong Kong Disneyland Resort, built by Disney in partnership with the Hong Kong government, was formally announced in November 1999 and officially opened on September 12, 2005. It consists of one Hong Kong Disneyland theme park, two hotels, and retail, dining and entertainment facilities covering 1.3 km (310 acres) on Lantau Island.

Disney invested US $ 316 million for a 43% equity stake in the project. The Hong Kong government invested US $ 2.9 billion for a 57% equity stake. Although Disney has a 43% stake in HKITP (the company formed between Disney and the Hong Kong government) it does not have any ownership of the land. Announcing the deal after several months of negotiations, the government forecast that the project would produce an estimated US $ 19.2 billion boost to the economy over 40 years, equivalent to 6% of gross domestic product. Construction of the resort provided more than 11,000 jobs with another 18,400 provided on opening. That number is predicted to grow to 35,800 over a 20 - year period.

Part 1: In a feature dated May 18, *The Standard* reports that shark fin soup, along with roast suckling pig and sliced abalone, will be included in the wedding banquets Disney is promoting at the two hotels at the Hong Kong Disneyland resort.

Eating shark's fin soup carries cultural significance and is seen as luxurious and a display of affluence and generosity. However, the process by which sharks are caught and killed to harvest the fins for the ingredients has long been criticised. A 2004 survey by the International Union for the Conservation of Nature (IUCN) found that out of 262 shark species around the world, 56 are endangered.

The Standard publishes a follow up to the story on May 23 and reports that Disney's plans to serve shark's fin soup have outraged local environmentalists. Brian Darvell, a professor at the University of Hong Kong and former Chairman of the Hong Kong Marine Conservation Society, provides a copy of a letter he sent to Disney Chief Executive Michael Eisner, in which he says, "I think this is a mistake of the highest order. No matter that such soup is perceived as prestigious by some consumers, from whom you simply wish to make money, shame on you."

Disney public relations manager Esther Wong says in a prepared statement, "Hong Kong Disneyland takes environmental stewardship very seriously and we are equally sensitive to local cultures. It is customary for restaurants and 5-star hotels to serve shark fin soup in Hong Kong as the dish is considered as an integral part of Chinese banquets."

Two days later, on May 25, *The Standard* reports that environmentalists have reacted angrily to Disney's "cultural sensitivity" reason for serving shark's fin soup. Victor Wu, a Singapore-based activist within the animal rights protection group Wild Aid, says in relation to the shark's fin protests, "This is a campaign initiated by the Chinese and

一场由中国人发起的、受到来自全世界各地中国人支持的运动。如果认为我们仅仅是具有环保意识,并未十分忧虑关于鲨鱼种群减少的问题,那是对中国人的轻视。"Brian Darvell 指责迪士尼公司在环保问题上自相矛盾,并且指责迪士尼集团环境政策高级副总裁 Kym Murphy,因为他是国家海洋避难基金会的信任理事会成员,以及非政府组织美国海洋保护协会成员。有旁观者指出,以生态保护为题材的电影例如《海底总动员》以及其他作品给迪士尼带来了巨大经济效益。

6 月 10 日《英文虎报》的新闻报道称,迪士尼公司决定将鱼翅羹从其婚礼宴会菜单中剔除。但在向顾客传达了有关这道菜可能会危害鲨鱼种群的知识后,酒店会按顾客的特殊要求保留该服务。公司计划向坚持使用鱼翅羹的顾客派发宣传手册,详细讲述扼杀鲨鱼对环境产生的影响,鲨鱼是如何被猎杀的,以及采集鱼翅的过程。同时,迪士尼公司声明,将只接受来自"可靠且值得信赖的供应商"提供的货源,坚持遵守相关国际条约。环保群体称他们对此决定表示很失望,并且立誓将继续抵制运动,直到该菜肴彻底消失为止。

有报道称几天后香港迪士尼公司与美国华特迪士尼总公司之间发生了一些冲突。在一封递交给《星期日南华早报》(6 月 12 日)的书信中,世界野生动物基金 WWF 香港区总裁 Eric Bohm 提到他已经与美国迪士尼公司于六月初进行了电话会议,会议同意其香港分公司将不再供应鱼翅,无论是常规菜单还是特制菜单中,直到 WWF 或迪士尼公司找到一个认可的、可持续的来源为止。

Bohm 声称在起草联合声明宣布讨论结果的过程中,有两种不同的声音,并且香港迪士尼公司的公告是继续供应鱼翅羹。这让人有些出乎意料。他发问道:"其子公司是否还在迪士尼掌控之下呢?""在迪士尼总公司向青年及大众承诺并宣告重视环境问题的大背景下,这个决定极具讽刺意味。难道迪士尼的环保政策只适用于美国本土吗? 离开美国本土,所谓的'文化差异'造成的环保政策不健全是大众可以接受的吗?"

当天的《南华早报》报道称,若干环保组织正在策划抗议游行活动,打算干扰 9 月 12 日香港迪士尼乐园开幕仪式,而其他组织呼吁直接联合抵制迪士尼产品。

6 月 24 日当天,出现了一个 180 度大转弯,香港迪士尼公司宣布将全面停止在中式婚宴上供应鱼翅羹。某发言人称,做出该决定是因为管理层"无法找到可持续的捕捞资源"来确保其出售的鱼翅产品不是远海大规模捕猎鲨鱼所得。

对于这一决策,香港迪士尼乐园集团管理总监 Don Robinson 评论道:"我们始终努力在文化敏感与环境保护之间寻求适当的平衡,我们相信这个决定与一直以来对环保的承诺和消费理念相辅相成。"当月晚些时候,有报道

supported by Chinese people around the world. It belittles the Chinese people to suggest that we are environmentally conscious but not concerned about shark decline." Brian Darvell accuses Disney of being contradictory regarding environmental protection, noting that Kym Murphy, Senior Vice President of Corporate Environmental Policy at Disney, sits on the Board of Trustees for the National Marine Sanctuary Foundation, an American marine protection NGO. Several observers point out that conservation-based films such as *Finding Nemo* and others have made Disney a lot of money.

On June 10, *The Standard* reports that Disney has decided to take shark's fin soup off its wedding banquet menu. However, its hotels will still serve it on request, after educating customers about the threat to sharks. The company plans to distribute pamphlets that detail the environmental impact of killing sharks, how they are killed and how the fins are harvested to customers who insist on having the soup; Disney also says it will only source shark's fins from "reliable and responsible suppliers" that adhere to relevant international treaties. Environmental groups say they are disappointed by the decision and vow to carry on campaigning until the dish is withdrawn entirely.

A report suggesting confusion between Disney in Hong Kong and its parent company Disney USA emerges a few days later. In a letter to *the Sunday Morning Post* (June 12), WWF Hong Kong Director Eric Bohm says he had conducted a teleconference with Disney USA in early June during which it agreed that its Hong Kong subsidiary would not serve shark's fin, either on the general menu or by request, until such time as the WWF or Disney were able to identify a certified sustainable source.

Bohm claims that two sides were in the process of drafting a joint press released to reflect these discussions, and that Disney Hong Kong's announcement was continuing to serve shark's fin soup came as a surprise. "Is Disney in control of its subsidiary," he asks. He continues, "In the context of Disney's commitment to youth and its public pronouncements of concern for the environment, this decision smacks of the grossest hypocrisy. Does Disney's environmentalism apply only in America? Outside America, do 'different cultures' make environmentally unsound practices acceptable?"

On the same day, *the South China Morning Post* reports that several green groups are planning a protest to disrupt the opening ceremony of Hong Kong Disneyland on September 12, while others are calling for an immediate boycott of Disney products.

On June 24, in a clear U-turn, Disney announces that it will not be serving shark's fin soup at its Chinese wedding banquets at all. A spokesman says the decision was taken because management was "not able to identify an environmentally sustainable fishing source" to ensure the fins sold were not products of large-scale butchering of sharks in open seas.

Commenting on the decision, Don Robinson, Group Managing Director of Hong Kong Disneyland, says, "Striking the right balance between cultural sensitivities and conservation has always been our goal, and we believe this decision is consistent with our

称当地学者和 20 名学生建立起一个非政府组织,以此来唤起大众对迪士尼相关行为的关注。该组织——自称"猎奇行动"——希望引起民众对迪士尼对环境、文化和劳动力所造成的影响的注意,并计划进行调查研究、监管劳动力权益、组织抗议活动。

第二部分:BBC 英国广播电视公司(7 月 26 日)报道,迪士尼公司召集当地官员围捕、驱赶并清除主题乐园内至少 40 只野狗。"我们认为这些野狗对我们的员工造成了威胁,所以请求政府将它们赶走。"迪士尼发言人 Esther Wong 如是说。Sally Andersen,香港救狗之家一员,向《南华早报》发消息称,乐园施工地内的野狗在工作人员的照料、饲养下过得很好,它们对人们友善,也习惯了人们的存在。许多评论员注意到迪士尼公司花费了大量金钱,让狗成为"人类最好的朋友"。

《英文虎报》(8 月 1 日)报道,迪士尼公司现在背负很大的社会压力,在考虑使用更安静、更环保友善的技术来降低其夜间烟火表演造成的污染。对此出现了众多质疑的声音:为何迪士尼公司拒绝使用空中发射技术进行烟火表演?该技术可以减少噪音,降低空气污染指数,这项技术在美国加州迪士尼乐园试用十分成功。有报道称在五月香港迪士尼乐园试验烟火表演后,离岛区议会(the Islands District Council)收到多达 31 次投诉。当月晚些时候,《英文虎报》(8 月 10 日)发布新闻报道称,迪士尼乐园夜间烟火表演和激光表演可能吓走了在那片区域繁殖生活的稀有鸟类,并称近期在主题公园附近发现白腹海雕巢穴——原本只有 10～20 对栖息在香港。

8 月 18 日一个自称"监察无良企业行为(SACOM)"的组织,由香港大学学生和工人运动者组建,隶属于"猎奇运动",与美国全国劳工委员会 NLC 联合发布了一份报告,主体是关于向迪士尼供货的工厂。

根据中文报纸《苹果日报》报道,来自 SACOM 的九名成员检查了位于广东的四家向迪士尼供应产品的工厂。标题为"寻求迪士尼良心的回归",报道了迪士尼供应商的员工,指出了这四家工厂共有的问题,包括工作场所状况不佳、工资支付不足、无法保障工人权利等,并指出诸多非常严重的问题,涉及工伤和劳动纠纷。报道表明,其员工被要求每天工作超过 12 小时,仅获得 40 元一天的酬劳。

迪士尼公司某发言人称,公司将进一步对此报道展开调查。她强调,迪士尼要求供应商遵守行为守则,守则规定了工作场所的条件、工资标准及工人权利。迪士尼将终止与违反规则的供应商的合作关系。该月晚些时候(8

on-going commitment to conservation and responsible consumption practices." Later that month, it is reported that a local academic and 30 students have established an NGO to raise public awareness of issues related to Disney. The group—which calls itself "Disney Hunter"—hopes to draw attention to Disney's influence on the environment, culture and labour. The group plans to conduct research and surveys, monitor labour rights and stage protests.

Part 2: The BBC (July 26) reports that Disney has called in local officials to round up and destroy at least 40 dogs roaming around the Disneyland theme park. "We felt that they posed a safety threat to our staff, so we asked the government to take them away," says Disney spokeswoman Esther Wong. Sally Andersen, of Hong Kong Dog Rescue, tells the South China Morning Post that dogs on the Disneyland construction site had been fed and looked after by construction workers and were friendly and used to humans. Many commentators note that Disney has made quite a lot of money out of films about dogs being "man's best friend".

The Standard (August 1) reports that Disney is facing pressure so it consider quieter and more environmentally friendly technology that can significantly reduce pollution from its nightly fireworks displays. Questions are asked about why the company refuses to use air-launch technology, which reduces noise and air pollution levels, at its Hong Kong park despite successfully adopting it at California Disneyland. Reports say that after Hong Kong Disneyland's fireworks trials in May, the Islands District Council received 31 complaints. Later that month *The Standard* (August 10) reports that Disneyland's nightly fireworks and laser shows could scare away a rare bird species that breeds in the area. The reports say that a nest belonging to a white-bellied sea eagle—of which only 10 to 20 breeding pairs are thought to inhabit Hong Kong—was recently discovered near the theme park.

On August 18 a group called Students and Scholars against Corporate Misbehavior (SACOM), formed by university students and labour activists in Hong Kong and affiliated with Disney Hunter, releases a report in conjunction with the US National Labor Committee (NLC) on factories supplying Disney.

According to the Chinese language newspaper *Apple Daily*, nine members of SACOM inspected four factories in Guangdong that supply products to Disney. Entitled "Looking for the Return of Disney's conscience: A report on labour in Disney suppliers", the report alleges problems in all four facilities, including poor workplace conditions, underpayment of wages and a failure to protect workers' rights. It alleges serious problems with regard to work injuries and labour disputes. It claims employees have been required to work for more than 12 hours per day, for only 40 yuan a day.

A spokesperson from Disney says the company will investigate the claims in the report. She stresses that Disney asks suppliers to follow a code of conduct that regulates working conditions, wages and workers' rights. Disney will terminate the contracts of any supplier that violates the code. Later that month, on August 30, SACOM and Disney Hunter activists hold a

月 30 日)SACOM 和"猎奇运动"参与者在迪士尼乐园举行了抗议活动,抗议迪士尼压榨内地工人的行为。《英文虎报》报道称,抗议活动中某学生肩扛米老鼠玩偶,手举横幅"剥削劳动工人,空谈社会关怀"。

SACOM 主席 Billy Hung 说道:"米老鼠坐在工人的肩膀上的形象代表着迪士尼乐园的权力凌驾于中国工人之上。"他补充说,卡通人物用手遮住了学生的眼睛和手,暗示工人被隐瞒着。抗议活动的时间恰巧与"社区关怀日"吻合,这个"社区关怀日"是由迪士尼公司和香港社会福利部门联合组织的,目的是在这两天里走进社区,免费发放 2 万张门票给社会弱势群体。

九月初有报道揭露说,有两位政府卫生部门检查员在进入迪士尼乐园区内进行食物中毒调查时被要求脱下帽子并摘去徽章。当地媒体揭露称该事件发生在 8 月 30 日。在收到食物中毒投诉后,两位"食物环境卫生署"检查员试图进入园区,对两处场所进行检查。一名员工回忆称,为了避免引起游园客人不必要的紧张,便要求检查员脱下帽子并摘去徽章后才可进入。

政府官员对此表示很生气。保安局局长 Ambrose Lee 说,主题公园无权越过法律规定。食物环境卫生署的助理总监 Rhonda Lo 描述该事件为"无法接受"。Lo 透漏,公园的管理层人员回应部门询问时将之解释为"误解"。然而在事件发生 10 天后迪士尼才做出官方道歉。乐园发言人 Maggie Lee 描述该事件为"沟通问题",并且向政府道歉。

随后涌现出对迪士尼员工待遇方面的不满。立法会议员 Lee Cheuk-yan 向《英文虎报》(9 月 10 日)透露,他正在说服迪士尼乐园的员工组建工会,因为他收到了不少对劳工政策的抱怨投诉。Lee 所在的"香港职工会联盟(HKCTU)"宣称,他们收到了来自迪士尼公司员工的多达 20 次投诉,称迪士尼公司忽视他们的健康需求以及其他需要。Lee 说道:"主要的投诉问题并不是关于薪资低或是员工福利方面的,更多是关于公司不尊重员工。"

根据 Lee 透露的信息,迪士尼乐园员工在园内不准使用手机,即使是在休息期间也不可以;女性员工必须身着短裙或紧身裙,但在美国园区是允许穿长裤的;除休息时间员工不得饮水,休息和用餐时间间隔过长;员工不准染头发,男士不许留长发、不许留胡子。同时《英文虎报》报道了迪士尼公司派 500 名一线员工 2005 年 1 月到 6 月前往美国佛罗里达迪士尼世界培训,教导

protest at Disneyland against what they claim is Disney's abuse of mainland factory workers. *The Standard* reports the protest, and includes a photo of a student carrying a Mickey Mouse doll on his shoulders and holding a banner that reads, "Exploits the Chinese workers, Empty Talks on Community care."

Billy Hung, Chairman of Students and Scholars against Corporate Misbehavior (SACOM), says, "Mickey Mouse sitting on a worker's shoulders signifies Disneyland's power over Chinese workers". He adds that the cartoon character was covering the student's eyes with his hands to imply that workers are concealed. The protest is timed to coincide with a "Community Caring Day", co-organised by Disney and the government's Social Welfare Department. It aims to reach the community over the two-day programme by giving 20,000 free tickets to the underprivileged.

In early September, reports emerge that two government health inspectors were asked to take off their hats and badges when entering Disneyland to conduct a food poisoning investigation. Local media reveal that the incident took place on August 30 when two officers from the Food and Environmental Hygiene Department attempted to enter the park to inspect two premises after receiving complaints of food poisoning. A staff member at the park asked the officers to take off their hats and badges before entering to avoid distressing guests at the park.

Government officials react angrily with the Secretary for Security, Ambrose Lee, saying that the theme park does not stand above the law, and the Assistant Director of Food and Environmental Hygiene, Rhonda Lo, describes the incident as "unacceptable". Lo reveals that in response to her department's inquiry, the management of the park explained that it was a "misunderstanding". However, a formal apology was only given 10 days after the incident happened. A spokeswoman for Disneyland, Maggie Lee, describes the incident as a "communication problem" and apologises to the government.

Complaints about Disney's treatment of its employees also begin to emerge. Lawmaker Lee Cheuk-yan tells *The Standard* (September 10) that he is urging Disneyland staff to organise a labour union because of complaints he has received about labour practices. Lee's Hong Kong Confederation of Trade Union claims it has received 20 complaints from workers, saying Disney is ignoring their health needs along with other problems. "The main complaint of the staff is not low salary or staff benefits. It is more about Disney not respecting them," Lee says.

According to Lee, Disneyland staff cannot use their cell phones inside the theme park, even during breaks; female workers must wear a skirt and tights, whereas trousers are allowed in the US parks; staff are prohibited from drinking water outside of breaks and the intervals between breaks and meals are too long; and employees are barred from dying their hair, growing it long or growing a beard. *The Standard* also reports that Disney sent 500 of its frontline staff to Disneyworld in Florida from January to June this year to teach them how to be "cultural representatives". One such worker says the training was demeaning. "I totally

他们如何成为"文化代表"。其中一位员工说该训练实在侮辱人格。"我完全丧失了自己对神奇王国的幻想,只把这当作一份工作而已。"迪士尼发言人 Esther Wong 回应称公司"将承诺陆续展开与演艺人员之间的公开对话,尊重他们的需要"。最终香港迪士尼乐园于 2005 年 9 月 12 日正式对外营业。

问　题

（1）当本地文化规则与其初始政策和规定相抵触的时候,公司应如何做出回应?

（2）你认为增加与利益相关者的对话和更完善的调查在多大程度上能缓和迪士尼出现的问题?

（3）你觉得这里报道的事件对迪士尼企业形象和名誉有怎样程度的影响?

（4）根据企业社会责任（CSR）,你认为香港迪士尼公司接下来应该怎么做?

案例研究 4-2 ▶▶▶▶▶

ABC 有限公司的全球化、伦理和企业社会责任

对 ABC 有限公司来说咖啡的品质很重要,但做一个良心企业同样重要。ABC 有限公司非常重视对社会的承诺。其网站如是写道:"承担企业社会责任,就是我们经营的方式。向社会和环境贡献积极力量是至关重要的,这也是我们履行使命的指导方针。在公司的每个层面,我们都与合作伙伴（员工）共同履行对社会的承诺,通过合作建立更强大的社会团体来保护自然资源。"以下是 ABC 有限公司承担企业社会责任的事迹:

- 要求其门店向当地事业和慈善机构捐款;
- 让其兼职员工有资格得到健康和 401(K) 福利;
- 致力于保护热带雨林;
- 2006 年年初引入可回收纸杯;
- 推广瓶装水产品"气质水",并将每瓶水所得的 5 分钱用来推动贫困国家干净水的供应;
- 在飓风"斯坦"于 2005 年 10 月肆虐墨西哥西南部、危地马拉西北地区后,向咖啡农提供援助;
- 启动国际项目来帮助提高咖啡农的收入,他们对待其工人和环境十分友善。

2001 年公司颁布了年度企业社会责任报告,其中强调公司的决策和行动需要与产品、社会、环境和工作场所有关联。这些报告并不是 ABC 有限公

lost my fantasy about the Magic Kingdom and just treated it as a job afterwards." Disney spokeswoman Esther Wong says the company is "committed to on-going open dialogue with our cast members and respecting their needs". Hong Kong Disneyland finally opens on September 12, 2005.

Questions

(1) How should a company respond when local cultural norms clash with its stated policies and principles?

(2) To what extent do you think increased stakeholder dialogue and better research could have mitigated Disney's problems?

(3) To what extent do you feel that the incidents reported here had an effect on the image and reputation of Disney?

(4) In terms of CSR, what do you think Disney should do next in Hong Kong?

Case Study 4 - 2 ▶▶▶ ▶▶▶

ABC Ltd. on Globalisation, Ethics and
Corporate Social Responsibility

Good coffee is important to ABC Ltd., but equally important is doing good. Starbucks takes that commitment seriously. Its website states, "Corporate Social Responsibility. It's the way we do business. Contributing positively to our communities and environment is so important to ABC Ltd. that it's the guiding principle of our mission statement. We jointly fulfil this commitment with partners (employees), at all levels of the company, by getting involved together to help build stronger communities and conserve natural resources". The following is a list of some of the things that ABC Ltd. has done in relation to its corporate responsibilities:

● requires its stores to donate to local causes and charities;

● made part-time employees eligible for health and 401 (k) benefits;

● works to protect the rainforest;

● introduced recycled-content paper cups in early 2006;

● introduced a bottled-water product called "Ethos" and donates 5 cents per bottle sold to boost clean-water supplies in poorer countries;

● provided assistance to coffee farmers and their families in southwest Mexico and northwest Guatemala after Hurricane Stan in October 2005; and

● launched an international programme to offer better pay to coffee farmers who treat their workers and the environment decently.

In 2001, the company began issuing an annual corporate social responsibility report that addresses the company's decisions and actions in relation to its products, society, the environment and the workplace. These reports are not simply a way for Starbucks to brag about its socially responsible actions, but are intended to stress the importance of doing

司单纯炫耀他们在社会责任方面的行动,而是用于强调负有责任感地进行商业经营的重要性,并且使员工和管理层对其行为负有强烈的责任感。

　　ABC 有限公司同样也很注重道德承诺。每位负有财务责任的高层主管都会签署一份"道德准则",确保他们对平衡、保护、维护股东利益的承诺实现度。每个门店的员工(合伙人)都有文件依据(《商业行为标准》《合作指南》《安全、治安及健康标准手册》)来帮助他们充满道德意识地展开工作。

问　题

　　(1) 请选择两个 ABC 有限公司在企业社会责任方面已经实施的政策,并从顾客的角度来评估 ABC 有限公司取得了怎样的成功。

　　(2) 现在由你来负责为 ABC 有限公司行政官开发一个全球文化意识的项目,他们负责引领公司国际事务拓展。请描述你认为哪些重要事项需要他们去了解。

business in a responsible way and to hold employees and managers accountable for their actions. ABC Ltd. also takes its ethical commitments seriously. Each top-level manager who has financial responsibilities signs a "Code of Ethics" that affirms his or her commitment to balancing，protecting and preserving stakeholders interests. All of the store employees (partners) have resources ("Standards of Business Conduct" "the Partner Guide" "the Safety，Security and Health Standards Manual") to help them in doing their jobs ethically.

Questions

（1）Choose two policies that ABC Ltd. has been practising in relation to its corporate responsibilities and evaluate how successfully Starbucks has achieved these policies from a customer's perspective.

（2）You are responsible for developing a global cultural awareness programme for ABC Ltd. executives who are leading the company's international expansion efforts. Describe what you think will be important for these executives to know.

第5章 职务分析与组织设计

📖 **学习目标**

■ 了解什么是组织设计及其特点

■ 了解什么是工作分析、岗位轮换、工作规范及其特点

■ 提供案例研究作为例子来帮助理解上述概念

许多组织机构正在改变和调整其结构以满足高度竞争市场的需求。它们追求更强的团队合作能力、更灵活有创意的设计、更短的产品研发周期、更优质的顾客服务、更高的生产力等。时代的变更需要更加灵活以及更具综合性的组织,能够提供高质量产品和优质服务,同时仍在不断创新,以在未来继续取得绩效。今天,组织面临大量不断变换的问题与机遇,且没有一种完美的方法去改造、管理它们。对每个机构而言,成功的关键在于找到最优设计方案来掌控具体情景下的需求和挑战(Stoner、Freeman 和 Gilbert,1995)。

组织设计是选择与实践结构的过程,是优化资源配置以服务组织的使命和目标。组织设计的最终目标是将其置入结构内来推动战略的实施。更重要的是,组织设计的过程也是解决问题的过程,应该以应急方式处理这一问题。也就是说,设计的结构必须符合组织或是其从属单位的特殊需求。

什么是组织设计

正式筹划和编排一个组织的各个部分就是组织设计。组织设计包括系统任务、工作流程、将个性化的个体与团体连接起来的沟通渠道。任何组织设计都应该借助劳动分工手段来进行任务分配,以及考虑到绩效结果的协调度(Stoner、Freeman 和 Gilbert,1995)。能够顾及这两方面的优秀组织设计是组织的一项重要资产(Stoner、Freeman 和 Gilbert,1995)。当然,并没有

Chapter 5   Job Analysis and Organisational Design

The objectives of this chapter

- Understand what is organizational design and its characteristics
- Understand what is job analysis, job rotation, job specification, and their characteristics
- Provide case studies as examples to help understand the above concepts

Many organisations are changing and adapting their structures to meet competitive market demands. They seek improved teamwork, more flexible and creative design, shorter product development cycles, better customer service, higher productivity etc. Changing times require more flexible and well-integrated organisations that can deliver high-quality products and services while still innovating for sustained future performance. Today, organisations face widely varying problems and opportunities, and there is no one way to best structure and manage organisations. The key to success is finding the best design for the particular situational needs and challenges of each organisation (Stoner, Freeman, & Gilbert, 1995).

Organisational design is the process of choosing and implementing structures that best arrange resources to serve an organisation's mission and objectives. The ultimate goal of organisational design is to put it into structures that facilitate the implementation of strategies. The process of organisational design is a problem-solving activity that should be approached in a contingency fashion. That is, structures must be designed to fit the particular needs of an organisation or subunit.

What Is Organisational Design?

The way in which the various parts of an organisation are formally arranged is usually referred to as the organisational design. This is the system of tasks, workflows, reporting relationships and communication channels that link together the work of diverse individuals and groups. Any organisational design should allocate task assignments through a division of labour and also provide for the coordination of performance results (Stoner, Freeman, & Gilbert, 1995). A good design that does both of these things can be an important asset to an organisation. There is no single best design that meets the needs

一种设计方案可以满足公司在所有情景下的需要。组织设计必须可以处理好各类突发情况。当环境和形势的变化时,结构也必须跟着变化。为了做出最优决策,经理人必须清楚备选方案,并且熟悉当下的趋势和发展方向。

正式与非正式组织结构

正式结构即为组织机构的官方结构,它代表着组织计划运行其职能的方式。组织系统图可以明确各类职能部门、职称,以及权力线、沟通渠道。从另一方面来看,非正式结构即为成员内非官方正式的组织关系。这类“影子”组织由非官方的、但往往是关键的组织成员之间的工作伙伴关系构成。非正式结构的界限可以横跨各个等级,在两端间摇摆(Stoner、Freeman 和 Gilbert,1995)。它可以表现在人们喝咖啡聊天中、小组活动中、朋友圈中以及其他可能场合中。

值得注意的是,非正式结构在帮助任何组织实现需要完成的工作任务的目标方面有很大的作用。在变革时期尤其如此,因为过时的正式结构不再能够为人们处理更多全新的、特殊的情况提供必要的支持。并且,由于改变或是调整正式结构需要耗费时间,这就成了一种普遍现象。通过非正式结构下紧急的、自发的关系,人们从情感性支撑的人际网络中获利,并且满足了具有重要社会性需求的友好关系。同时,也在必要的时候与能够帮助他们完成任务的个体进行人际接触,并使工作效能提升。这就是所谓的“非正式学习”(Dessler,2017),这个学习过程发生在人们每天非正式地交流来往之中,发生在各类广泛的非结构性情境中。

非正式结构同样具有一些潜在的弊端。由于它常存在于正式权威制度体系外非正式结构活动有时可以违背组织整体的最佳利益。同时它易受传闻谣言的影响,带有不准确信息,会产生变革阻力,甚至将工作从重要目标上转移开来(Dessler,2017)。

权力分散化与集权化

一个时常被经理人问起的问题——“制定决策应该由组织机构顶层管理者来完成,还是应该被广泛地授权给各个层级的管理人员?”前者指的就是集权化,而后者就是我们常说的分散。对这两者而言,并不存在经典性原则。传统管理往往呈现高度集中的决策结构,而分散化则是新型结构的特点之

of every firm in every circumstance. Organisational design must be developed in a contingent fashion; as environments and situations change, structures must also often be changed. To make good decisions, a manager must know the available alternatives and be familiar with current trends and developments.

Formal Structure vs. Informal Structure

Formal structure is the official structure of an organisation. It represents the way an organisation is intended to function. An organisational chart identifies various positions and job titles and the lines of authority and communication between them. In contrast, informal structure is the set of unofficial relationships among an organisation's members. This is a "shadow" organisation made up of the unofficial, but often critical, working relationships between organisational members. The lines of the informal structure may cut across levels and move from side to side (Stoner, Freeman, & Gilbert, 1995). They involve people meeting for coffee, exercise groups and in friendship cliques, among other possibilities.

It is important to recognise that informal structures can be very helpful in getting necessary work accomplished in any organisation. This is especially true during times of change when out-of-date formal structures may simply not provide the support people need to deal with new or unusual situations. Because it takes time to change or modify formal structures, this is a common situation. People benefit from the emergent and spontaneous relationships of informal structures by gaining access to interpersonal networks of emotional support and friendship that satisfy important social needs. They also benefit in task performance by being in personal contact with others who can help them get things done when necessary. This is known as informal learning (Deesler, 2017), which is learning that takes place as people interact informally throughout the work day and in a wide variety of unstructured situations.

Informal structures also have potential disadvantages. Because they exist outside the formal authority system, the activities of informal structures can sometimes work against the best interests of the organisation as a whole. They can also be susceptible to rumour, carry inaccurate information, breed resistance to change and even divert work efforts from important objectives.

Difference between Decentralisation and Centralisation

A question frequently asked by managers is "Should most decisions be made at the top levels of an organisation, or should they be dispersed by extensive delegation throughout all levels of management?" The former approach is referred to as centralisation, the latter is called decentralisation. There is no classic principle on centralisation and decentralisation. The traditional pyramid form of organisations may give the impression of being a highly centralised structure, and to be sure decentralisation

一，也是近来的组织管理趋势（Stoner、Freeman 和 Gilbert，1995）。今天的组织可以运行高度分散化模式却并不因此而失去集中控制力，这得益于信息技术的发展。借助计算机网络和高级信息管理系统，高层经理人能够更容易地对每天各个方面的绩效问题保持消息灵通。因为他们掌握着随时可用的结果信息，所以他们能允许更大程度的决策权分散化。

在分散化与集权化之间的抉择

对权力集中化与分散化两者的选择并不是绝对的。通常来说，决策的类型和企业的策略会影响一个公司决定哪些部分集中、哪些部分分散。虽然决策要依据具体情况而定，但是以下几点关键建议仍然具备一定的普遍性。

第一，关于公司整体策略的决策，主要是关于财政支出、财政目标和法律问题的决策，在大多数组织内由高层管理人员集权进行。执行类的决策，例如与产品、市场、研发、人力资源管理相关联的决策，根据公司整体策略和外部环境条件，也可能不进行集中化（Stoner、Freeman 和 Gilbert，1995）。

第二，当规模经济被认为是重要的因素时，则倾向于高度权力集中化（Stoner、Freeman 和 Gilbert，1995）。因此，关于采购和制造方面的决策常常集中化，以降低二次浪费并实现规模经济。与此相反的是，销售策略则倾向于权力分散化，那是因为在该问题上较少考虑规模经济的问题。

第三，当适应本土化显得十分重要时，则更偏好于选择分散化。由此说来，当本地市场情况内存在实质性差异时，关于市场和销售方面的决策权常被分散至本地市场及销售经理人。诸多跨国消费品公司在制造和采购方面采用集权化决策，以实现规模经济发展，但在不同国家采用分散化市场策略，将销售决策权给予本土品牌经理。这是因为市场竞争状况在不同国家间都有所差异，且适应本土化是十分必要的。

第四，在环境极其不稳定、变化急速的条件下，更倾向于选择分散化。当公司的市场竞争状况变化多端时，如伴随着新型科技、竞争对手的出现，市场状况多变，很难再采用权力集中化策略，这是因为集权化会减缓决策速度，将企业置于竞争劣势地位。这也是众多高科技企业与在更稳定、更易预测的环境下运营的公司相比采用权力高度分散化运营的原因。例如，阿里巴巴公司会赋予底层员工明确的职能权限去发展新的商业想法，他们有权游说高级主

is a characteristic of newer structures and recent organising trend (Stoner, Freeman, & Gilbert, 1995). Today's organisations can operate with greater decentralisation without giving up centralised control. This is facilitated by developments in information technology. With computer networks and advanced information systems, managers at higher levels can more easily stay informed about a wide range of day-to-day performance matters. Because information on results is readily available, managers can allow more decentralisation in decision making.

Choice between Decentralisation and Centralisation

The choice between centralisation and decentralisation is not absolute. Frequently, it makes sense to centralise some decisions and decentralise others, depending on the type of decision and the firm's strategy. Although the choice depends on the particular situations, a few important generalisations can be made. First, decisions regarding overall firm strategy, major financial expenditures, financial objectives and legal issues are centralised at the senior management level in most organisations. Operating decisions, such as those relating to production, marketing, R&D and human resource management, may or may not be centralised depending on the firm's strategy and the conditions in the external environment.

Second, when economies of scale are considered an important factor, there is a tendency towards greater centralisation (Stoner, Freeman, & Gilbert, 1995). Thus, purchasing and manufacturing decisions are often centralised in an attempt to eliminate duplication and realise scale economies. In contrast, sales decisions tend to be more decentralised, because economies of scale are less of a consideration in this area.

Third, when local adaptation is important, decentralisation is typically favoured. Thus, when there are substantial differences between conditions in local markets, marketing and sales decisions are often decentralised to local marketing and sales managers. Many multinational consumer products firms centralise decisions about manufacturing and purchasing to realise scale economies, but decentralise marketing and sales decisions to local brand managers in different countries because competitive conditions differ from country to country and local adaptation is required decentralisation dicisions.

Finally, decentralisation is favoured in environments that are characterised by high uncertainty and rapid change. When competitive conditions in a firm's market are changing rapidly, with new technologies and competitors emerging and conditions changing in ways that are difficult to anticipate, centralisation can put the firm at a competitive disadvantage because it slows down decision making. This is why many high-technology firms operate with a greater degree of decentralisation than firms operating in more stable and predictable environments. At Alibaba, for example, lower-level employees are given explicit permission to develop new business ideas and the right to

管来获得资金,以进一步使想法落地。这种分散决策权的策略不太会在运营环境较稳定、易预测未来的公司中采用。

当下的趋势是,虽然赋能授权和相关决策会推动组织的分散化,但信息技术的进展同时也能够帮助保持高层管理的集权控制。

直式(锥型)结构与扁平层级结构

直式层级结构具有较多的管理层次,而扁平层级则层次较少。许多公司起步时规模较小,常常只具有最多两个层级结构。然而,随着公司的壮大,经理人会发现日常运营中他们可以处理、掌控的信息量是相当有限的。为了避免控制力渐趋薄弱而逐渐失去控制力,他们开始倾向于增加管理层次,雇用更多的经理人,将决策权分散下去。换句话说,一个组织越壮大则层级结构越高。除此之外,随着组织的成长,其常常会从事更多的活动,例如扩大生产线、向新地区或是国家拓展市场。这些都将带来协调与控制方面的问题,通常也会通过增加管理层次的方式来解决。

控制(管理)幅度

控制幅度指的是直接向主管进行汇报的部署人数。控制幅度小,意味着只有少数人在主管的直接监督之下;控制幅度大,则代表着监管的人数多。具有较宽控制幅度的组织的层级结构较扁平,即拥有较少的管理层次;那些控制幅度较窄的组织的层级结构较高,即他们具有更多的管理层次。由于直式结构的组织拥有更多的经理人,所以花费较多。与扁平层级结构相比,直式结构通常更低效、灵活性更低、客户敏感度更低(Stoner、Freeman 和 Gilbert,1995)。控制幅度小就一定总是更好吗? 在决定缩小控制幅度之前,需要认真思考两个问题:由于增加管理层数带来的开支;增长行政管理环节可能引起的弊端。相反地,提高控制幅度将减少过度开销,员工获益于较少的直接监管,更具独立性。

当前的趋势就是,诸多组织正在向更宽的控制幅度、更小的行政管理系统和凸显"赋予授权"转变;主管个人正承担更多数量的下属责任,而下属则会受到更少的监管。

职位分析与设计

职位分析是对个人或团体特定工作的分配和安置,其以职位描述的形式

lobby top managers for the funds to develop those ideas. Such decentralisation of strategy is not found in firms operating in more stable and predictable environments.

The current trend is that whereas empowerment and related forces are contributing to more decentralisation in organisations, advances in information technology simultaneously allow for the retention of centralised control in top management.

Talland and Flat Hierarchies

Tall hierarchies have many layers of management; flat hierarchies have few layers. Most firms start out small, often with only one or at most two layers in the hierarchy. As they grow, managers find that there is a limit to the amount of information they can process and the control they can exert over daily operations. To avoid being stretched too thin and losing control, they add layers to the management hierarchy, hiring more managers and delegating some decision-making authority to them. In other words, as an organisation gets larger it tends to become taller. In addition, as organisations grow, they often start to undertake more activities such as expanding their product lines or expanding into new regional or national markets. This also creates problems of coordination and control, however, these problems are often solved by adding layers to the management hierarchy.

Span of Control

The span of control is the number of persons reporting directly to a manager. When a manager's span of control is "narrow", only a few people are under his or her immediate supervision; a "wide" span of control indicates that a manager supervises many people. Organisations with wider spans of control tend to be flat—they have few levels of management; those narrow spans of control tend to be tall—they have many levels of management. Because tall organisations have more managers, they are more expensive. They are also generally viewed as less efficient, less flexible and less customer sensitive than flat organisations (Stoner, Freeman, & Gilbert, 1995). Before making spans of control smaller, therefore, serious thought should always be given to both the cost of the added management overhead and the potential disadvantages of lengthening the chain of command. When spans of control are increased, overhead costs are reduced, and workers may benefit from less direct supervision and more independence.

The current trend is for organisations to shift to wider spans of control as chains of command are shortened and "empowerment" gains prominence; individual managers are taking responsibility for larger numbers of subordinates who operate with less direct supervision.

Job Analysis and Design

Job analysis is the allocation of specific work tasks to individuals and groups, which

呈现(Dessler,2017)。职位分析是在"适合"这一概念下以不同的方式进行的。一份优秀的职位分析需要让个体员工的价值观和工作任务的要求相匹配(Hon,2011)。任务需求包括简化工作、扩大职务范围、轮岗、职务丰富化。每个人的分工有多专业化,工作任务的定义就有多狭窄。

职位描述是关于某特定职位的目的、范围、职责、责任等大体的说明(Dessler,2017)。

工作规范则是一份详细讲解身体和心理活动的说明,内容与工作相关联,包括一些社会性和肢体性行为,例如员工的做法、使用哪方面知识解决问题、做出怎样的判断、在做决策时考虑了哪些因素等(Dessler,2017)。从人事角度出发,详细的工作职能清单是必不可少的。这其中最为重要的是选拔、晋升、评估、设定绩效标准、职能评估、培训。由此而言,工作规范在人事管理方面具有最基本的重要性,所以应用起来应当谨慎。当经理人与下属之间关系较差的时候,下属可能会将工作规范作为自我保护的工具,拒绝接受任务或指责,因为这些都没有在职责规范中明确显示。

工作规范应该指明在所有情况下员工要做什么和如何做。同样需要的是,大致指出花费在每项个人活动、团体活动的工作时间比例,以及临时职责出现的频率。工作规范应当始于对工作的描述,紧接着是更多详细的工作职能清单,例如:(1)主要职责与预期结果;(2)在该头衔下的常规职责;(3)在同一职称下的非常规职责或偶然突发的工作;(4)工作环境状况;(5)设备及材料应用;(6)个人联络方式(Dessler,2017)。

工作简化包括工作流程标准化以及雇用员工从事明确和高度专业化的任务。简化工作就是缩小工作职能范围——就是说限定个人承担任务的数量和种类。其逻辑很直接:如果工作不需要复杂的技能,工人们只需要进行更简单、更快的培训,更容易监管,若离职则较容易被取代。此外,因为任务具有精确性、界限明确,工人们应当能擅长反复从事同一个任务。使用高度简化作业的操作,并不总是奏效。这种工作会使员工处于不愉快的状态,因此,工人的旷工率上升、流失率上升、绩效较差,并提升生产成本,这些是对工作的厌烦与情感疏远造成的。尽管简化的工作可以吸引到一部分人,但其缺点在结构和重复任务方面愈演愈烈。由此而言,一种避免工作简化的方法就是通过增加任务的数量和种类来扩大工作职能范围(Dessler,2017)。这可以通过岗位轮换与职务扩大来实现。

are then compiled into a job description. A good job analysis is one that provides a good fit between the individual workers and the task requirements (Hon, 2011). Task requirements include job simplification, job enlargement, rotation, and job enrichment. Each varies in how specialised the division of labour becomes—that is, in how narrowly job tasks are defined.

Job description is a broad statement of the purpose, scope, duties and responsibilities of a particular job.

Job specification is a detailed statement of the physical and mental activities involved in a job and, when relevant, of the social and physical behaviour required, i.e. what the employee does, what knowledge he or she uses in doing it, the judgments he or she makes and the factors taken into account when making them (Dessler, 2017). For several personnel functions a detailed account of the job is necessary. The most important of these are selection, promotion, appraisal, setting performance standards, job evaluation and training. A job specification is therefore of fundamental importance in personnel management, though it should be used with discretion. When relations are poor between a manager and subordinates, the latter may use job specification as self-defensive weapons, refusing tasks or responsibilities because they do not appear in the specifications.

Whenever possible, the job specification should show what the person does, and how he or she will do it. It is also desirable to indicate approximately what proportion of working time is spent on each activity, or group of activities, and how frequently any occasional duties occur. The job specification should begin with the job description and then continue with a more detailed account of the job, including, for example, a) major responsibilities and results expected; b) routine duties under those headings; c) non-routine or infrequent duties under the same headings; d) working conditions; e) equipment and materials used; and f) personal contacts (Dessler, 2017).

Job simplification involves standardising work procedures and employing people in well-defined and highly specialised tasks. Simplified jobs are narrow in job scope—that is, the number and variety of different tasks a person performs are limited. The logic of job simplification is straightforward; if a job does not require complex skills, workers should be easier and quicker to train, less difficult to supervise and easy to replace if they leave. Moreover, because tasks are precisely and narrowly defined, workers should become good at doing the same tasks over and over again. Operations using highly simplified jobs are not always successful. Productivity can suffer as unhappy workers drive up costs through absenteeism and turnover and through poor performance caused by boredom and alienation. Although simplified jobs appeal to some people, there are disadvantages to the structure and to repetitive tasks. Thus, one way to move beyond job simplification is to expand job scope by increasing the number and variety of tasks performed by a worker (Dessler, 2017). This can be done through job rotation and job enlargement.

　　岗位轮换通过在不同岗位间进行周期性的人员轮换来增加任务变化度，包括不同的任务部署。岗位轮换可以依靠常规日程安排表来实现；也同样可以周期性或是不定期地进行。后一种方式通常用在培训员工时，以扩大人们对职位的了解。

　　职务扩大是通过结合两项或以上的任务来增加任务多样性，这些任务在此之前被分别安排给不同的员工。通常情况下，这些任务在原始职位上是在工作进行前或后立即完成的。并不是只完成一项任务，员工可以被指派多项任务。并且个体可以偶尔在不同职能部门间轮换岗位（Dessler，2017）。由于职务扩大与岗位轮换可以减少部分工作的单调性，还能简化职能，我们可以预期，这会提升员工个体的满意度和绩效表现。

　　职务丰富化是通过增加工作计划和职能评估来提升工作深度的，这通常由上级主管来执行。职务丰富化通过扩大其内容，创建更多的把满足感融入工作中的机会（Dessler，2017）。它是一项具有巨大潜力的重要管理策略，目的是在工作环境中提高个人绩效和工作满意度。

绩效标准

　　绩效标准需要明确特定工作在数量和质量上要达到的要求，它必须由该工作领域的专家来制定。在评估与培训期间绩效标准的使用频率最高。为了检验员工在其本位以及培训过后的表现，至关重要的是具有和平日实际绩效相比较的尺度规范。

　　能力标准是一项基准标杆，其表明在特定工作情境下人们应当有能力做的事情（Hon，2012）。典型的能力包括完成特殊任务的能力和主观意愿，以及能把一类工作的某些知识和技能推广到其他类型的工作中去。个人能力是个体能将其施展在各自职能之中的特性，例如领导能力或良好的沟通技巧。职业能力可以表述为是个人预期能取得的成果和绩效水平。

　　标准设定是工作评估的主要部分。在从事体力或技术活动时，绩效标准则是最容易设定的。这些标准可以表述为应该写出多少文章、完成多少文件、一天中打出多少个销售电话。当目标任务多变时，例如一天之中有多个类型的文章需要写，或是销售电话散布在很大区域内，该标准用简洁的条款来表述则会引起误解。同样地，一份绩效标准应当要涉及工作质量。

　　为经理和主管设定绩效标准要困难得多，因为他们的工作常变化莫测，且主要是脑力劳动。某些情况下，会有一些明确的任务目标，例如销售经理

Job rotation increases task variety by periodically shifting workers between jobs that involve different task assignments. Job rotation can be done on a regular schedule; it can also be done periodically or occasionally. The latter approach is often used in training to broaden people's understanding of jobs performed by others.

Job enlargement increases task variety by combining two or more tasks that were previously assigned to separate workers. Often these are tasks that are done immediately before or after the work performed in the original job. Instead of doing only one task, employees can be assigned to several tasks or individuals can occasionally switch jobs to work in a different functional department (Dessler, 2017). Because job enlargement and rotation can reduce some of the monotony in otherwise simplified jobs, we would expect an increase in an individual's satisfaction and performance.

Job enrichment increases job depth by adding work planning and evaluating duties that are normally performed by the supervisor. Job enrichment is the practice of building more opportunities for satisfaction into a job by expanding its content (Dessler, 2017). Job enrichment is an important strategy with the potential to improve individual performance and satisfaction in the workplace.

Performance Standards

Performance standards is sometimes necessary to specify the quantity or quality of work that should be attained by the holder of a certain job. The most frequent use of performance standards is found in appraisal and training; to assess an employee either in his or her normal work or after training it is essential to have a criterion against which to compare actual performance.

Competence standards are standards of competence used as benchmarks to indicate what people should be capable of doing in specific workplace situations (Hon, 2012). Competencies typically involve the ability and willingness to perform particular tasks and to transfer knowledge and skills from the performance of one type of work to others. Personal competencies are the individual characteristics that people bring to their duties, e.g. leadership ability or good communication skills. Occupational competencies are the outputs and performance levels that individuals are expected to attain.

Setting standards is an important part of job assessment. Performance standards are most easy to set when some kind of physical or technical activity takes place. They can state how many articles should be produced, how many documents completed or how many selling calls should be made in a day. When the task becomes varied, e.g. when articles of several different types are made during a working day or the calls are scattered over a large area, standards expressed in such simple terms become misleading. A performance standard should also contain some reference to the quality of work.

Standards for managers and supervisors are more difficult to set because their work is extremely varied and emphasises mental rather than physical activity. In some cases,

可能有固定的最低销售额需要完成,或是主管需要将他手下部门的等候时间控制在一定范围之内。诸如此类的标准,与"标准设定"部分的中心观点或紧急事件是相似的,当它可以用客观的手段来量化,且控制在负责人可以掌控的程度的时候,该标准具有相当特别的价值。

个人能力描述是依照适合某职位的某类人群、针对工作规范的详细阐述。它常被用在人才招聘、选拔、晋升的各个环节中,以便找出最适合该职位的人选。它包含一系列某职位候选人的所需属性;在某些情况下可能设立成果或是能力倾向测验,以获得关于岗位适合程度的精确结果。

个人能力描述通常必须建立在工作规范之上,其中的每个规定条款必须从在分析该职位后获得的事实依据角度来说是合情合理的(Dessler,2017)。有时候会在个人能力描述中出现像"具有积极主动性"这样的表述,不仅仅有些模糊不清,而且和实际的工作需要并没有直接关系。个人能力描述的目的是阐明该个体有能力胜任此工作,而不是不切实际的理想化。

假设要找到一名候选人,他完全精准地符合工作规范,或是经过培训后被准确地塑造成需要的类型,这是不切实际且相当困难的。通常情况下在经过分析后职责会有一些改变,有时是经过深思熟虑,有时是逐步地、潜移默化地随着职位负责人的个人能力、性格以及经验而变化。任何案例在任何情况下的职位分析都不可能给出一个完整、可靠的结果,岗位规则描述必须建立在具有灵活性的描述之上。

案例研究 5-1[①] ▶▶▶▶▶▶

作为一个在跨国酒店集团承担人力资源管理责任的经理人,你需要明确你的组织目标之一,就是通过有效地使用员工来实现生产力最大化。为了高效工作,你必须拥有牢固的组织机构,明确定义每一个所需要的工作任务,并指派员工们到合适的岗位去完成。除非每个人都非常明确工作的细节,否则就会遗留未完成的工作、产生职责争议、工作态度冷漠,甚至会引起大面积的

---

① 资料来源:Tanke,M.(2001). *Human Resources Management for the Hospitality Industry* (2nd. ed),72. Albany:Delmar Thomsson Learning.

there may be obvious targets, e.g. a sales manager may be expected to maintain sales at a certain minimum level, or a supervisor may be expected to keep waiting times in his or her section below a certain level. Criteria such as these, which are similar to the key points or critical incidents mentioned in setting standards, are particularly valuable when they can be measured objectively and are within the control of the person concerned. A target for a supervisor such as to "maintain satisfactory industrial relations within the section" would be valueless, first because of the subjective interpretation of the word satisfactory and second because the quality of industrial relations would depend on may factors outside the supervisor's control.

Personnel specification is an interpretation of the job specification in terms of the kind of person suitable for the job. A personnel specification is used above all in recruitment, selection and promotion as part of the process of utilisation, i.e. finding the most suitable person to fill a job. It is a list of a series of desired attributes against which candidates for a job are judged; in some cases, it may be possible to set an achievement or aptitude test to obtain a more exact measure of candidates' suitability.

The personnel specification must always be based on the job specification (Dessler, 2017); every statement in it must be justified by evidence obtained from the analysis of the job. Statements like "possessing outstanding initiative", which are sometimes found in personnel specifications, are not only vague but often have no relation to the actual demands of the job. The specification is intended to describe the person who is capable of doing the job adequately, not an impossible ideal.

It is unrealistic and somewhat difficult to suppose that a candidate will be found who fits the job specification exactly or can be precisely moulded into it by training. Quite often the job is changed after it has been analysed, sometimes deliberately, sometimes gradually and unconsciously by the job holder to suit his or her abilities, personality and experience. In any case job analysis can never produce a completely reliable result and job specifications based on it must always be interpreted flexibly.

Case Study 5 – 1[①] ▶▶▶▶▶▶

As a manager with human resources responsibilities in a large multinational hospitality corporation, you are aware that one of your organisational goals is to achieve maximum productivity through the efficient use of your employees. To achieve efficiency, you must have a solid organisational structure, and must identify each of the required job tasks and assign them to the appropriate job position. Unless each person knows exactly what his/her job entails, there will be work left unfinished, arguments over responsibilities, indifference and eventually a larger than desired turnover. Thus, the very heart of human resources

---

① Source: Tanke, M.(2001). *Human Resources Management for the Hospitality Industry* (2nd.ed). 72.Albany: Delmar Thomsson Learning.

人员流失。因此,人力资源管理的核心就是职位分析。

你所工作的公司旗下有酒店、度假村、独立的食物供应以及膳食供应设施。公司总部设立在美国,在欧洲包含超过 450 家的独立酒店,拥有数十家酒店地产。负责发展的高级副总裁向你传达了以下目标:"在两年内将酒店住宿运营产业扩展到经济型酒店市场,在进军美国中西部市场五年的周期之内,将产业扩大到五个州的范围。"

发展部门副总裁在顶着巨大的压力在两周后准备向公司总裁提交计划书。

由于你之前在职位分析程序和技术方面取得了经验,你被要求提供有关确定该项目人员工资预算的信息。为了向发展部门高级副总裁提供这些信息,你需要做什么? 副总裁要求从你这里得到的信息,将成为这个连锁酒店项目的定位、培训和发展等人力资源职能长期计划方案的基础。在此特别情况下,从上到下或是从下到上,哪种方式最适合你对此进行职位分析? 工作量化表这一方式是否适合该情境呢?

问　题

经过完整的职位分析之后,你发现有一个职位需要去填补,就是洗衣房服务人员。请给出详细的原因。

(1) 请为该职位设计一个职位规范。该职位需要个人具有怎样的技能水平和教育背景?

(2) 洗衣房服务人员的职位是否需要重新设计,以适应一些非传统劳动力来源的员工的技术水平以及教育背景? 为此你将如何进行设计?

案例研究 5 - 2 ▶▶▶▶▶▶

中国服装股份有限公司的组织设计

中国服装股份有限公司在全球为其服装连锁店生产服装产品及配件。Peter 和 Paul 两兄弟于 1980 年创立公司,且是公司最主要的股东。Peter 占

management is the job analysis.

The company that you work for has hotels，resorts，freestanding food service operations and catering facilities. The company is headquartered in the United States，where it maintains over 450 individual hospitality establishments and a dozen hotel properties located throughout Europe. The Senior Vice President of Development has shared with you the following organisational goals："To expand lodging operations into the economy hotel market within two years，with expansion into a five state region in the Mid-west with in a period of five years after entering the marketing."

The Senior Vice President of Development is under pressure to prepare a prospectus for the company president in two weeks.

Because of your previous experience with job analysis procedures and techniques you have been asked to provide information for which a projected payroll budget could be determined. What will you need to do to prepare this information for the Senior Vice President of Development? The information that the vice president is requesting from you will become the basis for the long-range plans for the human resources functions of orientation，training and development for this proposed chain of lodging properties. In this particular situation，would it be best to use a top-down approach or bottom-up approach for your job analysis? Would the job inventory approach be a suitable method of job analysis in this particular situation?

Questions

After you complete the job analysis，you find that one of the job positions that needs to be filled is that of laundry room attendant. Please explain why in detail.

(1) Develop a job specification for this job. What are the skill levels and educational background that will be required of the individual filling this job position?

(2) Could the job position for laundry room attendant be redesigned to accommodate the skill levels and educational background of some non-traditional sources of labour? How would you go about redesigning this particular job?

Case Study 5 – 2 ▶▶▶▶▶▶

The Organisational Design of China Clothing Inc.

China Clothing Inc. has been manufacturing clothes and clothing accessories for garment chain stores all around the world. Peter and Paul，who are brothers，established the company in 1980 and are still the principal shareholders. Peter owns a 60 per cent share of the stock，and Paul owns 20 per cent. Six employees，including two of the company directors，own the remaining shares.

The company employs 225 men and women，with 23 working in the offices. Peter is the president，and Paul is the treasurer and is in charge of all of the accounting，including the

有 60% 的股份，Paul 持有 20%。包括 2 名公司总监在内的 6 名员工持有剩余股份。

公司拥有男女员工 225 名，其中 23 名属于办公室人员。Peter 是公司总裁，Paul 是财务主管，且负责所有会计事项，包括薪资部门。Paul 一直试图说服 Peter 建立计算机网络。工厂经理也上交申请要求使用计算机网络进行工厂的质量控制。但 Peter 的反应却是计算机网络的建立和维护开销过高。

在某些场合，Paul 力劝他兄弟 Peter 雇用一名执行副总裁。Paul 觉得这将取代现有总裁的部分职能。

上个月，Peter 因为突发心脏病病了 24 天之久。Peter 的医生建议他必须减少工作量，并更多地授权给其他人。在 Peter 生病期间，公司失去了一笔巨大的合同。

他发现后，两名总监向他寻求解释。他们想知道为何总裁没有授权他的兄弟 Paul 或公司的其他人来协商这份合同。

问　题

(1) 中国服装股份有限公司的管理有什么问题？

(2) 谁应该要为这次损失承担责任？

(3) 针对该公司的管理，你会给出什么建议？

案例研究 5 - 3[①]　▶▶▶▶▶▶

Michael 是一名中型制造业小镇一流酒店的酒水经理。该酒店经营业绩稳定，现在正试图吸引本地消费者来酒店的餐厅及酒吧消费。餐厅将进行扩建，酒吧将从大堂中移除，扩建成带有餐桌服务的酒廊。Michael 负责该重建的所有事宜。

所有酒吧设备都将翻新，Michael 将与设计师一起商议决定需要哪些设备。将会有更多服务人员负责数十张餐桌，这些人员由 Michael 负责招聘和培训。除了酒吧内的消费者，调酒师将负责酒廊和餐厅的调酒，Michael 可能需要再增加一些调酒师。

Michael 明白现在的调酒师对这一变化会很忧心。他们会担心需要更努力地工作却只能换回更少的小费，这是因为他们将会和餐桌服务相竞争。同时他们也会很担心新的布局和设备。对他们来说，在全新的环境下工作感到自信、对新项目产生认同感以及接受新的人事调整是很重要的。

---

① 资料来源：Walker, J. R., & Miller J. E. (2009). *Supervision in the Hospitality Industry*: *Leading Human Resources*. Hoboken, NJ: John Wiley & Sons.

payroll department. Paul has been trying to persuade Peter to install a computer network. The plant manager has also submitted a request for a computer network for quality control purposes in the plant. Peter's response has been that a computer network costs too much to set up and maintain.

On several occasions, Paul has urged his brother Peter to seek the directors' approval to appoint an executive vice-president. Paul feels that this executive could take over some of the duties now performed by the president.

Last month, Peter was ill for 24 days because of a heart attack. Peter's doctor advised him that he must reduce his workload and delegate more authority to others. During Peter's illness, the company lost a big contract. When this was discovered, two directors asked the president for an explanation. They wanted to know why he had not authorised his brother, Paul, or someone else in the company to negotiate this contract.

Questions

(1) What is wrong with the China Clothing's management?

(2) Who should be held responsible for the loss of the big contract?

(3) What recommendations would you make to China Clothing regarding the management of the company?

Case Study 5 – 3[①] ▶▶▶▶▶▶

Michael is a beverage manager at the principal hotel in a middle-sized manufacturing town. The hotel has a steady business trade and is now reaching out to attract local customers to its restaurant and bar. The restaurant is to be enlarged and the bar next to the lobby is to be remodelled and expanded into a cocktail lounge with table service. Michael is in charge of planning all aspects of the change.

All of the bar equipment will be new, and Michael will work with the designer to determine what is needed. There will be a dozen tables served by waiters or waitresses whom Michael will hire and train. The bartenders will pour drinks for both the lounge and dining room servers in addition to customers at the bar, and Michael may have to add another couple of bartenders to the staff.

Michael knows the present bartenders will be worried about the change. They will be afraid that they will have to work harder for fewer tips, as they will be competing with the table servers. They may also be concerned about the new layout and equipment. It is important for them to feel confident about working in the new setup and to be committed to the project and accepting of the new personnel.

---

① Source: Walker, J.R., & Miller J.E.(2009).*Supervision in the Hospitality Industry*: *Leading Human Resources*.Hoboken, NJ: John Wiley & Sons.

问　题

（1）Michael 应该什么时候宣布这一消息？以怎样的方法宣布呢？

（2）他将如何应对新的人事变动带来的恐惧感？

（3）他需要做什么来增加他们的自信？

Questions

(1) When should Michael break the news, and how?

(2) How should he deal with their fears about the change of new personnel?

(3) What can he do to increase their confidence?

第6章　雇员招聘与选拔

学习目标

- 了解员工的招聘和选拔的过程
- 了解企业如何通过不同的渠道找到合适的人选
- 提供案例研究作为例子来帮助理解上述概念

由于在众多领域中出现技能短缺的现象,并且求职者供应数正在下降,吸引合适的候选人已成为诸多招聘人员主要的市场工作(Dessler,2017)。招募员工是填补该空缺的第一步,其包括对空缺岗位的检查、对合适候选人来源的考量、与这些候选人取得联系、然后从中吸引部分人选。接下来是选拔,例如借助各类手段对候选者进行测评、做出决定,紧接着就是给出招聘意向。如果需要一名新员工,且招聘是其中必要的途径,那么在获得填补该空缺的准许后,下一步就是搜索申请人。问题在于:可能适合这个职位的最佳候选人在哪呢? 需要通过内部晋升来完成还是使用外部资源?

内部招聘

扩张与增长是招聘需求的影响因素,其他因素包括辞职、解聘、退休、职位调动。许多组织会观察其内部来填补职位空缺(Dessler,2017)。内部招聘意味着在企业内部调动合适的候选人来填补空位。这一般通过晋升或从相似级别的其他岗位进行调动来实现。对组织和个人来说,内部招聘都具有优势。提供就业保障与借助内部提升的方式扩大职业晋升空间,可以提高员工的士气、忠诚度以及奉献度。同时也能降低开销,包括吸引合适的候选人、选拔"符合"组织的人选的开销,而且可以减少对入门培训的需求,使整个内部招聘变得更具吸引力。当然,员工要了解组织及其文化,同样,组织对他们

Chapter 6　Employee Recruitment and Selection

The objectives of this chapter

■ Understand the process of employee recruitment and selection

■ Understand how organizations find the appropriate candidate through different sources of commercial enterprises

■ Provide case studies as examples to help understand the above concepts

Attracting suitable applicants when skills shortages exist across a range of areas and the supply of job candidates is decreasing has become a major marketing exercise for many employers (Dessler，2017).Recruitment refers to the first part of the process，that is filling vacancies; it includes identifying the vacancy，considering the sources of suitable candidates，making contact with those candidates and attracting applications from them. Selection is the next stage，i.e. assessing the candidates by various means and making a choice followed by an offer of employment. If a new staff member is required，and approval to fill the position via recruiting has been acquired，the next step is to develop an applicant pool. The first problem is to identify where suitable applicants for this role are located. In particular，will the positions be filled by promotion from internal or from external sources?

Internal Recruitment

Expansion and growth contribute to the need for recruitment. Other factors include resignations，dismissals，retirements and relocation (Dessler，2017). Many organisations first look in-house to fill vacant positions. Internal recruitment means locating suitable applicants within the organisation to fill those positions. Positions may be filled by promotion or by transferring employees from a different job at a similar level. Internal recruitment has advantages for both the organisation and its employees. Providing employment security and career advancement through internal promotion improves employee morale，loyalty and commitment. The reduced costs involved in both attracting suitable applicants and selecting those who will "fit" the organisation，and the reduced need for induction and training，make internal recruitment attractive. And，of course，the employees know the organisation and its culture，and the organisation knows them.

也要有所了解。

然而，内部招聘并不是没有弊端的，部分没有得到晋升的员工可能感到不满；而且除非是组织正在裁员，否则一次成功的内部招聘将使得组织内部其他岗位空缺。

为了使内部招聘更高效，它应该要尽可能地更开放、更公平（Dessler，2017）。公开张贴岗位信息、在公司的信息平台上做广告等方式常用于邀请符合条件的职员来申请职位。如果潜在的候选人是由领导层选拔而得的，并非通过公开招标过程选定的，则应适当查阅人事记录，这些记录必须足够详细并妥善保存。

外部招聘

当内部招聘无法提供合适的候选人时，就需要开始外部招聘了。外部招聘意思是从机构外吸引参与者来申请空缺职位（Dessler，2017）。尽管内部招聘拥有很多优势，但大量职位都是由外部人员来填充的。外部招聘消耗时间、花费较高、不确定性大，尽管通过系统性规划可以一定程度减少这些缺点。可以将外部招聘分为两类：相对廉价，但选择有限的，例如由现有员工推荐；费用相对高昂的，但招聘者有机会接触更广泛的候选者，例如通过广告。以下是一些外部招聘的例子：

（1）由现任员工或是他们周围的熟人举荐；

（2）主动申请的候选人；

（3）与大学、学院、学校直接联络；

（4）本地就业服务中心和本地劳动力机构；

（5）专业团体的预约服务；

（6）私人招聘代理商；

（7）广告。

推荐与举荐

企业有时候会奖励成功推荐候选人的员工。这个招聘方法可选范围很有限，但花费较少。而且这些候选人通常具备良好的工作能力（Dessler，2017）。当他们听说公司有职位空缺的时候，亲戚朋友互相关照彼此。对于小型机构而言，口口相传的招聘既省时又高效。例如在香港，涉及雇用外籍

However，recruiting from within is not without drawbacks，such as discontent among those who are not promoted; also，unless the organisation is undergoing downsizing，a successful internal recruitment exercise will render another position vacant within the organisation.

For internal recruitment to be effective，it should be conducted openly and fairly as far as possible (Dessler，2017). Posting the job opening on notice boards，advertising it in a company newsletter etc. are some methods for inviting all of the qualified employees to apply for the post. In cases where potential candidates are selected by management rather than by an open bidding process，personnel records，which must be sufficiently detailed and well maintained，should be consulted properly.

External Recruitment

External recruitment may commence if internal recruitment does not provide a suitable applicant. External recruitment means attracting people from outside the organisation to apply for a vacant position (Dessler，2017). Although internal recruitment has many advantages，a lot of positions are filled by external applicants. External recruitment can be time-consuming，expensive and uncertain，though it is possible to reduce these disadvantages to some extent through systematic planning. External recruitment methods may be divided into two categories: those that are comparatively inexpensive，but offer a limited choice，i.e. recommendations by present employees，and those that are comparatively more expensive，but give the employer access to wider range of candidates，i.e. advertising. The following are examples of external recruitment methods:

(1) recommendations by present employees or by acquaintances of employers;

(2) unsolicited applicants;

(3) direct links with universities，colleges and schools;

(4) local employment service centres and local labour institutions;

(5) professional bodies' appointment services;

(6) private employment agencies; and

(7) advertising.

Recommendations and Referrals

Recommendations and referrals are sometimes encouraged by rewarding employees who introduce successful candidates. As a recruitment method，it gives a limited field of choice，but costs very little and the candidates are usually of good quality (Dessler，2017). Friends and relatives "look out for" each other and are willing to pass the word on when they hear about vacancies in the companies they work for. For small organisations，recruitment by word of mouth can be both efficient and effective. In Hong Kong，for example，recommendation is a popular method for hiring foreign domestic helpers (e.g.

佣人（例如菲律宾、泰国、印度尼西亚籍）时，举荐就是十分有效的方式。急需外籍佣人的招聘者可能会发现推荐这种方式比招聘代理商理商更高效。

自　荐

企业有时会收到申请者亲自打电话求职，或是写信询问工作事宜。对于刚从高等院校毕业的应届毕业生而言，这是常见现象，这成了他们最初求职的策略之一（Dessler，2017）。从招聘者角度来看，这是另一个相对廉价的途径，尽管提供的选择有限，候选人的能力也参差不齐。

与教育主体直接联系

校园招聘的主要功能在于筛选候选者以决定他们是否值得进一步考量，并吸引优秀人才进入公司。尽管这个过程花费时间，许多招聘人员与各个大学、学院或是学校都保持着良好的联系。通常这类候选者只会出现在一年中固定时段，也就是暑假前的数月内。教育机构可以成为管理培训生和专业技术人员的重要来源。

本地就业服务中心

本地就业服务中心是公开的职业介绍中心，其向求职者和招聘人员提供免费求职服务（Dessler，2017）。招聘人员若想在中心留下工作登记卡，只须提供详细的岗位信息，例如职务名称、工作地点、行业、工作时数、工资、职责、任职要求等，或者更常见的是通过电话，或是面对面。求职者若希望通过在距离自己最近的本地就业服务中心来获得更多就业机会，他们要填写注册申请表格，内容包括预期薪资、期望工作地点、语言能力、打字技能、驾驶技能等。站在招聘者的角度来看，该招聘途径具有以下优势：（1）免费；（2）能提供初步筛选，否则潜在申请者数量可能会很多。

专业团体

一些专业团体为注册的会员提供招聘服务，会员可以提供个人经历信息以及寻求岗位的类型。招聘者利用该项服务来确保所有提交简历的候选人都是符合专业资格要求的。如果某空缺的职位需要某些特定资历，有限的选

workers from the Philippine，Thailand or Indonesia）. Employers who are in urgent need of domestic help might find recommendations more efficient than employment agencies.

Unsolicited Applications

Applications are sometimes received from candidates who either call personally at the place of work or write letters of enquiry（Dessler，2017）. It is not uncommon for fresh graduates of universities and school leavers to adopt this approach as their initial job seeking strategy. From the employer's point of view，this is another inexpensive source，although it only provides a limited choice and the candidates are of variable quality.

Direct Links with Educational Bodies

The main functions of campus recruitment programmes are to screen candidates to determine if they are worth further consideration，and to attract good candidates to the firm. Although this can be time-consuming，many employers maintain connections with universities，colleges and schools. Candidates from these sources are usually available only at one time of the year—a couple of months before the summer break. Educational bodies can be an important source of management trainees and professional and technical employees.

Local Employment Service Centres

Local employment service centre are public employment agencies that offer free-of-charge services to job-seekers and employers（Dessler，2017）. An employer wanting to place a job card in a service centre only has to supply detailed information about the opportunity，such as job title，work location，industry，working hours，salary，job duties，qualification required of applicant etc.，either over the phone or in person. A job-seeker who wishes to secure employment through the local employment service centre may register with the service centre nearest to his/her home by filling out a registration form that requests information such as expected salary，preferred work location，language ability，typing skills，driver's license type etc. From an employer's point of view，this means of recruitment has the following advantages：（1）free of charge；and （2）provides an initial screening，without which the potential number of applicants might be very high.

Professional Bodies

Some professional bodies have an employment service；members can register by supplying details of their experience and the kind of job they are looking for. An employer who uses this service can be sure that all of the candidates are professionally qualified. If the vacancy requires a certain qualification，the limited choice offered is not

择项就显得很有优势。与其经营一家需要谨慎管理的招聘服务公司,诸多团体更倾向鼓励招聘者在其专业杂志上刊登广告(Dessler,2017)。例如香港人力资源管理协会 HKIHRM 在其发表的新闻的空白处张贴招聘广告,寻求人力资源管理方面的专业人才。

私人招聘代理机构

私人招聘机构的首要职责是进行职位匹配。向招聘者提供适合岗位的候选者的商业机构主要有三种类型(Dessler,2017)。

1. 办公室人员职位介绍所

办公室人员职位介绍所主要针对以下职位:文员、打字员、办公室助理、机械操作员、业务员等,它也常用来招聘临时救援工作者。并不令人惊讶的是大多数这类机构都聚集在香港中环地带,属于香港商业中心区。招聘人员首先通知各个机构空缺的职位,紧接着代理机构提交在已注册列表中找出的符合条件的候选者名单。一旦候选者确定入职,则招聘人员付给代理机构中介费用,通常是该职员一个月薪水的一半。如果该职员在特定时间内离职,则中介费用的一部分将会退回。通常对候选者来说不产生任何费用。当然,如果该候选人个人愿意的话,他也可以自由地在诸多代理机构内注册。

除非代理机构只负责提交合适的候选人给空缺岗位,否则他们的服务费将十分昂贵,因为招聘人员在面试、测试、申请过程中耗时很多。因此,对招聘人员来说,为了获得高质量的服务,与一两个私人招聘代理机构保持稳定、密切的伙伴关系是十分重要的。

2. 高层人员选拔机构

高层人员选拔机构通常负责承担招聘的整个过程,以及选拔管理层、专业人士的第一步。这些机构对岗位进行分析,准备岗位描述、技术细节、广告,派发申请表,面试选拔出来的候选者(Dessler,2017)。然后,招聘者可以得到筛选后的候选人名单以及他们的简历,以便招聘者做出最终选择。

这种招聘方式价格昂贵,因为通常情况下无论是否找到合适人选,招聘者都需要负担大量费用。它还有其他两个缺点:(1)对局外者来说,在短时间内很难深入了解到底怎样的人选才最适合现有公司的管理风格和管理架构;(2)机构很难随时跟踪候选人信息并进一步证实它推荐的有效性。而在没有证实和跟踪工作的情况下,随着时间的推移,选拔过程将得不到调整和改善。

a disadvantage. Other professional bodies, instead of running an employment service, which needs careful administration, prefer to encourage employers to advertise in their professional journals (Dessler, 2017). For instance, the Hong Kong Institute of Human Resource Management (HKIHRM) publishes a newsletter with space for recruitment advertisements for human resource management professionals.

Private Employment Agencies

Private employment agencies' primary function is job matching. Organisations that are run as commercial enterprises for supplying employers with candidates for jobs are of three main types (Dessler, 2017).

1. Office staff employment agencies

These agencies focus on jobs such as clerks, typists, office assistances, machine operators, merchandisers etc., and are popular with employers who are looking for casual or temporary relief workers. It is not surprising that most of these agencies are located in Central, which is Hong Kong's commercial centre. The employer first informs the agency of the vacancy, and the agency then submits a list of suitable candidates on its register to the employer. When a candidate is engaged, the employer pays a fee to the agency, usually to the tune of half a month's salary. Part of this fee is usually refunded if the employee leaves within a specified time. There is usually no charge to the candidate, who of course is at liberty to register with several agencies if he or she wishes.

Unless the agency takes care to submit only reasonable candidates for the vacancy, its services can be expensive because of the time taken up by the employer in interviewing, testing and processing applications. Hence, it is important for the employer to maintain a steady and close relationship with private employment agencies to obtain quality service.

2. Selection agencies for senior staff

These agencies usually undertake the complete recruitment process and the first stages of selection for managerial and professional vacancies. The agency analyses the job, prepares a job description and specification, advertises, sends out application forms and interviews selected candidates (Dessler, 2017). The employer is then presented with a shortlist of candidates, together with their career summary and qualifications, so that they may make the final choice.

This method of recruitment is expensive because the employer usually pays a substantial fee, whether or not a suitable candidate is found. There are two other disadvantages: (1) it is impossible for an outside body to understand in a short time what kind of a person will fit in with the present management style and structure of the company; and (2) it is difficult for the agency to follow up and validate its recommendations. Yet without validation and follow-up work, the selection process cannot be modified and improved over time.

3. 猎头

有时招聘高层管理人员的过程我们称之为"猎聘"或是"寻找决策人"。它所主张的观点是最佳候选人通常并不是向广告递交回复的或是其他主动寻求新工作的人,而是那些在现有职位相对成功的人士,是并无离职意向的人。在收到客户的佣金后,猎头将开始搜寻潜在候选者(Dessler,2017):(1)在竞争激烈的市场中(很有可能在公司报告或宣传册中获得他们的信息);(2)专业组织团体的会员名单中、交易协会年报中、新闻杂志报告中提到的行业成功经理人;(3)借助保密猎聘网络渠道。然后他们需要小心谨慎地接触这些候选者,并针对新职位的职责和酬劳进行讨论,这其中的一两位候选者将被推荐到客户公司(Graham 和 Bennett,1998)。

猎聘的优点:

(1)猎头应当具备关于薪资水平和额外福利的专业知识以吸引各方面的专业人才。同时,他们将分析空缺岗位,针对不同类型的个人需求给出见解,并负责进行最初的筛选和测试。这能节约客户许多行政和广告方面的开销。

(2)已受聘于具体岗位的高层管理人员通常工作忙碌,并无时间去阅读招聘广告、新闻或是其他社交平台,因此无法从这些途径接触到他们。

(3)有时高级经理准备有所行动,他们会让主要的猎头知道这个消息,尽管他们本人无法公开向竞争公司求职。

(4)猎聘公司能够确保推荐出去的候选人大多数都是十分胜任空缺职位的。

猎聘的缺点:

(1)猎头会对成功的企业造成一些不稳定影响,使它们失掉重金培养的高级经理人。

(2)被猎聘的个人可能时常会受到其他猎头的诱惑和吸引,而在短时间内离开新进入的公司。为了避免这一现象,许多公司给高层管理职位带上"金手铐",例如他们会支付高昂的现金奖励给猎头公司,但只有这些高级经理人在公司内任职数年后他们才会得到这笔奖赏。

(3)并不符合条件的候选者有可能贿赂猎头,从而让他们推荐自己。

(4)猎头人员可能会向潜在的候选者传递误导信息,说某职位可获得高薪,但实际情况并非如此。实际上薪资报价可能依赖于达到某个不切实际的目标。同样地,招聘公司可能期望猎头公司能找到解决他们所有问题和困难的合适人选,可现实是,当生意疲软不景气时,这是注定要失败的。

3. Headhunters

Very senior managers are sometimes recruited by a process known as "headhunting" or "executive search". Its advocates believe that the best candidates are not those who reply to advertisements or look for new jobs in other ways, but those who are successful in their present job and are not thinking of moving elsewhere. On receipt of a commission from a client, the headhunter will search for potential candidates (Dessler, 2017): (1) in competing businesses (possibly obtaining their names from company reports, brochures etc.), (2) in the membership lists of professional bodies, trade association yearbooks, newspaper and magazine reports that mention successful managers in the industry, and (3) through confidential headhunting networks. Selected candidates are then approached discreetly and, following a discussion regarding the job and its remuneration, one or two of them are introduced to the client firm (Graham & Bennett, 1998).

Advantages of Headhunting:

(1) Headhunters possess expert knowledge of the salary levels and fringe benefits necessary to attract professional candidates. They will also analyse the vacancy and offer an opinion about the type of person required, and will conduct initial screening and testing. This saves the client many administrative costs and advertising expenses.

(2) Top managers already in employment may be too busy to read job advertisements, newspapers and other conventional media, and hence cannot be reached by these means.

(3) Senior managers prepared to consider a move sometimes make this known to leading headhunters, even though they would not openly apply to competing companies.

(4) Recruiting firms can be confident that candidates presented to them will almost certainly be well equipped for the vacant position.

Disadvantages of Headhunting:

(1) Headhunting is highly disruptive to successful businesses, which stand to lose expensively-trained senior managers.

(2) A headhunted individual might subsequently be enticed by other headhunters to leave his or her new firm after a short period. To avoid this, some firms attach "golden handcuffs" to senior management positions, i.e. they pay large cash bonuses that are only available to executives who stay within the firm for a certain number of years.

(3) An unsuitable candidate might bribe the headhunter to recommend him or her for the vacant job.

(4) A headhunter might misleadingly suggest to potential candidates that a job carries a high level of salary when this is not actually the case. The salary quoted may in fact depend on meeting unrealistic targets. Similarly, a recruiting firm might expect a headhunter to find a candidate capable of solving all of its difficulties, but when the business is weak, it is bound to fail.

总的来说,招聘者应当仔细对选聘进来的专业人选和众多高级主管进行评估,在和猎头公司合作前确保获益远超过其不良的负面影响。在我国社会文化中小心谨慎尤为重要,无论是商业层面或是个人层面,都应十分注重和谐共处的人际关系。

广　告

时下最受欢迎的招聘手段就是发布招聘广告,邀请候选者前来申请。招聘广告应当把目标设定为尽可能快速且低价地招聘到符合条件的少数候选者。引起上百人前来申请的广告并不是一则好广告,因为招聘者随后将面对又漫长又昂贵的通过面试筛选参与者的过程。一则设计良好的广告可以具有第一轮选择的作用,通过对工作职责的全面描述,可以打消处于模棱两可状态的候选者申请的念头,也可以鼓励真正优秀的人前来申请。

招聘广告应该包括工作职责介绍和最低要求说明,涵盖以下信息:

(1) 职位名称;

(2) 职责和招聘者概述;

(3) 需要的经验、技能和资格;

(4) 工作地点、环境状况、额外福利等;

(5) 请说明培训(如果有的话);

(6) 候选人需要怎么做,例如撰写书信、电话预约、获取申请表格等。

应当向被拒的候选者送出及时通知和礼貌的回应;不顾及他人的处事方式终将有损公司声誉,反过来也会影响日后的广告宣传。希望保持匿名的大型企业可能要求猎头公司代表他们招聘员工。最后,纸质媒介并不是招聘者可以用来宣传的唯一平台,广播、电视或是其他媒介都可以(Dessler,2017)。进一步来说,大多数工厂区域建筑的外部都贴有空缺岗位的信息。用这种方式招聘半熟练工人既高效又低廉。超市的通知栏同样也是张贴职位广告的好地方,通常是兼职岗位,或是本地临时帮手或辅导人员(Graham 和 Bennett,1998)。

人才选拔

无论选择怎样的招聘方式,候选者都会被要求填写申请表格。表格首先要确保不遗漏重要信息,其次是有条理地按统一格式让候选者提供详细资

All in all，employers should carefully evaluate the pros and cons of recruiting senior executives through headhunters，and make sure that the benefits outweigh the dysfunctional side effects before engaging their services.Caution is particularly important in our society where harmonious relationships，both on a business level and on personal level，are highly valued.

Advertising

The most popular method of recruitment is to publicly advertise the vacancy and invite candidates to apply to the company. Job advertisements should aim at procuring a small number of well-qualified candidates as quickly and cheaply as possible. An advertisement that produces hundreds of replies is not a good one，as the employer will then be faced with a lengthy and expensive task of choosing a few candidates for interviews. A well-designed advertisement can become the first stage in selection by describing the job and qualifications required so that borderline candidates are deterred from applying and good candidates encouraged to do so（Graham & Bennett，1998）.

The advertisement should contain a job description and a specification that，in brief，includes the following pieces of information：

（1）job title；

（2）description of job and employer；

（3）experience，skills and qualifications required；

（4）work location，working conditions，fringe benefits，etc.；

（5）training，if any，that will be given；and

（6）the action the candidate needs to take，e.g. write a letter，phone for an appointment or to obtain an application form，etc.

Rejected candidates should be sent a prompt and courteous letter；inconsiderate treatment will eventually detract from a company's reputation and adversely affect the response to future advertisements. Large companies that wish to preserve their anonymity might ask selection agencies to recruit staff on their behalf. Finally，it is not just the printed medium that employers can use for placing job advertisements. Radio and television are other alternatives（Dessler，2017）. Furthermore，the exteriors of buildings in most of the factory districts are lined with job vacancy posters. This is both an effective and inexpensive way of recruiting semi-skilled manufacturing workers. Notice boards in supermarkets too are covered with job advertisements，usually for part-time and/or casual domestic helpers and tutors.

Selection

Whatever method of recruitment is used，the candidate should be asked to fill in an application form，first to ensure that no important details are omitted and second to provide information about the candidate in a logical and uniform order. The layout of

料。申请表的设置各式各样,但大多数都包含下列项目:

(1) 申请职位;

(2) 姓名、地址、联系电话;

(3) 生日、出生地、国籍;

(4) 教育背景;

(5) 培训经历和资格证书;

(6) 工作经历(过去雇主的姓名、岗位职责概述、所聘日期、离职原因);

(7) 申请者希望提供的其他信息或技能资料;

(8) 申请人签名;

(9) 签字日期。

申请表不仅仅是筛选人才的基础,也是受聘者个人人事记录的基本文件,在雇佣合同上具有法律重要性。

选拔方式

下一步需要经理人做的就是根据人事规范比较各个申请表的内容,寻找候选人明显适合该职位或有不足之处的某些特性或特征,这可以帮助排除部分候选者,或者可针对其不足的地方提供必要的培训。在这个对比的过程中经理人可以确定进入面试的候选人名单以及被拒者名单。后者需要给予未成功入选的通知。

在起草最终候选人名单之后,经理人将决定进行哪种类型的面试——个人面试或是小组面试,以及需要进行哪些测试,例如智力测试、能力测试、成果测试。面试是选拔过程中占有主要作用、不可或缺的一部分。

工作录取

假设在选拔过程中已经出现了合适的候选人,那么现在他(她)一定会收到录取通知。通常先给出口头通知,如果他(她)接受该职位,才会收到正式的书面通知。最初的工作录取通知需要特殊对待,尤其是以下几点(Dessler,2017):

(1) 给出的职位薪资不仅要恰当还需要具有吸引力,但要与现有员工薪资水平相一致。

(2) 职位名称必须确定,还要包括一些特别条款,例如"最初六个月内你需要参与公司某部门分支的培训"。

(3) 候选者必须知道该职位的基本条件,例如工作时数、假期、奖金和额外福利。

application forms varies, but most of them contain the following headings, usually in this order:

(1) job applied for;

(2) name, address, and telephone number;

(3) date and place of birth, nationality;

(4) education obtained;

(5) training and qualifications;

(6) employment history (names of previous employers, description of jobs held, dates of employments, reasons for leaving);

(7) any other information or skill the candidate wishes to provide;

(8) candidate's signature; and

(9) date.

The application form is not only the basis of selection, but is a fundamental document in an employee's personnel record that is importance in the contract of employment.

Selection Methods

Management's next step is to compare the application form with the personnel specification, looking for attributes that make the candidate suitable for the job and shortcomings that may either rule out the candidate from consideration or necessitate special training if he or she is engaged. From this analysis, the manager can make a list of candidates for interviews and a list of those rejected. The latter should be written to at once with letters expressing regret at their lack of success.

After the shortlist has been drawn up, the manager will decide what type of interview should be given—individual, successive or panel—and what tests should be used, e.g. an intelligence test, aptitude test or achievement test. The interview is the main and indispensable part of the selection process.

Job Offer

Assuming that a suitable candidate has emerged from the selection process, he or she must now receive an offer.Typically, a person is made an oral offer, and if he or she accepts it, the individual is given a written offer. The initial offer of a job needs special care, particularly with regards to the following points (Dessler, 2017).

(1) The wage or salary offered must not only be appropriate to the job and attractive to the candidate but consistent with the earnings of present employees.

(2) The job must be named and some special conditions stated, e.g. "for the first six months you would be under training at our ××× branch".

(3) The candidate must know the essential conditions of employment, e.g. hours, holidays, bonuses and fringe benefits.

（4）必须清楚标明附带条款，例如"须有合格的资信证明并通过体检"。

（5）必须清楚说明下一个步骤。如果候选者要求有考虑的时间，必须接受并保持联络。

如果口头通知已被接受，招聘者必须给出书面确认文件。他将重复之前已经说明的正式条款，确保条款的准确性，因为这将留作雇用合约的永久记录。在许多公司，书面录取通知只可能由人事经理或公司秘书来发出，以此确保其准确性。

案例研究 6-1 ▶▶▶▶▶

ABC Co., Ltd.是广州的一家中型企业（大概有150名员工）。这是一家试验所，负责进行纺织物、玩具、鞋类等的各类测试。其接近90%的主管或经理人都是从内部员工提拔上来的，他们大都在公司工作超过四年以上。Christine Ho是该公司的人事经理，他发现内部晋升会对员工产生激励效果，因为这向公司员工传递了这样的信息，即公司很赏识他们的忠诚，并且在公司服务的时间越久，未来前景越明朗。所有公开职位都张贴在通知栏内，认为自己胜任且有兴趣的人都可以申请。

该公司的外部招聘基本依赖于以下三个来源：（1）大学校园招聘；（2）报纸广告宣传；（3）推荐及引荐。专业或是技术岗位空缺可以通过纺织或化学工程专业应届毕业生来填补，该消息会在校园就业或咨询服务单元内公布。其他一般空缺岗位，例如打字员、文职人员、前台接待等大多将在本地报纸或招聘中心公开发布。同时也欢迎应征者个人推荐与引荐。成功推荐的员工将得到公司的奖赏。

问　题

（1）你认为ABC公司的招聘方式有效吗？

（2）你同意Christine Ho的观点，即内部晋升是选拔主管及管理人才的最佳途径吗？如果不是，为什么？如果是，你认为现行的内部招聘过程需要完善吗？

（3）你认为现行的外部招聘过程需要改进吗？

(4) Some provisos must be clearly stated, e.g. "subject to satisfactory references and medical examination".

(5) The next stage must be clearly defined; if the candidate asks for time for consideration, it must be agreed when he or she will get in touch.

If the oral offer has been accepted, the employer must confirm the offer in writing. The employer repeats in a formal letter the conditions already stated, taking great care that they are accurate because they will be on permanent record as the basis of the contract of employment. In many companies it is the rule that written offers may only be sent by the personnel manager or company secretary to ensure their confidentiality.

Case Study 6 – 1 ▶▶▶▶▶

ABC Co., Ltd. is a medium-sized (150 employees) firm in Guangzhou, China. It is a testing laboratory that carries out tests on fabrics, toys, footwear etc. Nearly 90% of its supervisors or managers are promoted from staff who have served the company for over four years. Christine Ho, personnel manager of ABC, feels that internal promotion has a motivational effect on employees. It conveys to members of the organisation the message that their loyalty is appreciated and that the longer they work for the company, the better are their future prospects within it. All internal openings are posted on notice boards for those who feel they are qualified and interested in applying.

For external recruitment, ABC Co Ltd. basically relies on three sources: (1) university recruitment; (2) newspaper advertisements; and (3) recommendations and referrals. Professional or technical vacancies that can suitably be filled by university graduates of textile or chemical engineering degrees are posted in career or counselling units in educational campuses. Other vacant general posts such as typist, clerk or receptionist are advertised in either the local newspapers or recruitment centres. Employees' personal recommendations and referrals are welcomed for all vacant posts. If these recommendations or referrals result in successful placements, the proposer is rewarded by ABC.

Questions

(1) Do you feel ABC's recruitment methods are effective?

(2) Do you agree with Christine Ho that internal promotion is best for supervisory and managerial posts? If not, why not? If yes, do you feel the current internal recruitment process could be improved?

(3) Do you feel the current external recruitment process could be improved?

案例研究 6 - 2[①] ▷▷▷▷▷▷

一位美国人 Jake Alberson 是一家加勒比海岸波多黎各岛上的小型豪华旅馆的经理。旅馆的生意通常是具有季节性的,吸引来自美国的高端旅客,从感恩节前后一直到春季末。Albertson 先生雇用了一小部分全年员工,大多数都是当地岛屿上的常住民,但在旺季时需要大量招聘人员,他倾向于招聘美国大学生,这是因为他们出色的英语能力。为了让旅馆的招聘计划有吸引力,他们向美国学生提供往返机票以及基本住宿,按周支付给他们合理的薪水,还提供全体员工的膳食。

为即将到来的旅游季节 Albertson 已经确定了他的大部分招聘对象,但他还需要雇用一名合格的调酒师,来打理旅馆外部忙碌的酒吧以及长廊。一天下午,Albertson 接到了波士顿 Louise Gang 的电话,她是酒店富有的主人。Gang 女士通知 Albertson,她朋友的侄女 Julie 想要过来,然后在该季"帮忙"。Albertson 已经明确地表示他想要寻找一名更合格的且有调酒经验的调酒师,但 Gang 女士说,"任何一个人都可以调酒"。"再说了",她补充道,"外貌出色的女生站在吧台能帮助增加收入。"她承诺会立刻将 Julie 的简历和成绩单传真过来。

Albertson 在看了 Julie 的简历后有些失望。她在大学主修的专业是服装设计,不仅成绩低于平均分,并且她过去的经验只有在大型连锁商店做了 6 个月的销售店员。几天后,Albertson 收到了一份写得很好的求职信和个人简历,一名 23 岁刚从新英格兰酒店学院毕业的学生,叫 David Chan,他有着 2 年在纽约酒店高端酒吧做调酒师的经历。Albertson 决定给他电子邮件,安排方便的时间进行最初的电话面试,就在他打开办公室电脑的时候,电话响了,是 Gang 女士的。"我朋友的侄女明早第一班飞机到,我告诉她这里有份工作给她。"

问 题

(1) 若总经理决定雇更为出色的 David Chan 而不是 Julie,他应该怎么向 Gang 女士交代?

(2) 作为私人所有、家族企业的经理人,当业务的需要和雇主的要求产生利益冲突时,Albertson 如何平衡?

---

① 资料来源:Sommerville, K. L. (2007). *Hospitality Employee Management and Supervision: Concept and Practical Applications*, 185 - 186. Hoboken, NJ: Jhon Wiley & Sons.

Case Study 6 – 2[①] ▶▶▶▶▶▶▶

Jake Albertson is an American who manages a small but luxurious inn on a Caribbean island near Puerto Rico. The inn's business is mostly seasonal, attracting high-end travellers from the United States from around Thanksgiving until late spring. Mr Albertson employs a small, year-round staff that is mostly made up of island locals, but hiring increases considerably during the busy season, and he prefers to hire American college students because of their superior English skills. To make the inn's hiring package attractive, American students are provided free round-trip airfare and basic onsite accommodations. They are paid a reasonable weekly salary, and the inn provides all of the employee meals free of charge.

Albertson has made most of his hiring decisions for the upcoming tourist season, but he still needs to hire a qualified bartender for the inn's busy outdoor bar and veranda. One afternoon, Mr Albertson receives a phone call from Louise Gang of Boston, the inn's wealthy owner. Mrs Gang informs Albertson that a friend's niece, Julie, would like to "come down" and "help out" for the season. When Mr Albertson makes it clear that he is looking for someone who is properly qualified and has previous bartending experience, Mrs Gang states, "Anybody can bartend, Albertson. And besides," she adds, "a good-looking girl behind the bar should help increase revenues." She promises to fax Julie's resume and transcripts right away.

Albertson is less than impressed after reading Julie's resume. Her major in college is fashion design, and not only are her grades below average, but her work experience includes only six months as a retail store clerk in a large department store chain. A few days later, Albertson receives a very well-written cover letter and resume from David Chan, a 23-year-old who has just graduated from a hospitality school in New England and has been working as a bartender in an upscale, New York City hotel for the past two years. He decides to email David Chan so that they can arrange a convenient time to conduct an initial telephone interview, and just as he logs on to the computer in his office, the phone rings and it is Mrs Gang: "My friend's niece is coming down on the first plane tomorrow. I told her you had a job for her".

Questions

(1) If the general manager decides to hire David Chan, who is more qualified than Julie, how should he deal with Mrs Gang?

(2) As the manager of a privately owned, family business, how should Albertson balance the needs of the business with the needs of the owner when the two sets of needs are in conflict with each other?

---

① Source: Sommerville, K.L.(2007). *Hospitality Employee Management and Supervision: Concept and Practical Applications.* 185 – 186. Hoboken, NJ: Jhon Wiley & Sons.

（3）如果小岛上并不缺乏符合条件的劳动力资源，情况会有怎样的不同？

（4）Gang 女士在旅馆工作的个人应具备怎样的能力方面与 Jake Albertson 持有不同意见吗？如果你的答案是肯定的，那么 Albertson 需要试图改变她的想法吗？为什么？为什么不？

案例研究 6 – 3[①] ▶▶▶▶▶▶

Mary 是名经验丰富的酒店夜间审计员，曾在阿尔戈斯酒店（Argos Hotel）全职任职接近 6 年之久。她在该酒店的工作成绩十分显著，几乎未出过错，无论是酒店宾客还是管理层都十分认可她积极的服务态度，她对夜间书面文件工作的细致入微的关注简直完美无缺。管理层已经非常信赖 Mary 了，但现在出现了一个问题。一名内部审计发现了偷窃的证据，矛头直指 Mary。

Jacobson 先生是酒店的总经理，当他意识到必须叫她来自己的办公室的时候，他感到十分哀伤，铁一般的事实证据摆在她的面前，在过去的 6 个月里她在酒店偷窃了将近 2000 美元。对质时，Mary 停下来啜泣，承认了一切。她告诉 Jacobson 自己最小的孩子得了严重的疾病，她和她的丈夫在经济上十分困难。她请求保住自己的工作，甚至承诺一定归还钱财。Jacobson 先生感到很痛心，但他告诉 Mary 自己将立即终止他们的雇佣关系。他觉得公司不会对 Mary 提起刑事诉讼，但她要收拾自己的个人物品，立即离开这里。

几周后，Jacobson 先生的助理告诉他正在电话上的是 Betty Li 打来了电话，坐落于 20 公里外城市里的高档房地产 WXY 酒店的人事总监。Betty 打电话来想要得到 Mary 的工作推荐，因为 Mary 向 WXY 酒店提交了全职夜班审计员职位的申请，"噢，不，"Jacobson 自言自语道，"她为什么偏偏让我来做她的推荐人呢？"他调整了一下情绪接着对助理说："好吧，把电话接进来。"

问 题

（1）看起来 Betty Li 不太可能向 Jacobson 先生询问 Mary 是否曾偷窃的事情，Jacobson 应当主动告诉她这个信息吗？如果应该，那么他该怎样传达？如果不应该，请给出解释。

---

①　资料来源：Sommerville，K.L.（2007）．*Hospitality Employee Management and Supervision：Concept and Practical Applications*．78 – 79．Hoboken，NJ：Jhon Wiley & Sons．

(3) How would this situation be different if there was not a shortage of qualified labour on the Caribbean island?

(4) Do Mrs Gang's perceptions of what qualifies an individual to work at the inn differ from those of Jake Albertson? If you answered yes, should Albertson attempt to change her perceptions? Why or why not?

Case Study 6 – 3[①] ▶▶▶ ▶▶ ▶▶

Mary is an experienced hotel night auditor who has been employed full time at the Argos Hotel for nearly six years. Her employment record at the Argos has been exceptional. She rarely misses work, both guests and management recognise her positive attitude towards customer service, and her attention to detail in the nightly paperwork are impeccable. Management has really come to rely on Mary, but now there is a problem. An internal audit has uncovered evidence of theft, and the evidence points directly at Mary.

Mr Jacobson, the hotel's general manager, is sick with grief when he realises that he must call Mary into his office and confront her with the hard evidence that she has stolen nearly \$2,000 over the past six months. When confronted, Mary breaks down sobbing and admits to everything. She tells Mr Jacobson that her youngest child has had serious health problems and she and her husband have been struggling financially. She begs to keep her job and even promises to pay the money back. Mr Jacobson is saddened, but he tells Mary that he is going to have to terminate her employment immediately. He says that he does not believe that the company wishes to file any criminal charges against Mary, but that she will need to collect her belongings and be escorted immediately from the building.

A few weeks later, Mr Jacobson's secretary comes into his office and says that she has Betty Li, the Human Resources Director at the WXY Hotel, an upscale property located in town about 20 miles away, on the line. Betty is calling to get an employment reference for Mary, who has submitted an application to the WXY Hotel for the position of full-time night auditor. "Oh no," Jacobson thinks to himself. "Why in the world did she ever list me as a reference?" He takes a moment to compose himself and then says to his secretary, "Okay, put her through."

Questions

(1) As it is unlikely that Betty Li will ask Mr Jacobson whether Mary is a thief, should Jacobson volunteer this information? If so, how should he present this information? If not, explain why not.

---

① Resource: Sommerville, K. L. (2007). *Hospitality Employee Management and Supervision: Concept and Practical Applications.*78 – 79.Hoboken, NJ: Jhon Wiley & Sons.

（2）如果 Jacobson 先生选择缄默，日后当 WXY 酒店在雇用 Mary 后发现事实的真相，他的酒店会面临任何指责吗？请给出解释。

（3）如果 Jacobson 先生决定向 Betty 说明 Mary 解除合约是由于偷窃行为，对阿尔戈斯酒店而言，可能会有什么法律上的后果？请给出解释。

（4）如果日后发现员工偷窃并解除合约关系，阿尔戈斯酒店应当在步骤和流程里增加哪些事项？请给出详细解释。

（2）If Mr Jacobson chooses not to volunteer the information, could his hotel possibly face any liability in the future if the WXY Hotel hires Mary and later learns the truth? Explain your answer.

（3）If Mr Jacobson decides to tell Betty Li that Mary's employment was terminated for theft, what might be the legal ramifications, if any, for the Argos Hotel? Explain your answer.

（4）What steps and procedures should the Argos Hotel implement in the event that any future employees are caught stealing and have to be terminated? Please explain in detail.

第7章　员工培训与开发

学习目标

- 了解酒店业的培训需求及其三种要素
- 了解培训的目标及其发展
- 了解培训效果评估的五个层次并通过案例研究解释管理的发展

　　培养发展员工的实用技能是组织工作的最重要的任务之一。这些组织机构通过对劳动力的有效利用来保持其自身的竞争优势。从这个角度我们可以断定，有效的培训对于企业在竞争中求生存、求发展，显得尤为重要。然而需要确保的是要将培训工作总量与质量区分开来。一个与企业经营策略不相关的、欠考虑的活动，不仅是时间和金钱上的浪费，而且很大程度上会导致员工消极怠工。多数员工都是期望组织向他们提供个人发展的机会，培养技能，学习掌握日后能够使用到的知识。本章提倡分四个步骤来理解培训过程的设计和开发，使得放在培训和开发活动上的时间和精力可以产生最高的成本效益。

培训需求分析

　　需求分析首先从对企业规划的评估开始。首选要评估该训练是否是实现既定目标的最佳手段。当需求分析得到相关主体的参与配合，并得到有效展开时，受训者往往极少会认为这样的培训是浪费时间。培训受到抵制的情况并不少见，但大部分不是针对培训技能的，而是产生于对培训需求和培训有效性缺乏沟通和理解。培训失效往往是由不理想的需求分析导致的，例如对真实的培训需求把握不准确，对培训是否是解决该组织问题的最佳途径缺乏判断，又或者没有把关键性的相关主体，如部门经理纳入培训过程中。这

Chapter 7　Employee Training and Development

The objectives of this chapter

- Understand hospitality training need analysis and its three elements
- Understand the objectives of training and its development
- Understand the five levels of training evaluation and managing development with case studies to help explanation

An organisation that uses its work force efficiently gains a competitive edge; therefore, effective training is an important part of an organisation's survival and growth. However, it is important to distinguish between the quantity and the quality of the training effort. An activity that is unrelated to corporate strategy is not only a waste of time and money, it is frequently a cause of demotivation. Most employees expect organisations to afford opportunities for personal development, and once they have developed skills and knowledge they expect to be able to use them. This study recommends a system of four steps for designing and developing cost-effective training processes.

Training Need Analysis

A need analysis starts with an assessment of the corporate plan; the first step is to determine whether training is the appropriate means to achieve a defined need. When training needs are managed effectively, with the involvement of line managers, there should be few instances in which trainees complain that training events are a waste of time. Resistance to training is common, and it is rarely the result of poor training skills. Failure arises from poor need analyses that do not accurately indicate training needs, do not determine whether training is the best response to the organisational problem and do not involve line managers in the analysis process, which can result in their lack of commitment (Noe, 2017).

Managers should take a systematic approach to training; it is essential that all training activities are the result of the identification of particular objectives. Identifying such objectives may be part of the organisation's appraisal system. Managers should be able to identify what lack of skills is currently causing problems. They should be able to

式的影响。需要着重强调的一个问题是"迁移",指的是将所有重要的传授的知识从所学之处迁移到工作中去。距离越远,受训者越少可能观察到这些知识与工作的关联性。很可能的情况是,培训内容太过抽象、太宽泛以至于很难应用于实际中。大体上说,最有效、最经济的培训是最接近实际工作的。以下列出了一些在实践中广受采纳的培训方法(Noe,2017)。根据特定的培训要求,它们可以用于培训员工、主管和高级经理(Stoner、Freeman 和 Gilbert,1995)。

1. 行动学习

将学习者,通常是高级经理人,组成小组,形成小组内自我管理的模式,互相担任彼此的咨询师。每个参与者将向整个团体提出一个实际生活问题,向大家寻求解决方案。因此团体里的每个成员扮演客户和咨询的角色。很重要的一点是每个人要领会学习方法的目的,掌握必要的互动技能,在类似的情景下可以实施。通常该方法主要适用于掌握实际决策权的经理人。经理人可以成功地互相学习,特别是问题中心学习法,且该问题处于他们的掌控之下(Noe,2017)。

2. 评估

这是发展管理能力最具成本效益的方式之一,因为所有经理人都要对他们的下属进行评估,同时也会得到来自各自上级管理者的评估。评估借助对经理人绩效的考察过程进行。该过程应当由受评人引导完成,将涵盖指出成功所在、审核进展、允许互相探索替代方案以及较多的高效工作行为。经理人收到的反馈结果、设定目标的整个过程以及下一个审核周期的可量化性指标,这三者都是极佳的以问题为中心的,个性化发展的最优方式。

3. 分配

这种方法通常用在培训项目的尾声阶段,它作为强化和测试已学内容是很有效的方法。当然该方法也可以用在其他情境下,特别是能够拓展受训者的经验。该部分需要按计划进行,以便它可以用可界定的、连贯一致的方式提高学习者的自身能力。

4. 案例分析

案例分析方法通常应用在管理培训中,例如大学的 MBA 项目。经理人通过对真实事件的研究,从中提取原理,日后可以应用到他们的工作中。是

question of "transference", which is the all-important carry-over of knowledge from the learning place to the workplace. The greater the distance, the less likely the trainee is to see the relevance of the training to the work; this occurs when the training is abstract and too generalised for easy practical application. Generally, the most effective and economical training occurs close to the job. The following training methods are in common use (Noe, 2017). Depending on the particular training needs, they can be used to train employees, supervisors or senior managers.

1. Action learning

Groups, usually of senior managers, meet in self-managed small work groups to act as consultants to each other. Each participant brings to the group a real-life problem to which he or she is committed to finding an answer. In the group, everybody acts as both a client and a consultant. It is important that each group member understands the objectives of the learning method and has the interactive skills necessary to operate in such an environment. This method is suitable for managers who have the power to make choices. Managers can learn successfully from each other, especially when the learning is problem-centred and under their control.

2. Appraisal

One of the most cost-effective methods of management development, appraisal is something that all managers should be both providing to their subordinates and receiving from their own manager. The process of reviewing a manager's performance—a process that should be led by the appraisee—will identify successes, review progress and allow for the mutual exploration of alternative, more effective work behaviour. The feedback that the manager receives and the process of setting objectives and quantifiable targets for the next review period are excellent problem-centred and individualised forms of development.

3. Assignments

This method is often used at the end of a training programme as a useful method of reinforcing the learning and measuring what has been learned. Assignments can, of course, be used in other circumstances, particularly to broaden the experience of trainees. They need to be planned so that they improve the competence of the learner in a definable and coherent manner.

4. Case study

These are commonly used in managerial training, for example in MBA university programmes. Managers can learn by studying real events and drawing from them principles that they can apply in their own work. Success depends on how the trainer

否能够成功做到这一点,取决于培训者如何管理该训练课程。有时受训者的思考会不充分,而不是着眼于对多变情境可能的应用上。

5. 辅导

辅导指的是在经理人与受训者之间进行的一系列非正式会议,其按照受训者的相关需要安排议程。它包括一些简单的技巧,例如如何提问、委托授权、项目的设定和分配等。需要注意的是要避免投入的下降,以及避免丧失学习任务目标(Noe,2017)。

6. 基于计算机的学习

信息技术的发展为学习者开辟了新天地。线上学习为全球范围的学习者提供了学习途径,这既可以节省时间和花费,也可以提供实时反馈,以强化学习者的动力。其中一个开放的在线学习平台是慕课网(MOOC),它让学习者能够随时随地在方便的时候学习。这个在线平台让学习者自己掌握学习进度。在学习者分散、培训者稀缺的情况下,将计算机和在线培训结合起来的方式值得推荐。

7. 演示

此类为"工作中"的培训。向学习者展示需要做的内容,然后尝试开展活动。该项培训具有可以立即反馈的以问题为中心的方法的优势。其潜在的缺陷是过度依赖技巧和知识的示范。缺少工作实践会容易被遗忘,也很难控制学习质量(Noe,2017)。

8. 岗位轮换

值得注意的是,学习者的岗位轮换是有计划和可监控的,而不是为了行政管理上的便利,去填补职位空缺。就他们自身而言,经历本身只有有限的知识潜力。重要的是所有经历要导向可界定的目标,且每部分都与目标相关联(Noe,2017)。

9. 讲座

讲座是教室里最普遍的学习方式,它对于那些享受抽象的概念化思考过程的学习者来说最为有效。讲座更适合针对有大量学习者的情况。因为讲座往往是一种被动学习,而学习者的注意力持续时间通常比讲座的长度短很多。

manages the session. As little is at stake, the thinking can be superficial and limited to the case rather than aimed at possible applications in a variety of situations.

5. Coaching

This method is usually conducted in a series of informal meetings between manager and learner and follows an agenda relevant to the learner's needs. It includes simple techniques such as asking questions, delegation and setting projects and assignments. Care must be taken to avoid a fall-off in commitment and the loss of learning objectives.

6. Computer-based learning

This technology has opened up new horizons for trainers. Programmed learning allows the learner to interact with the material, which both saves time and offers the opportunity for instant feedback that reinforces learning. Interactive video, such as Massive Open Online Course (MOOC), allows the learner to test different solutions to problems and to make sequential decisions based on the data provided on screen. The interactive techniques prevent the dangers of passive learning and give the learner some control of the learning process. In situations where learners are widely dispersed and trainers are in short supply, the combined use of computer and video training has much to commend it.

7. Demonstration

This is a kind of "on the job" training. The learner is shown what to do, then attempts the activity. This training has the advantage of being problem-centred with immediate feedback. The potential disadvantage is that much depends on the skills and knowledge of the demonstrator. Poor working practices can easily be passed on, as it is difficult to control the quality of the training.

8. Job rotation

In this well-established method of learning, it is important that the trainees' rotations are planned and monitored rather than used to fill gaps for reasons of administrative convenience. Experience for its own sake has only limited learning potential. It is important that the sum total of the experiences leads to a definable goal and that each part of the process is relevant to this achievement.

9. Lecture

This is not the most effective learning method, although it can be effective for those who enjoy the mental process of abstract conceptualisation. It is more suited to some subject areas than others. As it tends to be a passive experience, the learner's attention span is usually much shorter than the length of the lecture.

10. 团队开发

一名成功的经理人所具有的最出色的能力就是建立和保持团队工作的高效性。一个团队通常有 5～7 个人。团队动态性训练有三个目的：(1) 提升团队的整体效率；(2) 让团队成员能够知道为什么以及如何做好一个团队工作者；(3) 培养管理者的互动技能。好的培训者对于鼓励团队成员适应工作中人际反馈的强度和节奏、向他人学习等方面至关重要。

培训评估

将学习与反馈连接起来是具有重要意义的。基本要素包括评估培训项目，以及基于信息反馈基础上的必要修改。Hamblin(1974) 提出了一个最全面的评估分析方法，他将反馈信息描述为五个层级。

1. 反应(层级 1)

在接近培训尾声的时候，学习者会被要求提出对该活动的意见。这些信息通常通过问卷调查来获得。结果有用的信息量很少。这并不能向组织提供很多关于工作培训效果的有效信息。

2. 学习(层级 2)

数据本身并不直接明了。为了衡量培训的效果，对受训者在课程前后的表现进了量化测试。然而，该结果依旧无法告诉我们具体应采用哪一种学习方法。

3. 工作行为(层级 3)

这是收集信息最有效且最实际的层级。这里测量的是受训前后行为变化的差异程度。参与者和他们工作同事的观点也要收集进去。导致受训者在返回工作岗位时表现没什么改变是有众多原因的，其中有一项可能是培训本身不够充分。缺乏将新的想法付诸实践的机会、职务变化、不相关的奖励等都是可能的原因。该层级的评估十分重要，也切实可行。很令人失望的事实是最常用的两种评估类型是层级 1 和 2。其原因通常是在策划阶段缺乏部门经理的参与，并且缺少需求分析。

10. Team development

One of the most significant skills of successful managers is the capacity to build and maintain effective working teams, usually of around five to seven people. Group dynamics training has three purposes: (1) to improve the effectiveness of working groups; (2) to allow individuals to learn how they operate in groups and with what effect; and (3) to develop the interactive skills of managers. The services of a skilled trainer are essential to encourage the groups to work at the level of intensity needed for the giving and receiving of personal feedback and to encourage the group members to learn from their experiences.

Evaluation of Training

It is important to link learning to feedback. It is essential that training programmes are evaluated and that necessary changes are made in response to feedback. The most thorough analysis of evaluation methods has been provided by Hamblin (1974). He describes five levels of feedback.

1. Reactions (Level One)

At the end of the training experience learners are asked their opinions of the event. This information is usually collected through questionnaires. The participants have little to gain by saying the event was anything other than a success and the trainer is similarly placed. The resulting information is of limited use. It tells the organisation little about the effect of the training in the workplace.

2. Learning (Level Two)

The data are a little more pointed. To measure the effect of the training, the performance of a trainee before and after a course is tested in a quantifiable way. However, such tests do not indicate whether any of the learning will be applied.

3. Job behaviour (Level Three)

This is the most useful and practical level at which to collect information. What is measured here is the extent to which there has been any change in behaviour after the training. The views of the participants and their colleagues at work should be collected. There may be many reasons why the behaviour of a trainee has not changed on return to the workplace, only one of which might be the inadequacy of the training itself. Other possible reasons are limited opportunity to put new ideas into practice, changes in role and unrelated rewards. This level of evaluation is very important and is also feasible. Unfortunately, the most common types of evaluation are of the Level One and Two types, often due to the lack of involvement of line managers in the planning stages and the lack of effort made in the needs analysis.

4. 组织(层级 4)

该层级的评估显得更加复杂,但其结果可能很有价值。其着眼于培训,即其效果,是否与组织机构的目标相关联,例如是否可以带来成果、质量和员工士气的高涨。更重要的是,培训应该考虑到受训者来自的那个团体的战略计划,并要与该团体的文化相一致。如果不一致,则很可能带来负面影响。

5. 峰值(层级 5)

这个层及评估组织作为一个整体是否从培训中获益。它是否有助于企业生存?它会帮助组织朝着计划的方向发展吗?受训者现在能够更有助于企业实现利润的增长吗?在该评估层级上,受训员工需要在重要议题上与上层管理者保持更进一步的接触,例如战略计划等。但是要找到能把培训成果与组织目标构成直接关联的评估方法是很困难的。

管理开发

"培训"和"开发"有时候被视为近义词,有时又相反地被看作是互斥的、独立的活动(Noe,2017)。具体地说,培训可以看作是开发的一部分,也是开发的先决条件。术语"培训"一词常常与非常狭隘的计划活动相关。相反,管理开发计划必须作为企业规划进程的一部分。管理开发对企业整体来说具有广泛意义。当足够数量的管理人员成为同一个开发过程的一个部分,管理开发将成为组织发展的形式。

组织开发自己的企业文化,并以自己喜欢的方式去应对外部环境(Hon和 Leung,2011)。并没有一剂良药可以应对所有的管理开发。它将随着组织变化而变化。经理人通常认为管理开发只是为了改变个人行为。这可以通过向经理人提供新技能、态度观点和知识来实现。在此情况下,识别出哪一类知识是欠缺的,然后为每个经理人个体安排培训,这是管理开发的恰当形式。

4. Organisation (Level Four)

This level of evaluation is more complex, but the results can be valuable. Here the focus is on whether the training, however effective, is relevant to the departmental goals of the organisation; for example, has it led to improvements in output, quality or morale. It is important that training takes into account the strategic plans of the group from which the trainees are drawn and that it is consonant with the organisation's culture. If it is not, it will surely fail to have an effect.

5. Ultimate value (Level Five)

This level assesses whether the organisation as a whole has benefited from the training. Has it helped the organisation to survive and will it help it to develop in the directions planned? Is the trainee now able to contribute more to the goal of increased profit ability? What is good for the individual might not necessarily be good for the organisation. For this level of assessment, the training staff needs to be in close contact with top management as issues such as strategic planning are involved. It is difficult to find methods that can directly relate training outcomes to organisational goals.

Management Development

The terms "training" and "development" are sometimes treated as synonyms, or alternately, as mutually interactive activities (Noe, 2017). From an HRM perspective, they are better understood as being linked; specifically, training should be seen as both a part of and a precondition for development. The term training is often associated with a very narrow set of planned activities. In some organisations, training programmes are focused on meeting attendance targets for courses so that trainers appear credible at performance review time. In contrast, management development plans are part of the corporate planning process. Management development has wide implications for an organisation as a whole. When sufficient numbers of managers are part of the same development process, management development becomes a form of organisational development.

Organisations develop their own culture and preferred ways of responding to the external environment. There is no one right recipe for management development. It will vary from organisation to organisation. It is commonly felt by managers that the purpose of management development is to encourage changes in individual's behaviour (Hon & Leung, 2011). This can be achieved by providing a manager with new skills, attitudes or knowledge. In such cases, identifying what the manager lacks and then arranging for the individual manager to obtain it is an appropriate form of management development.

　　最后,另一个更高效的实现行为转变以提升业绩表现和工作态度的方法是,改变员工所处环境的文化。换句话说,发展工作团队并把团队目标和组织目标统一起来。例如,一个团队管理者视赋权他人为失去控制的威胁,因而不愿意下放权力和分配责任。在这种情况下,组织本身应当被视为变革的核心。一旦根源的问题得到解决,个人行为就会发生变化。

案例研究 7.1 ▶▷▷▷▷

　　北京东方君悦大酒店是知名酒店管理集团——凯悦国际酒店集团Hyatt International Hotels Corporation 下的重要成员之一。引人注目的"继任计划项目"为旗下员工提供了众多自我职业提升的机会,并且帮助酒店建立起强大的"集团人才储备"。最初由凯悦集团员工建立起来的凯悦的企业文化,受到全体员工的热烈拥护,从总经理到每一个员工。其企业文化营造出温馨、关爱、友好的工作环境,使得北京东方君悦大酒店的员工们有家一般的感觉。

　　Betty 张女士是大堂喷泉休息室的团队主管,为了满足客人的需求,她总是工作得很努力。客人对她最有代表性的评价是:"Betty 工作时总是充满热情,她的正能量会传染给周围的每个人。"而问题在于,在拥有 50 年历史的国际酒店管理集团下工作的普通员工,是如何拥有如此高涨的工作热情的呢?"当我刚涉足酒店业时,我只是个年轻稚嫩的女孩儿,并没有计划太多的未来。是凯悦点燃了我的梦想,给予了我很多机会。现在的我拥有清晰的职业目标,即成为一名出色的酒店管理领导者,为进一步的前进不断努力拼搏。"

　　在北京东方君悦大酒店超过 1300 名员工之中 Betty 仅仅是一个例子,而鼓励员工为了进步而持续地奋斗是人力资源部的目标。酒店的人力资源总监 Cheong Wai Meng 先生说道:"我们不仅向我们的员工们承诺提供一个良好的工作环境和有竞争优势的薪资,同时我们希望可以帮助他们实现个人职业生涯目标,辅助他们成就梦想。这其实反映了管理学的一句经典名言:'人力管理是为了能够管理人们的期待。'"

1. 我们鼓励个人成长,富于创新

　　Stella Sun 女士在酒店试营业开始时就是公司元老级员工之一,她 2001年 5 月加入凯悦,担任前台部门的团队领导。在这之后,10 月份酒店正式营

---

　　① 资料来源:Assisting employees to achieve greater professional success, reterieved from:https://beijing, grand, hyatt.com.

However, behavioural changes associated with better performance or improved attitudes can often be achieved more effectively by changing the immediate environment in which the individual works; in other words, by developing the whole work group. Take, for example, a manager who is reluctant to delegate responsibility to others, and even reluctant to fill vacancies, because immediate subordinates are seen as a threat.

Case Study 7 - 1 ① ▶▶▶▶▶

Grand Hyatt Beijing is one of the important hotels managed by the Hyatt International Hotels Corporation. The effective "Succession Plan Program" offers employees many opportunities for self-career advancement and helps the hotel to establish strong "talent group reserves". The Hyatt Culture, which was originally established by groups of Hyatt employees, is strongly embraced by all of the employees, from the general manager right down to each individual employee. It is the Hyatt Culture that creates the warm, caring and friendly environment that make employees feel at home in Grand Hyatt Beijing.

Ms Betty Zhang, a team leader in the Fountain Lounge located in the lobby, always works hard to satisfy guests' needs and wants. A typical compliment paid to her by guests is "Betty is a person who works with great enthusiasm and passion. Everyone around her will be infected by her positive energy". How does a normal employee maintain such a high level of enthusiasm for her work in this 50-year old international hotel management group? According to Betty, "When I first stepped into the Hotel Industry, I was just a young girl. I didn't plan much for my future. It was Hyatt that sparked off my dreams and gave me opportunities. Now I have a clear career objective, i.e. to become a successful hotel management leader, making continual efforts to achieve greater progress."

Betty is just one example of the over 1300 employees at Grand Hyatt Beijing, and encouraging the continuous striving for improvement is an objective of the Human Resources Department. Mr Cheong Wai Meng, Director of Human Resources says, "We not only commit ourselves to provide our employees with a favourable environment and competitive benefits, at the same time we hope to help them to achieve their individual career objectives and assist them to fulfil their dreams. This is truly reflective of a famous phrase in Management: 'People management is to be able to manage people's expectations.'"

1. We Encourage Personal Growth, We are Innovative

Ms Stella Sun, who has been an employee at the hotel since the preopening time, joined Hyatt in May 2001 as a team leader in the front office. She was promoted to duty manager in October during the Grand Opening. In January, 2004, Stella was further promoted to assistant

---

① Resource: Assisting employees to achieve greater professional success, reterieved from: https: // beijing, grand, hyatt.com.

业后她被提拔为值班经理。2004年1月Stella进一步被提拔为前台部助理经理，2007年1月她被任命为前台部经理，分管超过800间酒店客房。她负责协调前台、礼宾部、行李部、贵宾接待、俱乐部等的工作运转。她在酒店业的职业晋升速度之快是相当让人敬佩的。"管理团队切实真心地关注员工的成长和发展。我每天都会学到不同的技能。酒店鼓励本地员工的个人成长。他们愿意给员工机会去尝试。如果员工出任何错，他们会让我们知道学习的重点所在，以及应该如何提高。"

与Stella相似，大多数管理层员工都是从内部晋升的。甚至是外籍管理人员也有其在其他的凯悦酒店的成长经历。"我们已经建立起属于自己的'继任计划'来满足对人才的需求。"人力资源部门总监Cheong先生说道。"我们会训练自己的员工来展示他们的潜能；提供给他们必要的常规培训课程和材料；观察他们工作绩效表现，并给予建设性意见的反馈和指导，适时地帮助他们激发潜能，加快自我进步的速度。"

Betty在喷泉大堂任职，但她一直想要学习更多的知识技能。因此她找到自己的直属经理，向他表达了自己的意愿，希望能有机会去西餐厅交换培训两周。她的经理根据运营要求帮她安排了交换培训的相关事宜。很快Betty就获得了临时前往西餐厅工作的机会。她见识到诸多新鲜事物，也学到了很多新技能。身为酒店的一员，她对酒店理解、珍惜员工感到非常自豪。通过交叉培训后，Betty获得了更多的自信和经验。

事实上，交叉培训只是凯悦集团整个培训项目的一部分而已，在北京东方君悦大酒店，其享有盛誉的培训架构为"继任计划"打下了坚实的基础。酒店向员工们提供了众多类型、所有层级的培训项目，包括在职培训、跨部门培训、酒店内部交叉培训、酒店产品知识、管理技能培训和部门专业技能培训。与此同时，凯悦集团与哈佛管理学院联合启动了一系列线上课程，员工们可以通过网站开启自学之旅。

人力资源总监Cheong先生说道："这些有效的课程可以视作是3Cs，即简明、定制课程（consise，customised course）。"他还分享道，人力资源部有14名员工，其中7名从事培训工作。"我们希望我们的员工不仅专注在自己本职工作上，更重要的是他们能够获得与未来职业发展相关的知识技能。除此之外，我们也希望员工不仅仅把目标定位于成为一个经理人，很重要的一点是他们渴望成为一名专业的、高水准的领导者。"

随着凯悦国际集团的发展，特别是凯悦酒店在中国内地市场的快速扩张，北京东方君悦大酒店需要培训并建立起其自有的潜力人才储备。像其他

front office manager. By January 2007, Stella had become front office manager in this hotel with over 800 guest rooms. She is responsible for the smooth operation of the front desk, concierge, bell service, guest services, grand club etc. Her career advancement in the hotel industry has been incredibly fast and admirable. "The management team truly cares for the employees' growth and development. I learn different skills every day. The hotel encourages personal growth among local employees. They are willing to let the employees have their try. If the employees make any mistakes, they will then let the employees know the learning points and how they can improve from there."

Like Stella, most of the management employees are from internal promotions. Even the expatriate management employees had their growing up years at other Hyatt properties. "We have built our own 'Succession Plan' to meet the demands of talents," says the Director of Human Resources, Mr Cheong. "We will train our employees who show their potential; provide them with necessary regular training courses and materials; observe their working performance as well as giving them constructive feedback and guidance in due time so as to help them to unleash their potentials and accelerate their self-improvement."

Betty works at the Fountain Lounge, but she wants to acquire more knowledge and skills. Therefore, she has approached her manager and asked for an opportunity to be cross trained at a Western restaurant for two weeks. Her manager helps her to arrange the cross training schedule according to the operation requirements. Soon, Betty is offered this opportunity to work at the Western restaurant for a brief stint. She sees quite a lot of new things and learns new skills. She is very proud of being a member of this hotel that understands and appreciates the employees. From the cross training, Betty has gained more confidence and experience.

In fact, cross training is just one part of the training programme at Hyatt International. The renowned training structure creates a solid foundation for the "Succession Plan" at the Grand Hyatt Beijing. There are various types of training provided to employees at all levels including on-the-job training, departmental cross training, inter-hotel cross training, hotel product knowledge, management skills training and departmental professional skills training. At the same time, Hyatt International works with the Harvard Management School and has launched a series of online courses. Employees are able to access the website to start their self-learning journey.

Mr Cheong, Director of HR says, "These effective training offerings can be termed the 3Cs—'concise, customised course'." According to Mr Cheong, there are 14 employees in the HR department, and 7 are engaged in training. "We hope our employees will not only focus on their work, the most important thing is that they can obtain pertinent knowledge and skills that are required for their future career development. In addition, we hope our employees do not just aim for becoming a manager, importantly they strive to become a professional and highly effective leader."

With the development of the Hyatt International Corporation, particularly the rapid expansion of Hyatt Hotels in mainland China, the Grand Hyatt Beijing needs to train and build up a pool of potential employees. Like other Hyatt Hotels, it is also responsible for grooming

凯悦酒店一样,该酒店同样负有培养有潜力的员工的责任。成为一名领导并不是一个无法实现的目标。有一个先决条件:这个人应当慷慨不吝啬地将自己的知识技能分享给下属或同事。同时,他需要把握、珍惜机遇,去学习新技能,去发展自身能力,在自我进步的过程中承担更多的责任和使命。

2. 我们团队合作,互相照顾

一天晚些时候,当整个城市都进入梦乡时,北京东方君悦大酒店依旧灯火通明。总经理、值班经理、部门主管、经理与员工们都在加班,等待着 NBA 团队的到来。这个团队有大约 1000 名成员,因此需要大量的员工来迎接他们的到来。他们的航班理应在凌晨零点降落。然而飞机晚点了。听到这个消息没有人去休息,相反的是他们都很有耐心地在等待。直至客人到达,每个人以团队的形式一起工作,并协助他人工作。尽管非常忙碌,但员工们依旧很冷静地处理着所有的事情。几乎所有男员工们,包括行李部、客房服务、俱乐部、宴会厅的员工们都协同合作来帮助客人处理行李。

这样的情境对 Stella 来说不陌生,也不特殊。在北京东方君悦大酒店的日常运营中,这是稀松平常的事情,你常常可以看到部门之间合作互助。员工们能够互相帮忙也是因为他们有着交叉培训的经历,因此可以了解彼此的职能,有能力互助互惠。部门间并没有"距离"。

"酒店本身是一个整体,要求每个员工能够协调配合,以带来不同的效果。在员工们扮演各自职责时,他们也关注团队精神。这也是凯悦的企业文化——我们进行团队合作。"其他企业的文化可能由其所有者或管理团队来制定建立。与这些企业相比,Cheong 先生表示凯悦的文化是通过员工分享和认同而形成的。凯悦国际集团在听取来自旗下全球酒店员工反馈意见后,总结了 6 句话,构成了凯悦今天的企业文化。它们是:"我们关注顾客;我们多元化;我们鼓励个人成长;我们富于创新;我们团队合作;我们互相照顾。"

今天,凯悦集团的员工都很熟悉凯悦的企业文化,并引以为荣。该企业文化是基于员工的个人经验,代表着企业关心、尊重旗下的员工。Chong 先生的介绍表明,酒店管理团队是真切地关心、在乎、尊重下属。管理团队的成员总是愿意帮助员工排忧解难。

北京东方君悦大酒店的总经理 Christopher Koehler 先生就是管理团队的模范之一。他很乐意在酒店的各个场所与员工们问候、交谈,包括负责清洁洗手间的工作人员。员工们因此而感到管理团队的呵护和温暖,这也进一步强化了凯悦酒店集团的管理理念。

potential employees for Hyatt properties. Becoming a leader is not an unachievable goal. There is one prerequisite: employees should be generous enough to share their knowledge and skills with subordinates and co-workers. In the meantime, they need to grab and treasure the opportunities to learn new skills and prepare themselves for more responsibilities through self-improvement.

2. We Work in Teams, We Care for Each Other

Late at night, when the whole city is asleep, the Grand Hyatt Beijing is still glittering brightly. The general manager, deputy general manager, department heads, managers and employees are all working overtime and waiting for the arrival of the NBA group. There are around 1000 members in this group and thus many service employees are required for this group arrival. Their plane is supposed to touch down around 12: 00 am. However, it is late. No one sleeps when they hear the news. Instead, they wait with much patience and anticipation. Upon the guests' arrival, everyone works as a team. Although it is very busy, the employees are calm and everything is under control. Almost all of the male employees, including employees who work in bell service, housekeeping, Club Oasis and the banquet, work together as a team to help the guests with their luggage.

Such a scenario is definitely not unfamiliar or unusual to Stella. In the daily operation at Grand Hyatt Beijing, it is common to see departments cooperating and assisting each other. Employees are able to help in other departments because the hotel provides cross training between departments. There is no "gap" between departments.

As Mr Cheong says, "A hotel is a unit that requires all its employees to work together to make a difference. While the employees are playing their role, they pay more attention to the team spirit. This is also part of our Hyatt culture—we work through teams." The culture in other companies may be created by its owners or management teams. Comparing the Hyatt to such companies, Mr Cheong explains that the Hyatt culture is created by the sharing and concurrence of Hyatt employees. Six phrases drawn from the feedback of employees from different Hyatt Hotels worldwide form today's Hyatt culture. They are "We are customer focused", "We are multicultural", "We encourage personal growth," "We are innovative", "We work in teams" and "We care for each other."

Today, employees who work in any Hyatt property are familiar with and proud of the Hyatt culture. It is based on the personal experiences of the employees, and demonstrates that Hyatt respects its employees. Mr Chong's comments show that the hotel management team really cares about and respects their employees. The management team members are always willing to resolve employees' problems and worries.

Mr Christopher Koehler, general manager of the Grand Hyatt Beijing acts as an example to the management team members. He enjoys walking around the hotel meeting and warmly greeting his employees, including the attendant who is responsible for cleaning the restrooms. The employees can thus feel the care and warmth of the management team, which further enforces Hyatt's people philosophy.

3. 首先要满足员工的需求

为了落实凯悦的企业文化中"我们关注顾客，我们多元化"，并且满足顾客的期望，首先应满足自己员工的需求。这是北京东方君悦大酒店管理理念中十分重要的一部分，并被应用在各个领域中。举例来说，酒店翻新了员工通道，在员工到岗工作和下班回家时，给他们留下一个友好的印象。新的员工通道装饰着暖光灯、足够的家具、墙绘与充满活力的颜色。

为了保证员工在这里工作时感到满意，酒店不仅为员工提供令人愉快的工作环境、有竞争力的薪资和福利，还倾听他们的声音，关心他们，并向他们提供适当的机遇去实现个人职业晋升目标。我们都知道，酒店是 24 小时运转的，酒店会要求员工根据酒店运营需要调整日程安排，有时因为忙碌，员工需要超时工作。在这种情况下，酒店会根据政府规定给予超时工作津贴或调休。与此同时，根据酒店的业绩会给予员工季度奖金和年终奖金。

Stella 说："我在四家不同的酒店工作过，与它们相比，北京东方君悦大酒店更关注员工个人的需求。例如，在其他酒店，由于工作日程安排和工作经验的限制，我们很少有机会看到部门间员工调动。但在这里，经理支持员工的岗位调动的要求。他们会主动帮助员工分析他们的性格特征、兴趣爱好和能力。我的一位员工想要调去财务部门。他觉得财务工作可能更适合自己。6 月的时候他向上级提交调换申请，8 月份就已经在财务部就职了。"

在北京东方君悦大酒店，每个月都会举行"君悦会谈"。所有层级的员工们会坐在一起畅所欲言。开会期间，员工们可以自由谈论他们遇到的困难或挑战。酒店总经理与人力资源总监会仔细倾听他们的反馈。员工的建议和反馈是提高酒店运营质量的重要渠道。这同时也加强了员工们对酒店的归属感。除此之外，每个月还会举行生日派对。酒店管理团队和经理会一起庆祝。还有切蛋糕的活动，每月的寿星们聚集在一起唱生日祝福歌。场面十分温馨，令人愉悦。Betty 说："想一下，这么多人一起庆祝你的生日，我可以肯定寿星们会非常开心，会感到如大家庭般的温暖。"

此外，凯悦集团会由各个酒店和办公室分别举办大型年会活动，以奖励员工们的辛苦工作。在 1～2 周的活动期间，人力资源部门和员工团队一起组织各种活动，以促进员工的愉悦感和参与度。这些活动包括游戏、幸运抽奖、郊游和比赛活动。也会有管理团队准备的特别主题食物供应。Cheong 先生说："员工就是我们的核心财富，他们是人力资源部门的贵客。我们必

3. Satisfy the Employees First

To realise the Hyatt culture and to meet guests' expectations, it is necessary to first satisfy the employees. This is one of the important management concepts at Grand Hyatt Beijing and it can be applied in many areas. For example, the hotel has renovated the employee entrance to give its employees a welcoming impression when they report to work and leave for home. The new employee entrance is decorated with warm lights, adequate furniture, pictorial wall paintings and vibrant wall colours.

To ensure that employees are satisfied working here, the hotel not only provides employees with an enjoyable working environment and competitive payroll and benefits, it also listens to them, cares for their concerns and offers them suitable opportunities to achieve greater personal career advancement. As we know, hotels operate 24 hours, and employees are asked to change their schedules according to the hotel's operation requirements. Sometimes employees need to work overtime. In this situation, the hotel compensates employees with overtime allowance or a day off-in-lieu according to the government's policy. Furthermore, quarterly bonuses and year-end bonuses are given to employees based on the hotel performance.

Stella says, "I have worked in four different hotels. Compared to the hotels where I have worked, Grand Hyatt Beijing pays more attention to the employees' needs. For example, in other hotels, due to the restriction of the work schedule and work experiences, we seldom see employees having inter-departmental transfers. In Grand Hyatt Beijing, though, the managers hold a positive attitude toward the employees' transfer request. They will take initiative to help the employees to analyse their personalities, interests and abilities. One of my employees wanted to be transferred to Finance Department. He felt that financial work would be more suitable for him. He submitted his transfer request in June and reported to work in Finance in August."

In Grand Hyatt Beijing, there is a "Hyattalk" meeting each month. Employees at all levels attend this talk. During the meeting, employees are free to speak about the difficulties or challenges they face. The hotel general manager and director of HR listen to their feedback. They regard employee suggestions and feedback as a good channel for improving the hotel's operation. This also enhances the employees' sense of belonging to the hotel. In addition, there is an employee birthday party that is held each month. The hotel management team and mangers attend this celebratory party. There is a cake cutting ceremony and all of the birthday stars of the month gather around the birthday cake and sing happy birthday together. It is really a warm occasion. Betty says, "Think about it, with so many people celebrating your birthday, I am sure the birthday stars are very happy and are able to feel the warm touches from this big family."

In addition, Hyatt International carries out an annual event celebrated by every hotel and office in Hyatt International as a gesture of appreciation for the employees' hard work. Over the 1 to 2 week event, various activities are organised by HR and the union for the employees' enjoyment and participation. These include free massages, games, lucky draws, outings and competitions. Special themed food is also served to the employees by the

须牢记我们的职能——为我们的员工提供舒适愉悦的工作环境,协助他们实现各自的职业目标。"

问 题

(1) 请问你自己所在的组织有什么主要问题?

(2) 以凯悦国际集团为例,哪些政策是你想要学习和采纳的?

案例研究 7-2[①] ▶▶▶▶▶▶

Mary 刚刚受聘到一家位于市中心的拥有 450 间客房的大型酒店前台工作,工作时间是凌晨 3 点到上午 11 点。能接到这份工作她高兴极了,虽然这意味着她要离开在城市另一边的豪华酒店行李员的工作。她在那个岗位上工作了近两年,她的员工评语和顾客意见卡反馈都是很不错的。在原来的酒店,每当前台岗位有空缺的时候,她都会特别积极地申请,但出于某些原因,管理层总是选择了其他人。当 Mary 看到现在这个职位的招聘广告时,就迫不及待地前去申请,随后她收到了来自酒店前台经理 Betty 的面试邀请。

当 Betty 提供给 Mary 这个岗位的时候,她解释说酒店并没有"正式培训项目"。她让 Mary"跟着"Mark,她手下最强的 3—11 点值班的前台接待,大概一周后,她差不多就可以独立值班了。Betty 解释说,酒店马上会迎来非常忙碌的时节,所以对 Mary 的培训必须很快进行。"忙过了这段日子,等你通过了培训,我们就安排迎新会。"

第二天下午,当 Mary 到达酒店准备开始跟随着 Mark 培训时,前台没有人知道她是谁。过了一会儿,Betty 从她办公室出来,说道:"嗨,各位,这是 Mary。Mark 将带她今晚 3—11 点的夜班。等他到了的时候,各位确保跟 Mark 介绍一下 Mary,我得赶去银行了,晚上不会准时回来。"

Mark 到达办公室的时候,正巧晚上 7 点到凌晨 3 点值班的接待员准备打卡下班,"嗨,Mark,我得走了。你新来的培训生在前台,她叫 Sherry。"

"培训生?Betty 没说有个培训生要来。"Mark 有些困惑。

那个接待员说:"她看上去人挺好的,希望她能上手快点,你今晚有 184 名客人会到。"

然后 Mark 走到前台,介绍了一下他自己。"你好,我是 Mark。你就是

---

① 资料来源:Sommerville, K. (2007). *Hospitality Employee Management and Supervision: Concepts and Practical Applications*, 231-232, Hoboken, NJ: John Wiley & Sons.

management teams. Mr Cheong says，"Employees are our principal asset and they are the guests of HR department. We must always remember our duty——providing our employees with an enjoyable working environment and assisting them to achieve their career objectives."

Questions

（1）What are the major problems of your own organisation?

（2）What policies you would like to learn and adopt from the Hyatt International?

Case Study 7 – 2[①] ▶▶▶ ▶▶

Mary has just been hired to work the 3 to 11 shift at the front desk of a large，450-room downtown hotel. She is thrilled to have been offered the position，even though it means leaving her previous job as a bellhop in a luxury hotel on the other side of town. She held that position for nearly two years，and her employee evaluations and her customer comment cards have been excellent. Every time a front-desk position became available at her previous job，she would eagerly apply for it，but for some reason，management always seemed to select another candidate. When Mary sees the advertisement for the current position，she jumps on it，and she lands an immediate interview with the hotel's front-office manager，Betty.

When Betty offers Mary the position，she explains that the hotel does not have a "formal training programme". She says that Mary will be "shadowing" Mark，her strongest 3 to 11 clerk，and that after a week or so，she will be ready to work shifts by herself. Betty also explains that the hotel has a rather busy period coming up soon so Mary's training will be swift. "After this busy period and when you're through training，" Betty says to Mary，"we'll arrange a new meeting."

When Mary arrives the next afternoon to begin training with Mark，none of the other front-desk clerks know who she is. After a few moments，Betty comes out of her office. "Hey guys，" she says，"this is Mary. Mark is training her tonight on the 3 to 11 shift. Be sure to introduce Mark to Mary when he gets here；I have to run to the bank，and I won't be coming back on the property tonight."

Mark came into the back office as the last 7 to 3 clerk has just clocked out and is leaving. "Hey Mark，gotta run"，she calls out. "Your new trainee is out front，her name is Sherry."

"Trainee?" Mark explodes. "Betty didn't say anything about a trainee."

"She seems nice，" the clerk says，"but I hope she catches on fast；you've got 184 arrivals tonight."

As Mark comes behind the front desk，he introduces himself. "I'm Mark，" he says. "You

---

①　Resource：Sommerville，K.（2007）.Hospitality Employee Management and supervision：Concepts and Practical Applications，231 – 232，Hoboken，NJ：John Wiley & Sons.

Sherry 吧。"

"其实，我叫 Mary。"Mary 回答道，并主动伸出手去。

"好，随便吧。"他无视了 Mary 伸出的手，径直走到收银台开始工作。"我希望你在这方面有经验，"他一边数钱一边讲，"今晚会非常忙碌，可只有我们两个人。"

"好，没问题，"Mary 热切地回答说，"我在温泉酒店工作了快两年。"

"好，我拭目以待。"Mark 说道，"那家酒店很小，我怀疑他们从来没有和这里一样忙碌过。"

Mary 解释说即使温泉酒店规模不大，但服务水平和客户需求量还是让每个人忙得马不停蹄。"作为一名行李员……"Mark 突然打断了她。

"行李员!?"他大叫道，"是这样？Betty 到底是怎么想的，竟然让我一个人去带一个行李员！而且还是有 200 个客人到达的晚上？开玩笑的吧!"

问　题

（1）按照 Mary"跟着"Mark 培训第一个晚上事情的发展，你觉得 Mary 还会对到这里工作感到开心吗？她是否会开始找新的工作呢？请给出你的解释。如果 Mary 在 90 天试用期内决定离开，会给酒店带来哪些直接和间接的成本？

（2）对于让 Mary 跟着 Mark 进行培训这件事，Betty 犯了什么错？Betty 具体应该怎么做才能弥补整个前台培训项目？

（3）你会同情 Mark 的遭遇吗？还是你觉得他只是态度不好，不想培训新员工？请给出详细解释。

（4）如果 Mark 确实是培训前台 3—11 点夜班的最佳人选，Betty 需要做什么来确保 Mark 能够用更积极的态度来对待培训？请给出你的解释。

must be Sherry."

"Actually, it's Mary," Mary replies. She offers her hand.

"Well, whatever," he says, ignoring her hand and going directly to the cash drawer. "I hope you've got some experience," he says as he counts money. "We're going to be really busy tonight, and it's just me and you."

"Oh yes," Mary says eagerly. "I was with the Fountain Court Hotel for nearly two years."

"Well, we'll see," says Mark. "That's a much smaller hotel; I doubt they ever got as busy as this place gets."

Mary explains that even though the Fountain Court was smaller, the level of service and demanding guests kept everyone on their toes. "As a bellhop," she began, but Mark cut her off.

"Bellhop!?" he yells. "That's it? How in the hell does Betty expect me to train a former bellhop all by myself when we have nearly 200 arrivals tonight? What a joke!"

Questions

(1) Depending upon how things go during this first night of training, do you think that Mary will continue to feel good about her choice to work for this hotel, or will she begin looking for another job? Explain your answer. Should Mary decide to leave within her first 90 days of employment, what are the direct and indirect costs that the hotel will incur?

(2) What mistakes has Betty made with respect to setting up Mary's training programme with Mark? What specific changes should Betty make to the overall front-desk training programme?

(3) Do you empathise with Mark, or do you feel that he simply has a bad attitude and has no business training for new employees? Explain your answer in detail.

(4) If Mark is indeed the proper person to be conducting the training for new 3 to 11 desk clerks, what things could Betty do to ensure that Mark is able to approach his training duties with a more positive attitude? Explain your answer.

第8章　社会化、辅导与职业规划

学习目标

- 了解组织的社会化和定向及其特点
- 了解什么是职业生涯规划与管理
- 了解职业生涯规划对组织和员工的重要性

由于招聘和选拔在大多数情况下都花费高昂,考虑到公司利益,需要确保第一天或是第一周新人的不安情绪不会影响到这些新员工们,因为他们很可能成为长期服务于公司、有忠诚度、高效的员工。迎新会、入职培训、社会化以及辅导都将确保尽快消除他们来到一个新的、不熟悉的环境时的最初的焦虑,并且,随着信息技术和互联网技术的提升,人力资源经理人能够充分利用诸如社交媒体、虚拟现实(VR),甚至人工智能(AI)等技术,帮助培训、招聘、选拔、规划及管理员工(Dessler,2017)。

迎新、入职和辅导

迎新项目其实就是指从事人力资源管理的专业人士与各自的上级领导,向新员工概述公司的政策方针、规定、规章制度、员工福利等内容,发放员工手册和简介。

入职培训是指在员工开始正式工作时,接受新员工的整个过程,包括将他们介绍给全公司和他们的同事们,告诉他们各项活动、习俗以及公司的传统。它被视为培训的起点,或是选拔阶段的终点。事实证明,这个环节与劳动力流失率之间有紧密关系。入职介绍可以分为以下两个步骤(Dessler,2017)。

(1) 面向整个工作团队的入职介绍。这在员工心理层面上会起到很重要的作用,最好选择由员工的直属上司来进行。他应当将新成员介绍给同事

Chapter 8　Socialisation, Coaching and Career Planning

The objectives of this chapter

- Understand organizational socialization and orientation programmes and their characteristics
- Explain what is career planning and management
- Understand the importance of career planning for both organizations and employees

As recruitment and selection costs are usually high, it is to a company's advantage to make sure that first-day or first-week nerves do not scare away new employees who could potentially become long-serving, committed and productive workers. Orientation, induction, socialisation and coaching make sure that the initial anxiety that comes from entering a new and unfamiliar environment dissipates as quickly as possible (Dessler, 2017).

Orientation, Induction and Coaching

An orientation programme allows human resource management professionals and individual supervisors to outline the policies, rules, regulations and benefits of a job to a new employee and to provide him or her with a staff handbook and an introduction to fellow workers.

Induction is the process of receiving employees when they begin work, introducing them to the company and to their colleagues and informing them of the activities, customs and traditions of the company. It may be regarded as the beginning of training or the final stage of the selection process. It has been shown to have a close relationship with labour turnover. Induction may be divided into two stages (Dessler, 2017).

(1) Introduction to the working group is psychologically important and best done by the employee's immediate supervisor, who should introduce the recruit to colleagues and show him or her round the department.

(2) Introduction to the company background can be provided through lectures, films or visits. This should probably not be done in the first day or week of employment as the employee is at that time more concerned with his or her immediate surroundings and his or her own job. The employee will become interested in the wider scene two or three

们,并带他(或她)参观整个部门。

(2) 公司背景介绍。这可以以听讲演、看影片或参观的形式来进行。这部分不适宜在员工入职第一天或是第一周来进行,因为此时员工更在意的是未来自己的工作环境以及岗位。员工们在入职两三个月后开始对其他环境产生兴趣,然后可以进入入职培训课程的第二阶段。如果公司规模较大,这可能发生在公司的某个中心部门;如果是小公司,则可由直属领导与新员工进行一次非正式的谈话。

社会化指的是员工适应并接受组织文化的过程。社会化项目向新员工传授组织想要看到的态度、规则标准、价值观和行为表现。社会化将全体员工,即现有的和新员工,紧密联系在一起。期望的最终结果是形成一个合作、友好、实用以及生产性的劳动力队伍。

辅导包括给予员工一对一的指导来提高员工的知识技能水平,从而提高工作绩效。这通常需要一个经理辅导一个员工,这可以作为员工总体绩效管理计划的一部分。

答疑通常指一个高层人员帮助新进的员工发展他或她期望的职业发展计划所需的知识技能。这种方式有助于双方的职业规划和发展。

以上辅导和答疑步骤的时间范围从一小时到几天不等,甚至数月,取决于各个项目的复杂程度。为了获得更高的效率,行政官必须是名良师益友。除此之外,行政官训练员工的动机将取决于二者关系的质量。和其他人相比,一些行政官更擅长分配职责、提供增援和沟通,这也会影响结果。

职业规划与管理

传统人力资源活动主要关注于培训、选拔,训练和发展员工,根据员工各自不同的兴趣点、能力和技能安排职位。然而,在较先进的人力资源部门,这些活动通过战略性地着眼于雇主和员工的长期目标和利益得到支持。今天,普遍看法是雇主有义务充分激发员工的个人能力,并且给予所有员工成长的机会,去释放他们的所有潜能,发展成功的事业。这将引导企业把重心放在每个人的职业规划和发展上,这常常与员工绩效评估过程以及组织的连续发展规划紧密相联(Noe,2017)。

职业生涯指的是一个人一生中某个重要时期的一份职业,且有着进步的空间和机遇。职业生涯中的进步成长通常是通过担任一些工作职务来实现的,这能使员工发展未来职业需要的个人知识、技能及态度,同时带给他们职业成就感,以及体验成功的机会。职业生涯发展需要参与诸多活动,例如参

months after joining the company and can then take part in a second-stage induction course. If the company is large this may occur at some central point in the firm; in a small company, a supervisor may talk to the employee informally.

Socialisation is the process through which employees adapt to the organisation's culture. Socialisation programmes teach new employees the attitudes, standards, values and behaviour that are expected by the organisation. Socialisation also binds all of the staff members, existing or new, together. The end result, it is hoped, is a cooperative, friendly, functional and productive workforce.

Coaching involves giving one-on-one guidance and instruction to improve employee knowledge and skills and thus to improve work performance. It usually involves a manager coaching an employee and may form part of the overall performance management plan for the employee.

Mentoring usually involves a more senior member of staff helping a junior member of staff to develop the knowledge and skills necessary for his or her desired career development plan. The relationship that develops contributes to the career planning and development of both parties.

The time horizon for coaching and mentoring ranges from one hour to several days or months, depending on the comprehensiveness of the various programmes. To be effective, the executive has to be a good coach and mentor. In addition, the executive's motivation to train a replacement depends on the quality of their relationship. Some executives are better at delegating responsibility, providing reinforcement and communicating than others; this will also affect the results.

Career Planning and Management

The traditional roles of human resource departments are recruiting and selecting, training and developing employees and filling positions with employees who have the requisite interests, abilities and skills. However, in more advanced human resource departments, these activities are underpinned by a strategic focus on the long-term goals and interests of both the employers and employees. Today, it is commonly accepted that employers have an obligation to use their employees' abilities to the fullest and to give all of their employees a chance to grow, to realise their full potential and to develop successful careers. This has led to an increased emphasis on career planning and development for the individual, which is often closely linked to the performance review process and succession planning for the organisation (Noe, 2017).

A career can be defined as an occupation undertaken for a significant period of a person's life and with opportunities for progress. This progression is usually achieved through a series of work roles that enable employees to develop the knowledge, skills and attitudes required for future roles, while providing them with a sense of fulfilment and the opportunity to experience success. Career development involves activities such as

加工作坊、培训项目、由大学或学院提供的进阶学习。员工们通过认知其当前的技能、兴趣、知识和激励他们的当前工作的各个方面来参与职业规划；获得未来有可能选择的职业的各类信息（Noe，2017）；明确自己的职业生涯的目标；然后建立行动计划来实现这些目标。

明确职业发展阶段

不同职业发展阶段的活动、关系与任务是有区别的。组织必须清楚地了解不同的职业发展阶段，以及员工们在各自阶段的需求的不同。主要有四个职业发展阶段（Noe，2017）：探索、确立、维持和衰退。

1. 探索阶段

探索阶段指的是人们认真搜寻职业机会的一个阶段（大概在 15～24 岁）。他们试图将关于可选择的职业的知识与自己的兴趣和能力相匹配。尝试多种广泛的职业选择通常出现在这一阶段的早些时候。直至这一时期的尾端，人们会做出看似恰当的选择，然后开始递交他们的第一份工作申请。

2. 确立阶段

这个阶段大约在 24～44 岁，是大多数人职业生涯的核心阶段。该时期人们会努力在他们选择的专业上建立自己的地位。许多人会持续不断地对个人能力和职业志向进行考量，与他们最初的职业选择进行对比。

确立阶段又可以分为三个子时期。尝试阶段大致在 25～30 岁。在这个阶段人们会判断所选择的领域是否适合自己，如果不适合，可能会试图做一些改变。在 30～40 岁，人们会经历稳定期的子阶段。在这个阶段，他们在公司的职业目标已经确定，人们会做出更精确的职业规划来确定职业晋升的步骤、工作变更，或是参加教育类活动，以便尽可能地去实现这些目标。最终，人们可能会在 35～45 岁进入中期职业危机子阶段。在这一时期许多人会相对于其最初的志向和目标对其发展做出整体评估。在这一阶段，许多人会重新评估他们的工作和职业生涯。

3. 维持阶段

在 45～65 岁，许多人会从稳定期滑向维持期。在这个阶段人们一般已在工作中为自己创造了一个位置，而且大部分人的努力主要为了维持这个位置。

attending workshops, training programmes or courses offered by universities or colleges. Individuals engage in career planning by recognising their current skills, interests, knowledge and the aspects of their current job that motivates them; acquiring information about possible future opportunities (Noe, 2017); clearly identifying their career-related goals; and finally establishing action plans to achieve those goals.

Identify an Individual's Career Stage

Activities, relationships and tasks vary with career stages. Organisations must be aware of the different career stages and the differing needs of their employees at each stage. There are four main stages in a typical career (Noe, 2017): exploration, establishment, maintenance and decline.

1. Exploration stage

The exploration stage is the period (roughly ages $15\sim24$) during which people seriously explore occupational alternatives. They attempt to match their knowledge of available careers with their own interests and abilities. Tentative broad occupational choices are usually made during the early part of this period. Towards the end of this period, a seemingly appropriate choice is made and people apply for their first job.

2. Establishment stage

This stage spans roughly ages $24\sim44$ and is the heart of most people's working lives. During this period, people engage in activities to establish their standing in their chosen profession. Many people continue to test their capabilities and ambitions against those of their initial occupational choice.

The establishment stage has threes sub-stages. The trial sub-stage lasts roughly from ages $25\sim30$. During this period, people determine whether their chosen field is suitable; if it is not, several changes might be attempted. Between the ages of roughly $30\sim40$, people go through a stabilisation sub-stage. In this stage, firm occupational goals are set and more explicit career planning is conducted to determine the sequence of promotions, job changes and/or any educational activities that seem necessary for accomplishing these goals. Finally, between the mid-30s and mid-40s, people may enter the mid-career crisis sub-stage. During this period, many people conduct a major reassessment of their progress relative to their original ambitions and goals. In this stage, many people re-evaluate their work and career.

3. Maintenance stage

Between the ages of $45\sim65$, many people slide from the stabilisation sub-stage into the maintenance stage. During this period, people have typically created a place for themselves at work and most of their efforts are directed at maintaining that place.

4. 衰退阶段

接近退休年龄的时候(65 岁以上),一个人的职业生涯中通常会迎来减速期。不同国家有不同的退休年龄。在这个阶段许多人面临的前景是,不得不接受个人能力的降低和责任的减少,学会接受和发展新角色,成为年轻人的良师益友。随之而来的是彻底退休,然后,为他们原来花在工作上的时间和精力寻找不同的去处。

拥有职业规划和管理的理由

对新员工来说,在最初踏入职场的阶段,要建立起职业自信,学会与他们的第一个上司和同事们相处,学会接受责任和职责,最重要的是,对自己的才能、需要和价值有清晰的认知,因为这都与最初的职业目标有关联(Noe,2017)。

1. 规避现实冲击

职业初期阶段,有时会是很困难的甚至是灾难性的。在这个时期新员工最初天真的美好预期与残酷的企业现实相碰撞。这就是我们指的"现实冲击"。例如,工商管理硕士毕业生期待着他们的第一份工作能为他们提供富有挑战性的、比较刺激的环境,可以将他们在大学里学到的新技能应用其中,以证明自己的能力,从而得到晋升机会。然而现实是,对前途的展望和预期与现实的工作和生活相距甚远。新成员通常会因为人际冲突和官僚制度的残酷状况,因为不公正对待下属的上司而受到打击。

2. 提供具有挑战性的初始工作

人们普遍认为给新员工提供具有挑战性的初始工作是很重要的。但在大部分企业中现实并非如此。越来越多的组织开始意识到,在招聘、选拔和引导新员工上投入了许多金钱和精力后,必须给予他们展现才能的机会,这对留住员工是十分重要的。像安永和普华永道这样的咨询公司,他们期待年轻毕业生立刻对企业做出贡献,然后尽快在有挑战的项目团队中找到自我的位置。

3. 在招聘中提供真实的工作预览

向申请者提供真实可信的工作预览,内容包括在企业工作后有怎样的预

4. Decline stage

As retirement approaches (age above 65), there is often a deceleration period in a person's career. Different countries have different retirement ages and expectations. Many people face the prospect of having to accept reduced levels of power and responsibility and learn to accept and develop new roles as mentors and confidantes for younger workers. This is followed by full retirement, after which people find alternative uses for the time and effort formerly expended on their occupation.

Reasons to Have Career Planning and Management

In the initial stages of their careers people develop a sense of confidence, learn to get along with their first boss and with co-workers, learn how to accept responsibility and, most importantly, gain an insight into their own talents, needs and values as they relate to initial career goals (Noe, 2017).

1. Avoid reality shock

The career entry stage can be a difficult, even disastrous period, in which new employees' often naive expectations first confront the realities of organisational life. This is referred to as "reality shock". The young master of business administration graduate, for example, might expect his or her first job to provide a challenging, exciting environment in which to apply the new techniques learned in university and to prove his or her abilities, thereby gaining a promotion. Sometimes, however, the promises or the expectations do not match the realities of working life. New recruits are often demotivated by being relegated to unimportant, low-risk jobs, by the harsh realities of interdepartmental conflict and politicking or by a boss who is neither rewarded for nor trained in the mentoring tasks needed to supervise new employees properly.

2. Provide challenging initial jobs

Although it is generally agreed that providing new employees with challenging first jobs is important, this does not occur in many organisations. An increasing number of organisations are realising that after the effort and money invested in recruiting, selecting and inducting new employees, they must encourage them to remain by giving them an opportunity to demonstrate their abilities. In consulting firms such as Ernst & Young and Pricewaterhouse Coopers, young graduates are expected to contribute at once, and immediately find themselves on teams involved in challenging projects.

3. Provide realistic job previews in recruitment

Providing applicants with realistic previews of what to expect once they begin working in an organisation-previews that describe both the attractions and possible

期，描述日后工作有吸引力的地方和可能出现的困难，这都是将"现实冲击"降到最低的有效途径，从而提高员工长期绩效表现（Noe，2017）。招聘者和申请者通常在面试环节会给出和接收一些不切实际的信息。结果就是面试官没有向候选人描绘出清晰的职业目标，同时导致候选者对企业抱有不切实际的幻想。真实的工作预览可以提高员工的留任率，尤其是相对复杂的岗位，如管理培训生、销售人员或是寿险业务员。

4. 提供定期轮岗

新进员工测试自己最佳的方式就是尝试多种多样的挑战性的工作。通过不同岗位的轮换——例如从金融分析到生产再到人力资源——员工能够有机会评估自己的才能和兴趣。与此同时，组织也会得到一名具有广泛的、多功能视角的经理人。职能的拓展意味着仔细选择工作任务的顺序，以此来建立员工个人竞争力。

5. 开展职业导向绩效评估

经理人必须清楚了解，长期有效可信的绩效评估信息相比于短期保护直属下属的利益更为重要。因此，经理人需要关注每一个员工潜在的职业路径的具体信息，换句话说，是有关其日后工作职责的本质的信息，根据这些信息他们会对下属做出评估。这也有助于组织进行职业管理、开展继任计划，通过确定和培养潜力大、有天赋的职员，使个人目标与组织的使命和企业策略保持一致。

6. 提供接受指导的机会

组织指导是人力资源发展和职业管理与规划的重要组成部分。指导可以是正式的，也可以是非正式的。非正式的是指，管理者通常会主动向有潜力的员工提供指导，不仅训练他们，而且给予职业规划建议，帮助他们避开政治陷阱。正式的情况是，招聘者可能会把潜在的导师和学徒搭配起来，鼓励他们在工作中密切合作。可能会展开针对导师的培训，以便导师和学徒能更明确他们各自在师徒关系中的职责。

7. 管理晋升

招聘者必须确定提拔员工的基本准则，以及制定决策的方式，这都将对

pitfalls—can be an effective way of minimising "reality shock" and improving long-term performance. Recruiters and applicants often give and receive unrealistic information during job interviews. The result is that the interviewer may not form a clear picture of the candidate's career goals, while at the same time the candidate forms an unrealistically favourable image of the organisation. Realistic job previews can boost the retention rate among employees who are hired for relatively complex jobs such as management trainee, salesperson or life insurance agent.

4. Provide periodic job rotation

The best way for new employees to test themselves is to try out a variety of challenging jobs. By rotating to jobs in various specialisations—from financial analysis to production to human resources, for example—employees get an opportunity to assess their aptitudes and preferences. At the same time, the organisation gets a manager with a broader multifunctional view of the organisation. This may involve selecting carefully sequenced job assignments to build up employees' competencies.

5. Conduct career-oriented performance appraisals

Managers must understand that valid and reliable performance appraisal information is in the long run more important than protecting the short-term interests of their immediate subordinates. Thus, managers need concrete information about each employee's potential career path—that is, information about the nature of the future work for which they are appraising the subordinate or which the subordinate desires. This also assists the organisation with career management and succession planning, by identifying and developing high-potential and talented staff in a way that aligns the individual's goals with the organisation's mission and the changing business environment.

6. Provide opportunities for mentoring

Organisational mentoring is an important component of human resource development and career management and planning. Mentoring may be formal or informal. Informally, middle- and senior-level managers often voluntarily take up-and-coming employees under their wings, not only to train them but to give career advice and to help them steer around political pitfalls. In addition, many employers also establish formal mentoring programmes. In these programmes employers actively encourage mentoring relationships and may pair protégés with potential mentors. Training may be provided to mentors to aid both mentors and protégés in understanding their respective responsibilities in the relationship.

7. Managing promotions

Employers must decide on what basis to promote employees; the way these decisions

员工的动机、绩效和忠诚度产生影响。

（1）是资历还是能力起支配作用？

可能最重要的决策就是晋升是以资历为基础还是以能力为基础，还是两者的结合。为了给予员工动力，晋升最好以能力为基准。

（2）如何量化能力？

若晋升以个人能力为基准，那么如何定义和量化能力呢？定义和量化过去的绩效表现是相对直接明了的：定义工作、建立标准、单项或多项评估手段用来记录员工绩效。然而，在晋升时还需要对个人的潜能进行预测；因此，必须有有效的程序来预测候选人未来的绩效表现。许多招聘者仅仅参照之前的绩效，并假设一个人先前的绩效如何则在新工作中也会如此。这是最简单的途径。相反，另一些招聘者用测试或评估方式来衡量有可能晋升的员工，去确认他们是否具有经营管理的潜质（Noe，2017）。

（3）晋升程序正式还是非正式？

经理必须决定晋升程序是正式的还是非正式的。一些招聘者依赖于非正式的体系。在这种情况下任何公开职位的有效性和要求却是保密的。晋升决定由核心管理者做出，他们会从自己认识的或者拥有优秀能力的员工中选择候选人。

由此，许多招聘者建立正式的、公开的晋升政策和程序。这些组织会向员工阐述正式的晋升政策，说明作为奖赏的晋升的标准条件。正式的系统通常会公布岗位的政策。这表明空缺职位和职位要求将会对企业的主体员工公示和传播。许多招聘者也收集合格员工的详细信息，而有些人使用组织人员替换图。人力资源信息系统对于维护成千上万员工的资格证明、技能清单以及详细的继任计划特别有用。

（4）水平、垂直还是其他结构？

最后，招聘者越来越多地面对这样的问题：在一个更高一级的职位或晋升并不是常有的年代，如何提拔员工？进一步说，受到公司合并、全球化竞争的影响，缩减部门和裁员已经去除了许多高层管理职位，大多数组织结构都

are made affects employees' motivation, performance and commitment.

(1) Is seniority or competence the rule?

Probably the most important decision is whether promotion is based on seniority or competence, or some combination of the two. To encourage motivation, promotion based on competence is best.

(2) How is competence measured?

If promotion is based on competence, how is competence defined and measured? Defining and measuring past performance is a fairly straight forward matter: the job is defined, standards are set and appropriate appraisal tools are used to measure the employee's performance. However, promotion also requires predicting the person's potential; thus, there must be a valid procedure for predicting a candidate's future performance. Many employers simply use prior performance as a guide and assume that a person's prior performance indicates how he or she will perform in a new job. This is the simplest procedure to use. In contrast, some employers use tests or assessment to evaluate promotable employees and to identify those employees with executive potential (Noe, 2017).

(3) Is the process formal or informal?

Managers have to decide whether the promotion process will be formal or informal. Some employers depend on an informal system. In such cases the availability and requirements of any open positions are kept secret. Promotion decisions are then made by key managers who choose candidates from among the employees they know personally or who have, for one reason or another, impressed them. The problem is that when employees are unaware of the jobs that are available or the criteria for promotion, the link between performance and promotion is cut. The effectiveness of promotion as a reward is thereby diminished.

Many employers have formal, published promotion policies and procedures. In these organisations, employees are generally provided with a formal promotion policy statement that describes the criteria by which promotions are awarded. Formal systems often include a job-posting policy. This states that open positions and their requirements will be posted and circulated to all of the organisation's employees. Many employers also compile detailed information about the qualifications of employees, whereas others use workforce replacement charts. Human resource information systems can be especially useful for maintaining qualifications and skills inventories on hundreds or thousands of employees as well as details of succession plans.

(4) Vertical, horizontal or other?

Finally, employers are increasingly required to deal with the question of how to promote employees in an era in which higher-level jobs or promotions are not often available. Furthermore, retrenchments and downsizing due to mergers or global competition have eliminated many of the higher-management positions, as has the

发生了扁平化。除此之外,工人授权和相应地对专业技术的重视,产生了受过较高的专业技术培训的骨干以及渴望晋升到更高层级职位的一线工人,但缺乏开放的岗位阻挠了他们晋升的机会。

有一个选择就是,通过水平调动职位,甚至在已有职位范围内调动来向个人提供职业发展机遇。例如,一个生产线人员可能被调动去人力资源部门,给他们机会发展新技能,挑战个人的能力水平。扩招某些职位是有可行性的,公司可以提供相关培训来增加个人承担责任的机会。

8. 退休

退休可能是一个苦乐参半的经历。对一部分人来说这是他们职业生涯的顶点,是他们终于可以放松,享受劳动成果,不用再担心工作问题的时光。而对另一部分人来说,退休本身意味着一种创伤,习惯于忙碌的人们突然要应对"无产出"的状态和每天待在家里无所事事的不适感。对许多退休人士来说,在没有工作的情况下保持自我认知感和自我价值感是他们面临的重要问题之一。作为职业管理进程中最后一步,雇主努力试图帮助已退休的员工。

9. 退休前咨询

许多国家正面临两个问题,即劳动力老龄化与技能短缺。为了确保从工作到退休有一个健全合理的转换过程,组织能够选择的解决方式就是为那些即将退休的员工提供退休前咨询服务(Noe,2017)。这些选择将取决于组织方案以及辅导和退休规划等做法对老年雇员今后的发展及其退休决定和调整的影响。这些选择与组织的项目有关。随着信息技术的进步,特别是互联网技术的发展,组织可以向年长的员工提供通过远程办公继续工作的选择。

案例研究 8-1[①] ▶▶▶▶▶▶

酒店业职业规划与开发

在过去的两年里,四季酒店已经帮助超过 2000 名员工完成了他们的个

---

① 资料来源:Sommerville, K. (2007). *Hospitality Employee Management and Supervision: Concepts and Practical Applications*, 231-232, Hoboken, NJ: John Wiley & Sons.

flattening of most organisational structures. In addition，worker empowerment and a related emphasis on technological expertise have created cadres of highly trained professional technicians and front-line workers who aspire to higher-level positions but find their upward movement blocked by a dearth of openings.

One option is to provide career development opportunities for individuals by moving them horizontally or even within the position they currently hold. For instance，a production employee might be moved horizontally to HR to give them an opportunity to develop new skills and to test and challenge their aptitudes. Some job enrichment is usually possible，and the firm can provide training that increases the opportunity for assuming more responsibility.

8. Retirement

Retirement can be a bitter-sweet experience. For some employees it is the culmination of their careers，a time when they can relax and enjoy the fruits of their labour without worrying about the problems of work. For others，retirement is traumatic，as they try to cope with suddenly being "non-productive" and with having the strange experience of being home every day with nothing to do. For many retirees，maintaining a sense of identity and self-worth without a full-time job is a challenge and employers are increasingly trying to help retiring employees as a logical last step in the career management process.

9. Pre-retirement counselling

Many countries are dealing with both an ageing workforce and skill shortages. One approach organisations can take to ensure a sound transition from work to retirement is to offer pre-retirement counselling on the options available to those intending to retire (Noe，2017). These options will depend on organisational programmes and the effects that practices such as mentoring and retirement planning have had on older employees' later career development and their retirement decisions and adjustments. With advances in information technology，especially the growth of the Internet，organisations can provide older workers with the option of continuing in the workforce through telecommuting.

Case Study 8 – 1[①] ▶▶▶ ▶▶▶

Career Planning and Development in the Hospitality Industry

Over the past two years，the Four Seasons Hotels have assisted more than 2000

[①]　Resource：Sommerville，K.(2007).Hospitality Employee Management and supervision：Concepts and Practical Applications，231 – 232，Hoboken，NJ：John Wiley & Sons.

人职业规划。任何级别的员工，从客房服务员、助理到高层管理人员，都已经体验过这个由酒店大力推进的个人职业生涯规划项目。公司应当支持员工职业规划发展的想法是相对新颖的。传统上，员工个体职业发展计划是从上面传下来的。而今天，组织机构认识到其在促进个人职业规划建立中需要扮演更加积极的角色。在四季酒店，员工对于这种帮助的需求不断增加，与此同时，管理层发现酒店可以从提供帮助的过程中获益颇多。

四季酒店会进行常规的员工态度调查。这些调查持续显示其员工有着极高的忠诚度，处于各行业各类公司的最高位置。自从 1986 年以来，四季酒店就通过向员工提供对他们将来有用的机会的信息来帮助员工计划他们的职业生涯。职业规划不仅对员工有益，也在以下方面为四季酒店带来效益。

（1）员工能够在机会到来时做出明智的职业决策。

（2）员工对自己的职业愿景有更真实的认知。

（3）员工可以清晰地描述自己的专长、兴趣、目标、发展需求。这对管理发展与继任计划都会带来有价值的影响。

1. 制定更优的职业决策

很少有人可以在最初的工作时期就对自己的技能、兴趣和价值所在有着非常清晰的认识。大多数人都是边走边了解，经过一系列的尝试和犯错才能认识。最终他们会明确什么才是他们真正喜欢的，哪些才是其真正擅长的。而很不幸的是，这个尝试—犯错的过程对员工个人和组织而言，都是要有很大的付出的。个人会因为各种错误的原因做出错误的职业选择，进入他们感到不开心、表现不佳的岗位中。

例如，某餐饮部助理经理对自己一路晋升到总经理充满雄心壮志。为了获得必要的经验，她选择横向调动去客房部，但她开始发现客房服务十分无趣，并且对她的管理能力提出了极高的要求。之前她是相当出色的员工，现在她的评分只是居于平均水平。经过再三考虑，她终于意识到自己并不享受管理的过程，自己真正喜欢的还是在餐饮方面的工作。

一名德克萨斯四季酒店的员工申请调任去旗下位于加利福尼亚的酒店以获得升迁机会。但她并没有仔细思考过这个决定，只是单纯被晋升的美好前景吸引，她没有想清楚新工作地点的工作方式会很不同，包括生活方式、社会价值观、生活成本以及工作节奏，也没有考虑过自己是否愿意做出权衡。

employees in their personal career planning. Employees at every level, from housekeepers and secretaries up to senior management, have gone through the personal career planning programme, which is vigorously promoted by the organisation. The idea that companies should support employees in their career planning is relatively new. Traditionally, development plans for individual employees have been handed down from above. Today, however, organisations are realising they need to take a more active role in encouraging individual career planning. At Four Seasons, employees have been increasingly demanding such assistance and management has recognised that it can reap tremendous benefits from providing it.

Four Seasons conducts regular employee attitude surveys. These surveys consistently indicate a very high loyalty rating, among the highest of any company in any industry. Since 1986, Four Seasons has been helping employees to plan their careers by providing them with information about the opportunities that might be available to them in the future. Career planning is much more than just an employee benefit; it also benefits Four Seasons in the following ways.

(1) Employees are able to make better informed career decisions when opportunities become available to them.

(2) Employees are more realistic about their career prospects.

(3) Employees are much more articulate in describing their strengths, interests, goals and development requirements, resulting in valuable input for management development and succession planning purposes.

1. Making Better Career Decisions

Few people begin their working lives with a strong sense of their own skills, interests and values. Most learn as they go along, through a process of trial-and-error. Eventually, they identify what they really like and what they are good at. Unfortunately, this process of trial-and-error can be gruelling for both the employee and the organisation. Individuals may make career choices for all the wrong reasons, moving into jobs in which they are unhappy and perform poorly.

For example, an assistant food and beverages manager may be ambitious to advance all the way up to general manager. To gain the necessary breadth of experience, she takes a lateral move into rooms, but she finds the rooms function boring and highly demanding of her people management skills. Previously a superior performer, she now rates only average. On reflection, she realises that she does not really enjoy management. What she enjoys is specialising in food and beverages.

An employee at a Four Seasons hotel in Texas applies for a promotion involving a transfer to a California location, although she has not carefully considered the implications of the move. Attracted by the prospect of promotion, she gives little thought to the different life-styles, social values, living costs and pace of work in the new location. Furthermore, she has

在调动后的几个月内,她要求调回德克萨斯酒店。当员工做出了不佳的职业选择,周围的每个人都会受到牵连。员工自身会感觉痛苦,有时甚至会丢掉工作。与此同时,员工的同事和组织都会受到由于员工士气和绩效低迷带来的损失。

在四季酒店,管理层相信人们愿意好好工作,反之亦然。当有人做出不佳的职业选择时,正向强化循环就会逆转。当员工在新职位上感到不愉快,表现不佳时,他们会感到更不开心。组织的目的是为员工提供做出决策的框架,这样能为个人和企业节省因错误选择造成的在人力和财力上的开支。

2. 建立更切实际的职业目标

四季酒店正在茁壮成长,它有能力向员工的未来提供广泛的职业发展机遇。但这不意味着它能在当下就满足员工所有的职业晋升预期。在这个年轻的充满野心的群体里,当员工们对下一个机遇毫无耐心的时候,问题就浮现了出来。在某些情况下,他们觉得自己已经准备好上一个台阶了,而事实是他们还需要在现有职位磨合一段时间。其他情况是,员工已经一切就绪,但并没有合适的岗位空出来。有时这些员工就会变得十分没有耐心而选择离开,去其他的酒店,去小型企业或是离开这个行业。

组织并不想失去这些具有雄心壮志的员工。在许多情况下,这些员工往往发现外面的草地并不比这里的绿:他们进步的脚步并没有加快;小型企业并没有给他们足够的发展空间;或是他们开始想念本行业特别的工作氛围。事实上有时候,这样的员工又会回到原来的企业,并且比过去的忠诚度更高。然而,职业生涯规划可以避免这些失败的换工作经历造成的各方面的浪费。

根据公司的业务计划和人力资源要求,四季酒店提供职业生涯规划程序,帮助员工将个人技能和特长与他们将来有可能实现的机会相匹配的。经过职业规划,员工们会了解公司对自己的看法和建议,需要发展哪些技能来促进自己登上新台阶。带来的效果是,他们会对自己晋升所需的条件有更清晰的认知,即使他们并不知道什么时候会晋升。

3. 扶持管理发展与继任计划

通过引入职业生涯规划程序,鼓励员工保持与经理人之间常规的有关职业发展的讨论,公司将获得大量可用于管理发展和制订继任计划的自动的信

not considered whether she is willing to make the trade-offs involved. Within a few months of the move, she asks to be returned to Texas. Everyone suffers when employees make poor career choices. The employee suffers personal pain, and sometimes the loss of a job. The employee's co-workers and the organisation also suffer from the employee's declining morale and performance.

At Four Seasons, the management believes that people who like themselves do good work, and vice versa. When a person makes a bad career choice, the positive reinforcement cycle goes into reverse. Unhappy in the new position, the employee performs below par, which in turns makes him or her unhappy. The organisation's aim is to provide employees with a framework for making reasoned decisions, thus saving both the individual and the company from the human and financial costs that can follow a bad move.

2. Setting More Realistic Career Goals

Four Seasons Hotels is a growing organisation, able to offer its employees a range of future career opportunities, but that does not mean that it can meet all of its employees' expectations for career advancement at the moment they expect them to be met. In a young and very ambitious employee population, problems can arise when employees become too impatient for their next opportunity. In some cases, they think themselves ready to move up, when in fact they need more time in their current position. In other cases, the employee is ready, but no opening is currently available. Sometimes these employees become so impatient that they move on to other hotels, to small business or out of the industry altogether.

Organisations do not like to lose their ambitious employees and, in many cases, these individuals find the grass is not greener elsewhere: their progress is no more rapid, small business do not always allow them sufficient scope and they may miss the special atmosphere of the hotel industry. Sometimes, in fact, such individuals return to their original employer, more committed than before. However, career planning can prevent the upheaval of such abortive job switches.

The Four Seasons offers a career planning process that assists employees in matching their skills and strengths to the opportunities that will realistically be available to them in the future, given the company's business plans and human resource requirements. Through career planning, employees learn how they are currently viewed by the company, and what skills they may need to develop to advance further up the ladder. This gives them a much clearer sense of what they need to do to be promoted, even if they do not know when this is likely to occur.

3. Supporting Management Development and Succession Planning

By introducing career planning programmes, and by encouraging employees to hold regular career development discussions with their managers, the company gains a wealth of

息。他们会了解员工真正想去的位置,以及为了获得该职位员工应该具有哪些发展经验。

4. 推行职业规划

四季酒店的员工职业生涯规划项目是围绕由一家总部位于加拿大多伦多的 BBM 人力资源咨询股份有限公司总裁开发的《职业规划手册》进行的。《职业规划手册》(以下简称《手册》)对加拿大各行各业的许多重要组织都进行了业绩记录。该手册吻合下列职业规划进程的需求。

(1)从员工入手。职业规划的首要职责就是员工本身。每个人必须评估他们的技能、价值、目标,并且与经理和人力资源部人员一起进行信息收集,从而确切地阐述和检测他们的评估。故此《手册》着重强调职业自我管理的重要性。其他一些用来考察的方式,需要强制性的员工管理讨论、剥夺员工责任、冒险选择可能被视为不正当的手段进行绩效评估。

(2)灵活性。在四季酒店,职业规划的材料具有足够的灵活性,既可以方便员工自学之用,也方便研讨会使用。自学的方式更有利于员工在规划中负责地进行信息的沟通。向全体员工提供职业发展规划帮助也是性价比极高的方式。《手册》带给我们很大的弹性空间。

(3)广泛性。《手册》有适用于管理/专业与文书/技术的各种版本,可以用于公司的所有层级,从基层员工到高级管理人员,覆盖性强。

(4)实用性。一些职业规划的方式相当理论化、学术化。而该《手册》很实用,接地气,可以使阅读者直入主题。

(5)辅助经理人。大多数经理人希望帮助员工的职业发展。但通常他们工作忙碌,需要回应更具体的问题。"我很擅长管理人才,您同意这个观点吗?"和"如果我想成为客房部经理,如何获得一些必需的技能?"这样的问题要好于"您怎么看待我?"或"您认为我应该追求哪种职业?"《手册》可以在框架性问题上给员工很大的帮助,更便于经理人给出有效的反馈。

《职业规划手册》十分鼓励员工向他们的经理人或同事寻求反馈意见,了解他们眼中自己的优势和劣势。对经理人而言,这能更便于向员工提出绩效方面的忠告和建议,不像绩效评估那样有感情负担。四季酒店在职业规划项目开展的过程中,采用从上到下的手段,从职业计划和技能培训研讨会开始,

information for management development and succession planning purposes. They learn where their employees want to go, and what development experiences they require to get there.

4. Implementing Career Planning

The Four Seasons employee career planning programme is built around the Career Planning Workbook, developed by Dr Barbara Moses, President of Toronto-based BBM Human Resource Consultants, Inc. The Career Planning Workbook (hereafter, the Workbook) has an established track record with many leading Canadian organisations in a variety of sectors. The Workbook meets the following needs of a career planning process.

(1) Employee-initiated. The primary responsibility in career planning is the employee. Individuals must assess their skills, values and goals and initiate information-gathering sessions with managers and HR staff to formulate and test their assessments. The Workbook strongly reinforces this message of career self-management. Other approaches require mandatory employee-management discussions, taking the responsibility away from the employee and running the risk of being perceived as a kind of back-door performance appraisal.

(2) Flexible. At the Four Seasons, career planning materials are flexible enough to be used for self-study or in workshops. A self-study approach communicates the message that the employee is in charge of the process. It is also a cost-effective means of offering career planning assistance to all employees. The Workbook offers this flexibility.

(3) Portable. The Workbook, available in both managerial/professional and secretarial/ technical editions, can be used at all levels of the organisation, from entry-level employees up to senior management.

(4) Practical. Some approaches to career planning are extremely theoretical and academic. The Workbook is very practical and down-to-earth, and quickly gets the user involved in a no-nonsense fashion.

(5) Supportive of managers. Most managers want to assist their employees in their development. However, managers are busy people, and they need specific questions to respond to. "Do you agree that I'm good at managing people?" and "How can I acquire the additional skills I need to become Rooms manager?" are better questions than "What do you think about me?" or "What career do you think I should pursue?" The Workbook assists employees in framing meaningful questions, making it much easier for managers to give useful feedback.

The Workbook strongly encourages employees to seek feedback on what they see as their strengths and weaknesses from their manager and co-workers. This makes it much easier for managers to counsel employees about performance issues, outside the emotionally loaded atmosphere of the performance review. The Four Seasons uses a top-down approach to roll out the new career planning programme, starting with a Career Planning and Coaching

在每间酒店,提供给高级到中层经理,他们负责将手册介绍给员工。像这种一天的研讨会能够使经理人意识到什么是职业规划、如何与员工展开有效的职业发展讨论。

研讨会同时包含了很重要的个人职业规划内容。给予经理人个人职业规划的经验,可以使他们更致力于热心支持他们的员工的职业发展。在研讨会之后,经理人将向他们的员工介绍整个项目,在部门会议中,或是在一对一的交流中,告知他们在工作中可以参考《职业规划手册》。

5. 实现个人与企业目标

四季酒店的职业生涯规划项目取得了一些比较清晰的成果。

(1)态度调查表明,公司满足了员工对职业生涯的关心,员工感觉自己对职业规划的需求以一种有意义的方式得到了满足。

(2)员工制定出更优的职业决策。地域位置上的调动进行得更顺利、更成功。相似地,这表明员工权衡了潜在的利弊。经理将根据《手册》来帮助员工认清自己可能处在错误的职位上,从而使员工主动申请职位调动,化解了潜在的"定时炸弹"。

(3)员工更加实事求是。年轻的、有远大志向的员工从他们得到的机会中逐渐意识到实用性的重要意义,以及到下一次职位调动他们可能需要等待的时间。

(4)强化了人力资源规划进程。公司更好地掌握了有关员工发展需求和长期职业目标的信息。

(5)促进对个人和职位的了解正在成为企业文化的一部分。四季酒店的经理人和员工正开始讲一种从《职业规划手册》中衍生出来的新的"语言"。比如,人们会说"X 步调缓慢"或者"我很有归属感"。这些并不是什么职业术语。人们正在建立一种新的表达职业技能和个人兴趣、偏好的方式。他们对工作职位有着更广阔的眼界,更明确未来工作的关键基本技能和能力。文化的改变正在一步步进行中,这能极大地促进我们的工作,以确保合适的人处在合适的职位上。

当组织帮助员工进行职业规划时,每个人都会获益。公司通过培养员工来证明自己的承诺。员工制定更优的决策,避免走入职业误区的代价。与此同时,职业规划项目有助于让过高的晋升预期"冷却"下来,让员工对自己的处境有更现实的了解。并且这为管理发展和继任计划提供了至关重要的信息。

Skills Workshop for senior to mid-level managers, in each hotel, who then introduce the Workbook to employees. This one-day workshop educates managers on what career planning is and on how to hold effective career development discussions with employees.

The workshop also contains a strong personal career planning component. Giving managers a personal career planning experience makes them more committed to, and enthusiastic about, supporting their employees in their own career development. Following the workshop, managers introduce the programme to their employees, informing them of the availability of the Workbook either in departmental meetings or on a one-on-one basis.

5. Meeting Individual and Corporate Goals

The Four Seasons career planning programme has produced some very clear results.

（1）Attitude surveys show the company is meeting employees' career concerns. Employees now feel that their need for career planning is being met by the company in a meaningful way.

（2）Employees are making better career decisions. Geographical relocations are proceeding much more smoothly and successfully, indicating that employees are considering the potential trade-offs involved. Similarly, managers are reporting situations in which the Workbook helped an employee recognise that he or she is in the wrong job, resulting in a voluntary request for a transfer, and defusing a potentially explosive situation.

（3）Employees are becoming more realistic. Young, ambitious employees are gaining a more realistic sense of their opportunities, and of how long they may have to wait for their next move.

（4）HR planning processes are being strengthened. There is better information about employees' developmental requirements and longer-term career goals.

（5）Improved understanding of people and jobs is becoming part of the organisation's culture. Managers and employees at Four Seasons are beginning to speak a new "language" derived directly from the Career Planning Workbook. People say things like "X is low on pacing" or "I'm high on affiliation". This is not just jargon. People are developing new descriptive skills for talking about jobs and interests and preferences. They are also becoming much better at looking beyond their job titles to identify the key underlying skills and competencies they can bring to future work assignments. A cultural change is underway, one the greatly facilitates the organisation's efforts to ensure that the right person is placed in the right job.

When organisations assist employees with their career planning, everyone benefits. The company demonstrates its commitment to developing its employees. Employees make better informed decisions and avoid costly career blunders. At the same time, a career planning programme helps to "cool out" overheated expectations of advancement, giving employees a more realistic idea of where they stand. It also provides vital information for management development and succession planning activities.

问　题

（1）为什么酒店和旅游企业应当支持员工的职业规划？

（2）在四季酒店的职业规划项目中，有哪些具体的益处？

（3）执行员工职业规划项目时，四季酒店考虑了哪些标准要素？

案例研究 8－2① ▶▶▶▶▶▶

Rebecca Chow 是 XYZ 餐饮有限公司的人力资源经理。这是一家家庭式风格的连锁酒吧式餐厅，坐落于新英格兰区域的 6 个州内。Rebecca 遇到了一个问题。她需要三名新的总经理来负责公司未来 6 个月内即将开业的新餐厅。总经理职位要求具有 5 年管理经验。然而，计算机系统查看了所有助理经理的履历资格，只有一位目前任职于 XYZ 的员工具有必要的管理资历。人力资源副总裁要求 Rebecca 在这周末提交对这三个新职位的人事方案。

Rebecca 意识到 XYZ 的这个发展项目需要依靠自己进行开发。现在她要协调好管理发展项目，同时她也想发展小时工项目。在与一些员工探讨这个想法的时候，她遇到了一位 17 岁的洗碗工 Ben，他刚刚步入高三。Ben 希望在高中毕业后可以成为一名餐厅经理。

问　题

（1）请协助 Rebecca 做一份一页的计划书，来填补该职位的空缺。

（2）为了保证一个有效的发展项目，你需要什么样的信息？明确必要的假设。然后为 XYZ 餐饮公司管理项目设计一份纲要，以避免日后再次出现内部人才短缺的情况。

（3）你认为 Ben 的职业预期切实可行吗？为了最大化地实现 Ben 的职业目标，请具体明确地给出你的指导意见。

---

① 资料来源：Tanke, M. (2001). *Human Resources Management for Hospitality Industry* (2nd ed.), 214－215, Albany: Delmar Thomson Learning.

Questions

(1) Why should hospitality and tourism companies support employees in their career planning?

(2) What are some of the specific benefits of the Four Seasons career planning programme?

(3) What criteria do Four Seasons consider in the development of its employee planning programme?

Case Study 8 - 2[①] ▶▶▶▶▶▶

Rebecca Chow is the human resources manager of XYZ Restaurant Corp., a family style restaurantand bar, located in six states in the New England area. Rebecca is faced with a problem. She needs three new general managers for the new restaurants the corporation is planning on opening in the next six months. The job specification for general manager requires five years of management experience. However, a computer check of all of the assistant manager qualifications came up with only one person currently employed by XYZ with the necessary management qualifications. The Vice President of Human Resources has asked Rebecca to present by the end of the week an HR plan for filling the three new positions.

Rebecca recognises that the development programme at XYZ needs some development of its own. Now that Rebecca is more attuned to the importance of a development programme for management, she also wants to improve the programme for hourly employees. While discussing this idea with some of the employees, she meets a seventeen-year-old dishwasher, Ben, who is just entering his senior year in high school. Ben thinks that he would like to become a restaurant manager when he finishes high school.

Questions

(1) Assist Rebecca by coming up with a one-page plan to fill the necessary job vacancies.

(2) What kind of information do you need to ensure an effective development programme? Make and identify whatever assumptions are necessary. Then outline a development programme for XYZ Restaurant Corp. that will prevent this internal personnel shortage from happening again in the future.

(3) How realistic do you think Ben is in his career aspirations? Specifically, what guidelines would you suggest to maximise Ben's success in achieving his career goal?

---

① Resource: Tanke, M.(2001). *Human Resources Management for Hospitality Industry* (2nd ed.). 214 - 215, Albany: Delmar Thomson Learning.

（4）请指出 Rebecca 可以辅助 Ben 成功的几个步骤（短期和长期的）。

（5）假设 Ben 找到 Rebecca 时没有职业预期怎么办？Rebecca 要如何帮助他确定可能的职业兴趣和期望？

（6）如果你遇到一位没有职业预期的洗碗工，会提供给他哪一类职业发展机会，来最有效地挖掘他的潜能呢？

（4）Identify several steps（both short-term and long-term）that Rebecca could take to help ensure Ben's success.

（5）What if Ben had come to Rebecca with no career aspirations? How might Rebecca have helped him to identify possible career interests and expectations?

（6）What type of lateral career development opportunities might you provide for a dishwasher who came to you with no career aspirations that would maximise his or her potential?

第9章 绩效管理与评估

📖 **学习目标**

- 了解什么是员工工作绩效管理及其目标
- 介绍不同类型的评估员工的方法及其特点
- 通过案例研究了解如何建立组织公平的绩效管理

绩效管理体系可以将员工目标与组织目标联系起来,能够使组织获得竞争优势,超越对手,实现组织战略目标。通过向员工提供关于实际绩效标准和需要做到的行为的反馈,绩效管理系统能确保员工的绩效集中于有助于组织实现战略目标所需达到的绩效上。有效的员工绩效管理最终应当有助于组织的持续进步和改进。

有很多理由促使我们去建立一个详细周密的绩效管理体系(Noe,2017):(1)管理绩效中的评估,为制定晋升或薪资决策提供必要的信息。(2)它可以提供给上司及其员工每一个审查员工与工作相关的行为的机会。反过来,它又能够促使上司及其下属建立起可以纠正评估中可能暴露的缺陷的方案,强化员工正确的行为。(3)它提供了一个良好的机会,可基于员工表现出来的优势和劣势去审视员工职业规划。因而,绩效管理不仅能提供信息反馈,以促使员工个体提高绩效,而且它也是获得制定其他管理决策所需信息的途径。

绩效管理步骤

Graham 和 Bennett(1998)建议绩效管理体系包括以下三个主要步骤。

(1)工作的定义和了解。该步骤是要确定你及下属员工在他或她的工作职责和标准上达成一致意见。

Chapter 9   Performance Management and Appraisal

The objectives of this chapter

- Understand what is employee performance management and its objectives
- Introduce different types of employee appraisal methods and their characteristics
- Understand how to establish a fair performance management in organizations with case studies as examples

A performance management system that links employee goals with organisational goals enables an organisation to achieve an advantage over its competitors and meet organisational strategic goals. By providing feedback to employees about the actual standard of performance and behaviour they need to achieve, a performance management system ensures that staff performance is focused on the type of performance that will help the organisation achieve its strategic goal. Effective management of staff performance should ultimately improve an organisation and aid its continuous improvement efforts.

There are several reasons to develop a well-planned performance management system (Noe, 2017): (1) appraisals provide the information necessary for promotion and salary decisions; (2) it provides an opportunity for supervisors and employees to review each employee's work-related behaviour, which in turn enables both the supervisor and the staff member to develop a plan for correcting deficiencies and reinforcing the things the employee does right; and (3) it provides a good opportunity to review employees' career plans in light of their exhibited strengths and weaknesses. These reasons clearly show that performance management not only provides feedback that enables an individual to improve his or her performance, it is also a way of obtaining the information needed for other management decisions.

Steps in Managing Performance

Graham and Bennett (1998) suggested that a performance management system contains three main steps.

(1) Defining and understanding the job. This means making sure that you and your employee agree on his or her duties and job standards.

（2）选择评估方式。该步骤是指将员工实际绩效与既定标准相比较。这里通常包括不同种类的绩效考核表。

（3）考核面试。绩效管理通常要求一个或多个正式反馈环节,经常采用面试或"一对多"的形式。通常要讨论一个员工的绩效和进步,并依据发展的需要制订计划。

评估指的是对员工在该职位的绩效进行评判。它建立在诸多因素之上,并不是仅关注生产率。由于这个考核的唯一目的是在员工中决定是否允许加薪,有时它被称为人事考核。工作评估描述了该职位拥有者的相关优势及需要改进的方面。所有的经理人会不断对下属进行判断,从某种意义上讲,即不断给出评估结果。然而,绩效评估这个术语在人力资源管理的概念中,即为在规定方式下、以统一格式、在固定时间内做出正式的、系统的评价。因此,绩效评估涉及利用率（未来利用率及培训方面）和动机（薪资及反馈意见）两方面,两方面都与审核流程相关。

绩效评估通常分为四类（Graham 和 Bennett,1998）。

（1）绩效检讨（performance reviews）,分析过去所获成果和失败所在,给出改进日后绩效的建议。

（2）潜力评价（potential reviews）,评价晋升的合适程度或日后的培训及发展。

（3）奖励评估（reward reviews）,决定是否提高薪水。

（4）非正式评价,是对绩效进行持续性的评估。它们在本质上十分特殊,是自然产生的、介于受评者与评估者之间的副产品。

评估方法

通常评估本身的进行需要预先确定一个正式的方法,其一般包括组织和员工个人在目标与成果方面达成的战略性一致。这个方法应该向用户提供友好性、一致性、公平性、透明性。评估应该与薪资审阅、人力资源发展、培训指导以及继任计划有明确的联系。所有评估方法都要求员工的工作绩效与职务需求相匹配（Stoner,Freeman & Gilbert,1995）。因此,工作规范是必不可少的,其中应尽可能清楚地说明绩效标准。

1. 强制分布法

采用这种方法是在绩效分类中预订（评估）员工的百分率。这种方法对

(2) Choosing appraisal methods. This involves comparing your employee's actual performance to the standards that have been set; this usually involves various type of rating system.

(3) Conducting appraisal interviews. Performance management usually requires one or more formal feedback session, often referred to as interviews or "one-to-ones". Typically, an employee's performance and progress are discussed and plans are made for any development that is required.

An appraisal evaluates an employee's performance in a job based on factors other than productivity alone. Because its sole objective is to decide between employees in granting increases in wages or salaries, it is sometimes called a merit rating. Job appraisals identify the job-holder's relevant strengths and areas for improvement. All managers are constantly forming judgments about their subordinates and are in that sense continuously making appraisals. In a human resources management context, the term performance appraisal refers to a formal and systematic assessment made in a prescribed and uniform manner at certain times. Formal performance appraisal is concerned with utilisation (future use and training) and with motivation (pay and feedback), both of which are relevant to the review processes.

There are four common types of performance appraisal (Graham & Bennett, 1998).

(1) Performance reviews, which analyse past successes and failures with a view to improving future performance.

(2) Potential reviews, which assess suitability for promotion and/or further training and development.

(3) Reward reviews, which are used to determine pay raises.

(4) Informal reviews, which are part of a continuous assessment of performance. They are ad hoc in nature and are a natural by-product of the relationship between the appraises and the appraiser.

Appraisal Methods

The appraisal itself is generally conducted with the aid of a predetermined formal method, which usually includes the strategic alignment of organisational and employee goals and outcomes. The method should provide user friendliness, consistency, equity and transparency. There should also be clear links between the appraisal and salary reviews, human resource development, coaching and succession plans. All of the appraisal methods require the employee's performance to be matched against the demands of their jobs (Stoner, Freeman, & Gilbert, 1995), therefore, it is necessary to have job specifications that include clearly expressed performance standards.

1. Forced distribution method

With this method, predetermined percentages of rates (employees being evaluated)

同类小组的评价相当奏效,并且通常会在评论人之间达成基本一致。然而,需要尽可能避免较强的极端趋势(居中趋势),例如非常少的人被评估为很差。为了保证评估结果分布正常,有时会使用强制分布法,即评估人依照指示确保将评估结果按如表 9-1 所示的五个部分分布。

表 9 – 1　强制分布法等级分布

等　级	代表意义	比　率
A	良好的平均表现者	10%
B	中上表现者	20%
C	中等表现者	40%
D	中下表现者	20%
E	表现很差者	10%

在上面给出的例子中,得到高分的员工将可以得到相当可观的薪金提升,那些得分很低的则得到低于平均水平的加薪,同样重要的是,他们将得到策略上的帮助以提高他们的绩效。如果一段时间过后他们依旧无法提高其得分,则会鼓励他们在公司内部或外部另谋高就。

2. 平衡计分法

平衡计分法是一种基于测量的管理系统,可以将组织愿景与策略付诸行动(Stoner,Freeman & Gilbert,1995)。它的前提是,除财务状况之外,还有一系列变量作用于组织绩效,因此,这些变量都应被纳入测量范围。衡量客户满意度、增长度、留任率、内部运营(效能、速度、质量程序)、人力资源系统和发展的指标,都是公司绩效的主要指标,而财政是衡量成果的指标。最终,组织可以通过发展、测量、收集、分析企业内部流程与外部成果两方面的数据等手段追踪和改进其战略绩效与结果。该体系在战略意义上将员工绩效与增强组织生产力和竞争力连接起来。

3. 关键事件法

在该方法中,上级主管、在职者或是同事都有一个工作日志,记录每位员工工作行为中令人满意或不太理想的案例事件。然后,大约每 6 个月,主管和员工以这些具体事件作为案例,开会讨论绩效表现。该方法通常被用来补

are placed in performance categories. The method works reasonably well for a homogeneous group of employees, and a fair agreement among appraisers is usually obtained. There is, however, a strong tendency for extremes to be avoided (the central tendency), i.e. relatively few appraises are rated very good or very poor. To ensure that the assessment of merit is distributed normally, a forced distribution is sometimes used; appraisers are instructed to ensure that the appraises are distributed among the five categories in the proportions as shown in Table 9 – 1.

Table 9 – 1　Categories in the proportions with forced distribution method

Grade	Meaning	Percentage
A	Very good performers	10%
B	Good-average performers	20%
C	Average performers	40%
D	Poor-average performers	20%
E	Very poor performers	10%

The above company uses a forced distribution appraisal method. Employees with high ratings receive aggressive salary raises. Those with low ratings get below-average raises and, just as important, are helped with strategies for improving their performance. If they are not able to improve their rating over time, they are encouraged to find another job that might be a better fit, either inside or outside the company.

2. Balanced scorecard method

The balanced scorecard method is a measurement-based management system that translates organisational vision and strategy into action (Stoner, Freeman, & Gilbert, 1995). It is based on the premise that a range of variables contribute to organisational performance in addition to financial performance and should therefore be measured. Measures of customer satisfaction, growth and retention, internal operations (efficiency, speed, quality procedures) and human resource systems and development are leading indicators of company performance, whereas finance is a measure of outcomes. Ultimately, an organisation can track and improve its strategic performance and results by developing, measuring, collecting and analysing data from both internal business processes and external outcomes. This system strategically links employee performance to enhanced organisational productivity and competitiveness.

3. Critical incident method

With this method, the supervisor, incumbent or colleague keeps a log of desirable or undesirable examples of each employee's work-related behaviour. Then, every six months or so, the supervisor and employee meet and discuss the latter's performance using the

充其他评估技术,在这个层面上它有着许多优势。它能够给出具体的、无可动摇的事实依据来解释评估成果。它能确保对员工的评价反映了他(或她)全年的工作表现,而不仅仅是最近的表现。保留这些关键事件的生动的清单还可以提供具体事例,来说明一个员工如何做才能消除不利于绩效的因素。

关键事件法通常是用来补充排序法的。它可以有效地指出良好绩效或不良绩效的具体实例,并计划如何纠正缺陷。通过收集直接观察有效行为与无效行为的证据,且当它作为行为锚定等级评价法的基础时,关键事件法可以增强评估过程。但该方法单独用来比较员工行为时,并非有效,也不适用于制定薪资决策(Stoner,Freeman & Gilbert,1995)。

4. 期望行为分级法

该方法被称作"行为锚定等级评价法"(BARS)。它要求评价者选出受评者行为的某些方面,该方面是评估对象在某一工作中的典型表现(Stoner,Freeman & Gilbert,1995)。举例来说,受评估员工的上级主管在"应对压力的能力"范围下,会被要求完成一个表格,以"我期望该员工将按照以下方式展开工作"为开头,然后是评估者必须选择的一份表述清单(如表 9 - 2 所示)。

表 9 - 2 期望行为评估清单举例

表 述	分 数
工作中表现出强烈的创造力	5
工作中表现出创造力	4
工作中表现出普通水平的创造力	3
工作中表现出很少的创造力	2
工作中几乎没有表现出创造力	1

清单中每个表述旁边都有特定的分数,表明该行为的期望程度。给出的案例中,在压力下"工作中表现出创造力"给的分数为 4 分,而"工作中几乎没有表现出创造力"只有 1 分。这些刻度值被认为"固定"与每个表述所代表的典型的员工行为相对应。

该方法相对复杂、消耗时间、较难掌控。可能出现以下特别的难点:

(1) 选择评估行为的类别(称为"绩效维度");

(2) 每个类别给出明确的可接受与不可接受的行为事例;

specific incidents as examples. This method can be used to supplement another appraisal technique, and in that role it has several advantages. It provides the supervisor with specific facts for explaining the appraisal. It ensures that the employee's appraisal reflects his or her behaviour throughout the year not merely his or her most recent performance. Keeping a running list of critical incidents can also provide concrete examples of what an employee can do to eliminate any performance deficiencies.

The critical incident method is often used to supplement a ranking technique. It is useful for identifying specific examples of good and poor performance and for planning how deficiencies can be corrected. Through the collection of direct observations of effective and ineffective job behaviour, the critical incidents method can enhance the evaluation process, especially when used as the basis for behaviourally anchored rating scales. It is not as useful for comparing employees -nor, therefore, for making salary decisions (Stoner, Freeman, & Gilbert, 1995).

4. Behaviour expectation scales method

This approach, referred to as the "Behaviourally Anchored Rating Scale technique" (BARS), requires the appraiser to select an aspect of the appraisee's behaviour that is typical of the appraisee's performance in a certain aspect of a job (Stoner, Freeman, & Gilbert, 1995). For example, the supervisor of an employee being assessed for "ability to cope with stress" would be asked to complete a form that begins with the words, "I would expect this employee to behave in the following way", followed by a list of statements from which the appraiser must choose. A sample list of such statements might be as shown in Table 9 – 2.

Table 9 – 2　A sample list

Items	score
Strongly creativity at work	5
Creativity at work	4
Average creativity at work	3
Less creativity at work	2
Not creativity at all	1

Alongside each item is a score indicating the relative desirability of the behaviour. In the example given above, "Creativity at work" under stress earns a score of 4 points, whereas "Not creativity at all", earns only 1 point. These scale values are said to be "anchored" against the typical employee behaviour that each statement represents.

This approach is complex, time-consuming and difficult to administer. Specific challenges include the following:

(1) selecting the categories of behaviour (called "performance dimensions") for assessment;

(2) providing clear examples of acceptable and unacceptable behaviour within a category; and

（3）决定分配给每个行为事例的具体分数（例如针对描述期望行为的"固定"标准点）。

5. 目标管理法

该方法要求经理人给每位员工制定具体的衡量目标，然后定期和他们讨论关于目标的进展情况（Graham 和 Bennett，1998）。员工可以适当参与目标管理法，联合制定目标，定期提供反馈信息。目标管理法包括以下六个主要步骤（Graham 和 Bennett，1998）。

（1）制定组织目标。建立下一年组织级别的方案和目标。

（2）设立部门目标。部门主管与领导共同设定所属部门的目标。

（3）讨论部门目标。部门主管与全体员工讨论该部门目标任务，要求员工建立起自己的个人目标。换句话说，每名员工如何为实现部门目标做出相应的贡献？目标需要具体，明确表明预期结果，并且具有可测量性、可行性，不会过难或是过容易，且与经理和公司想要达到的目标相契合。最后，目标必须具有时效性，明确截止日期和转折点（Noe，2017）。

（4）定义预期结果。部门主管与员工制定短期绩效指标。

（5）绩效审查以测量结果。部门主管将每位员工的实际绩效与预期进行比较。

（6）给出反馈信息。部门主管保持定期的绩效审查，与员工会面讨论和评估其达到预期结果的进展。

现在只有少数企业在按每一个步骤践行目标管理法，但该方法是十分有用的起点，并确实形成了最新的评估方案。在这个方案中，更着重强调的是实现公司既定目标，而不是活力、合作与进取心这样很难定义的品质。现在很常见的是开放式的评估方法和绩效评估审查。目前，许多组织采用绩效管理方法将绩效评估与奖赏、晋升和培训相结合（Graham 和 Bennett，1998）。例如，高级经理的薪资或奖金会受到他们实现目标与否的影响。这些评估还决定了经理们需要参加怎样的培训和发展项目才能提高工作效能。

管理绩效的问题和争议

评估员工绩效对经理人来说是一项有风险的任务。一般来说员工对自

(3) deciding how many points to allocate to each example of behaviour (i.e. "anchoring" scale points against descriptions of desired behaviour).

5. Management by objectives (MBO) method

This method requires the manager to set specific measurable goals for each employee and then periodically discuss their progress towards these goals (Graham & Bennett, 1998). A modest MBO programme might entail jointly setting goals and periodically providing feedback. The typical MBO method consists of six main steps (Graham & Bennett, 1998).

(1) Set the organisation's goals. Establish an organisation-wide plan for the next year and set goals.

(2) Set departmental goals. Help department heads and their superiors jointly set goals for their departments.

(3) Discuss department goals. Department heads discuss the department's goals with all of the employees in the department and ask them to develop their own individual goal. Specifically, how can each employee contribute to the department's attaining its goals? These goals should be specific and clearly state the desired results. They must be measurable and achievable, and neither too tough nor too easy. They must also be relevant and clearly derive from what the manager and company want to achieve. Finally they must be timely, and reflect deadlines and milestones (Noe, 2017).

(4) Define expected results. Department heads and their employees set short-term performance targets.

(5) Performance reviews to measure the results. Department heads compare the actual performance of each employee to the expected results.

(6) Provide feedback. Department heads hold a periodic performance review meeting with each employee to discuss and evaluate the latter's progress in achieving expected results.

Few companies now practice every step in the MBO method, but it is a useful starting point and has definitely shaped more up-to-date appraisal schemes. In these schemes, the achievement of objectives is emphasised rather than the less definable qualities of energy, cooperation and initiative. Open-ended appraisal methods and performance appraisal interviews are now more common. Currently, many organisations use performance management to integrate performance appraisal with reward, promotion and training schemes (Graham & Bennett, 1998). For example, the salaries or bonuses of senior managers can be influenced by their performance against objectives. These appraisals can also determine what kind of training and development programmes managers need to improve their effectiveness.

Problems and Issues in Managing Performance

Appraising employees' performance is one of the more perilous tasks of a manager.

已得到的评估结果倾向于过度乐观,他们知道他们的加薪、职业进展及平和的心态都取决于评估结果。单是这些期望就使得评估绩效变得有些困难。更严峻的问题是有大量的结构性问题会使人对整个评估过程产生怀疑(Noe,2017)。

1. 应对评定量表绩效管理的五个主要问题

五个主要问题削弱了例如图尺度评价法那样的评估工具的效能:标准不明确、晕轮效应、居中趋势、宽松或严格、偏见。

(1)不明确的绩效标准

一个组织中的不同的主管可能对于如何界定"良好绩效""一般绩效"等有着不同的标准。同样,如"工作质量"或"创造力"这样的特性也很给界定。有诸多方式可以修正这个问题。最好的方式就是用描述性短语来清晰地定义每项标准,并使每个员工都能够了解这些描述。

(2)晕轮效应

晕轮效应指的是在评估某员工的一种特质(例如与他人相处融洽)时会对评价他的其他特质(例如工作能力)产生影响。该问题常常出现在对待上级主管特别友好(或特别不友好)的员工身上。例如,一名态度不友善的员工常常会被评估为所有品质都不令人满意,而不是仅仅在"与他人融洽相处"这一项。意识到该问题的存在就是朝着避免它出现的方向迈了一大步。监管培训是缓解该问题的手段之一。

(3)居中趋势

许多上级主管在填写量化评估表时会表现出居中趋势。例如,若评估量化区间从1到7,他们倾向于避免出现过高的分数(6或7)以及过低的分数(1或2),对下属的评估分数主要集中在3到5。如果使用图尺度评价法,居中趋势则意味着每一个员工都简单地被评定为"平均"。这种趋势会歪曲评估结果,使其对员工晋升、薪资方面都显得缺乏价值。

(4)宽松或严格

一些上级主管倾向于给员工始终很高(或很低)的分数,就像众所周知某些讲师/导师喜欢打高分,还有一些喜欢打低分一样。当上级主管并不被要求必须避免给员工过高或过低评分的时候,过于宽松或严格的问题会显得格外严重。

(5)偏见

由于评估人的偏见,员工个人的特征,例如年龄、种族、性别等,会影响对

Employees tend to overestimate their performance ratings and they know that their pay raises, career progress and peace of mind may hinge on these ratings. These expectations alone make it somewhat difficult to rate performance. Furthermore, there are numerous structural problems that can cast serious doubt on the fairness of the whole process (Noe, 2017).

1. Dealing with the five main rating scale performance management problems

Five main problems can undermine appraisal tools such as graphic rating scales: unclear standards, the halo effect, central tendency, leniency or strictness, and bias.

(1) Unclear performance standards

Different supervisors in the same organisation probably define "good" performance, "fair" performance and so on, differently. The same is true of traits such as "quality of work" or "creativity". There are several ways to rectify this problem. The best way is to develop and include descriptive phrases that define each standard clearly and make these descriptions available to all employees.

(2) Halo effect

The halo effect occurs when the rating of an employee on one trait (e.g. gets along with others) biases the way that person is rated on other traits (e.g. quantity of work). This problem often occurs with employees who are especially friendly (or unfriendly) towards a supervisor. For example, an unfriendly employee will often be rated unsatisfactory for all traits rather than just for the trait "gets along well with others". Being aware of this problem is a major step towards avoiding it. Supervisory training can also alleviate the problem.

(3) Central tendency

Many supervisors have a central tendency when filling in rating scales. For example, if the rating scale ranges from 1 to 7, they tend to avoid the highs (6 and 7) and lows (1 and 2) and rate most of their subordinates between 3 and 5. When a graphic rating scale is used, this central tendency means that every employee is simply rated "average". Such a tendency can distort evaluations, making them less useful for promotion, salary or counselling purposes.

(4) Leniency or strictness

Some supervisors tend to rate all of their employees consistently high (or low), just as some lecturers/tutors are notoriously high graders and others are not. This strictness/leniency problem is especially serious as supervisors are not necessarily required to avoid giving every employee a high (or low) rating. In systems that use ranking, supervisors must distinguish between high and low performers. Thus, strictness/leniency is not a problem with the ranking or forced distribution approaches.

(5) Bias

Characteristics such as age, race and sex can affect an employee's rating because of

其的评估。研究表明性别歧视在针对成功的女性经理人的绩效评估中存在，这意味着成功的男性经理人得到的评分高于成功的女性经理人。歧视会导致高额的诉讼费并损害组织的声誉。为了避免这些问题，高级经理人应当监控其绩效评估系统，以确保不会出现例如性别歧视或是其他歧视性偏见。

2. 规避绩效管理的问题

有许多方式可以将绩效管理问题的影响最小化，例如偏见歧视问题和居中趋势问题（Noe，2017）。

（1）确保让上级主管受到以上讨论过的问题的警示。明白问题所在可以帮助上级主管避免问题出现。

（2）选择正确的评估方式。每个方式，例如关键事件法、排序法，都有着各自的优势及劣势。例如，排序方法可以避免居中趋势，但当员工绩效确实都一样时，可能引起反感情绪。

（3）培训上级主管减少像晕轮效应、宽松、居中趋势这样的评估差错，可以帮助他们避免问题。

应当由谁进行评估

绩效评估应当公正、客观。不公正的评估会削弱员工的信心和士气，员工甚至可能针对公司提出法律诉讼。那么，应当由谁来进行评估呢？（Dessler，2017）

1. 由直属上司或经理进行评估

上司或经理人的评估依旧是整个评估体系的核心。上司通常应当站在观察及评估员工绩效的最佳位置，对他们的绩效表现负责任。大部分组织中一线经理人负责每天的管理活动，包括绩效管理。

2. 同级评估

由该员工的同级进行评估，可以有效预测未来管理的成功与否。越来越多的公司在使用自我管理团队方法，同级或团队评估开始流行起来。

bias in the appraiser. Research suggests that a gender-based bias exists against successful women managers in performance evaluations; this means successful male managers are evaluated higher relative to successful women managers. Discrimination results in high legal costs and damages the reputation of the organisation. To avoid these problems, senior management should monitor their performance appraisal systems to ensure that they do not exhibit such gender-related or other discriminatory biases.

2. Avoiding performance management problems

There are many ways to minimise the effect of performance management problems such as bias and central tendency (Noe, 2017).

(1) Be sure supervisors are aware of the problems discussed above. Understanding the problem can help supervisors to avoid it.

(2) Choose the right appraisal tool. Each tool, such as the critical incident method or ranking, has its own advantages and disadvantages. For example, the ranking method avoids the central tendency but can cause ill-feeling when employees' performances are in fact all equal.

(3) Training supervisors to eliminate rating errors such as the halo effect, leniency and central tendency can help them to avoid these problems. Training programmes may involve raters being shown a videotape of jobs being performed and then asking them to rate the workers' performance. The ratings made by each participant are then placed on a flipchart and the various errors are explained.

Who Should Do the Appraising?

Fair and objective performance management is important. Unfair appraisals can lead to legal action against an organisation and can undermine employees' confidence and morale (Dessler, 2017).

1. Appraisal by the immediate supervisor or manager

Supervisors' (or managers') ratings are still the heart of most appraisal systems. The supervisor should be—and usually is—in the best position to observe and evaluate employees' performance and is responsible for their performance. In most organisations, the line mangers are responsible for day-to-day people management activities, including performance management.

2. Peer appraisals

The appraisal of an employee by his or her peers can be effective in predicting future management success. With more firms using self-managing teams, peer or team appraisals are becoming more popular.

3. 自我评定

有时会要求员工对自己的表现进行自我评定（通常与上级评估结合起来）。自我评定的问题是，通常员工评价自己的结果都高于上司或同级评价的结果。要求使用自我评估方式的上级主管应当清楚他们的评估结果与自我评估结果可能会导致评估差异和立场僵化。即使没有被正式要求进行自我评估，员工在进入绩效考核时也会考虑到自己的自我评估，而结果通常会比上级的评价结果要高。

4. 由下属进行评估

现今越来越多的公司让员工对上级的绩效进行不记名评估，该过程可以收集反馈信息。当该方法在全公司展开时，这一过程能帮助顶层经理人诊断公司的管理风格、识别潜在的"人"方面的问题，需要时对个别经理人采取纠正措施。当被用于发展而不是单纯评估的目的时，这样的员工评估特别有价值。然而，员工觉得给出匿名的反馈信息更舒服，在评价自己时倾向于给出较夸张的评价。

5. 360 度（或多源）评估

用这个方法评估时，关于员工表现的信息会向上司、下属、同事、内部或外部客户收集（Noe，2017）。该反馈一般用来进行培训、发展，而不是用在薪资提升上。多来源员工绩效反馈信息相比于那些只由员工上司做出的评估，会提供一份更加深入全面的个人评估结果。

提供考核面试的反馈信息

考核面试是一场正式的谈话，期间上司主管与员工回顾审查员工的绩效，并制订计划以弥补不足、增强优势。首先，上司要让员工明白他现在工作得如何，并提出一个改进工作绩效的计划。其次，上级向员工展示审核结果，员工有机会对此做出回应，表达个人观点（Dessler，2017）。于是，上级主管

3. Self-ratings

Employees are sometimes asked to rate their own performance (usually in conjunction with a supervisors' rating). The problem with self-ratings is that employees usually rate themselves higher than they are rated by supervisors or peers. Supervisors requesting self-appraisals should know that their appraisals and the self-appraisals may accentuate appraiser-appraisee differences and harden positions. Even if self-appraisals are not formally requested, employees will enter the performance review meeting with their own self-appraisal in mind, and this will usually be higher than the supervisor's rating.

4. Appraisal by subordinate

More firms today let employees anonymously evaluate their supervisors' performance, a process many call upward feedback. When conducted throughout the firm, the process helps top managers to diagnose management styles, identify potential "people" problems and take corrective action with individual managers as required. Such employee ratings are especially valuable when used for developmental rather than evaluative purposes. Managers who receive feedback from employees who identify themselves view the upward appraisal process more positively than managers who receive anonymous feedback; however, employees are more comfortable giving anonymous responses, and those who have to identify themselves tend to provide inflated ratings.

5. 360 degree (or multi-source) appraisal

In this approach, performance information is collected "all around" an employee, from supervisors, employees, peers and internal or external customers. The feedback is generally used for training and development, rather than for pay raises. Most 360-degree feedback systems share several common features. Appropriate parties who are familiar with the employee being appraised and who understand the individual's job—peers, supervisors, employees and customers, for instance—anonymously complete survey questionnaires on an individual. Multiple sources of feedback on an employee's performance provide a more comprehensive evaluation of the individual than that of the employee's supervisor alone.

Providing Feedback in the Appraisal Interview

An appraisal interview is a formal discussion in which the supervisor and employee review the employee's performance and make plans to remedy deficiencies and reinforce strengths. First, the supervisor lets the employee know how he or she is doing and suggests a plan for improved job performance. Second, the supervisor presents the review results to the employee and the employee has an opportunity to respond to the review and present his or her own views (Dessler, 2017). A conclusion is reached between the

与员工间针对未来发展计划能够达成一个结论。

为了准备该面试,上级主管首先需要汇总数据,研究工作描述、对比员工实际绩效与职位标准、翻阅员工过去的评估结果档案。下一步,上级主管需要准备向员工解释说明如何为面对面考核做准备。给员工至少一周的时间来回顾他们的工作成果、仔细阅读他们的工作描述、分析问题、汇集员工们的问题及评论。最后,找到一个双方都适合的时间进行面试,并给整个面试留出足够充裕的时间。

在面试中,上级主管有四个注意事项需要牢记(Graham 和 Bennett,1998)。

(1)直接且具体。以客观数据说话。例如缺席率、质量记录、审查报告、生产率记录、出错率、顾客意见及其他客观信息。

(2)不能进行人身攻击。不能说"你写报告的速度太慢了"。相反地,试着将个人绩效与规范标准进行比较:"这些报告通常应该在十天内完成。"同样地,不要把员工表现与他人相比,例如"他效率比你快多了"。

(3)鼓励员工畅所欲言。主动倾听,询问开放式的问题,例如"你认为我们怎么做才能改善现在的状况?"使用命令句,如"请再说得详细一点"。将对方的上一个观点转述成问题:"你不认为自己可以完成这个工作吗?"

(4)不要聚焦在和表现评估面试无关的话题上。不要掺杂个人因素,但要确保员工离开时明白自己哪些行为是正确的,哪些不是。给出具体的例子;确保员工理解清楚,在员工离开之前就怎样以及何时才能有所改进达成一致。

案例分析 9 − 1[①] ▶▶▶▶▶▶

Peter Chan 是一家餐厅的总经理,这家餐厅隶属于一个大型全国连锁品牌。部门经理必须在 3 月份展开对每名职员的绩效评估,以便赶上该餐厅 5 月份的年度财务结算,及时给受奖励的员工加薪。Peter 和他的区经理 Jason Wu 针对每个员工的审查进行讨论,然后 Peter 需要与每个员工就其绩效评估结果,展开一对一谈话。按照预期,Peter 需要在 4 月份完成一对一评估反馈会面。这些会面的目的是向每位员工提供详细具体的绩效反馈信息,同时指出在绩效方面需要改进的地方。

同一部门级别的所有员工会使用统一的标准表格进行评估,这个表格由

---

① 资料来源:Sommerville, K.(2007). *Hospitality Employee Management and Supervision*: *Concepts and Practical Applications*.257 − 258, Hoboken, NJ: John Wiley & Sons.

supervisor and employee along with a plan for future development.

To prepare for the interview, the supervisor should first assemble the data, study the job description, compare the employee's performance with the standards and review the employee's previous appraisals. Next, the supervisor should prepare the employee by explaining to him or her how to prepare for a face-to-face interview. Employees should have at least a week's notice to review their work, read over their job description, analyse problems and gather their questions and comments. Finally, find a mutually agreeable time for the interview and allow enough time for a full discussion.

There are four things a supervisor should remember when conducting an interview (Graham & Bennett, 1998).

(1) Be direct and specific. Talk in terms of objective work data. Use examples such as absences, quality records, inspection reports, productivity records, number of errors, customers' comments and other objective information.

(2) Do not become personal. Do not say, "You are too slow in producing those reports". Instead, try to compare the person's performance with a standard: "These reports are normally done within ten days". Similarly, do not compare the employee's performance to that of others e.g. "He's quicker than you are".

(3) Encourage the person to talk. Listen to what the employee is saying; ask open-ended questions such as "What do you think we can do to improve the situation?" Use a command such as, "Tell me more". Restate the person's last point as a question: "You don't think you can get the job done?"

(4) Do not tiptoe around. Do not be personal, but do make sure the employee leaves knowing specifically what he or she is doing right and doing wrong. Give specific examples, make sure the person understands; and get agreement before he or she leaves on how things will be improved, and by when.

Case Study 9 – 1[①] ▶▶▶▶▶▶

Peter Chan is the general manager of a restaurant that belongs to a large, national chain. Unit managers are required to conduct a performance appraisal on every employee during the month of March, in time to recommend employee pay raises that are awarded at the end of the restaurant's fiscal year in May. Peter and his district manager Jason Wu discuss each employee's review, and then Peter is required to sit down with each employee to go over the employee performance appraisal. Peter is expected to have these one-on-one appraisal feedback meetings in April. The goal of these meetings is to provide each employee with specific feedback about performance and to address areas of performance that need improvement.

All of the employees at the unit level are evaluated using a standard form provided by the

① Source: Sommerville, K.(2007). *Hospitality Employee Management and Supervision: Concepts and Practical Applications*.257 – 258, Hoboken, NJ: John Wiley & Sons.

连锁品牌提供。表格包括评定标准;工作知识和技能储备;工作的质量及任务量;整齐度与准时率;遵守公司规章制度、工作态度、团队合作、与同事合作程度;主动性和随机应变能力。

Peter并不是很在乎他管理工作中的这个方面,因为他不喜欢面对偶尔出现的员工对评估结果有分歧的情况。同时,他认为很难保持客观。去年评估结束后,区域经理质疑Peter说:"每一年你的餐厅收到的顾客评价大量都是中等,但你给每个职员各个方面的评定都很高。我们可能需要重新审视一下你的评估过程了。"Peter清楚自己需要在对自己的员工进行评估方面有所改善,否则他自己的职位就可能会失去。

问 题

（1）为了使餐厅绩效评估体系更高效,Peter可以做些什么呢? 如果做出一些变化,员工们会获得哪些益处?

（2）如果Peter决定改变评估员工绩效的系统及方法,他可能会遇到什么问题?

（3）从现有的体系中员工是受益的还是不受益的? 请解释你的答案,并给出具体理由支持你的观点。

（4）在现有体系中,餐厅是否存在法律问题? 请给出详细解释。

案例分析 9-2 [①] ▶▶▶▶▶▶

Sandy正坐在她老板的办公室外等待自己第一次的评估面试。她有点紧张,却很自信。从三个月前到岗至今,也就是从她第一天在餐厅工作摔掉了整个托盘至今,她进步非常大。老板不再盯着她不放,不再告诫她这个不能做那个不能做,所以她觉得自己一切都做得很好。她和顾客相处得很好,事实上,有时候会有顾客特别要求由她服务。她的小费金额比其他大多数员工都高,这对她来说意义非凡。

门开了,老板招呼她进来坐下。"早上好,Sandy,"他说,"我们的时间有点紧,所以我们与你快速地过一遍评估表格。Sandy,请仔细读一遍,可以吗? 然后我们再来讨论。"Sandy扫了一下评分:平均、平均、平均,有待进步,好,她得承认自己在开红酒方面还有些问题,有时会弄坏瓶塞,平均、平均、平均。她叹了一口气,把表格递回给老板,坐回椅子上,紧握双手,低着头。

---

national chain. The form includes the following evaluation criteria: skills and job knowledge; quality and quantity of work; neatness and punctuality; adhering to company rules and procedures; attitude, teamwork and cooperation with coworkers; and initiative and resourcefulness.

Peter does not really care for this aspect of his job because he dislikes the confrontations that sometimes occur when an employee disagrees with the evaluation. Also, he feels it is hard to be objective. After last year's evaluations, the district manager questioned Peter and said, "Your restaurant gets a lot of average to mediocre customer comment cards each year, yet you rate each employee very high in practically every area when you evaluate them. We may need to take a look at your evaluation process." Peter knows that he needs to do a better job of evaluating his employees or his own job could be on the line.

Questions

(1) What could Peter do to make the performance appraisal system in his restaurant more effective? How will the employees benefit if changes are made?

(2) What problems might Peter encounter if he does decide to change the methods and rating system he uses when evaluating his employees?

(3) Are the employees benefiting or not benefiting from the system that is currently in place? Please explain your answer and give specific reasons for your opinion.

(4) Are there any legal issues that may present a problem for the restaurant based on the current system? Please explain in detail.

Case Study 9 – 2[①] ▶▶▶▶▶

Sandy is sitting outside her boss's office awaiting her first appraisal interview. She is nervous, but confident. She has improved tremendously since she dropped that whole tray of dinners when she first came to work three months ago. Her boss has stopped coming around and telling her not to do this and that, so she thinks that she is doing all right. She gets along very well with the guests; in fact, sometimes people ask to be seated at her tables. Her tips are higher than almost anyone else's and that must mean something.

The door opens and her boss motions her to come in and sit down. "Good morning, Sandy," he says. "We're a little bit rushed for time, so I'll just go through this evaluation form with you, Sandy. Read it over, won't you? Then we'll talk." Sandy glances through the ratings: Average, Average, Average, Needs improvement—Well, she has to admit she still has trouble opening wine bottles and sometimes breaks the cork. Average, Average, Average. She sighs, hands the form back to her boss, sits back in her chair, folds her hands tightly and looks down at them.

---

① Source: Walker, J., & Miller, J. (2009). *Supervision in the Hospitality Industry: Leading Human Resonrces*. Hoboken, NJ: John Wiley and Sons.

"你觉得怎么样,Sandy? 同意上面的说法吗? 我们需要制订一个计划来提高你在红酒服务方面的能力。我知道你有时候会请 Charlie 帮你开瓶,这并不是真正的好的客户服务。不妨让 Charlie 给你一些相关的建议,告诉你哪里做得不对。这样,可能下次你会得到好点的评分。对此你有什么问题或者想法吗?"

"'平均'代表什么?" Sandy 问道。

"嗯,我想它代表着和其他人相比,不好也不坏。实际上这表示你做得还可以,只是没有 John 和 Charlie 那么好。但是你肯定不用担心因此而丢了饭碗。你没问题的! 还有其他的吗?"

"哦……"Sandy 鼓起勇气,"我觉得自己不只是平均的水平,顾客会要求我来服务他们,我收到很多小费,所以一定是……"

"但你别忘了那次摔盘子的事情,Sandy! 我的确觉得现在你做得好多了,但我们说的是整个评估周期内的表现! 现在请你在这里签字……"

问 题

(1) 你认为老板给出的评分以及对此给出的解释如何?

(2) 你觉得 Sandy 会有怎样的感受? 她会因此受到鼓舞而有所提高吗? 你觉得知道自己不会丢掉工作足够了吗?

(3) 请列举出在评估面试中老板的错误。他要怎样才能处理得更好?

(4) 你认为老板提出的改进方案如何? Charlie 对此会有什么感受?

(5) 如果老板的上级领导听说了这次评估面试的内容,对此会有怎样的看法? 对于处理评估面试的方式,老板的上级负有哪些责任? 在评估面试中,可以设立哪些方式去评估上级领导?

案例分析 9-3[①] ▶▶▶▶▶▶

Hugo 的餐厅过去 12 个月以来员工流失率达到了 220%。这意味着每来一个人到餐厅工作就有 2 个人离开。Hugo 并不清楚造成该现象的具体原因,但他知道必须做出些改变。他雇用的经理 Joe 有着出色的推荐背景,但工作成果并不像 Hugo 预期的那样。许多老员工抱怨 Joe 在安排值班时有偏心,把小费最多的领班安排给他喜欢的人。

周六的晚上简直就是一场灾难——餐厅人满为患,还有很多人在等候,

---

① 资料来源:Walker, J., & Miller, J.(2009).*Supervision in the Hospitality Industry:Leading Human Resonrces*.Hoboken, NJ: John Wiley & Sons.

"Well，what do you think，Sandy? Do you agree? We need to make a plan for your improvement on wine service. I know you sometimes ask Charlie to open your bottles and that's not really what good customer service is all about. Why don't you get Charlie to give you some tips on what you're doing wrong? Then maybe next time you'll get a better rating. Now do you have any comments or questions?"

"What's average?" Sandy asks.

"Well，I guess it means no better and no worse than anyone else. Actually，it means you're doing okay，you're just not as good as John and Charlie. But you certainly don't need to worry about losing your job or anything like that—you're all set here! Anything else?"

"Well，" Sandy begins，gathering up her courage，"I thought I was really above average in customer service—people ask for me and they tip me a lot，so I must be..."

"But don't forget the time you dropped the dishes，Sandy! I do think you're doing very well indeed now，but we're talking about the whole evaluation period! Now，if you'll just sign this..."

Questions

(1) What do you think of the boss's ratings and his defence of them?

(2) How do you think Sandy feels? Will she be motivated to improve? Is it enough to know you are not going to lose your job?

(3) List the mistakes the boss makes in this interview. How could he have handled things better?

(4) What do you think of the boss's improvement plan? How will Charlie feel about it?

(5) If the boss's supervisor could have heard this interview，what would have been the supervisor's opinion of it? What responsibility does the boss's supervisor have for the way that interviews are handled? What means could be set up for evaluating supervisors on their interview?

Case Study 9 – 3[①] ▶▶▶▶▶

Labour turnover for the past 12 months at Hugo's restaurant has been 220 per cent. For every person who came to work at the restaurant，two others left. Hugo has no idea of the exact cost of this turnover，but he knows that some things have to change. The manager he has hired，Joe，had excellent references，but he has not worked out as Hugo hoped. Many of the older employees complain that Joe shows favouritism in scheduling，giving the better-tipping shifts to people he likes.

Saturday night is an absolute disaster—the restaurant is full，with a wait list，food is

---

① Source：Walker，J.，& Miller，J.(2009).*Supervision in the Hospitality Industry: Leading Human Resonrces*.Hoboken，NJ: John Wiley & Sons.

上菜的速度很慢,整个服务显得杂乱无章。服务生看上去像在餐厅里无秩序地走来走去,没有任何方向和定位。新进的员工本该向老员工们及顾客学习。但一切看起来就像是没有人真正明确需要做什么,什么时间该做,由谁来负责。

如此混乱的场面带来的是顾客的抱怨,以及顾客总数较去年同时期的下降。Hugo 请求你,以咨询师的角度,给出具体可实施的建议,如何才能让该餐厅获得成功。

问 题

请你给出 10 条建议。

案例分析 9-4① ▷▷▷▷▷▷

Ron Cheung 是一名受聘于美国东部一家大型企业的"职业神秘顾客"。该企业向美国及加拿大酒店和餐厅提供"顾客观察报告"。Ron 刚刚接到了公司调度人员的电话,同意他前往一家在他家乡附近新开的餐厅,完成"酒吧报告"。该餐厅属于一家快速发展的连锁餐厅,其定位于中高档牛排餐厅市场。

Ron 在该餐厅的酒吧需要停留 60 到 90 分钟时间,他要点酒水和开胃菜,在整个过程中要观察餐厅调酒师对酒品的掌握程度、潜在的偷窃问题、倒酒和量酒技术、一般性吧台维护和顾客服务。在完成报告后,Ron 将向公司发送邮件,报告将会被审阅、重新编辑成公司的统一格式,然后通过快递的方式交给餐厅的区域经理。Ron 对待这份工作十分认真,他了解自己报告中的信息很可能会影响到某个员工的去留。在不止一个场合中他报告过某餐厅不诚实的行为,结果一个调酒师被解聘,却发现同一个调酒师在几公里外的其他餐厅服务。"难道从没有人检查过介绍信吗?"他常常这么问自己。

当 Ron 到达他被派去的那家餐厅时,他得到了深刻的印象:由石头搭建的十分美丽的小溪;宽阔的平台俯视着小溪;柔和的灯光;每张餐桌都配有精美的瓷器和器皿,恰当地摆在挺括的白色餐布之上。他注意到,这里的顾客无疑都十分优雅,餐厅侍者和接待人员在宽敞的餐厅里快乐地忙碌着,招待已入座的客人和新到客人。"晚上好,先生,"侍者对着 Ron 说,"给您安排一

① 资料来源:Sommerville, K.(2007). *Hospitality Employee Management and Supervision*: *Concepts and Practical Applications*.306-308, Hoboken, NJ: John Wiley & Sons.

slow in coming out of the kitchen and the service seems to be disorganised. Servers seem to be wandering about the restaurant without any direction or station being allocated to them. New staff members are expected to learn what to do from existing servers and buyers. It seems as if no one has really determined what needs to be done, when it needs doing and who should do it.

The resulting chaos means that guests are complaining, and guest counts are down over the same period last year. Hugo has asked you, as a consultant, to make specific recommendations advising him what needs to be done to make the restaurant successful.

Question

What are your top 10 recommendations?

Case Study 9 – 4[①] ▶▶▶ ▶▶▶

Ron Cheung is a professional mystery shopper employed by a large East Coast company that provides "shopper-spotter reports" for hotels and restaurants throughout the United States and Canada. Ron has just got off the phone with the company's dispatcher, and he has agreed to complete a "bar report" at a new restaurant that recently opened near his hometown. The restaurant belongs to a fast-growing dinner chain that typically targets the mid- to upscale-steakhouse market.

Ron's visit to the restaurant includes 60 to 90 minutes at the bar, where he will order drinks and an appetizer and observe the restaurant's bartenders for alcohol awareness issues, potential theft, pouring and measuring techniques, general bar maintenance and customer service. After completing his report, Ron emails it to his home office, where it is reviewed, retyped in proper company format and sent to the restaurant chain's regional manager via overnight express mail. Ron takes his job seriously, and he realises that the information contained in his reports could possible cost an employee his or her job. On more than one occasion he has reported dishonest activity at a restaurant, which most likely resulted in a bartender's dismissal, only to discover the same bartender serving at a different restaurant a few miles away. "Doesn't anyone ever check references anymore?" he often wonders to himself.

As Ron arrives at the restaurant he has been assigned to visit, he is impressed: beautiful creek stone; a large, sweeping deck overlooking the river; warm lighting; and each table is set with what appears to be nice china and stemware, all perfectly placed on starched, white tablecloths. The clientele is decidedly upscale, he notes, and the wait-staff and greeters are cheerily bustling around the spacious dining room, tending to seated guests as well as new

---

① Source: Sommerville, K.(2007). *Hospitality Employee Management and Supervision: Concepts and Practical Applications.* 306 – 308, Hoboken, NJ: John Wiley & Sons.

张一人桌?"

"谢谢,不,"Ron 回答道。"我要在吧台会见一位朋友。"

"好的,这边请。"侍者答道。

Ron 来到了大厅,设法拉开了最后一个空着的高脚凳,它靠近吧台的正中央。"很好,"Ron 自言自语道,"我可以观察到吧台两边的情况,收银员就在我正前方,我能观察到这里的所有举动。"吧台有些忙碌,Ron 注意到有两位调酒师在工作:一位是高个子的金发男性,名牌上写着"Luke";另一位是个子矮小粗壮,有着深色头发的男性,名叫"Josh"。就在 Ron 等待其中一位向他走来时,他在脑海中记录下了整个酒吧的情况:吧台尽头堆放着很多脏玻璃杯;一些烟灰缸需要清空及清洁;有几个客人正试图引起调酒师的注意;一些侍者站在服务区的位置,很明显在等待他们的酒水订单制作完成。Josh 和 Luke 好像在忙于聊天,没人在意手头上的工作。

很快,Luke 走向 Ron 问道:"您今晚想要喝点什么?"

Ron 想了一下回答说:"嗯,我想,来杯波本吧。你都有哪些好的波本?"

"差不多通常的几种,"Luke 有点生硬地回答道。"火鸡波本、占边波本、老菲茨波旁威士忌、杰克绅士、威士忌,我总是这么说。"

"你们有伍德福威士忌吗?"Ron 问。

"8 美元一杯。"Luke 答道。

"好吧,"Ron 回答说,"加冰块,配一杯冰水,还有一小块青柠。"

Ron 看着 Luke 在玻璃杯中添了冰块,从吧台底部拿起一瓶波本,背对着 Ron,将波本倒入杯中,再将波本瓶放回吧台底部。在他将酒杯放在 Ron 面前时,他说:"8 美元。"

Ron 掏出了一张 20 元面值的钱放在了吧台上,然后问道:"男士卫生间在哪里?"

Luke 指向吧台的尽头说:"穿过那里,在你的左手边。"Ron 朝门口走去,但突然停下来,转过身,观察到 Luke 将 20 元钱放到自己的口袋里。然后他从现金收银机旁的一小堆纸币中拿走了几张,放在 Ron 的座位上。当 Ron 返回他的座位时,Luke 说:"喂,这是找你的零钱。谢谢。"

在剩下的全部时间里,Ron 观察到 Luke 给不同的顾客制作了 20～30 杯鸡尾酒。有时候 Luke 拉开收银机收钱,有时他迅速地转过身来背对顾客,把钱塞进自己的腰包,并从收银机旁边的一小堆钱中找零。Ron 还发现 Luke 不总是用量杯倒酒;有时他很随意地把酒倒进杯子里,有一次他看到 Luke 自己喝了一杯酒,好像是一杯龙舌兰。

Ron 还发现 Luke 似乎和坐在酒吧尽头的一位老先生很亲近,有三次,

arrivals. "Good evening，sir，" the host says to Ron. "Table for one?"

"Thank you，no，" replies Ron. "I'm just going to meet a friend in the bar．"

"Very good，" says the host，"right this way."

Ron arrives in the lounge and manages to grab the last open stool，which is positioned near the centre of the bar. "Good"，he thinks to himself. "I have a great view of both sides of the bar，and the cash register is straight ahead of me；I'll be able to observe all of the action." The bar is busy，and Ron notes that there are two bartenders working：one，a tall，blond male has a name tag that reads "Luke，" and the other，a stockier，dark-haired male，has a name tag that reads "Josh." As Ron waits for one of the bartenders to approach him，he makes mental notes about the overall condition of the bar：lots of dirty glasses stacked on the bar near the end；some ashtrays need to be emptied and cleaned；a few guests trying to get the bartenders' attention；and several wait-staff near the service area，apparently waiting for their drink orders to be filled. Both Josh and Luke appear to be engaged in conversation，neither of them making any concerted effort to tend to the business at hand.

Soon，Luke approaches Ron and says，"What can I get you tonight?"

Ron appears to think for a moment and says，"Oh，I think I'm in a bourbon mood. What kind of nice bourbons do you have?"

"Pretty much the usual，" Luke responds somewhat abruptly. "Turkey，Beam，Old Fitz，Gentleman Jack；whiskey's whiskey，I always say."

"Do you have Woodford Reserve?" asks Ron.

"It's $8 a shot，" says Luke.

"That's fine，" Ron replies. "On the rocks with a side of ice water and a wedge of lime please."

Ron watches as Luke fills a rocks glass with ice，removes a bottle from underneath the bar，and with his back to Ron，pours the bourbon into the glass then replaces the bourbon bottle underneath the bar. As he sets the glass in front of Ron，he says，"That'll be eight bucks."

Ron places a $20 bill on the bar and asks Luke，"Where's the men's room?"

Luke waves toward the end of the bar and says，"Right through there on your left." Ron walks toward the doorway but pauses momentarily，turns around，and observes Luke putting the $20 bill in his pocket. He then removes some bills from a small pile he has lying next to the cash register and places them at Ron's seat. When Ron returns to his stool，Luke says，"There's your change，man. Thanks."

Throughout the rest of his visit，Ron observes Luke make 20 to 30 cocktails for various customers. Sometimes，Luke rings the sale into the register，and sometimes he quickly turns with his back to the customers，pockets the money and makes change from the small pile lying next to the register. Ron also observes that Luke does not always use the jigger for measuring；sometimes he freely pours the alcohol into the glass，and on one occasion he observes Luke drinking a shot of what appears to be tequila.

Ron also observes that Luke seems to be pretty chummy with an older gentleman sitting

他看到 Luke 给老先生添酒,没有通知服务员,也没有加到吧台上放在他前面的顾客的账单中。那个顾客好像有些醉了,因为他开始大声讲话,笑个不停,面色泛红。Ron 看到那个顾客起身,摇摇晃晃地向洗手间走去。"哇,小心点,Johnson 先生。"一位很礼貌的服务员说道,他扶着客人的胳膊直到他稳住自己。

"他没事的,Eric,"Luke 对服务员说,"Johnson 有酒量。他还能再来两三杯呢!"

Ron 快喝完第二杯酒时,他注意了一下手表上的时间。他在吧台已经超过 80 分钟了,他认为已经有足够信息完成报告了。他向 Luke 表示感谢,然后离开吧台,一出门他就奔向他的车。"我需要今晚就上交这份报告,"他对自己说。他一边启动车,一边打开手机,打电话给公司的调度人员。"Sheila,"他说,"大概一小时后我会写一封'红色标记'的邮件给你,你可能需要派人过去,这样你就可以把这份报告在今晚就送出去。"

问　题

(1) 请列出并讨论 Ron 观察到的该酒吧所有潜在的问题。Ron 观察到的这些违规的行为有多严重?是否有某些行为严重到需要立刻给予警告?请具体指出是哪些行为。

(2) 当餐厅管理层收到 Ron 的报告时,你认为他会有哪些反应?为什么?你觉得管理层应该给予 Luke 一定的惩罚吗?若需要,他们应该如何进行?应当将 Ron 报告的内容分享给 Luke 吗?为什么,或为什么不?

(3) 如果管理层依据"神秘顾客"的报告决定解雇 Luke,需要给予"神秘顾客公司"哪些承诺呢?为什么?

(4) 依据本次案例分析中 Ron 的行为举止,他是值得信赖的人吗?他给出的报告是可靠的吗?请给出解释。一名成功的"神秘顾客"应当具备哪些独特的技能和个性?

at the end of the bar, and on three occasions he observes Luke refilling the gentleman's drink without ringing up a sale or adding the drinks to the gentleman's tab, which is lying on the bar in front of him. The customer seems to be somewhat inebriated, as he begins to speak loudly and laugh a lot, and his face is flushed. Ron watches the guest get up and begin to stagger toward the men's room. "Whoa, easy there, Mr Johnson," a friendly server says, and he takes the guest's arm until he steadies himself.

"He'll be fine, Eric," Luke says to the server. "Johnson can hold his liquor. He's probably good for another two or three rounds yet."

As Ron finishes his second drink, he notes the time on his watch. He has been at the bar more than 80 minutes, and he knows he has enough information to complete his report. He thanks Luke as he leaves the bar, and once outside, he sprints toward his car. "I need to turn this report around tonight," he says to himself. As he starts his car, he flips open his cell phone and calls his dispatcher at the home office. "Sheila," he says when the dispatcher answers, "I've got a 'red flag' coming to you via email in about an hour; you may want to get someone in there so that you can turn this report around and ship it out tonight."

Questions

(1) List and discuss all of the potential problems that Ron observed during his visit to the bar. How serious are the infractions observed by Ron? Are any of the infractions serious enough to warrant immediate termination? Be specific.

(2) When management receives Ron's report, what do you think the reaction will be? Why? Do you feel that management should discipline Luke? If so, how exactly should they approach him? Should the contents of Ron's report be shared with Luke? Why or why not?

(3) If management decides to terminate Luke's employment based on the contents of the mystery shopper's report, what assurances are needed from the mystery shopper company? Why?

(4) Based on Ron's behaviour in this case study, does he appear to be someone who is reliable and someone whose reports are reliable? Explain. What special skills and characteristics should a successful mystery shopper possess?

第 10 章　薪酬与员工福利

📖 **学习目标**

■ 了解什么是组织的薪酬和福利

■ 介绍不同类型的薪酬制度及其特点

■ 通过在中国环境下的案例研究介绍以能力为基础的薪酬制度的重要性

薪酬体系是管理中最重要、最具挑战性的人力资源职能之一,因为其涵盖了各项因素,对组织机构的战略目标有着深远影响。薪酬是公司向员工提供的所有奖赏的总和,来换取员工对企业的付出和服务(Hon,2012)。一个好的薪酬体系必须能吸引、保留、激励员工。薪酬体系包括经济报酬和非经济报酬两部分。经济报酬以工资、薪水、佣金、奖金的形式发放给个人。非经济报酬包括员工从工作本身或者从工作所处的组织环境中得到的体验和满足。非经济报酬涵盖了公司工作环境的心理层面和物质层面的因素,例如工作自主性、信息反馈、领导风格、互助型同事、工作环境等(Hon 和 Lu,2015; Leung、Wang 和 Hon,2011)。

在大多数薪酬方案中,通常使用工作评估来决定该职位的价值,以及依据个人在该职位的表现程度在该职务报酬范围内决定其薪资幅度。另一个相对较新的薪酬方向是依据个人的能力或特征,而不是职位本身来决定薪酬。其逻辑依据的一部分是为了更好地参与市场竞争,组织本身需要具有灵活性。因此,建立起能够鼓励个人发展对组织具有战略意义的知识、技能和能力的薪资体系,具有重要意义。两种新兴的薪资方法即为技能薪酬与能力薪酬。

技能薪酬

技能薪酬(skill-based pay,SBP)涉及员工相关技能的宽度与深度,这是

Chapter 10　Compensation and Employee Benefits

The objectives of this chapter

- Understand what are organizational compensation and benefits
- Examine different types of compensation methods and their characteristics
- Introduce the importance of competency-base pay through research findings in Chinese context and case studies

Compensation is one of management's most important and challenging HR functions because it contains many elements and has a far-reaching effect on an organisation's strategic goals. Compensation packages include all of the rewards provided to employees in return for their efforts and services (Hon, 2012). A strong compensation system is needed to attract, retain and motivate employees. Compensation systems include financial compensation and non-financial compensation. Financial compensation consists of the pay that a person receives in the form of wages, salaries, commissions and bonuses. Non-financial compensation includes the satisfaction that a person receives from the job itself or from the psychological or physical environment in which the person works. Non-financial compensation involves both psychological and physical factors such as task autonomy, feedback, capable managers, supportive co-workers, working conditions, etc (Hon & Lu, 2015; Leung, Wang, & Hon, 2011).

In most compensation schemes, job evaluation is used to determine the relative value of the job, and then individual job holders are paid a salary within the job's pay range based on how well they perform the job. One relatively new compensation orientation is to base pay on the competencies or characteristics of the person rather than on those of the job. Part of the underlying logic is that organisations need to be flexible to compete and it makes sense to establish pay systems that encourage individuals to develop the knowledge, skills and abilities that are strategically important to the organisation. Two emerging methods for basing pay on the person are skill-based pay and competency-based pay.

Skill-Based Pay（SBP）

Skill-based pay（SBP）compensates employees for the breadth and depth of the

对组织整体而言的,并不是指某一特定职位在某一时间点上可能需要的技能(Hon,2012b)。技能薪酬方法通常主要用于体力劳动者、操作员、技术人员和办公室人员,即针对那些可以给技能相对完整的详细说明和定义的工作岗位(Milkovich 和 Newman,1999)。技能薪酬分为五种类型方案。·

(1) 纵向技能方案考量在一个工作中技能输入和输出的获得情况(例如,钻孔机操作员掌握预防性保养和操作中检查的能力)。

(2) 水平技能方案奖赏横跨多份工作的互补技能的获得(例如个体掌握如何做应付账与应收账两个技能)。

(3) 深度技能方案奖赏有专长的人才(例如计算机程序员专长于数据库编程)。

(4) 基本技能方案奖赏员工发展在基本技能方面的专业水平(例如计划、组织、领导和控制这四种基本的人力资源功能)。这种类型的方案对分支遍及全球的跨国企业来说,尤其有利。

(5) 组合方案奖励以上讨论过的各项技能。这种方案最常用。

除了拥有具有灵活性的员工能带来的策略上的优势,还有诸多其他的采用技能薪酬方案的理由。第一,它有助于提高和维持生产效率,同时也可以贯彻更简洁和更加扁平化的组织结构。第二,在面临高缺勤率、流失率或是生产瓶颈时,它能更有效地保持生产能力。第三,它能提升员工参与度、对组织的忠诚度、团队合作力,并且丰富职位内容,这点也将有益于员工个体。

从期望值理论角度看,技能薪酬方案在突出强调预期方面有着显著的作用,因为技能训练通常能增强员工的信念,即个人的努力将导向其预期的绩效表现水平。技能薪酬方案下的员工通常会获得和同类工作在其他薪酬方案下相比较高的薪酬(Milkovich 和 Newman,1999)。因此,该体系还通过阐明掌握新技能与获得更高薪酬之间的关联性,大力注重员工的手段和价值。

在主要产品利润由拥有具有可互换的技能的员工而获得的环境中,技能薪酬方案似乎是最有效的。不过,技能薪酬方案的焦点主要在于对体系的投入,即员工发展(Milkovich 和 Newman,1999)。

relevant skills they bring to the organisation rather than for the particular job that they may be doing at a given point in time (Hon, 2012b). SBP is used mainly with manual workers, operators, technicians and office workers, in situations in which the skills can be fairly well specified and defined (Milkovich & Newman, 1999). There are five types of SBP plans, categorised by the type of skills tracked and rewarded.

(1) Vertical skill plans measure the acquisition of input/output skills (e.g. a drill press operator mastering preventive maintenance and in-process inspection) within a single job.

(2) Horizontal skill plans reward the acquisition of complementary skills (e.g. individual learns how to do both accounts payable and accounts receivables) across several jobs.

(3) Depth skill plans reward skill specialisation (e.g. computer programmer specialising in database programming).

(4) Basic skill systems reward employees for developing expertise in basic skills (e.g. four functions of math; reading, writing and speaking English). This type of plan is excellent for companies that have a large number of employees in the workforce who speak English as a second language.

(5) Combination plans reward any of the skills previously discussed. This type of SBP plan is the most common.

In addition to the strategic advantage of having flexible employees, there are several other reasons for adopting SBP. First, it helps to improve and maintain production efficiencies, while also implementing leaner and flatter organisational structures. Second, it can effectively maintain productive capability in the face of absenteeism, turnover or production bottlenecks. Third, it fosters involvement, commitment, increased teamwork and the development of enriched jobs that are more rewarding to employees.

From an expectancy theory perspective, SBP appears to be particularly useful in addressing the expectancy element, as the skills training is likely to enhance an employee's belief that his or her efforts will lead to the desired level of performance. SBP also typically creates a situation in which the employees under SBP plans make higher wages than employees in similar types of jobs in the local market (Milkovich & Newman, 1999). Thus, in the short run, the system also provides a strong focus on employee instrumentality and valence by spelling out the link between learning new skills and achieving higher pay.

SBP is likely to be most useful inenvironments where there is a major productivity benefit to be derived from having a staff with interchangeable skills. Nevertheless, SBP focuses on inputs to the system—that is, employee development. Unless the system is also combined with some means of measuring and rewarding outcomes, the long-term link to performance is likely to be tenuous apart from the retention of skilled workers because of the higher wages (Milkovich & Newman, 1999).

绩效薪酬

在绩效薪酬(payment by performance,PBP)体系下,在得到基本的评估结果后,员工的收入基于其绩效产出有不同程度的增加。业绩薪酬可以被广泛地定义为经济性奖赏与个人、团体或组织绩效之间的关联。每个职位标准的设定表达了一个时间段产出的数量,或完成工作所花费的时间;当员工超额完成任务时,则会给予一定的奖金(Milkovich 和 Newman,1999)。

业绩薪酬体系奖赏那些为企业成功做出贡献的员工。这里强调的是个体的绩效和功劳,而不是个体的奖金红利。有三种常见的业绩薪酬体系类型:(1) 个体功劳与绩效相关的体系,其使用各种指标评价个体,并将奖金汇总到基本工资里支付;(2) 奖金依据量化的产出单元与个人挂钩,分开支付;(3) 奖金和团队、部门或组织的绩效相联系,并不融合到基本工资之中,但加到集体基数上。以下步骤展示了公司如何建立一个绩效薪酬体系(Milkovich 和 Newman,1999)。

(1) 方案需要与员工进行沟通,可能在与员工代表协商后,做出适当调整。上级主管与经理人要就方案的使用进行培训。

(2) 每个职位的成果评分标准的设定都依据花费在完成每一个工作任务上的合理时间而定,并为员工休息和个人需要留出时间。

(3) 通过行政安排来记录每名员工的绩效成果,计算其奖金红利,并加入员工的基本薪资中。

实施业绩薪酬方案的费用,包括工作研究、行政工作、处理随之引起的争议等,都是需要考虑进去的。同时,有些方案计算起来相当复杂,且较难使人理解,这是因为奖金红利并不是随着绩效成果按比例提高的,可快可慢。

团体薪酬

在有些薪酬方案中,标准是建立在团体绩效之上的,而不是针对单人。由团体获得奖金,然后在其成员中分配。有时会平均分给每个成员,有时按基本工资的一定比例分配(Milkovich 和 Newman,1999)。团体奖金方案的优势有:

(1) 它可以涉及其他员工,例如工人、维护性员工等。

(2) 它可以提高团队精神。

(3) 它鼓励灵活性,因为个体更愿意在团队内进行职位调整。

Payment by Performance (*PBP*)

In these systems, the employee receives a basic rate to which is added a variable payment based on output. Payment by performance can broadly be said to provide a link between financial reward and the individual, group or organisation's performance. A standard is set for each job, expressed either as a quantity produced per unit of time or as the time taken to do the job, and a bonus becomes payable when the employee exceeds this standard (Milkovich & Newman, 1999).

PBP rewards deserving employees—those who have contributed to the success of the organisation. The emphasis is on individual performance and merit rather than on an individual's bonus. There are three common types of PBP systems: (1) individual merit and performance-related systems that appraise or assess individuals using various indicators and then integrate bonus payments into the base salary; (2) bonuses in the form of separate payments to the individual related to output as measured in units of production (piecework fits into this category); and (3) bonuses geared to the performance of the group, section, department or organisation, again not integrated into the base pay but added on a collective basis. The following three steps are generally needed to establish a PBP system (Milkovich & Newman, 1999).

(1) The scheme is communicated to employees with perhaps some modifications after consultation with representatives. Supervisors and managers are trained in its use.

(2) A standard rate of output is set for each job by measuring the reasonable time taken to complete each task and making allowances for rest periods and personal needs. There are various methods of setting standards, from intuitive judgment to detailed analysis of bodily movements.

(3) Administrative arrangements are made to record each employee's output, calculate his or her bonus and add it to the employee's basic wage.

The cost of running a PBP scheme, including work study, clerical work and dealing with disputes, can be considerable. Some schemes are also rather complicated to compute and difficult to understand because the bonus may increase at a faster or slower rate than output.

Group-Based Pay

In some compensation schemes the standard is based on the performance of a group rather than an individual. The bonus earned by the group is shared among its members, sometimes equally, sometimes in proportion to basic pay (Milkovich & Newman, 1999). The advantages of group bonus schemes are as follows.

(1) They can include indirect employees, e.g. labourers or maintenance employees.

(2) They improve team spirit.

(3) They encourage flexibility, because individuals are more willing to move to other jobs within the group.

（4）它特别适合于那些要由具有不同等级技能的员工组成的团队来执行的工作，例如电缆连接。

团队奖金不适合人数太多、成员不稳定或者团队内混杂着表现差距大的成员，因为在这种情况下会产生人际冲突或不公平感并最终削弱奖金对团队表现的影响力。

对高层管理人员的奖励

对高层管理人员的奖励水平相对于其他员工而言，近几年在许多国家急剧增长，这一现象引起了许多争议（Milkovich 和 Newman，1999）。有时，高级经理人会因支付给自己较高的薪水同时严重限制了低等级员工的薪资水平而受到指责。总监级别可能在设定自己薪水层级时，短期内会较少顾及市场的力量，对股东负有较小责任。当组织绩效与主管薪资之间没有关系时，批评就尤其严厉。向高级主管们提供极高的薪水主要有以下几个原因：

（1）这是十分必要的用来激励每个主管的手段（例如通过绩效相关工资）。

（2）高薪资意味着高地位，是对个人价值的认可。

（3）有能力的高层经理人通常供不应求，是猎聘的重点对象，因此高薪可以确保其对组织的忠诚度和长期承诺。

（4）高层管理职责包括承担做决策的风险，若决策失误，将会给组织和高管本身带来非常严重的后果。承担如此高的风险，就需要有高薪来补偿。

（5）高层管理人员通常拥有管理技巧、知识储备，以及在激烈竞争环境中获得成功的能力，市场本身供需的力量会自然地抬高这类人群的薪资水平。

（6）从长期来看，无法吸引到最优秀的管理人才会对公司造成损失。

（7）高级主管是管理层金字塔的顶端，因此需要高薪来维持其与他人的差距，这也有利于确保低层级员工可以获得合理的薪资。

（8）高薪会激励低层员工努力工作，实现目标。

能力薪酬

除了技能薪资或绩效薪酬方案以外，对于很难定义的工种来说，依据员工个人能力支付薪酬，而不是职位本身，这一理念正在被探索（Hon，2012）。这种类型的薪酬体系被称为能力薪酬（competency-based pay，CBP）。能力

(4) They are particularly suitable for jobs that are carried out by a team of employees of various levels of skill.

Group bonuses tend to be unsatisfactory in large groups, when group membership is constantly changing or when the group contains a mixture of very fast and very slow employees. Some companies have GBP schemes that are virtually group bonus schemes extended to cover a whole plant, with the bonus being proportional to the amount by which the factory output exceeds a given standard.

Rewards for Senior Executives

The reward levels of senior executives relative to other employees have increased sharply in many countries during recent years, a fact that has created much controversy (Milkovich & Newman, 1999). Senior managers are sometimes criticised for paying themselves very high salaries, while severely restricting the remuneration of lower ranking employees. Directors may be able to set their own pay levels with little regard to market forces in the short term and minimal accountability to shareholders. Criticism is particularly severe in situations where there is no relationship between organisational performance and executive pay. The reasons given for providing extremely high salaries to senior managers are as follows.

(1) They are necessary to motivate individual executives (e.g. through performance-related pay).

(2) High remuneration implies high status and recognition of individual worth.

(3) Competent top-level managers are in great demand and likely to be headhunted, so high wages are needed to secure their loyalty and long-term commitment to the organisation.

(4) Senior managers take risky decisions that, if wrong, have serious adverse consequences for both the organisation and the individual executive. A high salary is needed to compensate them for the assumption of such a high level of risk.

(5) Only a small number of executives possess the management skills, knowledge and capacity necessary to succeed in competitive situations, and market forces of supply and demand naturally raise the remuneration levels of these people.

(6) Failure to attract the best managerial talent will damage the firm in the long term.

(7) Senior management is at the top of the managerial pyramid, so high salaries are needed to maintain differentials, while still enabling lower levels to earn a reasonable reward.

(8) High salaries generate a culture of effort and achievement within a firm.

Competency-based Pay (CBP)

In addition to the proliferation of skill-based pay and performance-based pay plans, the concept of basing paying on the capabilities of the person rather than the job is currently being explored for work that is difficult to define. Pay systems of this type are called competency-based pay (CBP). Competency-based pay compensates knowledge

薪酬强调员工拥有的知识、能力、行为方式的广度和深度以及竞争力,而不是他们的资深度或者他们在特定时间占据的职位。虽然这种方式源于技能薪酬,但是这里的能力一词指的是更广泛的管理性和专业性的工作。Brown和 Armstrong(1997)将能力一词定义为个人显示出具备能使其有良好表现的知识、技能和行为方式。

对能力薪酬体系的兴趣在增加,部分原因是从战略角度看,组织更加注重提高核心竞争力。因此,能鼓励员工尽力发展对企业具有战略重要性的能力的薪酬体系会带来长期利益。具有知识的工人的重要性正逐步上升,这也是另一个促进组织依照个人能力支付薪酬,而不是单纯参考职位职责本身的因素。能力薪酬是一种可以降低复杂程度、增加生产力、提升整体能力的方式。它涉及识别竞争力,即将高水平者区别于其他平均水平的人。

一个能力薪酬体系需要从一个复杂的由角色、责任、目标、技能、知识、决定员工效能的能力等因素构成的网络中识别出核心竞争力(Hon,2012)。这些竞争力构成了由选拔、学习、奖励以及其他员工管理基础。能力薪酬体系还促进实现人力资源管理的功能、客户满意度、公司灵活性、员工创造力以及对员工职业生涯和个人生活的掌控力。

能力能为组织提供充分的价值,这点很重要,这可以证明能力薪酬体系在发展和薪资中产生的额外成本是合理的。否则组织会发现自身受到劳动力成本增加和在寻求新的薪酬模式上浪费精力的威胁。目前,许多组织正在尝试使用能力薪酬的方式,但还缺乏具体数据可以对其有效性进行评估。

在有可能识别出具有战略重要性的能力的情况下,能力薪酬是最有益的方式。理想地来说,个人能力是具体的、很难模仿复制的,对组织具有独特价值,因此组织机构会提供各类资源支持,包括薪资、个人发展等。同时,该体系与具体的目标、成果、相关奖赏相结合,也是十分重要的。否则,企业将无法从所获得的个人能力中受益。

研究发现[①]

能力薪酬获方法得了越来越多的关注,因为组织逐渐开始寻求发展员工

---

　　① 资料来源:Hon,A.,(2012).When competency-based pay relates to creative performance the moderating role of employee psyehological need. *International Journal of Hospitality Management*,31(1),130-138.

workers for the breadth and depth of the relevant knowledge, skills and competencies they possess, rather than the job they hold at a particular point in time. Although the approach has roots in skill-based pay, the term competency is used to denote the broader and more non-programmed nature of managerial and professional work. Brown and Armstrong (1997) has defined competencies as "demonstrable characteristics of the person, including knowledge, skills, and behaviors that enable performance".

Interest in CBP is increasing, in part because organisations are becoming more concerned with developing core competencies for strategic reasons. Hence pay systems that might encourage employees to develop competencies in areas of strategic importance to the organisation might have long-term benefits. The growing importance of knowledge workers is another catalyst for exploring pay systems based more heavily on the person rather than the specific job. CBP is an approach that reduces complexity, adds capacity and increases overall capability. CBP involves identifying the competencies that distinguish high performers from average performers.

A CBP system requires organisations to identify the core competencies in the complex web of roles, responsibilities, goals, skills, knowledge and abilities that determine employees' effectiveness (Hon, 2012). These competencies then form the foundation for selection, learning, rewards and other aspects of employee management. CBP also supports such imperatives as speed-to-market, customer satisfaction, flexibility, creativity and employees' control of their careers and personal lives.

It is important that the competencies add sufficient value to the organisation to justify the additional costs of CBP in both development and pay. Otherwise the organisation will find itself at a disadvantage because of higher labour costs and possibly also wasted efforts aimed at acquiring non-pivotal skills. At present, many organisations are experimenting with the competency approach, but there is a lack of concrete data with which to evaluate its effectiveness.

CBP is likely to be most beneficial in situations where it is possible to identify competencies that have strategic importance. Ideally, the competencies would be organisationally specific and difficult for others to imitate, making it particularly worthwhile for the organisation to provide the resources, including pay, for their development. It is important that such systems also be tied to specific goals, outcomes and related rewards. Otherwise, the potential benefits of the acquired competencies may not be realised.

Research Findings [①]

Interest in CBP is rising because organisations are increasingly seeking to develop the

---

① Source: Hon, A; (2012). When competency-based pay relates to creative performance the moderating role of employee psyehological need. *International Journal of Hospitality Management*, 31 (1), 130-138.

核心竞争力,这也是落实人力资源战略所需要的(Hon,2012b)。拥有有能力的员工的重要性的增加,以及更灵活的、应对顾客需求有求必应的需求压力,都使得工作任务更具变化性。这表明引入将员工个人能力与薪酬挂勾的奖励制度,有助于实现长期保持组织成功和达成有效的战略目标。尽管主张能力薪酬者认为能力薪酬体系可以促进商业策略的实施,以及帮助建立起拥有高水平绩效的组织,但关于该体系有效性的实证证据还十分有限。能力薪酬体系是否可以延伸到各个工作领域,这个问题还有待商讨。

　　一个关注个体工作能力的薪酬体系可以说在组织人力资源管理中意义重大,它能激发员工的创造力的发挥。能力一词被定义为产生有效业绩所需的"技能、知识储备和行为表现"(Brown 和 Armstrong,1997)。组成能力的诸多因素对于提高个人贡献度及帮助组织实现成功都很重要。Berman (1997) 提出,所需的技能及行为能力可以从工作任务中推断出来,因为个人能力通过个体成功地完成任务来体现,而完成这类任务的必要技能则表现为个人的行为模式。而知识是可以通过教育和从工作经验中获得的。由于能力展现在工作绩效之中,因此它可以在行为结果中有所显现,即表现出色者相对于其他一般职员而言,表现得更始终如一、更高效(Kochanski,1997)。组织可以借助能力薪酬体系向员工传递这样的信息——他们的知识、技能、持续行为是被高度评价的。因此,本节主要讨论能力薪酬体系中的两个方面——对知识和对技能的奖励。

　　知识主要依靠教育和工作经验积累来获得,工作经验能使个体将理论知识应用到实际工作任务中去;这类知识指的是隐性知识(Sternberg 和 Wagner,1991)。人力资本研究成果显示,学习和教育可以增加员工的知识储备和未来的收入潜力(Lawler 和 McDermottt,2003)。研究者们还指出,个体的创造力可以习得知识并激发动机。举例来说,在一个复杂的工作环境中,比如一个要求高水平的参与力和创造力的工作任务,个人知识和才智对于预测较好的绩效来说都是最重要的因素(Dierdoff 和 Surface,2008)。因此,那些在个人兴趣领域具备高水平知识和经验的个体,在完成工作任务中表现更出色,特别是会有独具创造力的表现。由此来说,当能力绩效体系和与知识相关的绩效关联时,个体更倾向于表现出高水平的创造力。

　　员工的技能和持续的行为表现同样可以促进创造力的发挥。个体技能

core competencies required to implement human resources strategically（Hon，2012b）. The growing importance of capable workers and the pressure to be more flexible and responsive to customers' needs have also made job tasks more dynamic. Thus，introducing reward systems that align employee competencies with remuneration can contribute to the strategic goal of maintaining organisational success and effectiveness over the long run. Although competency advocates argue that competency-based pay（CBP）can facilitate the implementation of business strategies and help build high-performance organisations，there is limited empirical evidence for the effectiveness of competency reward systems. Whether CBP systems can be extended to the workplace remains an open question.

A compensation system that emphasises individual competence is arguably the most significant human resource management system an organisation can implement to encourage employee creativity. Competency is defined as "the skills，knowledge，and behaviors that need to be applied for effective performance"（Brown & Armstrong，1997）. These components of competency are important for enhancing personal contributions and for helping an organisation to succeed. Berman（1997）stated that skills and behaviour can be inferred from job tasks，in that personal competence is demonstrated when an individual successfully performs a task and the skills and ability to perform such tasks are demonstrated by an individual's patterns of behaviour. Knowledge，however，is acquired through education and work experience. As competence represents performance in the workplace，it can be seen as a behavioural outcome that excellent performers exhibit more consistently and more effectively than average performers（Kochanski，1997）. CBP is a tool through which organisations can indicate to their employees that their knowledge，skills and consistent behaviour are highly valued. Accordingly，two aspects of CBP are considered in this study：reward for knowledge and reward for skill.

Knowledge is mainly acquired through education and work experience that enables individuals to apply their theoretical knowledge to practical job tasks；this kind of knowledge is referred to as tacit knowledge（Sternberg & Wagner，1991）. Human capital research has shown that learning and education increase employees' knowledge experience and future earning potential（Lawler & McDermottt，2003）. Researchers have also argued that individual creativity is a function of knowledge acquisition and motivation. For example，in a complex job environment，such as job tasks that demand a high level of involvement and creativity，personal knowledge and intelligence are the most important factors for predicting superior performance（Dierdoff & Surface，2008）. Thus，individuals who are believed to have advanced knowledge and experience within the domain of interest perform better in their work tasks，especially in terms of creative performance. Individuals are thus likely to demonstrate a higher level of creativity when CBP is linked to knowledge-related performance.

Employees' skills and consistent behaviour also help to facilitate creativity.

和持续性行为来自于工作任务。如果能持续完成一项任务,一个员工就被视为具完成工作任务的必要技能和能力(Berman,1997)。具有必要的技能和能力的员工能够在他们的工作中表现出持续一致的行为模式,而且能在标准水平或是超过标准要求的水平上完成许多基本的职责。具备执行该任务所需要的技能和能力,并在他们的工作范围内表现得很能干的员工,会表现出持续的行为模式,并且需要获得新技能来增强其个体创造力。Redmond 和他的同事(1993)指出,对于自己的技能和能力具有强烈自信的人,在面对挑战和变化的环境时会更努力地去应对。因此,基于能力的奖励显得更适合那些对自己工作能力很自信的人。这一心理层面上的信念会促进创造性行为。依据个人技能和持续表现来进行奖励,强调了不断学习、个人进步、保持高效的重要性,这进一步可以使员工积累创造性能力。因此,当组织采用的能力薪酬体系与个人技能联系起来时,员工可能表现出较高水平的创造力。

相关研究也考察了个人特征与能力薪酬体系的相互作用对员工创造力的影响。每个组织机构都有一套任务(例如能力薪酬体系),这是其企业核心价值的基础(例如创造力)。首先,尽管员工无法创造他们自己的就业状况,但个人看法与需求将会影响他们对既定状况的反应。过去的研究发现,具有较高成就需要和权力需要的人,更倾向于成果导向的工作环境,在该情境下员工能够通过个人努力获得成功或权力(McClelland,1985;O'Reilly、Chatman 和 Caldwell,1991)。Fodor 和 Carver(2000)进行了一项实验,选择大学生为实验对象,观察具有较高成就需要和权力需要的人与任务反馈之间的互动,从而预测其创造力。研究结果显示,相比较于收不到任何任务反馈信息而言,拥有较高成就需要和权力需要的人在接收到正面积极的任务反馈时会产生更多的创意和想法。同样,采用能力薪酬体系有可能增强员工的创造力,这是因为能力薪酬体系关注的是高效能劳动力,这是具有较高成就需要和权力需要的人的突出特点,而他们倾向于成果导向的奖励方式。由此而言,能力薪酬体系可以作为精神激励源,它能强化员工对于成功的认知,赋予他们力量,鼓励他们在工作中更有创造力。

尽管能力薪酬体系有很多优点,但它也有局限性,就员工个体层面而言,这显然是一种高开销的方式,在许多员工做一样的工作的企业,它并没有产生大规模的经济效益。组织可能需要投入大量的时间和金钱在每个个体身

Individual skills and consistent behaviour can be inferred from job tasks. By consistently performing a task, an employee is demonstrating that he or she has the necessary skills and capabilities to perform the job task (Berman, 1997). Employees who have the necessary skills and capabilities are able to demonstrate consistent patterns of behaviour in their work and are likely to perform many essential duties at or above the standard required. Individuals who have the skills and abilities required to perform capably in their task domains are likely to demonstrate such skills in a consistent pattern of behaviour and to acquire new skills that enhance their creativity. Redmond and his associates (1993) stated that individuals who strongly believe in their skills and competence make a greater effort to master the challenges they face and the dynamic environments in which they operate. Thus competency-based rewards appear to be more suitable for individuals who are confident of their own capabilities, a psychological belief that contributes to creative behaviour. Rewarding individuals for their skills and consistent behaviour emphasises the importance of continuous learning, personal improvement and maintaining proficiency, which in turn allows individuals to accumulate creative competence. Individuals are thus likely to demonstrate a higher level of creativity when CBP is linked to individual skills.

Studies have examined how individual characteristics and CBP interact to affect employee creativity. Every organisation has a set of tasks (e.g. CBP systems) that are the foundation of its core values (e.g. creativity). Although employees do not, in the first instance, create their own employment situation, their individual perceptions and needs affect their responses to a given situation. Previous studies have found that individuals with a high need for achievement and a high need for power prefer outcome-oriented environments and situations in which they can attain success or power through their own efforts and abilities (McClelland, 1985; O'Reilly, Chatman, & Caldwell, 1991). Fodor and Carver (2000) conducted an experiment using college students to examine how individuals with a high need for achievement and a high need for power interact with task feedback to predict creativity. Their results showed that individuals with a high need for achievement generate more ideas and initiate more activities when they receive positive task feedback than when they receive no feedback. In a similar vein, the adoption of a CBP-based compensation system is likely to enhance employee creativity, because CBP emphasises a high-energy workforce, a feature that particularly appeals to people with a high need for achievement and a need for power, who prefer outcome-oriented reward practices. Thus, CBP may serve as a source of emotional arousal that enhances individuals' perceptions of their achievements, gives them power and encourages them to be more creative at work.

Despite the advantages of adopting CBP, there are also limitations associated with a competency-based approach. At the individual employee level, it is clearly a high-cost approach without the economies of scale that are available in systems where many individuals hold the same job. An organisation may invest considerable time and money in

上,相应地使他们获得较高的薪资。除非他们所获得额外技能,和其他竞争企业的员工相比,能够增加更多的生产价值,否则组织有可能是承担了比其他竞争企业更高昂的薪资成本。

或许选择改用能力薪酬方式的最大问题是需要做出大量的改变。显然,比起改变已有的组织形式,在新的组织设置中采用该方式更容易。许多非常成功的能力薪酬体系都出现在新公司中,这些公司从最初就设计了员工参与导向的管理风格,强调个人技能和技能的发展。在已有组织中,整个人力资源管理架构都要做出变更或替换。很显然这是一项重大的任务,可能受到许多在传统薪酬体系下感到舒服的员工的阻挠,以及官僚管理体系的干扰。事实上,他们当中许多人可能并没有在强调以能力为基准的企业中需要具备的高效的执行能力。这很有可能导致实施新体制最初,要度过一段艰难时期,并有可能导致人员流动率的上升。在这个关键点上,实际出现的问题大小是无法预估的,因为很少有研究关注这类问题的代价和结果。

总而言之,采用能力薪酬体系的组织的增加肯定会增加有关企业发展、实施、人力资源管理体系、最终效益的研究课题数量的机会。这些研究有助于理解在实行能力薪酬体系的企业中如何实现高效运转。需要有进一步的理论和研究开发出能使实行能力薪酬体系的企业更有效益的实践指南。围绕个体和他们的技能的组织,显然代表了一个新的模式,它需要有新的系统。一个特别有意思的问题是,在能力薪酬体系的组织里员工将如何定位于特定的任务和活动,他们在哪里可以找到明确的目的意义。

案例研究 10 - 1[①] ▶▶▶▶▶▶

悦榕庄酒店及度假村[②]

对 Timothy Cheong 来说,激励和赞赏是显然不同的。"对我来说激励主要就是与金钱有关,奖励针对的是你做的事,且是做得正确的事情。而赞赏更多是在精神层面。"他如此说道。然而尽管看上去二者很容易区分,但在

---

① 资料来源:Zolkifi, S., (2013). Case study: Banyan Tree Hotels & Resorts, reterieved from http://www.humanresourcesonline.net/features/case-stualy-banyan-tree-hotels-resorts/.

② 资料来源:Timothy Cheong, group HR director at Banyan Tree Hotels and Resorts, shares the challenges of providing incentives and recognition in the hospitality industry. By Sabrina Zolkifi.

individuals, which in turn may lead to them being more highly paid. Unless the additional skills that they acquire allow them to add more value to the product than employees in competing firms, this can create a situation where an organisation has higher overall wage costs than their competitors.

Perhaps the biggest issue in moving to a competency-based approach is the amount of change required. It is clearly much easier to establish such an approach in new organisational settings than it is to change an existing compensation system. Some of the most successful systems are in new firms that have been designed from the beginning to have employee involvement-oriented management styles and to emphasise skills and skill development. In existing organisations, the entire HRM infrastructure needs to be altered or replaced. This is clearly a large task and may be resisted by the many employees who are comfortable with the traditional compensation system and the bureaucratic approach to management. Indeed, many employees may not be able to function effectively in an organisation that emphasises the competency-based approach. This may lead to a difficult initial period after the approach is installed and may potentially result in an increased turnover rate. At this point, the actual size of the problem is unknown because there is little research on the cost of such a conversion and its outcomes.

To conclude, the increase in the use of the CBP approach promises to raise a number of research opportunities concerning their development, implementation, HRM systems and ultimate effectiveness. Such studies are needed to understand what is likely to be effective in a competency-based organisation. Further theory and research is also necessary to develop useful guidelines for the practices that are needed to make competency-based organisations effective. Organising around individuals and their skills clearly represents a new paradigm that requires new systems. A particularly intriguing question is how individuals can be allocated to particular tasks and activities and where they will find their sense of purpose in an organisation that is competency based.

Case Study 10 – 1[①] ▶▶▶▶▶

Banyan Tree Hotels & Resorts[②]

For Timothy Cheong, there is a clear difference between incentives and recognition. "Incentives, for me, are predominantly cash-related, where you get rewarded for what you're doing, and for doing it right. Recognition is a lot on the heart part," he says.

---

① Source: Zolkifi, S., (2013).Case study: Banyan Tree Hotels & Resorts, reterieved from http://www.humanresourcesonline.net/features/case-stualy-banyan-tree-hotels-resorts/.

② Source: Timothy Cheong, group HR director at Banyan Tree Hotels & Resorts, shares the challenges of providing incentives and recognition in the hospitality industry. By Sabrina Zolkifi.

酒店业谈到激励和赞赏,这二者要复杂得多。Cheong 承认鉴别酒店或度假村基层员工的工作是十分简单的事情,因为"前台员工会立即得到反馈信息,且他们的工作更具有可辨识度"。

"企业办公室工作属于后台的工作,在看到工作成果前有很长一段酝酿时间。某种程度上说,那里的工作很难进行实时辨别。"Cheong 说。但这并没有阻止悦榕庄在鉴别企业办公室员工工作成果上花费心思。公司有一份内部杂志 *MAD*,它代表"与众不同(make a difference)"。该杂志公布收到的奖赏,突出强调出色的顾客体验。*MAD* 的内部编辑人员来自公司的市场部。*MAD* 一周出三期,帮助提高整个组织员工的认可度,同时也尝试使赞赏成为更自发的行动。Cheong 说,这是前台经理人掌握的事情,而不在公司设定以内。

"为什么要等到杂志出版再去表达呢?"他问。一个一线经理人应当学会在需要的时候给出适当的赞赏;一顿简单的午餐,或是轻拍一下背就足够了。"赞赏需要尽可能及时自然地表达出来。它不应该是制度化的,但激励可以是制度化的。"他说。当涉及员工激励时,悦榕庄实施了一个由三个部分组成的结构,并且独立于公司的奖金方案。

员工奖金通常在年末发放,并且会有些不定的波动,这是因为它直接与整个公司的绩效挂勾。在三月份财政年结束时,在所有的法定数额和关键业绩指标都已审阅完毕后,就会发放奖金。奖金被分成了两个部分——对商业运营的激励和对个体员工的奖励。"举例来说,如果营业额设定为 1000 万美元,那么奖励就与此相关联。有一种数学方法可以基于关键业绩指标数据,计算员工所能得到的奖金比例。"Cheong 说道。因此,公司每年坐下来制定其业务目标是很重要的。

"如果我们实现了那个任务,员工将会得到 X 额度的奖金。然后我们再看员工个体绩效,将会得到 Y 额度的个人奖金鼓励。最后有一个部分就是和软实力相关的——你比其他所有人都擅长之处,那么就构成了 Z。因此 X 加上 Y 再加 Z 就构成了员工得到的全部奖金。"Cheong 认为,尽管 Z 部分相比于 X 和 Y 更难进行量化,那是因为后两者与具体的关键业绩指标挂勾,但公司更重视对员工软实力的奖赏。

Cheong 说:"由于在奖励中涵盖这个部分,在工作时可以促使员工牢记他们个人的软实力是受到企业的赏识的,例如团队协作、工作热情、领导力

However，although they are easy to tell apart，the challenges of providing both incentives and recognition in the hospitality industries are complex. Cheong admits it is easier to recognise staff working at the ground level of the resorts and hotels because "front-end staff gets immediate feedback and their work is more identifiable."

"Corporate office work tends to be behind the scenes，and it has a longer gestation time before you see the outcome. In a way that is where it is harder to have real-time recognition，" says Cheong. This has not stopped Banyan Tree from recognising the staff in its corporate offices. The company's internal magazine *MAD*，which stands for "Make a Difference，" publishes awards that have been given out and highlights great guest experiences. *MAD*，whose internal editor works in the company's marketing team is produced about three times a week and helps increase recognition for employees throughout the organisation. It is also an attempt to make recognition a more spontaneous activity，something Cheong says front end managers have mastered，but not those in corporate settings.

"Why wait until the magazine comes out?" he asks. A line manager should learn to give recognition when it's due; just a simple lunch or a pat on the back is enough. "Recognition should be as spontaneous as possible so that it is immediate. It should not be too institutionalised，whereas incentives can be，" he says. When it comes to employee incentives，Banyan Tree has implemented a structure with three components that are separate from the company's bonus scheme.

Employee bonuses are often rolled out at the end of the year. The amount fluctuates because it is linked directly to the overall performance of the full group of companies. The monetary incentives are given out in March at the end of the fiscal year after all of the statutory numbers and business KPIs have been reviewed. The total incentives package is then broken into two parts—there are incentives for the business and for individuals. As Cheong explains，"For example，if a business is supposed to make \$10 million，the incentive will correlate to that. There's a mathematical way of calculating the percentage of monetary incentive the employee will get based on those KPIs." Therefore，it is important that the company sits down at the beginning of every year and defines its business objectives.

"If we hit that，employees get X amount. Then there is the individual performance we look at，which will be the Y amount in individual monetary incentives. Lastly，there is a component linked to the soft skills—things you do that no one else can do better—and that makes up Z. So X，plus Y，plus Z becomes the total monetary incentives the employee receives." Cheong admits that although the Z component is harder to quantify than X and Y because the latter two are linked to solid KPIs，the company sees the importance of rewarding employees for their soft skills.

According to Cheong，"Having it as a component in the process helps employees keep in mind that they are being graded based on their soft skills like teamwork，compassion and

等。"同时他还强调了绩效评估的重要意义。公司每年进行两次评估,尽管奖金只是按年度发放的。"年中绩效回顾是重新调整最初设定的关键业绩指标的时间点,因为很多事情会发生变化。其次,对员工来说是一次现状核查,使一部分员工意识到自己并不适合这个岗位,是时候该离开了。"Cheong 说道。

企业办公室有一个称作"相关事件识别"的项目,又称为 ARE,它通常在中国的春节时进行。"每个人被邀请前往 KP(Ho Kwon Ping,悦榕庄的执行总裁)的家中,大家一起享受赞赏每个人在工作中的良好表现的美好时光。这不仅仅是一项对于长期服务的奖励——我们同时认识到了周围人的工作能力,就像 Bintan 一样,他被派往新加坡。我觉得这能给大家归属感。"ARE项目在酒店和度假村也在实施,在这里公司认可长期服务的员工,给予奖励,例如"最佳厨师""最佳行李员"。

"当然,对他们我们会给予奖金,但没什么能比得上和执行总裁或者总监同台更感到荣誉的了,并从他们的手上接受荣誉。"无论员工是在酒店或是在企业办公室工作,Cheong 说,"使员工感到被认可是相当重要的事情。"他将像对 ARE 项目这样的表彰算作对经济奖励的补充。酒店业的很多的员工薪水都不高,因此他们会很重视金钱奖励。

"另外一件需要注意的事就是你还要给员工们面子,这在亚洲文化中显得尤其重要,这也是 ARE 发挥作用的地方。特别是在我们这个行业,既要给他们经济上的鼓励,也要有面子上的认可,这是很重要的。"悦榕庄发觉针对前台员工,需要平衡金钱激励与心理层面的认可二者的关系,因此其确保所有服务费都给予员工。

正如 Cheong 所说,"这是我们在悦榕庄感到十分骄傲的一件事情。虽然服务费并不一定总是给予员工的,但我们大多数人的立场是坚信公司应该不拿取服务费。对我们来说,服务费只是激励和认可服务质量的一种形式,这一点可能对很多人来说并不了解,很多人可能已经忘记了。当我们进入中国或是其他国家时,有些酒店所有者曾尽力扣留服务费。无论什么时候当我们与酒店主签署新的协议时,我们都会把这个条款加入其中,即所有服务费将给予员工。如果他们不同意该条款,我们就拒绝签署协议。"

随着公司的持续扩大并向更多的城市拓展业务,走进"那些金钱优先的市场",Cheong 称提供经济上的激励会面临一项新的挑战,"因为我们想要尽可能实现平等"。他补充道,自己还不确定这个形势会如何发展下去,但他常

leadership." He also emphasises the importance of performance reviews, which the company does twice a year, although bonuses are only given annually. "Mid-year performance reviews is a time to readjust some of the KPIs you initially set because the things have changed. Secondly, it's also a reality check for the employee in the sense that they may realise this isn't the place for them and that it's time to go."

The corporate office has a programme called Associate Recognition Events, or ARE, which usually occurs during the Chinese New Year. "Everyone is invited to KP's (Ho Kwon Ping, Banyan Tree's Executive Chairman) house and we have a good time recognising everyone for their good job. It's more than just giving out long service award—we also recognise people who are nearby, like those in Bintan who come to Singapore, and I think that gives them a sense of belonging." The ARE events also occur at the hotels and resorts; the company recognises long service staff, and gives out awards like Best Chef and Best Bellboy.

"Of course for them, we give them a cash reward, but it's nothing like standing on stage with the Chief Executive or Executive Chairman, who always makes it a point to be there, and personally receive their awards." Regardless of whether the employee is working in the hotel or in the corporate office, Cheong says, "It's really important staff feel recognised." He adds that recognition efforts like the ARE programme complement monetary incentives. In the hospitality industry, many of the staff are not highly paid, so they do appreciate the monetary rewards.

"The other thing is, you also have to give employees face, especially in an Asian culture, which is where the ARE comes in. It's important, especially in our industry to give them both money and face recognition," Cheong adds. Banyan Tree may have found the balance between providing monetary incentives and recognition for the front-end staff, making sure that all service charges are given to the workers.

As Cheong says, "That is one thing we're very proud of at Banyan Tree. It is not always true that service charges go to the staff, but we stand out in a crowd by believing that the company should get zero service charges. That, to us, is a form of incentive and a recognition of quality service that is probably not known to many people, and one that I think a lot of people have forgotten about. When we expanded into China and other countries, some of the hotel owners fought tooth and nail to keep their service charges. Whenever we write a new agreement with owners, we include this clause where all service charges will go to the employees. If they don't agree, we'll walk away from the agreement."

As the company continues to grow and move into more city areas "where the cash element takes precedence," providing monetary incentives will begin to pose a challenge "because we want to be as egalitarian as possible," says Cheong. He adds that he is not yet sure how the situation will develop, but tells himself to "really try and emphasise recognition more; not because you want to save money, but because things that hit the heart are more

常告诉自己"真正地去尝试,更多地强调赞赏;这并不是因为你想要节省资金,是因为比起口袋里的金钱,打动人的心灵会更持久"。

"那些只涉及钱袋子的事情很快会被人们忘记,但打动人心的事将一直被铭记。如果你要讨论参与度,这是让员工参与的最佳方式,很显然你不能克扣他们的薪水,但你也不需要总是支付最高的价格。"他补充说道,重要的是有关认可度的工作是发自内心的,是真诚的。"这不是一件幻想的、遥不可及的事情,一个简单的举动就足以让员工们相信我们是如此珍惜我们的员工。"

问　题

（1）你认同该公司激励和认可员工的策略吗?

（2）请评价该公司政策的优缺点。

案例研究 10-2[①] ▶▶▶▶▶▶

假设你是一名掌管 90 间客房、非协会会员、坐落于美国南卡罗来纳州的酒店人力资源经理。该酒店拥有一间菜品有限的、咖啡厅类型的餐厅,那里不提供酒精类饮料。在你酒店的地理区域内离你很近的还有另一家酒店,足够和你竞争这里的顾客和员工。该区域市场上劳动力十分紧俏,失业率低至5.7%。你支付给小时工的最低工资标准为每小时 7.7 美元,在该区域内这是最低的水平。

过去,你从未将薪酬直接与绩效评估或是生产力水平挂钩。你觉得就当前的劳动力市场形势来看,采用绩效薪酬方案(对非豁免员工)更有益。然而总经理却并不那么乐观。她觉得你在转变为绩效薪酬方案时会遇到大量问题,这些难题将远超所获利益。

问　题

（1）你要如何说服总经理接受绩效薪酬方案将获益更多的想法?请预测她关心的问题,指出问题所在,并为每一个问题创建解决方案。

（2）请准备一份两页纸的关于短期执行绩效薪酬体系的变革方案交给总经理。请确保你的方案强调了员工可能关心的问题。

---

① 资料来源: Tanke, M.(2001). *Human Resources Management for Hospitality Industry* (2nd ed.). 214-215, Albany: Delmar Thomson Learning.

sustaining than things that hit the pocket."

"Things that hit the pocket will soon be forgotten but things that hit the heart will always be remembered. If you talk about engagement, that's the best way to engage staff, and obviously you mustn't underpay them but you don't always have to pay top-end." He adds that it is also important that such recognition efforts come from the heart and are genuine. "It doesn't have to be something fanciful, but a simple act is enough to convince people we do value our employees."

Questions

(1) Do you agree with this company's incentive and recognition policy?

(2) Evaluate the pros and cons of the company's policy.

Case Study 10 − 2[①] ▶▶▶▶▶

You are the human resources manager of a 90-room, non-unionised hotel located in South Carolina. The property has a limited menu, coffee shop-type restaurant with no alcoholic beverage service. There is one other hotel property in your geographic area that is close enough to compete with you for both guests and employees. The labour market in the area is very tight, with unemployment at a low 5.7 per cent. The lowest wage you pay to your hourly employees is $7.70 per hour. No one in the area will work for any less.

Historically, you have never linked compensation directly to performance appraisals or productivity levels. You believe that in the current labour market situation a pay-for-performance compensation plan (for non-exempt employees) would be beneficial. The general manager, however, is less than enthusiastic. She feels that you will encounter a number of difficulties in switching to a pay-for-performance plan and that the problems will outweigh the benefits.

Questions

(1) How will you convince the general manger that a pay-for-performance plan will be beneficial? Anticipate her concerns, identify them and develop solutions for each of them.

(2) Prepare a two-page transition plan to present to the general manager for the short-term implementation of a pay-for-performance system. Make sure that your plan addresses any potential concerns your employees may have.

---

① Source: Tanke, M.(2001). *Human Resources Management for Hospitality Industry* (2nd ed.).214 − 215, Albany: Delmar Thomson Learning.

案例研究 10 - 3[①] ▶▶▶▶▶▶

ABC 酒店集团每年员工流失率为 123%。你是一名人力资源总监,公司总裁要求你进行一项广泛的员工调查,找出员工流失率如此高的原因以及为降低流失率可采取的措施。调查结果显示大多数(86%)小时工要么属于不合格员工(17%),要么没有从公司的福利计划中得到好处。

酒店总裁还想了解这么高的员工流失率的代价是什么。在仔细的分析后,你指出员工流失费用对于每一个按小时支付薪水的岗位是 5000 美元,对于每一个主管或管理层职位是 1 万美元。总裁要求你拿出降低员工流失率的建议方案。特别是他希望给出修订福利计划的建议,以及如何将这个建议方案传达给时薪在 8~14 美元的各种员工群体。

问　题

(1) 调查中你会选择问哪些问题?

(2) 请给出减少因劳动力流失带来的费用的建议方案。

(3) 你将如何展开要与各种团体成员进行的必要信息的交流?

---

① 资料来源:Walker,J.,& Miller,J.(2009).*Supervision in the Hospitality Industry:Leading Human Resonrces*.Hoboken,NJ:John Wiley & Sons.

Case Study 10 – 3① ▶▶▶ ▶▶▶

ABC hospitality group's annual employee turnover is 123 per cent. The company's president has asked you, the HR director, to conduct an extensive employee survey to find out why the turnover rate is so high and what can be done to reduce it. The findings reveal that most (86%) of the hourly employees are either not eligible (17%) for or not taking advantage of the benefits programme.

The president also wants to know what the cost of such high employee turnover is. After careful analysis, you determine the cost of employee turnover to be $ 5000 for an hourly paid position and $ 10000 per employee for a supervisor or managerial position. The president is asking for your recommendations to reduce employee turnover. Specifically, he would like you to make suggestions about modifying the benefit programme and how to communicate the recommendations to a diverse group of employees earning between $ 8 and $ 14 per hour.

Questions

(1) What questions would you ask on the survey?

(2) Make recommendations for reducing the cost of labour turnover.

(3) How do you recommend communicating the necessary information to the diverse group of associates?

---

① Source: Walker, J., & Miller, J. (2009). *Supervision in the Hospitality Industry: Leading Human Resonrces*. Hoboken, NJ: John Wiley & Sons.

第 11 章　员工关系管理(动机与压力)

学习目标

- 了解员工关系管理在组织中的重要性
- 了解员工激励理论的原则
- 通过研究和案例了解员工会从事职场反生产行为的原因及其可能的解决办法

每个组织机构都会意识到组织对顾客满意度和忠诚度的需求。顾客提供的资金使得组织机构存活下去。然而,并不是每个经理人都明白在一般员工中产生满意度和忠诚度的必要性。当有新晋员工加入时,他们可能立即就开始考虑离开的事情。在酒店业,经理人十分清楚人员流失率带来的巨大开销。因此,组织和管理者需要不断地向员工提供表达意见的机会。工作满意度和留任率是与组织绩效有着密切关联的。例如,工作不愉快、不满意的员工通常会造成大量满意度低的顾客的出现。员工关系构成了人力资源管理活动,它与组织内部的员工活动有所关联(Hon,2013)。这些活动包括解决冲突、公平原则、晋升、降级、解聘、停职、人员流失、退休。

了解员工需求与满意度

心理学家在解释人类行为时将人类的需求视为基本假设。美国心理学家亚伯拉罕·马斯洛将人类需求分为以下五种类别。

1. 生理或基本需求

人类必须满足这些最基本的需求来维持生命。例如,其包括饥饿、口渴与睡眠。在工作环境中,工资或薪水的基本目的就是满足基本需求。

Chapter 11 Employee Relationship Management (Motivation and Stress)

The objectives of this chapter

- Understand the importance of employee relationship management in organizations
- Understand the principles of employee motivation theories
- Investigate the reasons why employees engage in counterproductive behaviors in organizations with possible solutions through research findings and case studies

Every organisation recognises the need for satisfied and loyal customers. Customers provide the financial resources that allow the organisation to survive. However, not every manager understands the need to generate satisfaction and loyalty among employees. When new employees join a company, they may immediately begin to think about leaving. In the hospitality industry, managers are aware of the high cost of turnover. Therefore, organisations need to constantly give employees reasons to stay. Job satisfaction and retention are related to organisational performance; for example, unhappy and disgruntled employees often create large numbers of dissatisfied customers. Employee relations comprise the HRM activities associated with the movement of employees within an organisation (Hon, 2013). These activities include conflict resolution, principles of justice, promotion, demotion, discharge, layoff, turnover and retirement.

Understanding Employee Needs and Satisfaction

Psychologists take human needs as basic assumptions when interpreting human behaviour. Abraham H. Maslow (1943) divided human needs into the five classes.

1. Physiological or basic needs

People must satisfy these needs just to stay alive. They include, for example, hunger, thirst and sleep. In the work environment, the fundamental purpose of a wage or salary is to provide the means of satisfying basic needs.

2. Security safety needs

These are concerned with self-protection, with the avoidance of harm and, to some

2. 安全需求

安全需求与自我保护、避免伤害有着密切关联,某种程度上说也是对未来的保护。例如住房、取暖、自卫都是安全需求。在工作中,对保障稳定职业的需求、限制竞争的出现,行业工会的诸多方面都是员工试图满足这种需求的例子。

3. 归属或有爱的需求

每个人,在不同程度上,都期待给予和得到友谊。通过与他人保持友情、关爱的关系来获得愉悦感,就是这种需求的例子。人们融入群体部分是为了满足情感需求,部分是为了寻求更多的安全感。

4. 尊重或自尊需求

尊重或自尊需求包括成为独立个体、获得他人的尊重、拥有支配权和占有权的需求。由于这类需求可以通过社交活动来满足,它与 3 的需求有重叠的部分。在职场拥有权力、公务车、办公室地毯或是其他各种特殊的东西,这些都能满足这类需求。

5. 自我实现的需求

这是最高层次的需要,它包括将个人的能力发挥到最充分,发展自我,充满创造力。工作环境中大多数员工不太有机会满足这个层次的需求;有技能的操作工、专业工人和经理人是最有可能获得该层级的满足感的。

马斯洛指出,人们倾向于按照一定的先后顺序来满足个人需求。一般来说在生理与安全需求得到满足后,更高层次的需求(归属感、尊重、自我实现)将会依次变得重要。这个需求层级理论被广为接受,容易理解,可以对很多但并非全部的职场行为做出解释。克雷顿·奥尔德弗(1969)对此提出了修正理论,其常常被称为 ERG 理论,它由三个层次的需求组成。

(1) 生存需求。其与马斯洛的生理和安全需求几乎相同。

(2) 相互关系需求。它包括情感需求和涉及人际关系的尊重需求。

(3) 成长需求。它包括自我实现需求和涉及个人努力的尊重需求。

与马洛斯理论一样,ERG 理论指出,当低层级的需求得到满足时,上一级层级的需求才会变得重要。但它进一步提出,如果某一层级的需求没有得到充分满足,低于该层级的需求将变得更加重要。例如,对晋升产生失望感

extent, with provision for the future. Examples are the needs for shelter, warmth and self-defence. At work, the need for security of tenure, the existence of restrictive practices and many aspects of trade unionism are examples of how employees try to satisfy needs of this kind.

3. Belonging or affection needs

Everyone, to various degrees, wishes to give and receive friendship. Companionship and association with others for recreational purposes are examples of these needs. People may join groups partly to satisfy affection needs and partly for greater security.

4. Esteem or ego needs

These include the need to be independent, to receive the esteem of others, to dominate and to acquire possessions. As it is possible for needs of this kind to be satisfied through social activities, there is an overlap between groups 3 and 4. At work, a position of authority, a company car, an office carpet or a special type of overall may satisfy these needs.

5. Self-actualisation needs

This final group includes the need to make the fullest use of one's capabilities, to develop oneself and to be creative. In a working environment, the majority of employees find few opportunities to satisfy needs in this class; skilled operatives, professional workers and managers are the most likely to be satisfied in this way.

Maslow suggested that people tend to satisfy their needs in order of precedence. In general, when physiological and security needs have been satisfied, the higher needs (belonging, esteem and self-actualisation) become important, in that order. This hierarchy of needs is widely accepted, easy to understand and can be used to explain much, but not all, behaviour at work. Clayton Alderfer (1969) proposed a modification of the theory, often known as the ERG theory, which consists of only three levels of need.

(1) Existence needs. These are approximately equivalent to Maslow's physiological and security needs.

(2) Relatedness needs. This group includes affection needs and esteem needs that are concerned with personal relationships.

(3) Growth needs. This group includes self-actualisation needs and the esteem needs that are concerned with individual effort.

Like Maslow's theory, the ERG theory proposes that as one level is satisfied the level above becomes important, but adds a further proposition that if one level is not sufficiently satisfied the level below becomes more important, e.g. a disappointment in promotion (growth needs) may produce a greater wish for social involvement

(成长需求)后,就可能对社会参与产生出极大的愿望(关系需求)。奥尔德弗声称,他的理论与马斯洛的理论相比,给出了对人类行为更深刻的解释。

对成就、权力和归属感的需求

戴维·麦克利兰(1987)提出了三种重要的人类需求,即成就需求(nAch)、权力需求(nPow)、归属需求(nAff)。成就需求者的特点是:(1)喜欢独立承担责任的工作;(2)追求成功;(3)不断监控自己行为和影响。具有强烈成就需求的人工作极其努力,不断力争提高个人绩效。相反地,对于追求权力的人来说,激励他们的是未来可以控制下属。而归属需求者希望与同事有令人愉悦的关系,渴望帮助别人。他们寻求与他人建立友好关系。他们强烈渴望得到同伴的认可,因此他们在团体协作中会采取保守的态度。成就需求者通常会是经营自己企业的出色企业家,或是在一个大型企业的独立部门的经理。然而,他们并不一定都是高效的管理者。他们会顾虑到个人的成就,因此可能无法鼓励他人获得成功。

弗鲁姆的期望理论

根据期望理论(Vroom,1964),一个人为满足需要而付出的努力取决于他认为努力会得到一定的结果并带来期望的回报(Vroom,1964)。依据该理论,个人行为受到以下三个信念的影响:

(1)个人想要发生的情况;

(2)对事件发生概率的估计;

(3)个人相信该事件将满足其需求的强烈程度。

通常个体对未来情况的预测是建立在过去发生情况的基础之上的。因此,当员工在并没有先前经验可以参考的新环境中时(例如工作的变换、新的工作环境),会感到不确定,由此可能降低员工的工作动机。例如,有三名员工都希望得到晋升机会,但不确定怎样才能取得成功。第一位员工认为在公司的社交俱乐部里面获得杰出荣誉是获得晋升的最佳途径,因而花费了很多时间在这上面,很自信自己可以被选中获得名誉职务。第二名员工认为专业资格能力才是最佳途径,因此晚上也十分努力地工作。第三位员工也认为专业能力是最优途径,但并没有花费精力去学习,因为他不相信自己有能力通过考试。他也不努力为功社交俱乐部的荣誉成员,因为与第一位职员不同,他不觉得这是获得晋升机会的一种方式。

(relatedness needs). Alderfer claimed that his theory provides a more comprehensive explanation of behaviour than Maslow's.

Needs for Achievement, Power and Affiliation

David McClelland (1987) identified three important human needs: need for achievement (nAch), need for power (nPow) and need for affiliation (nAff). Achievement-oriented people (1) prefer tasks for which they have sole responsibility; (2) have a drive to succeed, and (3) monitor continuously the effects of their actions. People with a high need to achieve work extremely hard and constantly strive to improve their performances. Conversely, power seekers are motivated by the prospect of controlling subordinates. People with high nAff want pleasant relationships with colleagues and want to help others. They also have a strong desire for the approval of peers and consequently tend to adopt conformist attitudes when working in groups. Individuals with high achievement needs often make good entrepreneurs running their own businesses, or managers of self-contained units within large companies. However, people with nAch are not necessarily effective managers. They are concerned with their personal advancement, but may not be capable of encouraging others to succeed.

Vroom's Expectancy Theory

According to expectancy theory (Vroom, 1964), the amount of effort a person devotes to satisfying needs depends on the person's perception that the effort will achieve a certain outcome and bring desirable rewards. According to this theory (Vroom, 1964), an individual's behaviour is affected by three beliefs:

(1) what the person wants to happen;

(2) his or her estimate of the probability of the thing happening; and

(3) how strongly the person believes that the event will satisfy a need.

Individuals normally base their predictions of what will happen in the future on what has occurred in the past. Consequently, new situations that employees have not previously experienced (e.g. job changes, new working environments) cause uncertainty and thus may reduce employee motivation. For example, take a situation in which three employees wish to obtain a promotion, but are not sure how to achieve it. The first employee decides that prominence in the firm's social club is the best route and spends much spare time there, confident that he or she will be voted into honorary office. The second employee believes that a professional qualification is the best way and works hard in the evenings to achieve one. The third also perceives a professional qualification as the best way to advance, but does not make the effort to study because he or she is not confident of his or her ability to pass the examinations. The third individual also does not try to become an honorary officer of the social club because, unlike the first employee, he or she does not perceive this as a way of getting a promotion.

管理层人员应当向员工表明什么是他们真正期待的。员工应能够看到个人努力与奖励之间的关联。奖励应可以满足员工的需求。员工期待着,努力工作将带来令人满意的奖励。因此,只有当员工认为某个特殊奖励越吸引人,而且努力工作才有较大的可能获得奖励,个人才会把更多的精力投入工作中(Vroom,1964)。

赫茨伯格的激励—保健理论

弗雷德里克·赫茨伯格(1968)提出了一种应用于工作的激励理论。该理论从工作环境中分出了两类不同因素:激励因素或满意因素;保健因素或维护因素。赫茨伯格指出,格外满意的经验并不是格外不满意的经验的对立面。赫茨伯格从他的分析中得出的结论是,提升工作满意度的因素是"成就、认可、责任、晋升机会以及工作本身"。他称之为激励或满意因素。

工作中下列因素如果缺乏或不充足会导致不满意:"薪资、与他人的关系、管理监督类型、公司政策、物质上的工作环境以及额外福利。"他称这些为保健因素。一名员工可能因为他不喜欢工作环境或认为薪酬方案不合理而选择离职,但若以上因素都有所改善,员工也并不会因此受激励而更努力地工作。

然而,例如成就感与责任感的缺乏,不一定会导致员工离职,但若提升员工的成就感与责任感,那么员工则会更有动力投入工作。赫茨伯格指出,个体在激励或保健因素的相对重视程度各不相同,一部分人更关心实现成功、获得认可等,但另一部分人可能格外关注薪资、人际关系等。

公平理论

激励公平理论主张,员工对自己是否被公平对待做出的评价是影响激励的主要因素(Stoner、Freeman 和 Gilbert,1995)。员工被认为会将他们获得的奖赏和努力程度与其他同事相比较,如果他们相信他们获得的奖赏相对较低,就会感到愤愤不平。如果回报被认为与其他人相等——与个体所付出的努力成正比,则会认为是"分配公平"。否则,如果个人感到奖赏/努力之间的关系不一致,或失去平衡,就会出现"认知失调"。导致的结果就是员工感到不安、不愉快,他的努力程度和动机就会随之减弱。

Management should make it clear to employees what exactly is expected of them. Employees should be able to see a connection between their efforts and the rewards these efforts generate. Rewards should satisfy employees' needs. Employees' expect that working hard at a job will lead to satisfying rewards. Thus, the more attractive an employee considers a particular reward, and the higher the probability that the exertion of effort will lead to that reward, then the more effort the individual will put into his or her work (Vroom, 1964).

Herzberg's Theory of Motivational and Hygiene Factors

Frederick Herzberg (1968) propounded a theory of motivation at work that divides the factors of the work environment into two classes: motivators or satisfiers; and hygiene or maintenance factors. Herzberg noted that experiences that are regarded as exceptionally satisfying are not the opposite of those that are exceptionally dissatisfying. From his analysis, Herzberg concluded that the elements in a job that produce satisfaction are "Achievement, recognition, responsibility, promotion prospects and work itself". He called these motivators or satisfiers.

The elements of a job that produce dissatisfaction when they are absent or inadequate are "pay, relations to others, type of supervision, company policy, physical working conditions and fringe benefits". He called these hygiene factors. An employee might leave a firm because he or she disliked its working conditions or thought the compensation scheme inadequate, but the employee would not be motivated to work harder or better if working conditions or the compensation scheme were improved.

However, the absence of achievement or responsibility, for example, would be unlikely to cause an employee to leave, but if these could be increased, the employee would be more motivated at work. Herzberg recognised that individuals varied in the relative importance they attached to motivators or hygiene factors; some were very concerned with achievement, recognition etc., in their jobs, whereas others were interested in pay, personal relationships etc.

Equity Theory

The equity theory of motivation asserts that an employee's own assessment of whether he or she is being fairly treated is a major factor influencing motivation (Stoner, Freeman, & Gilbert, 1995). Employees are assumed to compare their personal reward/ effort situations with those of colleagues and to feel aggrieved if they believe they are relatively under-rewarded. If returns are regarded as equal to those of other employees— proportionate to the effort expended by the individual—a state of "distributive justice" is said to exist. Otherwise, "cognitive dissonance" occurs, whereby the individual perceives the reward/effort relationship as inconsistent and out of balance. Consequently, the worker feels uncomfortable and discontented, and his or her effort and motivation may diminish.

员工动机的实践技能

在众多用来激励员工的技能中,下面一些是特别有效的(Dessler,2017):

- 保证员工有受到重视的感觉
- 高层管理人员树立良好榜样
- 双向沟通
- 对员工尊重、信任、赋予授权
- 将员工视为负有责任感的人,而不是当作可利用的资源对待
- 创造努力才会获得公平的奖励这样的企业文化
- 尽可能使工作让员工感到有趣
- 设定挑战目标(借助分配给员工必要的资源来实现目标)
- 对于员工的绩效及时提供反馈信息
- 告诉员工,为了实现他们的职业抱负,他们到底需要做什么
- 确保经理人会听取员工的意见
- 通过组织工作使员工可以预测到工作活动的结果
- 建立公平的员工意见渠道
- 给予员工获得新技能的机会,给合适、有能力胜任的员工提供晋升机会

工作扩大化、工作丰富化、工作轮换

工作扩大化指的是员工执行了更大范围的和以前相比几乎具有同样难度和责任的任务(Dessler,2017)。工作丰富化指的是员工被赋予更大的责任并需要在更大的范畴内做决定,需要他采用过去未曾用过的工作技能。两者都是工作拓展的例子。

两者都是试图将为员工创造自我实现的机会。范围更大的任务和要做更多的决定会使员工感到自我的重要性,获得成就感,更充分地发挥个人能力。因此员工将从工作本身(内部)和薪资及福利(外部)获得满足感。

工作轮换即向员工提供一些次要技能的培训,并允许他们隔段时间互相交换岗位。员工对工作过程有了更深刻的理解,从而获得了更大的满足感,而且多才能员工的增加,对于管理工作也是有用的。

并不是每个员工对工作扩大、丰富或轮换都持有欢迎的态度。有些人在

Practical Techniques for Building Employee Motivation

Among the numerous techniques known to be useful for motivating employees, the following have been found to be particularly successful (Dessler, 2017):

- ensuring that employees feel they are valued;
- senior management setting a good example;
- two-way communication;
- respecting, trusting and empowering employees;
- treating people as responsible human beings rather than as resources to be exploited;
- creating an organisational culture in which effort is seen to result in fair rewards;
- providing leadership training to managers and supervisors;
- making the work that employees complete as interesting as possible;
- setting challenging goals (through allocating to employees the resources necessary for the attainment of goals);
- providing rapid feedback on employees' performance;
- telling employees what exactly they need to do to achieve their career aspirations;
- ensuring that managers listen to employees' opinion;
- organising work so that employees see the end results of their activities;
- establishing fair employee complaints procedures; and
- giving employees opportunities to acquire new skills, and offering promotion to suitably qualified people.

Job Enlargement, Job Enrichment and Job Rotation

A job is enlarged when the employee carries out a wider range of tasks of approximately the same level of difficulty and responsibility as before (Dessler, 2017). A job is enriched when the employee is given greater responsibilities and scope to make decisions, and is expected to use skills not used before. Both are examples of job extension.

Both are attempts to build opportunities for self-actualisation into an employee's work. A greater range of tasks and more decision making will make an employee feel more important, give a sense of achievement and make more use of the person's abilities. The employee will therefore receive satisfaction from the job itself (intrinsic satisfaction) and money and fringe benefits (extrinsic satisfaction).

Job rotation provides employees with training in several minor skills and allows them to exchange jobs with each other at intervals. Greater satisfaction is obtained because the employee has a greater understanding of the work process, and the increased versatility of the employees is useful to management.

Not all individuals respond favourably to job enlargement, enrichment or rotation.

更高的要求面前并不能受到强烈的激励,或并不期望在工作中获得满足感(Dessler,2017)。另一些人拒绝任何改变,或拒绝接受赋予他们更大的决策制定权,他们认为这些职能是经理的职责所在。

员工反生产行为

成功企业的另一个标志就是当员工有反生产行为或偏差行为时具备解聘员工的能力和意愿。偏差行为指的是工作中主动参与的违反规范的行为,其目的通常是危害组织或成员(Bryant 和 Higgins,2010)。它可以采取组织或人际偏差的形式。前者威胁整个组织(例如雇主),包括像偷窃这样的行为,而后者有害于表现好的个体成员(例如同事),典型的行为表现如撒谎、对他人粗鲁(Bennett 和 Robinson,2003)。工作场所的偏离行为和员工反生产行为都会给组织整体带来巨大的损失。因此,留住生产率高的员工的关键之一就是确保这些员工不会受到那些从事非生产性、破坏性、危险行为的同事或上级领导的不公平对待或虐待。为了实现高效运行,组织必须采取措施以确保表现好的员工被鼓励留在组织内,表现弱者可以允许留任、给予鼓励,但必要时可以强制其离开。

公平原则

对于持续进行的意见反馈和绩效评估来说公平显得十分重要,它在做最终决定时则表现得更为关键。员工获得的公平感有三种类别——分配公平、程序公平和互动公平(Hon 和 Lu,2010;Hon、Yang 和 Lu,2011)。分配公平指的是人们依据他人所获得的成果与自己所获得的相比较(参照他人)而做出的评判。某个人丢掉了工作但其他类似的人却没有丢掉,这样的情形,容易在被解雇的员工群体中产生分配不公平的感觉。然而,这种潜在的不公平的行为是否会转化为暴力或诉讼的报复行为,则取决于程序公平与互动公平。

分配公平注重结果,而程序公平和互动公平则更关注手段。程序公平尤其侧重在方法和过程上,用来判定收获结果的多少。如果在做出对员工有负面影响的决策时采用的方法和过程看上去是公平的,其得到的反应可能会正面些。尽管被解聘的员工会产生诸多负面情绪,但如果做出这个决定的过程

Some do not appear to be motivated very strongly by the higher needs, or do not expect to satisfy them at work (Dessler, 2017). Others resist any change or attempt to give them decision-making functions; they say that managers are there for that purpose.

Employee Counterproductive Behaviour

Another hallmark of successful firms is their ability and willingness to dismiss employees who are engaging in counterproductive or deviant behaviour. Deviance refers to voluntary counter-normative workplace behaviour, frequently aimed at harming the organisation or members within it (Bryant & Higgins, 2010). It can take the form of organisational or interpersonal deviance. The former threatens organisations (e. g. employers) and includes actions such as theft, whereas the latter is detrimental to the well-being of individual members (e.g. co-workers) and is exemplified by behaviour such as lying or rudeness towards others (Bennett & Robinson, 2003). Workplace deviance and employees' counterproductive behaviour have significant costs for organisations. Thus, one of the keys to retaining productive employees is ensuring that these people are not being treated unfairly or being mistreated by supervisors or co-workers who are engaging in unproductive, disruptive or dangerous behaviour. To compete effectively, organisations must take steps to ensure that good performers are motivated to stay with the organisation, whereas low performers are allowed, encouraged or if necessary forced to leave.

Principles of Justice

Fairness is an important part of on-going feedback and performance appraisal, but is even more critical in the context of a final termination decision. The three types of fairness perceived by employees are distributive justice, procedural justice and interactional justice (Hon & Lu, 2010; Hon, Yang, & Lu, 2011). Distributive justice refers to the judgment that people make with respect to the outcomes they receive relative to the outcomes received by other people with whom they identify (referent others). A situation in which one person loses his or her job while other similar employees do not, is conductive to perceptions of distributive injustice on the part of the discharged employee. The degree to which this potentially unfair act translates into retaliation in the form of violence or litigation, however, depends on perceptions of procedural and interactional justice.

Distributive justice focuses on the ends, whereas procedural and interactional justice focus on means. Procedure justice focuses specifically on the methods and procedures used to determine the outcomes received. If the methods and procedures used to arrive at and implement decisions that affect the employee negatively are seen as fair, the reaction is likely to be much more positive than if this is not the case. Even given all of the negative ramifications of being dismissed from one's job, the person being dismissed may accept

是始终如一的、无偏见的、准确的、可校正的、有代表性的、符合伦理的,被解雇的那个人就会以最小的愤怒接受这个决定。

程序公平处理的是如何制定决策,而互动公平指的是人际关系本质中怎样实现该结果。如果某决策得到了充分的解释并以一种社会敏感、善解人意和有同情心的方式执行时,就有助于平复由解聘一个员工的决定的而引起的员工产生的不满情绪。事实上,在组织内部促进程序公平、互动公平的系统,会带来更高的满意度和更高效的生产力。

冲突解决

在当代商业世界里,团队合作的重要作用越来越凸显,因为许多服务型组织需要更高效地协调其组织行为(Hon 和 Chan,2013);然而,以团队为形式的高效工作面临大量的挑战。其中一个主要的挑战就是冲突问题,这些团队成员之间的冲突是由于任务关系的复杂性、过度的工作要求、内部人际间的争执而引起的。因此越来越多的组织正在引入冲突解决技术,该技术承诺可以以及时的、建设性的、成本效率高的方式解决争执。

冲突解决在处理工作场合中与绩效和人际差异相关的问题方面非常有效(Hon 和 Liu,2016)。冲突解决呈现为许多不同的形式,但一般来说,其过程包括以下四个阶段。每个阶段都反映出不同的人在某种程度上更广泛地参与。我们希望看到的是这些冲突在最初的阶段中可以得到解决,而不需要经历所有四个阶段。

(1)敞开式政策。当两个人陷入冲突之中(例如上级与下属之间)试图努力达成共识。若最终无法达成一致,那么他们会进入下个阶段。

(2)同行互查。由来自组织的各个部门与产生争执的员工处在同一级别的代表组成一个小组,听取情况,然后试图帮助那一对人达成一致。若最终无法达成一致,则他们会进入下一个阶段。

(3)调解。一个来自组织外部的中立的第三方组织,听取情况,试图帮助冲突的双方达成共识。若最终无法达成一致,则进入下一个阶段。

(4)专业仲裁。一位来自组织外的专业仲裁员听取情况,并单方面做出具体决定或裁决。大多数仲裁员是经验丰富的律师或退休法官。

the decision with minimum anger if the procedures used to arrive at the decision are consistent, unbiased, accurate, correctable, representative and ethical.

Procedural justice deals with how a decision is made, whereas interactional justice refers to the interpersonal nature of how the outcomes are implemented. When the decision is explained well and implemented in a fashion that is socially sensitive, considerate and empathetic, this helps defuse some of the resentment arising from a decision to discharge an employee. Indeed, systems that promote procedural and interactive justice across the organisation result in a more satisfied and more productive workforce (Colquitt, *et al*., 2001).

Conflict Resolution

In the contemporary business world, teamwork is increasingly important because many service organisations feel the need to coordinate their activities more effectively; however, there are considerable challenges to working effectively in teams (Hon & Chan, 2013). One major challenge is conflict, which can arise between team members due to the complexity of task relationships, excessive work demands, interpersonal disputes. Hence, more and more organisations are adopting conflict resolution techniques that show promise in resolving disputes in a timely, constructive and cost-effective manner.

Conflict resolution is effective in dealing with problems related to performance and interpersonal difference in the workplace (Hon & Lui, 2016). Conflict resolution can take many different forms, but in general the process involves the following four stages. Each stage reflects a somewhat broader involvement of different people, and the hope is that the conflict will be resolved in the earlier steps and will not need to proceed through all four stages.

(1) Open door policy. The two people in conflict (e.g. supervisor and subordinate) attempt to arrive at a settlement together. If none can be reached, they proceed to the next step.

(2) Peer review. A panel composed of representatives from the organisation who are at the same level as the people in the dispute hear the case and attempt to help the parties arrive at a settlement. If none can be reached, they proceed to the next step.

(3) Mediation. A neutral third party from outside the organisation hears the case and, via a nonbinding process, tries to help the disputants arrive at a settlement. If none can be reached, the parties proceed to the next step.

(4) Professional arbitration. A professional arbitrator from outside the organisation hears the case and resolves it unilaterally by rendering a specific decision or award. Most arbitrators are experienced employment attorneys or retired judges.

研究发现 1[①]

在团队或组织工作中冲突是避免不了的,这是由于工作任务相当复杂,工作关系互相关联。然而研究人员并不认为冲突对组织有害或有益(Hon和 Chan,2013b)。研究人员认为一些形式的冲突对工作结果有正面影响,另一些则有负面影响(De Dreu,2008;Simons 和 Peterson,2000;Tjosvold,2007)。例如,一些专家学者指出,当团队在预先讨论前对自己的偏好有不同意见时,可以做出更佳的决策(Schulz-Hardt、Mayer 和 Frey,2002)。另一学者认为,冲突对团队效能和满意度会产生负面影响(Simons 和 Peterson,2000;Wall 和 Callister,1995)。

团队内产生的冲突涉及任务和关系两个层面(Amason 和 Schweiger,1997;Jehn,1995;Kabanoff,1991)。任务冲突(例如关于过程和政策、判断、对事实情况的解读等)涉及工作任务与工作绩效之间的分歧。这种类型的冲突导致了信息的交换,考虑对方的观点,并且能够对工作现状进行详细的评估,推动团队产生新的创意(De Dreu,2008;De Dreu 和 Van de Vliert,1997;Jehn,1997;Xia 和 John,1995)。相反地,关系冲突(例如关于个人品位、政治倾向、价值观、个性等的冲突)将不利于许多工作成果,因为此类冲突会引起情感上的负面反应,例如焦虑、烦躁、恐惧和愤怒。此外,人际关系不和谐的副产品(如压力、愤怒、报复行为、打斗)会导致个人和团队的较差的绩效。(Amason 和 Schweiger,1997;Jehn,1995;Simons 和 Peterson,2000)。由此来看,对个人和组织来说,冲突有益也有害。

1. 挑战压力源与阻碍性压力源

冲突的两种类型(任务冲突和关系冲突)都可以在工作环境中造成紧张和压力(Amason 和 Schweiger,1997;De Dreu 等,1999;Langfred,2007);不过,冲突对组织是有益还是有害取决于压力的类型。工作压力可以归类为"好压力"或"坏压力"。Cavanaugh 等(2000)是第一批界定两种类型的工作压力的:挑战导向型压力与障碍导向型压力。挑战导向型压力可以视为好的一类,只要该压力不是太大,因为其可以提升工作满意感,增强员工留任的意愿;障碍导向型压力则可以视为不好的一类,因为它与不佳的绩效表现相关联,且会增加员工流失率(Lepine 等,2005)。

[①]　资料来源:Hon, A., & Chan, W. (2013). The effects of group conflict and work stress on employee performance. *Cornell Hospitality Quarterly*,54(2), 174 – 184.

Research Findings 1 [①]

Conflict is inevitable in work teams and organisations because work tasks are highly complex and work relationships are vastly interdependent. However, researchers have disagreed about whether conflict is harmful or beneficial to organisations (Hon & Chan, 2013b). Researchers have posited that some forms of conflict are positively related to work outcomes, whereas others are negatively related (De Dreu, 2008; Simons & Peterson, 2000; Tjosvold, 2007). For example, a number of scholars have proposed that teams make better decisions when they disagree about their preferences in pre-discussion (Schulz-Hardt, Mayer & Frey, 2002). Others have suggested that conflict is negatively related to team effectiveness and satisfaction (Simons & Peterson, 2000; Wall & Callister, 1995).

Conflict in teams can focus on tasks or on relationships (Amason & Schweiger, 1997; Jehn, 1995; Kabanoff, 1991). Task conflict (e.g. conflicts about procedures and policies, judgments and interpretation of facts) involves disagreements about how the work task is related to work performance; this type of conflict leads to information exchange, considers opposing opinions and enables the exploration of the status quo and thorough evaluation of the focal work activity, helping people generate new ideas (De Dreu, 2008; De Dreu & Van de Vliert, 1997; Jehn, 1997; Xia & John, 1995). In contrast, relationship conflict (e.g. conflicts about personal taste, political preferences, values and interpersonal style) is detrimental to a variety of work outcomes because this type of conflict causes negative emotions, such as anxiousness, annoyance, fear and anger. Moreover, the by-products of interpersonal discord (e.g. stress, anger, retaliatory behaviour, fights) lead to poorer individual and group performance (Amason & Schweiger, 1997; Jehn, 1995; Simons & Peterson, 2000). Therefore, conflict can both benefit and hamper individuals and organisations.

1. Challenge stressor vs. hindrance stressor

Both types of conflict (task or relationship) can cause tension and stress in the workplace (Amason & Schweiger, 1997; De Dreu, *et al*., 1999; Langfred, 2007); whether the conflict is beneficial or detrimental depends on the type of stress. Work stress can be classified as either "good" or "bad" stress. Cavanaugh, *et al*. (2000) were among the first to define the two types of work stress: challenge-oriented stress and hindrance-oriented stress. Challenge-oriented stress can be seen as good, if it is not too high, because it can increase job satisfaction and intention to remain; hindrance-oriented stress can be seen as bad because it is associated with poor performance and increasing turnover (Lepine, *et al*., 2005).

---

① Source: Hon, A., & Chan, W.(2013).The effects of group conflict and work stress on employee performance. *Comell Hospitality Quarterly*,54(2), 174 - 184.

近来关于组织行为和管理的研究表明,任务冲突具有较大的功能性,是一种正向的激发动机的力量,并伴随着任务成就感(Selye,1982;De Dreu等,1999)。任务冲突增加了团队成员的工作量和时间压力,鼓励员工深入地、深思熟虑地参与任务相关的信息的思考的过程。整个过程花费了更多的努力和精力在工作任务之上,将新的,有时是更富有创造性的观点注入挑战性压力中,引领团队做出更优的决策,增强组织效能(De Dreu 和 West,2001;Jehn,1995)。任务冲突通常导致正面的动机激励,而障碍导向型压力会阻碍个体实现自我价值与能力的发挥。因此,任务冲突与挑战导向型压力呈正相关,与障碍导向型压力呈负相关。

相反,关系冲突属于功能性失常,与负面情绪有关(Robbins,2000;Rolinson,2002)。该类型的冲突限制了团体寻找和处理与任务相关信息的能力,因为团体成员将他们的时间和精力花费在彼此身上,而不是与团队任务有关的问题上。此情形会引起障碍导向型压力,因为关系冲突可以产生紧张气氛和对立,在执行任务时会分散团队成员的精力。关系冲突与障碍导向型压力呈正相关性,它会给工作成果带来负面影响,因为此类冲突限制了团队成员仔细观察任务相关问题的意向(De Dreu 和 Weingart,2003)。在之前我们提到过,挑战导向型压力可以创造挑战和成就感。它与障碍导向型压力完全不同,后者无法创造挑战,也无法获得成就感。因此,关系冲突与障碍导向型压力呈正相关,与挑战导向型压力呈负相关。

2. 不同类型的工作类型将导致不同的绩效结果

经理人热衷于研究工作相关的压力问题,以及它对员工心理健康和工作绩效的影响。一项关于服务行业职业压力的调查显示,88%的人表示压力过高,其中大多数人感觉有前所未有的压力感(Cohen,1997;Jex等,2001)。和该假设相反的是,Cavanaugh 等(2000)提出工作压力是一种多维度的概念,而不是单一维度的变量。他们认为与一些压力因素(例如关系冲突)相关的工作压力可能带来负面结果,而与其他因素(例如任务冲突)相关的工作压力则可能带来正面影响。为了证实这一两面性,研究人员指出,压力的类型由其是挑战导向型压力(良好的压力)还是障碍导向型压力(不良的压力)决定。

与挑战相关的压力常被定义为良好的压力类型,它可以产生满足感、挑

Recent research in organisational behaviour and management has suggested that task conflict is largely functional, is a positive emotional motivating force and is accompanied by a sense of task achievement (Selye, 1982; De Dreu, *et al.*, 1999). Task conflict increases group members' workload and time pressure, encouraging them to engage in the deep and deliberate processing of task-relevant information. This process fosters more effort on and attention to job tasks and the development of new and sometimes highly creative insights into the challenging stress, leading the group to make better decisions and increasing organisational effectiveness (De Dreu & West, 2001; Jehn, 1995). Although task conflict in general leads to a positive emotional motivating force, hindrance-related stress is associated with job constraints that hinder an individual's ability to achieve a goal. These undesirable constraints will prevent an individual from achieving a sense of fulfilment. Thus, task conflict is positively associated with challenge-related stress, but negatively associated with hindrance-related stress.

In contrast, relationship conflict is dysfunctional and associated with negative emotions (Robbins, 2000; Rolinson, 2002). This type of conflict limits the group's ability to seek and process task-related information, as group members are spending their time and energy focusing on each other, rather than on the group's task-related problems. This situation causes hindrance-related stress because relationship conflict produces tension and antagonism, and distracts group members from performing the task. Relationship conflict is positively associated with hindrance-oriented stress and results in negative work outcomes because such conflict limits group members' tendency to scrutinise task-related issues (De Dreu & Weingart, 2003). As previously mentioned, challenge-related stress can create challenges, but also a sense of achievement. Challenge-related stress is different than hindrance-related stress, which does not create challenges or lead to feelings of achievement. Thus, relationship conflict is positively related to hindrance-oriented stress and negatively related to challenge-oriented stress.

2. Different types of work stress lead to different performance outcomes

Managers are interested in studying work-related stress and its effect on employees' psychological health and work performance. In a survey of occupational stress among service workers, 88% reported elevated levels of stress, and most reported feeling more pressure than they could ever remember (Cohen, 1997; Jex *et al.*, 2001). In contrast to this assumption, Cavanaugh, *et al.* (2000) proposed that work stress is a multidimensional construct rather than a unidimensional variable. They argued that work stress associated with some stressors (e.g. relationship conflict) may result in negative outcomes, whereas work stress associated with other stressors (e.g. task conflict) may result in positive outcomes. To clarify this ambiguity, researchers have suggested that the types of stress are based on whether they are challenge-related (good stress) or hindrance-related (bad stress).

Challenge-related stress has been defined as good stress that creates feelings of fulfilment,

战感、刺激感、成就感,其产生的原因包括工作量过大、时间压力、责任的增加(LePine 等,2005;Podsakoff 等,2007)。研究结果表明,挑战性的工作需求或工作环境可以产生正向的情感,尽管可能充满压力。挑战型压力通常与积极的工作结果(即较高的工作绩效和满意度)相关,因为它有可能使个人获得利益或促进成长。挑战型压力因素可以引发正向的情绪,触发积极的行为方式或解决问题的应对方式(例如增加努力程度和工作时间),从而可以提高绩效。先前的研究结果表明,挑战型压力因素与组织承诺和工作反应呈正向相关(Boswell、Olson-Buchanan 和 LePine,2004;Cavanaugh 等,2000;Podsakoff 等,2007)。

障碍导向型压力常被定义为不良的压力,它与工作需求或工作环境相关联,包括过多的、不想要的约束和限制,其在实现目标的过程中干扰了个人能力的发挥(Boswell、Olson-Buchanan 和 LePine,2004;Cavanaugh 等,2000;Podsakoff 等,2007)。障碍导向型压力因素还包括职务模糊、职位冲突、官僚作风、缺乏职业安全感。因此,障碍导向性压力与负面工作结果相关联,例如较低的工作绩效和工作满意度。障碍导向型压力因素可能激发负面情绪和态度,这是因为人们往往认为职位模糊和职位冲突可能威胁到他们的个人的成长和目标的实现(Cavanaugh 等,2000;LePine 等,2005)。对个人成长的威胁能够导致人们不再付出过多心力在工作任务之中,从而产生较差的工作绩效和较低的满意度。研究表明,障碍型压力因素与组织承诺和工作满意度呈负相关,与员工流失率和退缩行为呈正相关(Boswell,等,2004;Podsakoff 等,2007;Watkins,2003)。

挑战型压力可以刺激个人努力工作,来改善他们不良的环境,从而使他们更有可能从工作中获得满足感。相反地,障碍型压力会阻碍人们实现有价值的目标和成果,像不良的人际关系这样的压力因素,会分散人们的工作注意力,从而导致较差的绩效表现和较低的工作满意度(Hon 和 Chan,2013b)。

研究发现 2[①]

员工创造力、职业满意度和内部地位感知

员工创造力会显著影响个人成就。例如,员工创造力可以增加新员工对

[①] 资料来源:Kim,T. Y.,Hom,A. H. Y.,& Corant,M.(2009). Proactive personality,career satisfaction,and perceived insider status:The mediating roles of employee creativity. *Journal of Business and Psychology*,24,93 - 103.

challenge or achievement; sources includes job overload, time pressure and increased responsibility (LePine, *et al.*, 2005; Podsakoff, *et al.*, 2007). Research has suggested that challenging job demands or work circumstances produce positive feelings, although they may be stressful. Challenge-related stress is generally associated with positive work outcomes (i.e. high job performance and satisfaction). As they have the potential to promote personal gain or growth, challenge stressors trigger positive emotions and an active or problem-solving style of coping behaviour (e.g. increasing effort and time), which can improve performance. Previous studies have shown that challenge stressors are positively associated with organisational commitment and job responses (Boswell, Olson-Buchanan, & LePine, 2004; Cavanaugh, *et al.*, 2000; Podsakoff, *et al.*, 2007).

Hindrance-related stress is defined as bad stress that is associated with job demands or work circumstances involving excessive or undesirable constraints that interfere with an individual's ability to achieve goals (Boswell, Olson-Buchanan, & LePine, 2004; Cavanaugh et al., 2000; Podsakoff *et al.*, 2007). Hindrance-related stressors include role ambiguity, role conflict, red tape and concerns about job security. Hindrance-related stress is associated with negative work outcomes such as lower job performance and lower job satisfaction. Hindrance stressors tend to evoke negative emotions and attitudes because people tend to appraise role ambiguity and role conflict as potentially threatening to their personal growth and goal attainment (Cavanaugh, *et al.*, 2000; LePine, *et al.*, 2005). Threats to personal growth cause people to withdraw personal effort from job tasks, resulting in poor job performance and low satisfaction. Studies have shown that hindrance stressors are negatively associated with organisational commitment and job satisfaction, and positively related to turnover intentions and withdrawal behaviour (Boswell, *et al.*, 2004; Podsakoff, *et al.*, 2007; Watkins, 2003).

Challenge stress can stimulate individuals to work harder to improve their undesirable circumstances, and they are more likely to be satisfied with their jobs. In contrast, hindrance stress can prevent people from achieving desirable goals and outcomes; stressors such as poor interpersonal relationships can distract them from working on task-related issues, leading to poor performance and lower satisfaction on job tasks (Hon & Chan, 2013b).

Research Findings 2 [1]

Employee Creativity, Career Satisfaction and Perceived Insider Status

Employee creativity significantly influences individual outcomes. For example,

---

[1] Source: Kim, T. Y., Hom, A. H. Y., & Corant, M. (2009). Proactive personality, career satisfaction, and perceived insider status: The mediating roles of employee creativity. *Journal of Business and Psychology*, 24, 93 – 103.

职业的满意程度。新晋员工最初都缺乏对工作及他们周围活动的认可度,也很少能理解他们的环境中哪些事件与他们的职业生涯有关(Kim、Hon 和 Crant,2009)。应对如此缺乏控制和不确定的一种方式,就是调整工作内容的各项要素(Ashford 和 Black,1996;Caplan,1983)。此类行为包括改变工作目标、任务分配、工作方法、流程、任务设计、安排分配、任务合作以及互动交流(Janssen 等,2004)。那就是说,员工创造力可以为新员工提供有效的应对策略来改善他们的工作环境,这也将影响情感行为。与此相一致的是,Zhou 和 George(2001)发现,员工创造力行为可以使他们通过找到新的更好的工作方法来降低工作不满意的程度。Seibert 等(1999)也指出,创新行为与员工职业成功具有正相关性。因此,在复杂的社会系统内通过合作来创造有用的新思想、新程度或新过程的员工,会获得较大的职业满足感,这是因为他们创造并影响了他们工作的环境。此外,当新员工的创造力行为正向影响了同事和整个工作过程,那么他们会在工作和职业生涯中体验到一定的满足感。创造力行为可以帮助新晋员工有效适应其职位,使其获得较高的职业满足感(West 和 Farr,1989)。由此来看,员工创造力与职业满足感是有关联的。

员工创造力与新进员工对企业内部地位的感知也是有关联的。内部地位感知可以捕捉到在多大程度上员工认为自己是特定的组织内部圈子内的一员(而不是圈外人士)(Stamper 和 Masterson,2002)。圈子内外的员工之间的区别有助于了解员工关系、劳动力效能、竞争优势方面的情况(Pfeffer 和 Baron,1988)。内部地位的功能之一就是职员能感受到自己对工作做出的有效贡献程度的高低。例如,与兼职员工相比,全职员工更可能觉得自己是内部人员(Stamper 和 Van Dyne,2001),因为全职员工通常比兼职员工获得更多的福利、培训和晋升机会,从而,基于社会交互关系,感到有义务将更多的精力投入组织工作中(Blau,1964)。该激励/贡献模式可以让全职员工在组织中变得更加活跃。

某种程度上因为员工创造力与所感到的贡献度有关联,因此它也和感受到的内部地位有关。富有创造力的人关于自己对于组织的贡献,会获得更多正面的感受,他们富有创意的想法会影响其社会地位和社交网络。根据个人控制理论(Greenberger 和 Strasser,1986),在工作中具有创意的员工对工作

employee creativity can increase the extent to which new employees are satisfied with their careers. New employees initially lack identification with their jobs and the activities going on around them, and are less likely to understand how the contingencies in their environments are related to their careers (Kim, Hon, & Crant, 2009). One way to cope with this lack of control and uncertainty is to modify the elements of the work context (Ashford & Black, 1996; Caplan, 1983). Examples of such behaviour include changing task objectives, task assignments, working methods, procedures, job design, allocation and coordination of tasks, and interpersonal communication (Janssen *et al*., 2004). That is, employee creativity can provide new employees with effective coping strategies for improving their job environments, which will influence affective behaviour. Consistent with this, Zhou and George (2001) found that employees' creative actions can reduce levels of job dissatisfaction by finding new and better ways of doing things. Seibert *et al*. (1999) also showed that innovative behaviour is positively related to employees' career success. Thus, employees who create a useful new idea, procedure or process by working together in a complex social system receive greater career satisfaction because they have created and influenced the situations in which they work. Moreover, when new employees' creative behaviour positively influences fellow employees and work procedures, they experience satisfaction with their jobs and careers. Creative action can help new employees adapt effectively to their jobs, leading to greater career satisfaction (West & Farr, 1989). Thus, employee creativity is associated with a sense of career satisfaction.

Employee creativity is also associated with new comers' perceptions of insider status. Perceived insider status captures the extent to which employees believe that they are insiders (rather than outsiders) within a particular organisation (Stamper & Masterson, 2002). The distinction between insider and outsider has been used to understand employment relationships, labour efficiencies and competitive advantages (Pfeffer & Baron, 1988). Insider status is in part a function of the extent to which employees perceive that they are making positive contributions to the workplace. For example, full-time employees are more likely to perceive themselves as insiders than part-time employees (Stamper & Van Dyne, 2001) because full-time employees generally receive more benefits, training and promotion opportunities than part-time employees, and thus feel obligated to contribute more work and effort to the organisation based on social exchange relationships (Blau, 1964). This inducement-contribution cycle can make full-time employees feel more accepted within their work organisation.

In part because employee creativity is associated with perceived contributions, it is also associated with perceived insider status. People who are creative at work will experience positive feelings about their contributions to the organisation, and their creative ideas will affect their social status and social networks. According to personal control theory (Greenberger & Strasser, 1986), employees who perform creatively at

具有更高程度的控制力,以及更多的向他人展示个人创造力和技能的机会。展现创造力技能和能力对个人是否感到是组织中有价值的一员有积极影响,可以增强他们作为组织内部人员的感觉。此外,员工创造力是组织机构非常重视的一个方面,因为这对组织的生存和长期效能都具有十分重要的意义(Amabile、Conti、Coon 等,1996;George 和 Zhou,2001;Oldham 和 Cummings,1996)。由此说来,组织会提供更多的奖励和刺激(例如培训和晋升)给具有创造力的员工,这些员工可以贡献更多的富有创造性的活动。这些特殊的刺激会增强员工对自我创造力的认知,视自己为组织中有价值(而不是可能会被抛弃的)的一员(Stamper 和 Masterson,2002)。

案例研究 11－1①　▶▶▶▶▶▶

　　Barry Du 在他打开放在桌面上的第一封信时,双手止不住地颤抖,这封信是他的秘书 Hickton 女士今早整齐地摆在层层文件之上的。Barry 是市区 Royal Arms 酒店的总经理,他在八年任职期间常常要处理大量邮件,但他从来没有像这次这般惊恐过。他颤抖着双手拿起电话,拨给他的秘书,"Hickton 女士,"他声音颤抖地说道,"请让人力资源部的 Franks 立刻到我这里来一下,然后给我们的代理律师去电话,我们被起诉要赔偿 450 万美元!"

　　Barry 一遍又一遍地阅读着这封来自全国最大法律公司的诉讼信。他正在估量事件的严重程度,这时 Leo Franks 冲了进来,他是酒店人力资源总监。"怎么回事 Barry?"Franks 问道。"Hickton 说她觉得你要突发心脏病了。"Barry 一句话都没说,把信递给了 Franks。他快速地扫了一遍内容,找了把椅子坐下,抬头看着 Barry,疑惑地说道:"为什么他要起诉我们几百万!太疯狂了! 就算曾经有这样的人,我们也都已经解聘得干净利索了。"

　　"嗯,我不是律师,"Barry 说,"但就算我们赢了这场官司,也会让公司损失掉一笔巨大的资金。我们都有可能因此丢掉饭碗。"Barry 告诉人力资源总监,酒店的代理律师要求立刻将信传真给他。"同时,"Barry 说,"我们需要把这家伙的全部档案调出来,准备一份详细的报告,看看这件事到底是怎么发展到这一步的。"

　　10 个月前,两名女性宴会厅服务员指控酒店宴会厅经理 Justin Elliott,说他在女性服务员在布置和打扫宴会房间时用手机拍摄淫秽照片。"他让我

　　① 资料来源:Sommerville, K. (2007). *Hospitality Employee Management and Supervision: Concepts and Practical Applications*, 130 - 132. Hoboken, NJ: John Wiley & Sons.

work gain a high degree of control in their jobs and the opportunity to demonstrate their creative abilities and skills to others. Demonstrating creative skills and abilities positively influences individuals' feelings as valuable members of the organisation, enhancing their perceptions of being organisational insiders. In addition, employee creativity is highly valued by organisations because they need creative employees to survive and to have long-term effectiveness (Amabile, Conti, Coon, Lazenhy, & Herron, 1996; George & Zhou, 2001; Oldham & Cummings, 1996). Thus, organisations will offer more rewards and inducements (e.g. training and promotions) to creative employees who can contribute more creative activities. These special inducements will enhance the creative employees' perceptions of themselves as valuable (rather than expendable) members of the organisation (Stamper & Masterson, 2002).

Case Study 11 – 1[①] ▶▶▶▶▶

Barry Du's hands begin to shake as he opens and reads the first letter on the neatly stacked pile that his secretary, Mrs Hickton, had placed on his desk earlier that morning. Barry, the General Manager of the downtown Royal Arms Hotel, has dealt with a lot of mail during his eight-year tenure, but he cannot remember any letter frightening him quite as much as this one. His hands are still trembling as he picks up the phone and rings his secretary's outer office: "Mrs Hickton," he says in a shaky voice, "get Franks from human resources up here right away, and put in a call to our attorneys: we're being sued for $4.5 million dollars!"

Barry reads and rereads the letter from one of the state's largest law firms. He is just starting to grasp the magnitude of it when Leo Franks, the hotel's Director of Human Resources, bursts into his office. "What is it, Barry?" asks Franks. "Mrs Hickton said she thought you were about to have a heart attack." Barry, without saying a word, hands the letter to Franks. As Franks quickly scans the letter's contents, he locates a chair, looks up at Barry, and says in disbelief, "Why, he's suing us for millions! This is crazy! That was a clean termination if ever there was one."

"Well, I'm no lawyer," says Barry, "but even if we can win this, it's going to cost the company a ton of money. We could all lose our jobs over this." Barry tells the HR director that the hotel's attorneys has asked that they immediately fax them a copy of the letter. "In the meantime," says Barry, "we need to pull this guy's entire file and prepare a full report of just how all this went down."

Ten months ago, two female banquet servers accused Justin Elliott, one of the hotel's banquet managers, of using the camera on his cell phone to take lewd photographs of the female servers while they were setting up and cleaning up the hotel's banquet rooms

---

① Source: Sommerville, K.(2007). *Hospitality Employee Management and Supervision: Concepts and Practical Applications*, 130 – 132. Hoboken, NJ: John Wiley & Sons.

钻到桌子下面,捡起地上的垃圾。"一个服务员在交给人力资源部的报告开头这样写道。"他明明知道在这样的动作下酒店规定的着装会使我们走光,他总是站在我们身后盯着我们偷笑,嘲弄我们。"

"但是这次不一样,"另一名服务员在她的报告中指出。"我看到他拿着手机,放在低于他腰部的位置,我就知道他肯定在拍我们趴在地上的照片。"服务员在报告中声明,她们和Justin对质过照片的事情。她们说:"他告诉我们立刻回去工作,不许抱怨,否则他就将照片发布到个人网页上让全世界都看到。"

那时候,Barry和Franks都一致同意立刻解聘Justin——没有书面或口头警告——立刻解聘。尽管该宴会厅经理已经在酒店服务了超过10年了,但没有人觉得如果允许他继续保留职位,他们能够承担性骚扰案件带来的风险。在解聘面谈中,他们告诉Justin,未经许可使用手机对女性员工拍照是十分恶劣的,并说,如果他明智的话,以后不要再考虑酒店的工作。

"我没觉得这里有什么问题。"Franks说道,"正如我之前提到过的,就算曾经有这样的人,这次解聘也都解决了。"

"我也这么认为,"Barry答道。"可是,在上次事件发生前,关于员工使用手机在工作场合拍摄其他员工的行为,我们从来没有书面的政策规定。"

"那么性骚扰问题呢?"Franks争辩说。"我们已能置他于死地,尤其是我们有两位服务员提供的报告。"

"你又错了,Franks,"Barry闷闷不乐地答道,"我们在此之后根本没有跟进有关性骚扰的条例,我在Justin的档案里找不到任何文件能说明,他完成了我们最新的性骚扰培训。"

"我要找到员工手册的底本,"Franks说,带着一些挫败感。"这次我们一定要认真细致地梳理一遍,大幅度地更新一次!"

"我巴不得这些律师打电话过来。"Barry回答道。

问 题

(1) 如果Justin Elliott在官司中声称自己被"不正当解雇",因为酒店员工手册中没有明确提供关于使用手机在工作场合拍照的相关规定,他有多大的胜诉概率? 酒店代理律师在陈词中可能给出哪些论据?

(2) 由于工作场合中电子技术的使用率越来越高,对于员工滥用电子技术的问题,酒店应该在书面规定中明确哪些政策? 对于互联网、手机、即时通

before and after functions. "He told me to get down under a table and pick up some trash that was on the floor," stated one of the servers in her report to human resources. "He knows these dresses we're required to wear get all hiked up when he makes us do that, and he usually just stands back and gawks and snickers at us, making fools of ourselves."

"This time it was different, though," the other server had noted in her report. "I saw him holding his cell phone down by his waist, and I knew right away that he was taking pictures of us crawling around on the floor." The servers stated in their reports that they confronted Justin about the pictures he had taken. They said that "He told us to get back to work and to quit complaining or he'd post them on his personal Website for the whole world to see".

At the time, both Barry and Franks had agreed that they would terminate Justin's employment immediately—no written or verbal warnings—immediate termination. Even though the banquet manager had been with the hotel for more than 10 years, neither executive felt that they could run the risk of a sexual harassment lawsuit if they allowed him to remain in his position. During the termination interview, they told Justin that using his cell phone to photograph his female employees without their permission was particularly egregious and that he would be wise not to use the hotel as an employment reference in the future.

"I don't see the problem here", says Franks. "As I mentioned before, this was a clean termination if ever there was one."

"I do", replies Barry. "We never had a written policy about employees using their cell phones at work to take pictures of other employees until after this all happened."

"But what about the sexual harassment issue?" argues Franks. "We got him dead in the water there, especially with the statements those two servers gave us."

"Wrong again, Frank", says Barry glumly. "We didn't even follow our own sexual harassment policy on this, and I can't find any documentation in Justin's file that indicates that he even completed our updated sexual harassment training."

"I'm going to pull my master copy of the employee handbook', says Frank, somewhat defeated. 'We're going to have to go through it with a fine-toothed comb and update it big time!'"

"I wish to hell those attorneys would call", says Barry.

Questions

(1) If Justin Elliott's lawsuit is claiming "wrongful termination" because the hotel's employee handbook did not specially provide a policy regarding the use of cell phone cameras at work, what are his chances of prevailing? What arguments might the hotel's attorneys present in its defence?

(2) Because of the increased use of technology in the workplace, what policies should the hotel have in writing with respect to employee abuse of these technologies?

讯、电邮的使用,应该给出独立的规范吗? 请给出解释。

（3）为什么酒店总经理说酒店甚至没有遵循自己的性骚扰规范这一点很重要? 他们要如何继续下去?

（4）请解释记录员工是否接受,例如性骚扰、饮酒等方面的各项规定的培训的重要意义。如果 Justin Elliott 事实上确实错过了最新的性骚扰培训,那么在他案件中可能对酒店造成怎样的影响? 请给出全面解析。

Should there be separate policies on Internet use, cell phone use, instant messaging and email use? Explain.

（3）Why is it important that the hotel's general manager says that the hotel did not even follow its own sexual harassment policy? How should they have proceeded?

（4）Explain the importance of documenting employee awareness training with respect to such things as sexual harassment, alcohol awareness and so forth. If Justin Elliott did in fact miss the updated sexual harassment training, how might this affect his lawsuit against the hotel? Explain in full.

第 12 章　国际人力资源管理

- 探讨人力资源管理的未来问题
- 了解在中国环境下霍夫斯泰德（Hofstede，1980）的五个文化维度
- 了解在劳动力全球化的环境下，与外派员工相关的问题将成为人力资源工作的重要方面

商业组织必须实现全球化，否则只有灭亡一条道路，这是对 21 世纪经济趋势最恰如其分的描述。亚洲是一个全球市场，对许多公司都有经济影响。日本占据经济实力强国地位已经超过 20 年之久，其他国家例如新加坡、马来西亚逐渐凸显出重要的经济实力（Ivancevich 和 Lee，2002）。除此之外，中国拥有超过 13 亿人口，正逐渐打开其市场面向外国投资者，展现出巨大的商品市场前景。

大多数公司最初展开全球化业务时主要是通过出口、授权许可或特许经营。出口需要直接或间接向国外销售，并需要保留国外代理商和经销商（Dessler，2017）。这是许多小型企业进入国际市场的方法之一。授权许可是通过机构授权给外国企业，许可其使用知识产权，例如专利、著作权、制作工艺过程，或在特定时期使用其商品名称。它通常限于制造商。特许经营是指母公司授予其他公司依照规定方式从事商业行为。和授权许可相比较，特许经营必须遵循更严格的运营规范。特许经营多用于服务型企业，例如酒店或餐厅。

尽管出口、授权许可、特许经营都是最初拓展业务的良好选择，但为了最大限度地利用全球机遇，公司最终必须在其他国家进行大量资本投资。公司参与全球业务的程度可能差别很大。跨国企业是设在一个国家（母国或原籍

Chapter 12　International Human Resource Management

The objectives of this chapter

- Investigate the future issues of human resource management
- Understand Hofstede's（1980）five cultural dimensions in Chinese context
- Understand expatriate-related issues will be an important HR aspect in a global workforce environment

In the twenty-first century，business organisations must either globalise or die. Asia is a global market with economic consequence for many firms. Japan has been a dominant economic force for over 20 years，and other countries such as Singapore and Malaysia have more recently become significant economic powers（Ivancevich & Lee，2002）. In addition，China，with its population of over 13 billion and with markets that are opening up to foreign investors，presents a tremendous potential market for goods.

Most companies first enter the global market through exporting，licensing or franchising. Exporting entails selling abroad，either directly or indirectly，and involves retaining foreign agents and distributors（Dessler，2017）. Many small businesses enter the global market in this way. Licensing is an arrangement whereby an organisation grants a foreign firm the right to use intellectual properties such as patents，copyrights，manufacturing processes or trade names for a specific period of time. Licensing is usually limited to manufacturers. Franchising is an option whereby a parent company grants another firm the right to do business in a prescribed manner. Franchisees must follow stricter operational guidelines than licensees. Franchising is popular with service firms such as restaurants and hotels.

Although exporting，licensing and franchising are good initial entry options，to take full advantage of global opportunities，companies must eventually make a substantial investment in other countries. Firms can vary greatly in their degree of global involvement. A multinational corporation（MNC）is a firm that is based in one country （the parent or home country）and produces goods or provides services in one or more foreign countries（host countries）. A multinational corporation directs manufacturing and marketing operations in several countries；these operations are coordinated by a parent

国家),在一个或多个外国(东道国)生产产品或提供服务的企业。跨国企业在诸多国家指挥管理生产制造和市场运营。这些运营都由母公司协调管理的,通常是在原籍国家(Hon & Lu,2015)。

世界正在经历全球化劳动力增长时期。全球人力资源管理就是将人力资源散布在全球,不受地理界限的限制,以实现企业目标。处理全球人力资源问题的个体面临许多挑战,远超过国内同仁(Dessler,2017)。这些挑战包括文化障碍、全球人员配置和国际问题,例如薪酬体系。

文化问题

影响国际人力资源管理的最重要因素就是企业入驻的国家的文化背景。它通常决定了各种人力资源管理政策的效果和作用。在美国奏效的政策,可能在其他文化价值背景下并不奏效(Hofstede,1980)。例如,美国企业十分依赖对于个人绩效的评估,且其奖励也与此紧密相关。但在日本,个人应当服从大局或组织整体的意愿和需要。

霍夫斯泰德文化维度

吉尔特·霍夫斯塔德(1980)指出,不同的文化应该被分为五个维度。这五个文化维度可以帮助我们了解在管理来自不同文化地区的员工时的潜在问题。

1. 个人主义—集体主义

这里指的是整个社会中个体与其他个体之间的关系强度,就是说人们充当单一个体角色而不是集体一员角色的程度高低。在个人主义文化背景下(例如美国、英国、荷兰),人们应该照顾自己的个人利益和直系亲属的利益。个人要独立自主而不是受到集体的保护。在集体主义文化背景下(例如中国、哥伦比亚、巴基斯坦),人们需要关照的是大的社会群体的利益,在个人遇到困难时群体会保护个体成员。

2. 权力距离

权力距离关注的是在一种文化背景下等级体系中的权力关系——特别是权力的不平等分配。它描述通常存在的权力不平等的程度。在权力距离小的文化背景下(例如丹麦、以色列),追求的是尽可能缩小权力和财富的差距,而权力距离大的文化背景下(例如印度、菲律宾),注重的是保持此差异

company, usually based in the firm's home country (Hon & Lu, 2015).

The world is experiencing an increasingly global workforce. Global human resource management (GHRM) is the use of human resources without regard to geographic boundaries to achieve organisational objectives. Individuals dealing with global human resource matters face many more challenges than their domestic counterparts (Dessler, 2017). These challenges range from cultural barriers to global staffing to international issues such as compensation.

Cultural Issues

The most important factor in international HRM is the culture of the country in which a company is located. This often determines the effectiveness of various HRM practices. Practices found to be effective in the US many not be effective in a culture that has different beliefs and values (Hofstede, 1980). For example, US companies rely heavily on individual performance appraisals, and rewards are tied to individual performance. In Japan, however, individuals are expected to subordinate their wishes and desires to those of the larger group.

Hofstede's Cultural Dimensions

Geert Hofstede (1980) identified five dimensions on which cultures could be classified. The five cultural dimensions help us to understand the potential problems of managing employees from different cultures.

1. Individualism-collectivism

Individualism-collectivism describes the strength of the relationship between an individual and other members of a society—that is, the degree to which people act as individuals rather than as members of a group. In individualist cultures (e.g. the US, Great Britain, the Netherlands), people are expected to look after their own interests and the interests of their immediate families. The individual is expected to stand on his/her own two feet rather than be protected by the group. In collectivist cultures (e.g. China, Colombia, Pakistan), people are expected to look after the interest of the larger community, which is expected to protect people when they are in trouble.

2. Power distance

Power distance concerns the hierarchical power relationships in a culture—particularly the unequal distribution of power. It describes the degree of inequality that is considered normal. Cultures with small power distances (e.g. Denmark, Israel) seek to minimise inequalities in power and wealth, whereas countries with large power distances, (e.g. India, the Philippines) seek to maintain those differences. Differences in power distance often result in miscommunication and conflicts between people from different

性。权力距离的不同通常会导致交流中存在误会,使得不同文化背景的人产生冲突。例如,在墨西哥和日本,通常称呼个人的工作职位头衔。而在美国,个体则认为互相称呼名字可以最小化权力距离。尽管这在美国是非常普遍正常的事情,但在其他文化中这可能被视为是冒犯的、失礼的行为。

3. 不确定性规避

这个维度描述了某种文化中的人们对于结构化情境相对于非结构化情境的偏爱程度以及他们对于未来无法被准确预测这一事实的态度。一些文化(例如新加坡、牙买加)拥有较弱的不确定性规避。他们使人们接受不确定性,并接受每天的不确定性。在该文化背景下的人们对待不同观点更随和、更灵活。其他文化(例如希腊、葡萄牙)使人们凭借科技、法律、宗教信仰来寻求安全感。因此,这些文化向人们提出了明确的规则来指导人们如何做到举止得当。

4. 男性主义—女性主义

这里指的是在社会上男女性别角色的界限。男性主义文化(例如德国、日本)视传统的男性为主体价值——炫耀卖弄、获得可观的成果、挣钱——这种文化渗透于社会的每个角落。这些社会强调自信、表现、成功、竞争。女性主义文化(例如瑞典、挪威)提倡视女性为主要价值取向,例如视人际关系重于金钱、互相帮助、保护环境。这样的文化强调服务、关爱弱者、团结。

5. 长期倾向—短期倾向

具有长期倾向文化的社会(例如日本、中国)更关注未来,看重那些从眼前利益来看并不是很必要的有价值的事情,例如节俭(省钱)、持久性。而具有短期倾向的文化(例如美国、俄罗斯、西非)则面向过去和现在,促进尊重传统和履行社会义务。

全球市场下的外派雇员

战略性方案、猎聘、全球外籍人才选拔都是在当今社会企业成功的至关重要的因素。外派雇员一词一般用来指公司派遣往其他国家进行业务管理的雇员。选择外派经理人的主要问题就是要决定在不同文化背景下,组织内谁才是最能胜任该任务的人选。外派经理人必须在其管理运作领域拥有技

cultures. For example，in Mexico and Japan individuals are always addressed by their titles. Individuals from the US，however，often believe in minimising power distances by using first names. Although this is perfectly normal in the US，it can be offensive and a sign of disrespect in other cultures.

3. Uncertainty avoidance

Uncertainty avoidance describes how cultures seek to deal with the fact that the future is not perfectly predictable. It is defined as the degree to which people in a culture prefer structured over unstructured situations. Some cultures（e.g. Singapore，Jamaica） have weak uncertainty avoidance. They socialise individuals to accept uncertainty and take each day as it comes. People from these cultures tend to be rather easy-going and flexible about different views. Other cultures（e.g. Greece，Portugal）socialise people to seek security through technology，law and religion. Thus，these cultures provide clear rules as to how one should behave.

4. Masculinity-femininity

The masculinity-femininity dimension describes the division of roles between the genders within a society. In masculine cultures（e.g. Germany，Japan），the traditional masculine values—showing off，achieving something visible and making money— permeate the society. These societies stress assertiveness，performance，success and competition. Feminine cultures（e.g. Sweden，Norway）promote values that have been traditionally regarded as feminine，such as putting relationships before money，helping others and preserving the environment. These cultures stress service，care for the weak and solidarity.

5. Long-term and short-term orientation

Cultures with long-term orientations（e.g. Japan，China）focus on the future and hold values that do not necessarily provide an immediate benefit，such as thriftiness （saving）and persistence. Cultures with short-term orientations（e.g. the US，Russia， West Africa）are oriented towards the past and present and promote respect for tradition and for fulfilling social obligations.

Expatriates in Global Markets

Strategic planning，recruitment and the selection of global expatriate talent are essential elements of modern-day corporate success. Expatriate is the term generally used for employees sent by a company in one country to manage operations in a different country. One of the major problems in selecting expatriate managers is determining which individuals in an organisation are most capable of handling an assignment in a different culture. Expatriate managers must have technical competence in the area of operations；

术能力,否则他将无法赢得下属的尊重和信服。一名成功的外派经理人必须对当地国家文化规范十分敏感,有足够的适应能力去接受它,有足够强大的内心去应对不可避免的文化冲击(Leung、Wang 和 Hon,2011)。除此之外,经理人的家庭也要具有这样的能力去适应新的文化。这些适应技能可以分为三个维度(Dessler,2017)。

(1) 自我维度。该技能可以使经理人始终保持正面的个人形象和心理幸福感。

(2) 关系维度。需要培养和当地人建立友好关系的技能。

(3) 感知维度。该技能能够使经理人对当地文化有准确的感知和评价。

Arthur 和 Bennett(1995)在他们对国家外派人员的研究中指出,以下五种因素的重要性呈降序排列：家庭情况、灵活性和适应性、工作知识储备和动机、人际关系技能、文化的开放性。

外派人员的培训和发展

一旦外派经理人选定,接下来为应对接踵而至的任务而展开的准备工作就显得必不可少了(Hon & Lu,2015;Leung,Wang & Hon,2011)。由于这些人已经具有相关的工作技能,因此一些公司会关注其在跨文化方面的培训。这些培训包括培养对于所前往国家文化的欣赏和认知能力,从而使外派人员能表现得体。有必要强调有关文化敏感度的几个方面。

(1) 外派人员必须清楚自己的文化背景,尤其是聘用国国民的文化背景。对本国文化具有准确的自知,经理人可以调整个人行为来突出有效的特征,而尽可能缩小不和谐因素的影响。

(2) 外派人员必须清楚了解其新的工作环境中的组织文化。这包括识别哪些类型的领导行为和交际风格在商务会议和社交场合是合适的。举例来说,东方文化认为"沉默是金"。如果和中国客户谈判,对于出现的长时间的静默不要惊慌,这只是单纯地代表他们正在认真思考你的提议。

(3) 外派职员必须学会在新文化背景下进行准确的沟通。一些企业会为外派职员提供语言培训,以帮助他们更快地适应新的文化环境。尽管该假设可能准确,但极少数聘用国家人们可以流利使用母国语言。因此,外派经

otherwise they will be unable to earn the respect of subordinates. A successful expatriate manager must be sensitive to the country's cultural norms, flexible enough to adapt to those norms and strong enough to make it through the inevitable culture shock (Leung, Wang, & Hon, 2011). In addition, the manager's family must be similarly capable of adapting to the new culture. These adaptive skills have been categorised into three dimensions (Dessler, 2017).

(1) The self dimension. The skills that enable a manager to maintain a positive self-image and psychological well-being.

(2) The relationship dimension. The skills required to foster relationships with the host-country nationals.

(3) The perceptions dimension. The skills that enable a manger to accurately perceive and evaluate the host environment.

Arthur and Bennett (1995), in their study of international assignees, found the following five factors to be important in descending order of importance: family situation; flexibility and adaptability; job knowledge and motivation; relational skills; and cultural openness.

Expatriate Training and Development

Once an expatriate manager has been selected, it is necessary to prepare that manager for the upcoming assignment (Hon & Lu, 2015; Leung, Wang, & Hon, 2011). As these individuals already have job-related skills, some firms focus development efforts on cross-cultural training. This includes creating an appreciation of the host country's culture so that expatriates will behave appropriately. This entails emphasising a few aspects of cultural sensitivity.

(1) Expatriates must be clear about their own cultural background, particularly as it is perceived by the host nationals. With an accurate cultural self-awareness, managers can modify their behaviour to accentuate the effective characteristics while minimising those that are dysfunctional.

(2) Expatriates must understand the organisational culture in their new work environment. This includes identifying the types of leadership behaviour and interpersonal styles that are considered acceptable in both business meetings and social gatherings. For example, in Eastern culture, silence really can be golden. So do not panic if long periods of silence form part of your meeting with Chinese clients. It simply means they are considering your proposal carefully.

(3) Expatriates must learn to communicate clearly in the new culture. Some firms attempt to use expatriates who speak the language of the host country, and a few provide language training. However, most organisations simply assume that the host-country nationals all speak the parent-country's language. Although this assumption might be true, seldom do these nationals speak the parent-country language fluently. Thus, expatriate

理必须接受培训,以便在有语言障碍的情况下也能与他人进行交流。

外派人员薪酬

许多跨国企业在发展中国家(例如中国)建立业务点以利用当地廉价的劳动力资源和潜在的市场资源(Leung、Wang 和 Hon,2011)。为了确保经营的效力,外派职员通常被安排在关键岗位。管理的挑战之一就是外籍雇员是依据其本国的劳动力市场薪资水平获取薪酬的,而本地劳动力的薪酬依据的是本地薪资水平,这导致两群体间相对较大的薪酬差距。对于双重工资系统的研究表明,当一组职员的薪资始终比另一组低时,处于劣势的群体倾向于视其薪酬水平是不公平的(Leung、Wang 和 Hon,2011)。本地职员和外籍职员的薪酬差距远超本地的双重薪资体系,因此可以预见到其负面影响十分显著。

外籍职员和本地员工间巨大的薪酬差距使后者认为这的确是不公平的(例如,Chen、Choi 和 Chi,2002;Toh 和 Denisi,2003)。这是有问题的,因为不公平的感觉会滋生大范围的负面反应,从较低的工作士气、不合作、较差绩效表现,到退缩行为、离职、工作越轨行为(Colquitt、Conlon、Wesson 等,2001)。该现象在中国大陆尤为严重,因为外籍职员的薪资是本地劳动者的数倍(Choi 和 Chen,2007)。由此,很重要的一点是去探究可能改善或者加剧其负面影响的非经济类因素(Toh 和 Denisi,2003)。

跨国公司的薪酬差异

先前对于本地职员和外籍职员薪酬差距的研究表明,若外派职员对本地员工具有人际敏感度,那么由于薪酬差异带来的负面影响就会有所减少(Leung、Wang 和 Hon,2011)。例如,如果外籍职员被本地职员视为办事是公正的,这就能改进他们之间的关系。当人们的结果不佳时,他们需要知道背后的原因。高层次的程序公平可以确保他们对决策制定者的信赖,从而增强其对决策的接受度,这也解释了为什么感知到公平会降低不良结果带来的负面效果。

中国环境下的跨国企业,薪酬差距十分明显,许多本地劳动者将此巨大差距视为极度不公平(例如 Choi 和 Chen,2007;Leung 等,2009)。研究确认了一种可以判断薪酬差距的可接受性和合理性的人力资源管理实践:为本地职员创造一种包容的氛围。氛围通常由领导者的行为来营造,其为员工提供了即时的组织环境,汇集员工的认知和感受来进行度量(Schneider、 managers must be trained to communicate with others when language barriers exist.

Expatriate Compensation

Many multinational corporations（MNCs）have set up operations in developing countries（e.g. China）to take advantage of the low labour costs and market potential （Leung, Wang, & Hon, 2011）. To ensure the effectiveness of these operations, expatriates are typically placed in key posts. A challenge for management is that expatriates are paid at a level commensurate with their home labour market, whereas locals receive a local salary, resulting in a relatively large compensation gap between the two groups. Research on two-tier wage systems, in which one group of employees is paid substantially less than another, has generally shown that the disadvantaged group tends to regard its level of compensation as unfair （Leung, Wang, & Hon, 2011）. The compensation gap between locals and expatriates is much larger than in domestic two-tier wage systems, and thus its negative consequences are significant.

The large compensation gap between expatriate and local employees is indeed a source of perceived injustice for the latter（e.g. Chen, Choi, & Chi, 2002; Toh & Denisi, 2003）. This is problematic, because perceived injustice breeds a wide range of negative reactions, ranging from low morale, uncooperativeness and poor performance to withdrawal behaviour, turnover and workplace deviance（for a review, see Colquitt, Conlon, Wesson, Porter, & Ng, 2001）. This issue is serious in mainland China, where expatriates typically earn several times more than their local counterparts（Choi & Chen, 2007）. Hence, it is important to explore the non-financial factors that may ameliorate or intensify the negative effect associated with this gap（Toh & Denisi, 2003）.

Compensation Difference in MNCs

Previous research on the compensation gap between locals and expatriates has suggested that if expatriates are seen as interpersonally sensitive toward locals, then the negative effects of the locals' compensation disadvantage is reduced. For example, if expatriates are perceived by the locals as practicing procedural justice, this improves the quality of their relationship. When people have poor outcomes, they need to know why. A high level of procedural justice can assure them of the trustworthiness of decision makers and enhance their acceptance of decisions, which explains why perceived justice can cushion the negative effect of a poor outcome.

In the MNC context in China, the compensation gap is obvious and many locals see this large gap as highly unfair（e.g. Choi & Chen, 2007; Leung, et al., 2009）. Studies have identified one HRM practice that is diagnostic of the acceptability and legitimacy of the compensation gap: an inclusive climate for locals. Climate is often shaped by leadership behaviour, which provides the immediate organisational context for employees and is typically measured by aggregating employee perceptions（Schneider, Salvaggio, &

Salvaggio 和 Subriats,2002）。一个包容的环境氛围可以定义为本地职员可以分享这样的感知和理解,即由外籍职员执行的自由任意决策为本地员工们提供了参与决策制定的机会。一个包容的氛围和我们有两个清晰定义在薪酬水平之上的团体这样的环境息息相关,这种划分使跨国企业的包容成为一个显著的问题。如果跨国企业的外派职员将本地员工纳入决策制定的过程中,那么当地雇员将认为这种组织范围内的自由决策是一种强烈的信号,即外派职员对他们有着强烈的信任感和承诺感,而且没有剥削的动机。与该推理一致的是,Wayne 等(1997)认为,包容性传达出管理层对员工的承诺和信赖,员工感受到组织对自己的支持和鼓舞,就会反过来对组织忠诚度和组织成员行为产生正相关影响。在本土企业环境中,经理人在下属参与制定决策过程中所表现出来的包容能够建立起信任,以及良好的上下级关系。因此,一个由外籍职员营造的对于本地职员的包容的氛围与本地员工的工作态度呈正相关,同时会对外籍职员产生积极反应。

中国环境下的组织文化

组织文化这一概念被定义为一个体系内共享的价值观和价值形式的纲要,它指导组织如何运转。个体特征的某些方面(例如需求和动机)与组织文化产生互动,来预测组织态度和行为(Hon 和 Leung,2011)。因此,组织的人对文化的适应性与理解不同组织文化下不同个体的适应性的重要性息息相关。这些不同点可以帮助我们预测员工建立积极的工作态度和对自我角色的认知的可能性。

个体需求动机的差异可能影响其对"适应性"的感知,这也可以解释和其他人相比,为何一部分人比另一些人更内在地受到激励,为何不同的人进行同一项任务时会得到不同的结果。只有当工作环境可以满足员工个人的需要、欲望和偏好时,员工对其工作才会感到满意。否则,他们并不会受到内在动机的驱使,相反地,他们会继续例行公事,或者每天机械地重复。

人一文化一致性对员工创造性绩效的影响

内在激励/动机指的是人们倾向于从事他们认为有趣、有挑战性和充满满足感的任务(Hon 和 Leung,2011)。这是驱使每个人所有行为的潜在力量,代表着个人从完成任务中所获得的满足感。研究表明,受内在激励/动机驱使的个体往往在认知上更具灵活性和适应性,这促使他们参与到工作活动

Subriats，2002）. An inclusive climate is defined as one in which local employees' share a perception that the discretionary practices implemented by expatriates provide the locals with the opportunity to participate in decision-making processes. An inclusive climate is particularly relevant in a context that includes two clearly defined by compensation levels. Such divisions make inclusion across group boundaries a salient issue. If the expatriates of an MNC involve local employees in decision-making processes，then local employees will see this organisation-wide discretionary practice as a strong signal that the expatriates trust and are committed to them and lack an exploitive motive. Consistent with this reasoning，Wayne，*et al.*（1997）argued that inclusion conveys management's commitment to and trust of employees and confirmed that inclusion is antecedent to perceived organisational support，which in turn is positively related to organisational commitment and organisational citizenship behaviour. In the context of domestic firms，managers' inclusion of subordinates in the decision-making process serves to build trust and establish good supervisor-subordinate relationships. Hence，an inclusive climate initiated by expatriates for locals will positively relate to job attitudes and also create positive reactions towards expatriates.

Organisational Culture in Chinese Context

Organisational culture has been conceptualised as a system of shared values and norms that guide how an organisation operates. Certain aspects of an individual's characteristics（i.e. needs and motives）interact with organisational culture to predict work attitudes and behaviour. Hence，the person-culture（PC）fit is relevant for understanding the importance of fit for different individuals under different organisational cultures（Hon & Leung，2011）. These differences help predict the likelihood of employees developing positive work attitudes about the organisation and their roles within it.

Individual differences in need motivations may influence perceived "fit"，and this helps explain why some people are more intrinsically motivated than others and why different people can perform the same task but achieve different outcomes. Employees are satisfied with their tasks only if the work environment is able to fulfil their needs，desires and preferences. Otherwise，they are not intrinsically motivated；instead，they will adopt a habitual routine or daily activity pattern in performing tasks.

Effect of Person-Culture Congruence on Employee Creative Performance

Intrinsic motivation is the tendency for people to engage in tasks that they find interesting，challenging and satisfying（Hon & Leung，2011）. It is the driving force behind all of an individual's actions and represents the personal satisfaction derived from completing tasks. Studies have shown that intrinsically motivated individuals tend to be cognitively more flexible and adaptive，and this enables them to participate in activities

中,找到乐趣,促进创造力的发挥(Amabile,1997)。

McClelland(1985)的动机理论研究指出内在动机有三种形式:成就感需要、权力需要和亲和/归属感需要。首先,成就感需要是对成功的一种渴望,期望有超乎寻常的表现。具有成就感动机的个体拥有的是追求杰出绩效表现和通过个人努力获得自尊、地位、成就满足感的内在动力。他们倾向于独立工作,或者和与自己相似的人群一起协作,他们更偏好强调创造力的、解决问题的、获得成就的组织文化。其次,权力需求者渴望对权力的控制,使用强有力的行动来影响他人。在工作环境中,高度权力激励者寻求的是地位和名誉,以此来获得满足感(McClelland,1985)。他们会追求个人抱负,例如获得管理权力和政治地位(House、Spangler 和 Woycke,1991)。第三,亲和力需要倾向的是与他人建立热情的合作关系。具有强烈亲和动机的个体会表现得助人为乐、乐于帮助他人(Stahl 和 Harrell,1981)。研究结果发现具有高度亲和动机的人们在团队工作中表现更佳,团队成员由善于合作的人组成,因此会出现集体主义文化,从而推动集体目标的实现和合作努力,并视集体荣誉和利益为首要。

研究揭示了三种类型的组织文化——创新文化、合作文化和传统文化,这与员工内在动机之间可能有所联系(Hon、Bloom 和 Crant,2014;Hon 和 Leung,2011)。

1. 创新文化

从广义上讲创新文化需要承担风险,以结果为导向,具有刺激性、挑战性,营造了富有进取精神的工作环境。提到动机,员工被鼓励成为具有创造性、适应动态变化的人(Wallach,1983),同时员工本身也会期望企业赏识、奖赏个人的充满创造力和活力的行为。其形式和价值表现强调的是如新颖、成员间平等、开放、灵活性等,这些都可以促进创造力。这种文化被视为可借助所发出的强有力的信号来提升创造力,它暗示给员工无论是冒险、探索、做出可能失败的行为,都是安全的行为(Amabile 等,1996;George,2007;Shalley 等,2004)。过去的研究结果发现,高度的成就感动机与创新文化良好地契合(Wallach,1983;Koberg 和 Chusmir,1987)。因为追求高成就感的人渴望的是出色、偏爱冒险,他们在创新文化环境中会有更佳的表现(McClelland,1961)。由此来说,可以预见的是,拥有高成就感

that they find interesting and facilitates the use of creativity (Amabile, 1997).

McClelland's (1985) motivational study identified three forms of intrinsic motivation: a need for achievement, a need for power and a need for affiliation. The need for achievement (nAch) is a commitment to strive for success and a desire to show standards of excellence. An achievement-motivated person possesses an inner drive towards outstanding performance and a need to achieve esteem, status and feelings of personal accomplishment through personal efforts. They prefer to either work alone or with others who are like themselves, and they express preferences for organisational cultures that emphasise creativity, problem solving and accomplishment. The need for power (nPow) is the desire to control and to use vigorous action to influence the behaviour of others. In the workplace, highly power-motivated individuals seek to acquire status and reputation and gain satisfaction from exercising their influence (McClelland, 1985). They have a tendency to pursue their own individualistic aspirations, such as attaining management and political positions (House, Spangler, & Woycke, 1991). The need for affiliation (nAff) is the desire to establish warm and cooperative relations with others. Individuals with strong affiliation motives tend to be supportive and helpful in their relationships with others (Stahl and Harrell, 1981). Research has found that people with high affiliation motives work well in teams that are composed of cooperative people, and thus a collectivistic culture emerges that promotes collective goals and cooperative efforts and places priority on maximising collective welfare.

Studies have identified three types of organisational culture—innovative culture, cooperative culture and traditional culture—that might correlate with employees' intrinsic motivation (Hon, Bloom, & Crant, 2014; Hon & Leung, 2011)

1. Innovative culture

An innovative culture creates a risk-taking, results-oriented, stimulating, challenging and enterprising work environment. In terms of motivation, employees are encouraged to be creative and dynamic (Wallach, 1983) and the employees themselves expect to be rewarded for their creativity and dynamism. Norms and values that emphasise things such as novelty, equality of members, openness and flexibility are thought to promote creativity. This kind of culture is thought to promote creativity through the powerful signals indicating that it is safe for employees to undertake the risky, exploratory and failure-prone activities that are associated with creativity (Amabile, et al., 1996; George, 2007; Shalley, et al., 2004). Previous research has found a good match between high nAch and innovation (Wallach, 1983; Koberg & Chusmir, 1987). Because high achievers seek to excel and have a propensity to take risks, they are likely to do well in a more innovative cultures (McClelland, 1961). Thus, it is predicted that individuals with a high nAch are likely to work well in an innovative

动机的个体更倾向在创新文化中有出色的表现,该文化需要他们达到更高的组织标准。

2. 传统文化

在中国,传统文化根植于人心,并居于统治地位达数世纪之久。传统文化指的是对传统习俗礼节有坚守的义务,尊重并接受礼俗,以及传统文化价值(Schwartz,1992)。传统文化中强调的是对传统的尊重,个体服从更高等级的权力,遵守规则,人际关系受到严格的行为准则的管理和控制。保持个人的谦虚感来维持人际间和谐共处是传统文化倡导鼓励的价值观,同时通过强烈的社会约束力来维持社会稳定(Fahr 等,1997;Zhang、Zheng 和 Wang,2003)。同时,严格强烈的文化禁令使人们不能挑战现状或批判根深蒂固的行为模式。因此,传统守旧的保守主义抵制新的做事方式,以此来保护传统价值。传统文化可能因此而束缚了个人创造力的发挥,因为传统文化鼓励个体使用安全保险的、系统的、可预测、可控的方式来解决问题(Kirkman 和 Shapiro,1997)。当传统文化足够强大时,具有高度权力动机的个体将会感到权力减少,因境况不同而受限,只能在现有的权力线范围内制定政策。相反地,当传统文化力量削弱时,具有高度权力动机的个体感到更自由,不受教条刻板规矩的约束,其创造力增强,因为他们此时拥有更多的机会去掌控一切,和他人协作实现目标,尽其所有努力来施展权力,以此来影响那些更高等级位子上的人。这表明高度权力动机和较弱的传统文化间可能互相作用,最终指向更高水平的创造力。

3. 合作文化

合作文化是由执行任务、政策和整个流程构成的,其目的是鼓励团队协作、分享信息和经验(Scott 和 Bruce,1994)。合作文化以自发意愿和个体能力为特点,通过在社交网内分享信息和专长来互相帮助,提供有效的信息反馈,从而直接帮助到员工改进工作任务。这些合作性行为不仅为员工提供了及时的帮助,同时强化了社会安全网络,使得员工在未来的创造性活动中可以得到依靠。同事间的帮助、寻求、付出同样提供了解决问题的一种方式,使得员工更愿意参加创造性活动。具有高度亲和动机的员工偏爱帮助和支持团队中的其他人,在工作中有最佳的表现,这强化了合作文化的意义(McClelland,1985)。在关于需求和文化的研究中,Koberg 和 Chusmir

culture that requires them to meet high organisational standards.

2. Traditional culture

Respect for tradition has deep roots in China and was the dominant cultural orientation for many centuries. In a traditional culture, there is a commitment to, respect for and acceptance of the customs and norms of traditional values (Schwartz, 1992). In traditionalist cultures, there is an emphasis on respect for tradition, subordinating oneself to those higher in authority, rule following and relationships governed by strict, prescribed codes of conduct. Maintaining interpersonal harmony and acting with personal modesty are the cherished values of traditionalist cultures and there are strong social sanctions to protect against social discord (Fahr, *et al.*, 1997; Zhang, Zheng, & Wang, 2003). There are also strong cultural injunctions against challenging the status quo or criticising entrenched patterns of behaviour; hence, conservatism, defensiveness against new ways of doing things and protecting traditions are strong social mores. Traditional culture may therefore hamper individual creativity because tradition encourages individuals to seek solutions to problems in a safe, systematic and predictable manner (Kirkman & Shapiro, 1997). When traditional culture is strong, individuals with a high power motive will experience a sense of powerless and be constrained by the status differences and established practices that exist within the lines of authority. In contrast, when traditional culture is weak, individuals with a high power motive feel less bound by rigid rules and policies, and their creativity is enhanced because they have more opportunities to control others, to coordinate others to achieve social objectives and to make vigorous efforts to exercise their power to influence those in senior positions. This suggests that high nPow and less traditional culture may interact, thus leading to higher levels of creativity.

3. Cooperative culture

A cooperative culture is made up of operating tasks, policies and processes that are designed to encourage team work and the sharing of knowledge and experience (Scott& Bruce, 1994). A cooperative culture is characterised by the willingness and ability of individuals to help one another by sharing knowledge and expertise within social networks and providing useful feedback that may direct members towards ways of improving work tasks. This collaborative behaviour not only provides immediate assistance to employees, it may also reinforce a social safety net that members can rely upon during future creative efforts. Helping, seeking and giving among co-workers can also provide a means of problem solving, which makes employees more likely to engage in creative efforts. Employees with a high affiliation motive like to help and support others in a team and perform best in an organisation that emphasises a cooperative culture (McClelland, 1985). In a study of needs and culture, Koberg and Chusmir (2002)

(2002)发现支援型组织文化与高度亲和动机相结合,与工作满意度、参与度显著呈正相关,而与离职意愿呈负相关。因此,当员工感受到组织文化鼓励彼此合作、实现集体目标时,高度亲和动机和创造力之间有强烈的正相关作用。

延伸阅读① ▶▶▶▶▶▶

中国酒店、旅游业人力资源面临的问题

中国的酒店和旅游业正面临着许多人力资源方面的挑战和问题。关键问题在于:执行层面和管理层面都缺乏能胜任的员工、较高的员工离职率、应届毕业生进入该行业意愿程度低、校园课本知识和行业实际间的巨大差距。本研究通过对业内经理人和学术专家的采访以及作者本人在中国的教学和研究经历来探索出现的问题。我们希望的是,这些问题可以引起中国政府和业内领军人物、学术专家的注意,当然这需要所有人倾力合作才能实现。

引 言

为了应对中国酒店和旅游业人力资源方面的挑战,浙江大学和香港理工大学国际企业培训中心在 2004 年联合组织了圆桌讨论会议。来自酒店、旅行社、学术机构的与会者参与了研讨。圆桌讨论会议的议题是"中国酒店和旅游业人力资源面临的挑战"。这次圆桌会议的小组焦点座谈会由香港理工大学酒店及旅游管理学院的张邱汉琴教授主持。超过 20 个代表积极参与了讨论。

酒店视角

业界各方都有所共识的是现今中国在酒店业人力资源管理方面面临诸多挑战和问题。参与研讨者们指出,酒店业人力资源短缺,很难招募到有能力胜任的职员去填补空缺。几年前,如果某家酒店有 300 个空缺岗位,会有近 3000 人前来申请。但现在,一样的空缺数量,却只有大约 200 名申请者。

---

① 资料来源:Hanqin Qiu Zhang,Professor at the School of Hotel and Tourism Management,The Hong Kong Polytechnic University, Hong Kong, China;Ellen Wu, Assistant Lecturer at the College of Tourism, Zhejiang Gongshang University, Hangzhou, Zhejiang, China.

found that in supportive organisational cultures high nAff is significantly related to job satisfaction and involvement and negatively related to intention to leave. Thus, there is a strong positive relationship between a strong nAff and creativity when employees perceive that the organisational culture encourages cooperation among co-workers in meeting organisational goals.

Focus Group Case Study[①] ▶▶▶▷▶▷

Human Resources Issues Facing the Hotel and Travel Industry in China

There are many human resource challenges facing China's hotel and tourism industry. The key issues are the lack of qualified staff at both operational and managerial levels, high staff turnover rates, the unwillingness of university graduates to enter the industry and the gap between what is taught in school and college and the realities of the industry itself. This study explores these issues by interviewing industry executives and academics and through the authors' own experiences of teaching and research in China. The Chinese government, industry leaders and academics must make a collaborative effort to address these issues.

Introduction

To address the human resource challenges facing China's hotel and travel industry, a roundtable discussion is held at Zhejiang University in conjunction with the Hong Kong Polytechnic University International Executive Development Centre in 2004. Participants from hotels, travel agencies and academic institutions attend the discussion. The theme for the roundtable discussion is "Human Resource Challenges Facing the Hotel and Travel Industry in China". The discussion is led by Prof Hanqin Qiu Zhang, Professor of the School of Hotel and Tourism Management, Hong Kong Polytechnic University. More than 20 representatives actively participate in the discussion.

Hotel Perspectives

All of the parties agree that there are many human resource challenges facing China's hotel industry. The participants point out that there is a shortage of human resources and it is very difficult to recruit qualified personnel to fill vacancies. A few years ago, if a hotel had 300 vacant posts, there would be some 3,000 applications. But now, if a hotel has 300 vacant posts, there are likely be around 200 applications. This is due to the rapid increase in

---

① Source: Hanqin Qiu Zhang, Professor at the School of Hotel and Tourism Management, The Hong Kong Polytechnic University, Hong Kong, China; Ellen Wu, Assistant Lecturer at the College of Tourism, Zhejiang Gongshang University, Hangzhou, Zhejiang, China.

这是因为随着中国酒店数量的迅速增加，相应地对员工的需求也大大增加。20 世纪 90 年代，中国许多受过良好教育的年轻人认为酒店可以提供良好的工作环境、更高的薪资水平。在那段时间，酒店招募到态度积极、具有较高能力的人员比较容易。但现在，酒店业的社会地位受到其负面声誉以及像信息技术和银行业这样的新兴产业的全球化的影响而逐渐下降。现状就是受过优质教育的年轻人会更倾向于考虑在能给予更好的职位、更高的薪水和福利的行业工作。酒店业较差的经济状况意味着大多数酒店都无法实现他们的预期。

由于员工能力有所欠缺，就会导致服务标准日渐降低，特别是在四星或五星级酒店。导致这一现象的主要原因如下。首先，本地人力资源短缺使得酒店不得不从欠发达地区招聘受教育水平较低的职员。总的来说这些员工受到文化障碍的限制很难接受培训。其次，由于合适且有能力的候选人十分稀缺，酒店管理者不得已在其尚未具备能力胜任或承担管理职责前提下提升内部员工。再次，上面已提到过，酒店一般无法提供具有竞争力的薪酬和福利给员工，因为许多酒店效益不佳。此外，大多数一线员工都是因为职位空缺而招聘进来的，他们可能缺乏实践经验和作为服务性人员的积极态度。而且显然现在的年轻一代将酒店工作视为进入"高社会地位"的门槛，而不是考虑将其作为终身职业。

结合以上所谈，我们不难发现招聘到合格的人力资源经理是很难的。大多数现在在职的人员缺乏设计制定综合人力资源体系的经验。这会进一步弱化酒店业人力资源的境况，因为其无法建立起专业化的管理方式和手段。酒店员工离职率日益增长，一些有名的酒店品牌（例如香格里拉和假日酒店）通过建立和运营自己的培训中心来应对此问题。这一举措受到了广泛的欢迎，因为它强化了培训理念和职业发展。这种方式对酒店业整体、雇主和职员都有益处。然而，这里的问题是完成高级培训的经理人可能用培训经历作为寻求更高薪酬或更优工作环境的筹码。经过良好培训的酒店经理或具有较高英语水平和管理技能的管理人员很受银行和其他机构的欢迎。某种程度上说，这也是一些刚刚建立不久的新兴酒店不愿意在员工培训上做过多投资的原因，可能的话他们愿意招聘有过培训经历、经验丰富的员工。中国酒店产业正在快速发展。

经理人们认为这是个严重的问题。为了有所改善，他们提出了一些保留策略。其中一个例子是以继任计划原则为基础的。即，只要其中一名员工得

the number of hotel properties in China and the related rise in demand for employees. In the 1990s, many young people with a good education background in China believed that hotels provided a good working environment and higher than average salaries. It was comparatively easy for hotels to recruit high calibre staff with a positive attitude to service during that period. But now, the hotel industry's social position has been undermined by negative publicity and the globalisation of emerging industries such as IT and banking. The current reality is that young people with good educational qualifications prefer to work for industries that offer better paid positions and benefits. The poor financial situation in the hotel industry means that most hotels cannot meet their expectations.

As employees are less well qualified, this tends to further undermine service standards, especially in 4-and 5-star hotels. First, the local human resource shortage has forced hotels to recruit employees with lower educational attainments from undeveloped regions such as rural areas. In general, these employees are more difficult to train due to cultural barriers. Second, as there are too few suitable and qualified candidates, hoteliers have had to promote employees before they are ready to take on supervisory and/or managerial responsibilities. Third, as noted above, hotels cannot generally offer competitive salary and benefit packages as many hotels are not trading profitably. Further, most line employees have been recruited as needed and available and they tend to lack practical experience and a positive attitude towards service roles. It is also apparent that the current young generation sees hotel work as a gateway to a job in a "higher status" industry rather than as a life-time career commitment.

Coupled with the above, it is difficult to recruit qualified human resource managers. Most who are currently employed in this role lack the experience of designing an integrated human resource system. This further undermines the hotel industry's human resource situation, as the ethos of professionalism in management methods and approaches is not well established. Hotel staff turnover rates are increasing and some well-known hotel brands (such as Shangri-la and Holiday Inn) are responding by operating their own training centres. This development is greatly welcomed as it advances the concept of training and career development in a way that benefits the industry, employers and employees in equal measure. However, the problem is that managers who have completed advanced training tend to use this to secure a higher salary and/or better work environment elsewhere. Well-trained hotel managers or supervisors with good English language and management skills are very much welcomed by banks and other organisations. In part, this is the reason why those running newly opened hotels are unwilling to invest in developing their employees; where possible, they will recruit pre-trained and experienced staff. The Chinese hotel industry is growing at a rapid pace and this will make the current situation even worse.

The managers themselves, view this as a serious problem. To solve it, some retention strategies have been developed. One example is based on the principles of succession planning. Here, as soon as one staff member is promoted, his successor is selected. Some

到晋升,那么他的继任人选就会被选拔出来。一些酒店集团正在寻求终身的职业规划,来作为留住其优质经理人的方式。

圆桌讨论中行业代表们提到,政府在人力资源发展方面并没有给予足够的重视,尽管在旅游局已经建立起人事教育部门。该部门向各个部门主管和总经理提供每年的培训项目,但大多数行业专家认为这是表面功夫,效果低下。代表们认为需要由政府资助进行持续的培训计划,如果想要该计划有效,计划就应该成体系并被很好地组织起来。

各位业界代表们在圆桌讨论中达成共识,即从酒店学院或大学毕业的应届生缺乏实践经验和积极的服务态度。大多数应届生对薪酬、监管、工作环境、培训、团队环境都不满意。进一步说,经验显示高学历者流动率极高——通常会在指派为酒店某职位后的数星期内。他们认为自我发展受到了上级(那些看起来技能不足的上岗培训者或是在激励团队方面经验老道者)的阻碍,并抱怨他们看不到清晰的、从执行到管理角色延伸的职业生涯发展之路。代表们一致认为士气和动机水平很低是造成较高的员工离职率的关键因素。

一些人认为中国的"独生子女"政策在新一代的问题上起到了反作用。业内代表人士认为,总体上讲这些年轻人不具备适应工作环境压力的能力,因为他们不习惯酒店的辛苦工作和较长的工作时间。从历史角度看,大多数现有的年龄在30～40岁的高级主管和经理人只是高中毕业,他们得不到接受高等教育的机会。新招募的毕业生会在他们的管理之下。这会引起一些不满情绪,因为前者注重实战经验,而后者重视的是高等教育带给他们的观点和看法。

一些人同意,高素质的员工应当给予相应的薪酬,因为如果缺乏提高薪水以及提供一定的福利待遇的政策,很多酒店几乎不可能招聘到好员工。但很不幸的是,大多数酒店总经理受聘于短期合约,他们被要求将注意力集中在降低劳动力成本上,而不是培养合格的员工上,以此来确保他任职期间酒店的利润。

外籍经理人占据了中国跨国酒店的大部分管理职位。大多数中国经理人缺乏进一步提升的机会,即使他们可能是有能力提高的。一些人抱怨称培训项目太过注重业务,面向本地职员的关于监管、管理方面的培训过少。

hotel companies are looking at life-time career planning as a means of retaining their best managers.

The industry representatives at the roundtable argue that the government is not giving sufficient priority to human resource development, although a personnel education department has been set up in the tourism bureau. The department offers an annual schedule of training programmes for heads of departments and general managers, but most industry professionals think these are superficial and ineffective. Representatives feel that on-going local government-sponsored training is needed and that if this is to be effective, it needs to be systematic and well organised.

The roundtable consensus from industry representatives is that graduates from the hotel schools and universities lack "hands on" experience and a positive attitude towards service. Most graduates are dissatisfied with pay, supervision, working conditions, training and the team environment (among other things). Further, experience shows that degree holders rapidly move on—typically within several weeks of being appointed to a hotel role. Graduates feel undermined by their supervisors (who are unlikely to be skilled on-the-job trainers or experienced in motivating their team) and claim that they cannot readily see a career path from hotel operations through to managerial roles. As morale and motivation levels are low, the consensus is that these are key contributory factors to the high employee turnover levels.

Some argue that the "one-child" policy in China has had an unfavourable influence on the new generation. Industry representatives feel that in general, young people do not possess the ability to adapt to the pressures of the work environment because they are unused to the hard work and long hours of the hotel industry. For historical reasons, most of the current senior supervisors and managers aged from 30 – 40 completed middle school, but did not have the opportunity to continue on into higher education. Newly recruited undergraduates are under their supervision. This causes resentment, because the former place greater emphasis on practical experience, whereas the latter value the insights that higher education has given them.

Some agree that high calibre staff should be paid accordingly, as without improvements in pay and benefits packages, it is almost impossible for hotels to recruit good staff. Unfortunately, most hotel general managers are employed on short-term contracts and they are required to pay more attention to reducing labour costs than developing qualified people, so as to secure profitability during their contract periods.

Expatriate managers occupy the majority of managerial positions in China's international hotels. Most Chinese managers lack the opportunity to progress, despite the fact that they might be qualified for advancement. Some complain that training programmes are too operations oriented and that supervisory and managerial training is rarely given to local employees.

旅游视角

　　所有业界代表们都认为,旅行社市场正面临严峻的人力资源短缺问题,缺失高水平人才会造成长期的影响。在中国,旅游业始终被高流动率困扰,特别是在导游和中层管理人才层次上,因此继任问题一直让人忧心。而且,留任策略还未发展到能解决这些问题。和酒店情形相似,一些旅行社经理人抱怨称没有职业提升培训的机会提供给他们,因为管理层将缩减成本视为重中之重。除了留任问题,这样的短期思维也会造成员工情绪低落和缺乏工作满足感。

　　还有一个问题是招聘人员进入旅行行业本身就有很大的难度。旅行社市场在吸引优秀年轻的、有英语或酒店教育背景的毕业生方面十分困难,这有如下原因。从历史上来看(大致在 20 年前),成为一个国际导游对毕业生来说是很好的选择,因为导游的平均月薪等同于甚至高于其他行业的薪资标准。但如今,导游的月薪,即使算上佣金,相对低于各行业平均收入水平。大部分有资质的国际导游都拥有英语或旅游专业本科学位,对他们来说,在银行业、信息技术或商贸业找到一个月薪为旅游行业两三倍的工作很容易。这种情况意味着在转行前,导游停留在旅游业的时间平均只有 2～3 年。

　　和酒店情况相似,旅行社也很难留住人才。对此有诸多原因可以解释。第一,旅行社倾向于尽可能低成本运营。如果一名导游一天带一个团的游客,按规定他必须要支付给旅行社按人数计算的费用(按人头收费是业内认可的),这就会导致较高的导游流失率。第二,大多数导游和旅行社经理都描述其工作为"例行公事",缺乏职业发展前景。第三,国际旅行社总经理的平均年龄在 50 岁左右。尽管他们通常都具有良好的教育背景,但大部分人并没有参与到专业方向的发展计划中。可是,对他们来说提高知识水平和技能水平、调整管理策略来适应新形势是必不可少的,毕竟中国在过去的 20 年里有着翻天覆地的变化。众人皆知的是,旅行社平均规模在不断缩减,这使得员工们担心企业不能长期发展。这才是旅游业并不被看作是作为终身发展的职业而只作为转向其他行业的垫脚石的关键原因。

　　最后,业界代表们都认为,未来中国的旅行社会面临许多困难,尤其是因为互联网已成为旅游产品分销、游客通信、信息传递和商业交易的方便、经济的工具。

Travel Perspectives

All of the industry representatives feel that the travel agency sector is facing a serious human resource shortage and that the shortage of high-calibre employees will have a long-term effect. In China, the travel sector has been plagued with high turnover, particularly among tour-guides and middle-level managers, and so succession issues are a serious concern. Further, retention strategies have not been developed to tackle the problem. As with hotels, some travel agency managers complain that there is no career advancement training available to them, as general management see cost reduction as the higher priority. Aside from the retention issues, this type of short-term thinking is the cause of resentment and job dissatisfaction.

Adding to the problem is the difficulty in recruiting people to work in travel agencies in the first place. The travel agency sector has difficulty in attracting young graduates in English and Tourism for the following reasons. Historically (up to 20 years ago), working as an international tour guide was viewed as a good choice for graduates, as a guide's averagy monthly salary is similar to or higher than salaries in other industries. Today, a guide's monthly salary, even with commissions, is relatively low in comparison to average income levels. Most qualified international guides graduate with a bachelor's degree in English or Tourism. Thereafter, it is easy to secure a job in banking, IT or commerce, with a monthly salary two to three times of in tourism.

As with hotels, travel agencies find it difficult to retain employees for a number of reasons. First, travel agency businesses tend to operate at the lowest possible cost. If a tour guide leads a group one day, he/she is obliged to pay the travel agency per-person fees the following day (this is known as the *rentou* fee system) and this contributes to high tour guide turnover. Second, most tour guides and travel agency managers describe their work as "routine", with limited career development prospects. Third, the average age of general managers in international travel agencies is around 50 years. Although they typically have a good educational background, the majority do not engage in professional development. Yet it is essential for them to improve their knowledge and skills and/or adjust their managerial strategies to suit the current situation, as China has changed dramatically over the past 20 years. The average size of travel agencies is diminishing and employees are worried that this will affect sector development in the long run. This is a key reason why travel agency work is not viewed as a lifetime career, but as a stepping stone to something else.

Finally, industry representatives agree that travel agents are likely to face a difficult future in China, not least because the Internet has become a convenient and cost-effective vehicle for tourism product distribution, guest communications, information delivery and commercial transactions.

大学视角

学术界代表们十分忧心大量的主修旅游及酒店管理的学生并不愿意在这个行业工作。教师报告称,大多数学生对自己未来想从事什么职业并不清晰,选择酒店及旅游管理专业是因为:

- 学习这些课程的门槛较低(专业的入学要求较其他专业更低);
- 毕业后容易找到工作;
- 酒店通常会有舒适的工作环境;
- 父母引导他们进入这条职业道路。

在他们进入大学前,大多数学生对酒店和旅游业了解甚微,当他们了解了酒店的运营,尤其是他们必须从基层运营职位开始起步时,许多人会经历强烈的"现实冲击"。所以,许多教师预计他们的毕业生并不会申请酒店业的工作。

一部分大学教师感到进入酒店业的初级职位并不需要本科学位。大多数学生觉得适应工作环境有些困难,尤其是最初的六个月时间。对绝大多数毕业生而言,在酒店工作最初的两至三年太辛苦,他们无法承受。还有一部分大学教师认为,酒店管理层对招聘进来的大学毕业生缺乏关怀和关注。进一步说,大部分酒店并不提供管理培训项目,或者持续的职业发展支持。简言之,多数毕业生辞职是因为应对巨大的压力时感到不适。

员工赋权的概念在中国尚未被采用,尽管朝这个方向已经有一些试验性的措施。当下,一个本地酒店管理的品牌公司已决定给予员工更大的员工赋权,因此一线员工可以为了顾客满意度在一定程度上的开销范围内做出任何决定。

从 20 世纪初起,一系列中国的大学和学院开始开办酒店及旅游管理专业,还建立了一些硕士学位项目。然而,要满足行业的教育需求,优秀的教职人员还不足够。这里有许多原因。首先,大多数在旅游学院的教职人员的专业是历史、统计、地理,并没有正式的酒店和旅游方面的培训或经历。他们在教授课程的时候,通常只是照本宣科。其次,教职人员中高学历者(拥有研究生及以上学历)的数量十分有限。

中国的旅游学院虽然有工商部门的参与和投资,但也存在诸多问题。首先,地方政府在教育投资方面施加了限制。其次,私立学校很难招聘到合格

University Perspectives

Academic representatives are concerned that a high proportion of students who are majoring in tourism and hotel management do not want to work in this industry. Teachers report that most students are unclear about their futures, having opted for tourism and hotel management courses for the following reasons:

- it is easy to gain entry to these courses (educational prerequisites are lower than for other subjects);
- it is easy to find a job after they graduate;
- hotels are perceived as offering a nice working environment; and
- their parents guided them to this particular career path.

Most of them know very little about hotels and tourism before they enter college and many of them experience a "reality shock" when they find out more about hotel operations, especially when they learn that they must start their careers in operative roles. As a result, most teachers expect that their graduates will not apply for jobs in hotels.

Some university teachers feel that it is unnecessary for an undergraduate with a BA degree to start their hotel career at the most junior level. It is also felt that most students find it difficult to adapt to the working environment, especially in the first six months. For most graduates, the initial two to three years of hotel work is hard and they are not able to endure it. Some university teachers feel that hotel management give very little care and attention to the graduates they recruit. Further, most hotels do not provide management training programmes or on-going career development support. In short, most graduates resign because they are ill-equipped to cope with the pressures they experience.

The concept of staff empowerment has yet to be adopted in China, although there are tentative steps being made in this direction. Currently, a local brand hotel management company has determined that greater employee empowerment should appeal to the staff and that line employees should be able to make any decisions involving guest satisfaction.

Since the 1990s, an array of Chinese universities and colleges have offered degree courses in hotel and tourism management, and some master's degree programmes are well established. However, the calibre of some of these faculties is not sufficient to meet the education requirements for a number of reasons. First, most faculty members in tourism departments are subject specialists in history, statistics or geography, with no formal hotel and tourism training or exposure. When they deliver lectures, they typically read from a textbook. Second, higher level qualifications among faculty (at master's and doctoral levels) are very limited.

There is some involvement and investment from industry and commerce in China's tourism colleges but there are problems here too. First, local government imposes some

的院长,尤其是同时具有强大的学术能力和行业经验的人选。

业界对教育的期望

所有圆桌会议的代表们一致认为,现存的学院和大学无法满足业界的诸多期望。这有以下原因。

第一,旅游专业学生在开始正式课程前缺乏方向指导。此外,学业第一年的所有科目都属于基础学科,例如英语、数学、大学语文、政治、经济学以及党史。学生在第二和第三年才开始学习专业主修课程。这些课程大多数专业资料都已经过时老旧,而教职人员因为资源有限没有能力开发更优质的教学材料。第四年,学生开始在酒店和旅行社实习。但这些实习项目缺乏足够完善的设计来满足行业的需求和教育需求。

第二,合格有能力的教师资源稀缺,大多数教师缺少实践经验。这也就是教师在教授课程时只能照本宣科的主要原因。在教室里可以展开的案例分析数量较少,而教师本身需要提高学术能力及实践技能。

第三,有人提议大学、学院或者其他酒店类学校应当与酒店和旅游业的企业建立起更多的联系。举例来说,教育部门可以邀请更多的业内精英代表来举办讲座,他们通过这个方式与学生们分享实践经验和技巧。此外,在设计课程和课程架构时应积极寻求业内人士的观点。由行业专家人士组成的顾问委员会可以帮助确保课程内容真正反映行业内的"最佳实践方法"。除此之外,学术专家应与行业强强联手,应用研究和咨询项目的成果,这对整个行业的长期发展十分有益。如有可能,应当鼓励学生参观酒店和旅游部门。这有助于他们更好地理解行业实际现状,以及雇主对毕业生的真实期望。

结 论

本次专题小组研讨得出了诸多结论。首先,尽管中国的酒店和旅游业正在快速发展,但其面临的人力资源方面的挑战会带来负面影响。主要的挑战是员工留任问题、人力资源人才短缺、缺乏合格的经理人、教育和行业预期的差距问题。其次,中国的旅行社系统也面临着严重的人力资源问题。急切地需要适当的留任策略,尽管很多经理人并不将其视为重中之重。有人认为国

restrictions on educational investment. Second, it is very difficult for private colleges to recruit a qualified dean with both strong academic and industrial experience.

The Industry's Expectation of Education

All of the roundtable representatives agree that the colleges and universities are currently unable to meet the industry's expectations for the following reasons.

First, tourism students lack orientation before they start their courses. Furthermore, in the first year, all of the subjects are basic ones, like English, Mathematics, Chinese, Politics, Economics and Party History. The students only start their major courses in the second and third years. In these courses, most of the specialist materials are outdated and the teaching faculty are not able to develop better teaching materials due to limited resources. In the fourth year, students commence internship programmes in hotels and travel agencies, but these internship programmes are not designed to integrate the needs of industry and education.

Second, qualified teachers are rare and most teachers are short of practical experience. As a result, they deliver their lectures by reading from textbooks. Very few of the case studies was used in the classroom and faculty needs to improve either academic or practical skills.

Third, universities, colleges and other hotels schools need to build more links with the hotel and travel industry. For example, the education sector might invite more industry representatives to give guest lectures, so that they can share practical experiences and skills with the students. Further, the views of industry representatives might be actively sought when designing curriculum and course structures. An advisory board of industry professionals would help to ensure that the curriculum reflects the industries "best practices". In addition, academics should seek to collaborate with industry on applied research and consultancy projects that would benefit the whole community in the long run. Where possible, students should be encouraged to participate in educational visits to hotels and travel sector operations. This will help them to better understand the practical realities of the industry and employers' expectations of graduates.

Conclusion

Several conclusions can be drawn from this focus group study. First, although China's hotel and tourism industry is developing rapidly, it seems that human resources challenges are having a negative effect on this development. The major challenges are employee retention, human resource shortages, shortages of qualified managers and the expectations gap between education and industry. Second, China's travel agency sector is facing serious human resources problems. Retention strategies are urgently needed, although it is not considered to be the top priority by general managers. It is felt that

家和省级的旅游行政部门应尽快参与帮助解决该问题。需要为旅游部门经理人和上级领导组织在职培训,制定继任方案的规定和条款。第三,旅游教育方面与行业间存在着巨大的预期差距。业内管理者和经理人对毕业生的绩效表现并不满意。该行业不再是毕业生首选的职业方向也使得情况不断恶化。缩小二者间差距是个战略性问题,需要全体利益相关者的重视,特别是行业内人士、学术专家和政府。现有的教育课程内容老旧、过时,急须植入由行业人士组成的顾问委员会提供的内容,这尤其是因为才能出众的教育者十分稀缺。最后,在中国乃至全球,还有很多事情需要去完成,以帮助教育者们不断加强其个人技能和获得行业经验。

案例分析 12 – 1① ▶▶▶▶▶▶

　　万豪国际是全球盈利最佳的酒店和提供住宿业务的全球运营商和特许经营商。本案例研究是依据万豪国际的人力资源战略,去了解是什么促使它成为"最佳雇主",并分析"最佳雇主"和"最佳提供者"之间的联系。该企业是出色的人力资源管理和战略规划实例,因此值得对其组织战略进行深入细致的研究。万豪国际建立了很高的目标以及清晰的愿景,这成就了它现在的一切。它的成就包括优质的客户服务、独特的市场策略、长远的愿景和使命、低投诉率、杰出的服务和员工激励、准确的培训和对初中高不同等级员工的培训和发展。

　　首先要讨论的是客户服务的实现,这是酒店业的重中之重,可以说要实现完美的客户服务,最重要的因素就是完美的员工或完美无缺的员工培训,这也是万豪国际的首要优势所在。其旗下员工接受高度训练和激励,并总是在寻求发现酒店业的新特质。如此新颖的创意给企业在竞争市场中带来了巨大的优势。万豪国际旗下的华美达国际是首家提供无反向脂肪菜单的酒店连锁企业。其因向顾客提供最舒适、奢华的服务而广受欢迎,其舒适、奢华的服务也使其斩获诸多殊荣。

　　① 资料来源:Bernadine,H.(2010).*Human Resource Management—An Experiential Approach*(5th ed).New York:McGraw Hill;Ulrich,D.(1997). *Human Resource Champions—The Next Agenda for Adding Value and Delivering Results*.Boston:Havard Business School Press;Marriott J.W.,Diversity and Inclusion,A Global Factsheet. reterieved from http://www.marriott.com/Multmedia/PDF/Corporate/Diversity Factshe et.pdf.

national and provincial tourism administration should be involved in helping to resolve this problem in the short term. On-the-job training needs to be organised for travel sector managers and supervisors and provisions made for succession planning. Third, there is a significant expectations gap between tourism educators and the industry. Industry executives and managers are not satisfied with the performance of graduates. This situation is made worse by the fact that the industry does not appeal to graduates as a career choice. The challenge of narrowing the gap is a strategic problem that needs the attention of all of the stakeholders, and especially industry, academia and government. The current curriculum is old and out-dated and inputs from industry-based advisory panels are urgently needed, especially as high calibre educators are rare. Finally, more needs to be done to help educators to enhance their own skills and experiences both of the industry in China and internationally.

Case Study 12 – 1[①] ▷▷▷▷▷▷

Marriott International is a worldwide operator and franchisor of the most lucrative and profitable business in the world i.e. hotel and lodging. This case study is based on the HR strategies followed by Marriott International, to find what have enabled it to become an "employer of choice". The case study also analyses the connection between being an "employer of choice" and being a "provider of choice". The organisation is a living example of management and strategic planning and its organisational strategies are well worth researching. Marriott International had to establish high goals and a defined vision to become what it is now. The achievement is a convergence of high customer service, uniqueness in marketing strategies, prolonged vision and mission, low complaints, excellent service by motivated employees and proper training and development of employees at the higher, middle and junior level.

Customer service delivery is critical in the hotel business and perfect customer service delivery requires perfect employees or perfectly trained employees, which is the first advantage of Marriott International. The employees are highly trained and motivated and are always seeking to discover new features in the hotel industry. Such new ideas give the firm a competitive advantage. Marriott International owns Ramada International, which was the first hotel chain to offer a menu without trans fats. It also became popular for its excellent and luxury service delivery and has won many awards for both service delivery and extravagant luxury.

---

① Source: Bernadine, H. (2010). *Human Resource Management—An Experiential Approach* (5th ed). New York: McGraw Hill; Ulrich, D. (1997). *Human Resource Champions—The Next Agenda for Adding Value and Delivering Results*. Boston: Havard Business School Press; Marriott J.W., *Diversity and Inclusion, A Global Factsheet*. reterieved from http://www.marriott.com/Multmedia/PDF/Corporate/Diversity Factshe et.pdf.

　　该企业拥有出色的市场占有率以及在招聘时广受青睐的关键因素,是其具有远见卓识和战略性的人力资源决策。第一个因素是它的"目标招聘活动"。在这个战略性招聘程序中,工作要求被全面审查,并从公司内部招聘合适的人员,这样,不仅有助于企业保持住高质量的人才,还可以最小化解决内部摩擦问题的额外费用。

　　万豪国际始终坚持这样一个原则:为了达到其长期目标,它需要在招聘每一个新人时,都选择业内最好的人。万豪的招聘过程包括多轮考核,包括心理测验、性格测验、个人面谈、小组讨论以及严格的推荐人审核。尽管其他许多企业也采用这些招聘方法,但万豪国际在招聘过程中还考虑内在核心能力和个性活力。

　　万豪国际的人力资源方面的专家重视创造力和绩效,这使得他们轻易地击败了全球市场上的竞争对手,无论是新兴的酒店还是老牌的先锋。他们成功地收购了一些有名的连锁酒店,并帮助他们达到新标准。该企业最大的成就要数其超越了文化和地理界限,获取客户的能力以及在全球范围能进行人才竞争的能力。一旦这两方面相结合,就使其成为"最佳雇主"和"最佳提供者"。

　　在万豪集团的愿景中,他们声称自己是一个以人为主体的企业。工作中的人必须受到尊重、尊敬、激励、感到温暖,反过来这将激励员工使客户有一样的感受。这就是该企业激励员工增加工作乐趣的主要方式,它间接地引导员工在服务客人时报以温暖、快乐之情,使得万豪国际对于员工和顾客来说都是更优的选择。

　　万豪国际的人力资源团队是相当聪明的,其一直在寻找新的机会。这产生了不断的变化,而管理层最大限度地尊重支持每个新的策略,这点尤为重要。万豪的竞争者们对其服务质量很难构成威胁,这是因为万豪的人力资源团队具有较强的创新和采用新技术的动力。企业拥有一个卓越的委员会,其

The reasons for the organisation's excellent market capture and its popularity as a place to work are its far-sighted vision and strategic HR decisions. The first factor is its "target recruitment campaign". In this strategic recruitment process, job requirements are fully scrutinised and suitable people are recruited from within the firm, which not only helps the organisation to maintain quality people, it also minimises the extra cost involved in managing attrition problems.

Marriott International works on the principle that to achieve their long-term goals they need to choose the best in the industry with every new person recruited. Marriott's recruitment process has many rounds involving psychometric checks, personality checks, personal interviews, group discussions and also strict referral checks. These methods are also used by many other organisations but Marriott International's recruitment process considers both inner ability and personality dynamism.

HR professionalsat Marriott International value creativity and performance and they easily beat the competition in the global market of emerging new hotels and old market pioneers. They have successfully acquired some renowned hotel chains and helped them reach new standards. The biggest achievement of the organisation could be its ability to reach people, i.e. customers, across cultural and geographical borders and to compete for people and talent worldwide. When these factors come together, the result is "employer of choice" and "provider of choice".

In their vision and mission, they claim they are an organisation that stands by its people; the people on the job must be respected, honoured, motivated and feel at home, which in turn motivates them to make the customers feel the same way. This is a powerful way to motivate employees and make them happy at work; it indirectly leads employees to serve customers with grace and happiness, making Marriott a better place for both employees and guoots.

The HR team at Marriott International is extremely talented and is continually looking for new opportunities. It makes regular changes, and management supports each and every new strategy with utmost respect, which is very important. Marriott International's competitors cannot easily imitate this diversity, as the HR team at Marriott is highly motivated to innovative and adopt new techniques. The organisation has a committee for excellence that works on diversity objectives and monitors progress at each and every level of organisation. This committee has a special team of people who work on regional diversity in local markets. The committee ensures diversity in communication, in leadership development programmes for local employees, in strategic partnerships and in conferences that reach a customer base all over the world.

Marriott International's HR policies are based on the recognition that their international expansions and global operations require long-term commitment from employees and they are committed to diversity management in a global market. The retention rate is very high compared to their competitors, and they have a committed, dynamic and diverse workforce

致力于实现不同方面的目标,在组织内的每个层级监管每项进程。该委员会有一个专门的小组负责本地市场的区域多样性分析。该委员会确保沟通的多样性、本地员工的领导力发展项目的多样性、战略合作伙伴的多样性以及面向全球顾客的对外交流会议的多样性。

万豪国际的人力资源政策基于这样一个认识,其全球扩张和运营要求员工给予长期承诺,他们需要承诺在全球市场上进行多样化管理。相比较业内市场的竞争对手,其员工留任率极高。他们拥有一支敬业、充满活力、多元化的员工队伍,员工来自 66 个国家、可以使用超过 60 种语言。而且,他们的员工中 61% 是少数民族,50% 是女性。所有这些员工都具备较高的专业素养,而且都在万豪国际寻求长期的职业生涯发展。

万豪国际专注于对员工进行熟练的语言培训,尤其是熟练掌握英语,企业长期设置的"求知欲"项目,致力于培训员工讲西班牙语或英语的能力,使其员工在英语口语流畅度上达到较高水平。人力资源被视为每个组织的重要财富,而万豪国际将所有员工看作合伙人,其与供应链或其他供应商之间也保持紧密的联系。其在供应链方面也努力达到多样性。公司供应链多样化项目使得其供应商中有 15% 为少数民族或女性拥有的企业。为了实现这一目标,他们在地方、区域和全国供应商市场开展工作。他们努力支持少数民族和女性拥有的小企业,也帮助他们的企业成长和发展。这同时带给公司稳定、繁荣的发展,因为企业希望企业股东和多样化的合作伙伴可以共同成长、繁荣壮大。

结　论

对万豪国际集团来说获得"最佳供应者"和"最佳雇主"的荣誉着实是巨大的成就。如此高的成就背后的核心就是其广泛、独有的人力资源劳动力,他们为企业保持酒店业佼佼者的地位做出了持续的贡献。

公司的人力资源政策是其成功占领全球市场和实现全球多样化经营的基础。出色的战略性招聘借助招聘活动、供应商多样性的项目、员工培训与发展、个性发展方案、英语流畅度培养项目、高水平的货币与非货币奖赏,有助于员工保持良好的积极性,也使得万豪成为"最佳雇主"。

除了出色的市场占有率、酒店的多样化、得体的员工队伍、完美的服务、时间管理、全球扩张中文化和区域意识,最重要的是高质量。奢华的酒店设施、健康的住宿和餐饮设施,使得万豪成为"最佳供应者"。

这两者的平衡依仗着企业优秀的人力资源团队,能为顾客带来正能量的被高度激励的员工,以及能在国际市场上强化组织归属感的多样化的劳动力。

这个平衡的获得也与企业把雇佣少数民族和女性作为其多样化的管理项目的一部分的策略相关,也与企业致力于承担其他社会责任相关。这一切

who can speak more than 60 languages and belong to more than 66 countries. Furthermore, 61 per cent of their workforce are minorities and 51 per cent are women; all of their employees are highly professional and seek long-term careers at Marriott.

Marriott focuses on training employees in language proficiency, specifically English language proficiency. Its long-standing "Thirst for Knowledge" programme, which focuses on training employees in Spanish and English, has given its employees a high level of English language proficiency. Human resources are considered an asset in every organisation, but Marriott considered its employees as partners and also has strong links with supplier chains and other vendors. They work on achieving diversity in the supplier chain as well. Their company-wide supplier diversity programme has resulted in 15 per cent of their suppliers being minority-or women-owned businesses. To reach this goal, they worked on local, regional and national supplier markets. Their effort to support minority- and women-owned small businesses has helped them to grow and develop. It also brings stability and growth to the firm, as the company wants the stake owners and diversity partners to grow and prosper with them.

Conclusion

It is a great achievement for Marriott International to be recognised as both a "provider of choice" and "employer of the choice". Both titles are big achievements for the firm and the key to both successes is a wide and exclusive HR workforce that continuously works to make the firm a leader in the hotel industry.

The company's HR policies are the foundation of its success in capturing the market globally and diversifying worldwide. Excellent strategic recruitment through recruitment campaigns, suppliers diversity programmes, training and development of employees, personality development programmes, English language proficiency programmes for employees and high levels of monetary and non-monetary rewards help employees to always remain motivated and makes the firm an "employer of choice".

In addition to this excellent market capture, the hotels' diversified and graceful workforce, perfect service delivery, time management, cultural and regional awareness in international expansions and most importantly its quality, luxurious and healthy facilities for lodging and eating makes the organisation the "provider of choice".

The balance between the two is achieved by an excellent HR team, highly motivated employees who give positive energy to the customers and a diverse workforce that enhances the organisation's sense of belongingness even in the international market.

The balance may also be related to the company's strategy of using minorities and women as part of its diversity management programme and the company's focus on its other social responsibilities. These things lift the standard of the firm and make it

都将企业标准提升到了新高度,获得了全球市场的认可,取得核心竞争优势,即使在如此严峻的市场条件下。万豪国际的经营范围不只局限在美国本土及附近地区的酒店领域,其已是酒店业的领军人物,凭借多样化的管理成为最著名的国际连锁酒店品牌。它凭借其正直、高收益、社会责任感以及名望和美誉,获得了极高的全球认可度。

问 题

（1）你同意万豪国际拥有"最佳雇主"和"最佳供应者"的荣誉吗？

（2）请评价该企业人力资源政策的正反两个方面。

globally acceptable and competitive even in stiff and adverse market conditions. The business of Marriott International is not limited to the hotel industry in US or nearby areas，but it is considered a pioneer in the hotel industry，and its international chain of hotels is best known for diversity management. It has gained worldwide recognition for its integrity，profitability，social responsibility as well as fame and popularity.

Questions

(1) Do you agree that the Marriott International is an "employer of choice" and a "provider of choice"?

(2) Evaluate the pros and cons of the company's HR policies.

参考文献

References

Ajzen, I., & Fishbein, M.(1980). Understanding attitudes and predicting social behaviour.

Amabile, T. M., Conti, R., Coon, H., Lazenby, J., & Herron, M.(1996). Assessing the work environment for creativity. *Academy of management journal*, 39(5), 1154 – 1184.

Amabile, T. M.(1997). Motivating creativity in organizations: On doing what you love and loving what you do. *California management review*, 40(1), 39 – 58.

Amason, A. C., & Schweiger, D. M.(1997). The Effects of Conflict on Strategic Decision Making Effectiveness and Organizational. *Using conflict in organizations*, 101.

Ahearne, M., Mathieu, J., & Rapp, A.(2005). To empower or not to empower your sales force? An empirical examination of the influence of leadership empowerment behavior on customer satisfaction and performance. *Journal of Applied psychology*, 90(5), 945.

Arnold, J. A., Arad, S., Rhoades, J. A., & Drasgow, F.(2000). The empowering leadership questionnaire: The construction and validation of a new scale for measuring leader behaviors. *Journal of Organizational Behavior*, 21(3), 249 – 269.

Arthur, W., & Bennett, W.(1995). The international assignee: The relative importance of factors perceived to contribute to success. *Personnel Psychology*, 48(1), 99 – 114.

Aziz, A., Goldman, H. M., & Olsen, N.(2007). Facets of Type A personality and pay increase among the employees of fast food restaurants. *International Journal of Hospitality Management*, 26(3), 754 – 758.

Bandura, A.(1986). *Social foundations of thought and action: A social cognitive theory*. Prentice-Hall, Inc.

Bannister, B. J., Chan, A. W., Mak, W. M., Ng, C. W., & Bennett, R.(1998). Managing human resources in Hong Kong(2nd edition). Sweet & Maxwell Asia: Thomson Company.

Barber, N., Ghiselli, R., & Deale, C.(2007). Assessing the relationship of CEO compensation and company financial performance in the restaurant segment of the hospitality industry. *Journal of Foodservice Business Research*, 9(4), 65 – 82.

Baron, R. M., & Kenny, D. A.(1986). The moderator-mediator variable distinction in social psychological research: Conceptual, strategic, and statistical considerations. *Journal of personality and social psychology*, 51(6), 1173.

Bennett, R. J., & Robinson, S. L. (2003). The past, present, and future of workplace deviance research.

Berman, J. A. (1997). *Competence-based employment interviewing*. Greenwood Publishing Group.

Bernadine, H. (2010). Human resource management-an experiential approach (5th ed). New York: McGraw Hill.

Bhaskar-Shrinivas, P., Harrison, D. A., Shaffer, M. A., & Luk, D. M.(2005). Input-based and time-based models of international adjustment: Meta-analytic evidence and theoretical extensions. *Academy of Management Journal*, 48(2), 257 – 281.

Bharwani, S., & Jauhari, V.(2013). An exploratory study of competencies required to co-create memorable customer experiences in the hospitality industry. *International Journal of Contemporary Hospitality Management*, 25(6), 823 – 843.

Bies, R. J., & Shapiro, D. L.(1987). Interactional fairness judgments: The influence of causal accounts. *Social Justice Research*, 1(2), 199 – 218.

Blau, P. M.(1964). *Exchange and power in social life*. Transaction Publishers.

Bono, J. E., & Judge, T. A. (2003). Self-concordance at work: Toward understanding the motivational effects of transformational leaders. *Academy of Management Journal*, 46(5), 554 – 571.

Bowe, R.(2005). Going green: Red stripe, yellow curry and green hotels. *The Environmental Magazine*, 16(1), 52 – 53.

Brewster, C., Carey, L., Grobler, P., Holland, P., &Warnich, S. (2008). Contemporary issues in human resrouce management: Gaining a competitive advangate (3rd edition). Oxford University Press Ourthern Africa(Pty) Ltd.

Brislin, R. W. 1986. "The Wording and Translation of Research Instrument". *Fields Methods in Cross-Cultural Research*, 137 – 164.

Brockner, J., & Wiesenfeld, B. M.(1996). An integrative framework for explaining reactions to decisions: interactive effects of outcomes and procedures. *Psychological bulletin*, 120(2), 189.

Brown, D., & Armstrong, M., (1997). Terms of enrichment. *People Management*, 36 – 38.

Brownell, J.(2008). *Building Managers' Skills to Create Listening Environments*. Cornell University, School of Hotel Administration, The Center for Hospitality Research.

Brownell Ph D, J.(2009). Fostering service excellence through listening: What hospitality managers need to know.

Butcher, K., Sparks, B., &McColl-Kennedy, J. (2009). Predictors of customer service training in hospitality firms. *International Journal of Hospitality Management*,

28(3), 389 – 396.

Bryant, M., & Higgins, V.(2009). Self-confessed troublemakers: Aninteractionist view of deviance during organizational change. *Human relations*.

Chan, B., & Coleman, M.(2004). Skills and competencies needed for the Hong Kong hotel industry: The perspective of the hotel human resources manager. *Journal of Human Resources in Hospitality & Tourism*, 3(1), 3 – 18.

Chan, E. S.(2011). Implementing environmental management systems in small- and medium-sized hotels: Obstacles. *Journal of Hospitality & Tourism Research*, 35(1), 3 – 23.

Chan, E., Hon, A., Chan, W., & Okumus, F. (2014). What drives employees' intentions to implement green practices in hotels? The role of knowledge, awareness, concern and ecological behavior. International Journal of Hospitality Management, 40, 20 – 28.

Chan, E., Hon, A., Okumus, F., & Chan, W. (2017). An empirical study of environmental practices and employee ecological behavior in the hotel industry. Journal of Hospitality & Tourism Research, 41(5), 585 – 608.

Chen, C. C., Choi, J., & Chi, S. C.(2002). Making justice sense of local-expatriate compensation disparity: Mitigation by local referents, ideological explanations, and interpersonal sensitivity in China-foreign joint ventures. Academy of Management Journal, 45(4), 807 – 817.

Chen, C., Kasof, J., Himsel, A., Dmitrieva, J., Dong, Q., & Xue, G.(2005). Effects of explicit instruction to "be creative" across domains and cultures. *The Journal of Creative Behavior*, 39(2), 89 – 110.

Chen, G., Kirkman, B. L., Kanfer, R., Allen, D., & Rosen, B.(2007). A multilevel study of leadership, empowerment, and performance in teams. *Journal of Applied Psychology*, 92(2), 331.

Chen, L. C., & Tseng, C. Y.(2012). Benefits of cross-functional training: three departments of hotel line supervisors in Taiwan. *Journal of Hospitality and Tourism Management*, 19, e11.

Chand, M.(2010). The impact of HRM practices on service quality, customer satisfaction and performance in the Indian hotel industry. *The International Journal of Human Resource Management*, 21(4), 551 – 566.

Chiang, C. F., Back, K. J., & Canter, D. D.(2005). The impact of employee training on job satisfaction and intention to stay in the hotel industry. *Journal of Human Resources in Hospitality & Tourism*, 4(2), 99 – 118.

Choi, J., & Chen, C. C.(2007). The relationships of distributive justice and compensation system fairness to employee attitudes in international joint ventures. *Journal of Organizational Behavior*, 28(6), 687 – 703.

Colquitt, J. A., Conlon, D. E., Wesson, M. J., Porter, C. O., & Ng, K. Y.(2001).

Justice at the millennium: a meta-analytic review of 25 years of organizational justice research. *Journal of applied psychology*, 86(3), 425.

Cavanaugh, M. A., Boswell, W. R., Roehling, M. V., & Boudreau, J. W.(2000). An empirical examination of self-reported work stress among US managers. *Journal of applied psychology*, 85(1), 65.

Caplan, R. D.(1983). Person-environment fit: Past, present, and future. In C. L. Cooper(Ed.), Stress research(pp. 35 – 78). Wiley: New York.

Chan, S. H., &Kuok, O. M.(2011). A study of human resources recruitment, selection, and retention issues in the hospitality and tourism industry in Macau. *Journal of Human Resources in Hospitality & Tourism*, 10(4), 421 – 441.

Croes, R., & Tesone, D. V.(2007). The indexed minimum wage and hotel compensation strategies. *Journal of Human Resources in Hospitality & Tourism*, 6(1), 109 – 124.

Cheng-Hua, T., Shyh-Jer, C., & Shih-Chien, F.(2009). Employment modes, high-performance work practices, and organizational performance in the hospitality industry. *Cornell Hospitality Quarterly*.

Costen, W. M., & Barrash, D. I.(2006). ACE-ing the hiring process: a customer service orientation model. *Journal of Human Resources in Hospitality & Tourism*, 5(1), 35 – 49.

Chan, W. W., & Ho, K.(2006). Hotels' environmental management systems(ISO 14001): creative financing strategy. *International Journal of Contemporary Hospitality Management*, 18(4), 302 – 316.

Chang, W., &Madera, J. M.(2012). Using social network sites for selection purposes: An investigation of hospitality recruiters. *Journal of Human Resources in Hospitality & Tourism*, 11(3), 183 – 196.

Costen, W. M., & Salazar, J.(2011). The impact of training and development on employee job satisfaction, loyalty, and intent to stay in the lodging industry. *Journal of Human Resources in Hospitality & Tourism*, 10(3), 273 – 284.

Chew, Y. T., & Wong, S. K.(2008). Effects of career mentoring experience and perceived organizational support on employee commitment and intentions to leave: A study among hotel workers in Malaysia. *International Journal of Management*, 25(4), 692.

Chang, Y. C., Chang, H. T., Chi, H. R., Chen, M. H., & Deng, L. L.(2012). How do established firms improve radical innovation performance? The organizational capabilities view. *Technovation*, 32(7), 441 – 451.

Cohen-Charash, Y., & Spector, P. E.(2001). The role of justice in organizations: A meta-analysis. *Organizational behavior and human decision processes*, 86(2), 278 – 321.

Davies, D.,&Wei, L.(2011). Human resources management in China: cases in HR practice. Oxford England: Chandos Pub.

DeDreu, C. K. (2008). The virtue and vice of workplace conflict: Food for (pessimistic) thought. *Journal of Organizational Behavior*, 29(1), 5 – 18.

Denison, D. R.(1996). What is the difference between organizational culture and organizational climate? A native's point of view on a decade of paradigm wars.*Academy of management review*, 21(3), 619 – 654.

Deci, E. L., & Ryan, R. M.(2000). The "what" and "why" of goal pursuits: Human needs and the self-determination of behavior. *Psychological inquiry*, 11(4), 227 – 268.

Deci, E. L., & Ryan, R. M.(1985). The general causality orientations scale: Self-determination in personality. *Journal of research in personality*, 19(2), 109 – 134.

Dierdorff, E. C., & Surface, E. A.(2008). If you pay for skills, will they learn? Skill change and maintenance under a skill-based pay system. *Journal of Management*, 34(4), 721 – 743.

Dermody, M. B., Young, M., & Taylor, S. L.(2004). Identifying job motivation factors of restaurant servers: insight for the development of effective recruitment and retention strategies. *International Journal of Hospitality & Tourism Administration*, 5(3), 1 – 14.

DiPietro, R. B., & Condly, S. J. (2007). Employee turnover in the hospitality industry: An analysis based on the CANE model of motivation. *Journal of Human Resources in Hospitality & Tourism*, 6(1), 1 – 22.

DiPietro, R. B., Murphy, K. S., Rivera, M., & Muller, C. C.(2007). Multi-unit management key success factors in the casual dining restaurant industry: A case study. *International journal of contemporary hospitality management*, 19(7), 524 – 536.

DiPietro, R. B., & Pizam, A.(2007). Employee alienation in the quick service restaurant industry. *Journal of Hospitality & Tourism Research*.

Deng, S. M., & Burnett, J.(2002). Water use in hotels in Hong Kong. *International Journal of Hospitality Management*, 21(1), 57 – 66.

Dessler, G. (2017). Human resource management (15th ed). Boston: Pearson Higher Education.

Ellis, J. D., Arendt, S. W., Strohbehn, C. H., Meyer, J. and Paez, P.(2010). Varying influences of motivation factors on employees' likelihood to perform safe food handling practices because of demographic differences. *Journal of Food Protection*, 73 (11), 2065 – 2071.

Evans, M. G.(1985). A Monte Carlo study of the effects of correlated method variance in moderated multiple regression analysis.*Organizational behavior and human decision processes*, 36(3), 305 – 323.

Fodor, E. M., & Carver, R. A. (2000). Achievement and power motives, performance feedback, and creativity. *Journal of Research in Personality*, 34 (4), 380 – 396.

Fodor, E. M., & Greenier, K. D. (1995). The power motive, self-affect, and creativity. *Journal of Research in Personality*，29（2），242 – 252.

Farh，J. L.，Earley，P. C.，& Lin，S. C.（1997）. Impetus for action：A cultural analysis of justice and organizational citizenship behavior in Chinese society. *Administrative science quarterly*，421 – 444.

Fjelstul，J.，& Tesone，D. V.（2008）. Golf and club entry level management competencies. *International Journal of Contemporary Hospitality Management*，20（6），694 – 699.

Fassina，N. E.，Jones，D. A.，& Uggerslev，K. L.（2008）. Meta-analytic tests of relationships between organizational justice and citizenship behavior：testing agent-system and shared-variance models. *Journal of Organizational Behavior*，29（6），805 – 828.

Frash，R.，Antun，J.，Kline，S.，& Almanza，B.（2010）. Like it! Learn it! Use it? A field study of hotel training. *Cornell Hospitality Quarterly*.

Gagné，M.，& Deci，E. L.（2005）. Self-determination theory and work motivation. *Journal of Organizational behavior*，26（4），331 – 362.

George，J. M.（2007）. Creativity in organizations. *Academy of Management Annals*，1：439 – 477.

George，J. M.，& Zhou，J.（2001）. When openness to experience and conscientiousness are related to creative behavior：an interactional approach.*Journal of applied psychology*，86（3），513.

Gilson，L. L.，& Shalley，C. E.（2004）. A little creativity goes a long way：An examination of teams' engagement in creative processes. *Journal of management*，30（4），453 – 470.

Gilson，L. L.，Mathieu，J. E.，Shalley，C. E.，& Ruddy，T. M.（2005）. Creativity and standardization：complementary or conflicting drivers of team effectiveness? *Academy of Management Journal*，48（3），521 – 531.

Gladwin，T. N.，& Walter，I.（1980）. How multinationals can manage social and political forces. *Journal of Business Strategy*，1（1），54 – 68.

Glick，W. H.（1985）. Conceptualizing and measuring organizational and psychological climate：Pitfalls in multilevel research.*Academy of management review*，10（3），601 – 616.

Gong，Y.，Huang，J. C.，& Farh，J. L.（2009）. Employee learning orientation，transformational leadership，and employee creativity：The mediating role of employee creative self-efficacy. *Academy of management Journal*，52（4），765 – 778.

Graham，H. T.，& Bennett，R.（1998）. Human Resources Management（9th edition）. A Division of Pearson Professional Limited. Pitman Publishing，London.

Greenberger，D. B.，& Strasser，S.（1986）. Development and application of a model of personal control in organizations. *Academy of Management Review*，11（1），164 – 177.

Gröschl, S. (2007). An exploration of HR policies and practices affecting the integration of persons with disabilities in the hotel industry in major Canadian tourism destinations. *International Journal of Hospitality Management*, 26(3), 666 – 686.

Guillet, B. D., Kucukusta, D., & Xiao, Q. (2012). An examination of executive compensation in the restaurant industry. *International Journal of Hospitality Management*, 31(1), 86 – 95.

Gursoy, Maier, & Chi. (2008). Generational differences: An examination of work values and generational gaps in the hospitality workforce. *International Journal of Hospitality Management*, 27(3), 448 – 458.

Hamblin, A. C. (1974). *Evaluation and control of training*, Maidenhead: McGraw-Hill.

Haven-Tang, C., & Jones, E. (2008). Labour market and skills needs of the tourism and related sectors in Wales. *International Journal of Tourism Research*, 10(4), 353 – 363.

Hackman, J. R., & Oldham, G. R. (1980). *Work redesign*.

Hinkin, T. R., & Schriesheim, C. A. (2004). "If You Don't Hear from Me You Know You Are Doing Fine" The Effects of Management Nonresponse to Employee Performance. *Cornell hotel and restaurant administration quarterly*, 45(4), 362 – 372.

Hofstede, G. (1980). Motivation, leadership, and organization: do American theories apply abroad? *Organizational dynamics*, 9(1), 42 – 63.

Hon, A. (2011). Enhancing employee creativity in the Chinese context: The mediating role of employee self – concordance. International Journal of Hospitality Management. 30(2), 375 – 384.

Hon, A. H. (2012a). Shaping Environments Conductive to Creativity the Role of Intrinsic Motivation. *Cornell Hospitality Quarterly*, 53(1), 53 – 64.

Hon, A. H. Y. (2012b). When competency-based pay relates to creative performance: The role of employee psychological need. *International Journal of Hospitality Management*, 31(1), 130 – 138.

Hon, A. (2013). Does job creativity requirement improve service performance? A multilevel analysis of work stress and service environment. International Journal of Hospitality Management, 35, 161 – 170.

Hon, A. H. Y., Bloom, M., & Crant, M. (2014). Overcoming resistance to change and enhancing creative performance. *Journal of Management*, 40(3), 919 – 941.

Hon, A. H. Y. & Chan, W. W. H. (2013a). Empowering leadership and team creative performance: The roles of team self-concordance, team creative efficacy, and team task interdependence. *Cornell Hospitality Quarterly*, 54(2), 199 – 210

Hon, A. H.Y. & Chan, W. W. H. (2013b). The effects of group conflict and work stress on employee performance. *Cornell Hospitality Quarterly*, 54(2), 174 – 184

Hon, A. H. Y., & Leung, A. S. M. (2011). Employee creativity and motivation in the

Chinese context: The moderating role of organizational culture. *Cornell Hospitality Quarterly*, 52(2), 125 - 134.

Hon, A. H., & Lu, L. (2010). The mediating role of trust between expatriate procedural justice and employee outcomes in Chinese hotel industry. *International Journal of Hospitality Management*, 29(4), 669 - 676.

Hon, A. H.Y., & Lu, L.(2013a). Be nice for money or for love? The roles of justice in the Chinese hotel industry. *International Journal of Contemporary Hospitality Management*, 25(6), 883 - 902.

Hon, A. H. Y. & Lu, L.(2015). Are we paid to be creative? The effect of compensation gap on creativity in an expatriate context. *Journal of World Business*, 50(1), 159 - 167.

Hon, Alice H. Y, & Lu, L. (2016). When will the trickle - down effect of abusive supervision be alleviated? The moderating roles of power distance and traditional cultures. Cornell Hospitality Quarterly ,57(4),421 - 433.

Hon, A. H. Y., &Rensvold, R. B.(2006). An interactional perspective on perceived empowerment: The role of personal needs and task context. *The International Journal of Human Resource Management*, 17, 959 - 982.

Houtenville, A., & Kalargyrou, V. (2012). People with disabilities employers' perspectives on recruitment practices, strategies, and challenges in leisure and hospitality. *Cornell Hospitality Quarterly*, 53(1), 40 - 52.

Hurrell, S. A., & Scholarios, D.(2014). "The People Make the Brand" Reducing Social Skills Gaps Through Person-Brand Fit and Human Resource Management Practices. *Journal of Service Research*, 17(1), 54 - 67.

Hsieh, Y. C.(2012). Hotel companies' environmental policies and practices: a content analysis of their web pages. *International Journal of Contemporary Hospitality Management*, 24(1), 97 - 121.

Jasper, C. R., &Waldhart, P.(2013). Employer attitudes on hiring employees with disabilities in the leisure and hospitality industry: Practical and theoretical implications. *International Journal of Contemporary Hospitality Management*, 25(4), 577 - 594.

Janssen, O., Van deVliert, E., & West, M.(2004). The bright and dark sides of individual and group innovation: A special issue introduction. *Journal of Organizational Behavior*, 25(2), 129 - 145.

Jex, S. M., Bliese, P. D., Buzzell, S., & Primeau, J.(2001). The impact of self-efficacy on stressor-strain relations: Coping style as an explanatory mechanism. *Journal of applied psychology*, 86(3), 401.

Kabanoff, B. (1991). Equity, equality, power, and conflict. *Academy of Management Review*, 16(2), 416 - 441.

Kalargyrou, V., & Woods, R. H. (2011). Identifying Training Challenges in Hospitality Industry: An Exploratory Approach. *Hospitality Review*, 29(1), 1.

Kalargyrou, V., & Woods, R. H.(2011). Wanted: training competencies for the twenty-first century. *International Journal of Contemporary Hospitality Management*, 23 (3), 361 – 376.

Kanter, R.(1985). Managing the Human Side of Change: Making Employees Feel Good about Change Is a Challenge for Today's Managers. *Management Review*, 74(4), 52.

Karatepe, O. M. (2011). Do job resources moderate the effect of emotional dissonance on burnout? A study in the city of Ankara, Turkey. *International Journal of Contemporary Hospitality Management*, 23(1), 44 – 65.

Karatepe, O. M., & Demir, E.(2014). Linking core self-evaluations and work engagement to work-family facilitation: a study in the hotel industry. *International Journal of Contemporary Hospitality Management*, 26(2), 307 – 323.

Karatepe, O. M., Keshavarz, S., & Nejati, S.(2010). Do core self-evaluations mediate the effect of coworker support on work engagement? A study of hotel employees in Iran. *Journal of Hospitality and Tourism Management*, 17(01), 62 – 71.

Kim, T. Y., Hon, A. H. Y. & Crant, M (2009). Proactive personality, career satisfaction, and perceived insider status: The mediating roles of employee creativity. *Journal of Business and Psychology*, 24, 93 – 103.

Kim, T. Y., Hon, A. H. Y. & Lee, D. R(2010). Proactive personality and employee creativity: The effects of job creativity requirement and supervisor support for creativity. *Creativity Research Journal*, 22, 37 – 45.

Kim, W. G., & Brymer, R. A.(2011). The effects of ethical leadership on manager job satisfaction, commitment, behavioral outcomes, and firm performance. *International Journal of Hospitality Management*, 30(4), 1020 – 1026.

Kim, T. G., Lee, J. H., & Law, R.(2008). An empirical examination of the acceptance behaviour of hotel front office systems: An extended technology acceptance model. *Tourism management*, 29(3), 500 – 513.

Kline, S., & Hsieh, Y. C. J.(2007). Wage differentials in the lodging industry: A case study. *Journal of Human Resources in Hospitality & Tourism*, 6(1), 69 – 84.

Kirkman, B. L., & Shapiro, D. L.(1997). The impact of cultural values on employee resistance to teams: Toward a model of globalized self-managing work team effectiveness. *Academy of Management Review*, 22(3), 730 – 757.

Kirton, M.(1980). Adaptors and innovators in organizations. *Human Relations*, 33 (4), 213 – 224.

Kochanski, J.(1997). Competency-based management. *Training & Development*, 51 (10), 40 – 45.

Kochanski, J. T., & Risher, H. (1999). Paying for competencies: rewarding knowledge, skills and behaviors. *Aligning Pay and Results: Compensation Strategies that Work from the Boardroom to the Shop Floor. American Management Association*.

Lawler, E. E., & McDermott, M. (2003). Current performance management practices—Examining the varying impacts. *World at Work Journal*, 12(2), 49 – 60.

Ledford, G. E.(1995). Paying for the skills, knowledge, and competencies of knowledge workers. *Compensation & Benefits Review*, 27(4), 55 – 62.

Lema, J. D., &Agrusa, J.(2009). Relationship of WWW usage and employee learning in the casino industry. *International Journal of Hospitality Management*, 28(1), 18 – 25.

Leong, F. T., & Chang, W. C.(2003). Guest Editors' Introduction: Traditionality/Modernity as a psychological construct: Current research and future directions. *Asian Journal of Social Psychology*, 6(1), 1 – 4.

LePine, J. A., Podsakoff, N. P., & LePine, M. A.(2005). A meta-analytic test of the challenge stressor-hindrance stressor framework: An explanation for inconsistent relationships among stressors and performance. *Academy of Management Journal*, 48(5), 764 – 775.

Leung, K., Wang, Z., & Hon, A. H.(2011). Moderating effects on the compensation gap between locals and expatriates in China: A multi-level analysis.*Journal of International Management*, 17(1), 54 – 67.

Li, A., & Cropanzano, R.(2009). Do East Asians Respond More/Less Strongly to Organizational Justice Than North Americans? A Meta-Analysis. Journal of Management Studies, 46(5), 787 – 805.

Luo, Y.(2001). Dynamic capabilities in international expansion. *Journal of World Business*, 35(4), 355 – 378.

Madera, J. M.(2012). Using social networking websites as a selection tool: The role of selection process fairness and job pursuit intentions. International Journal of Hospitality Management, 31(4), 1276 – 1282.

Madera, J. M., Neal, J. A., & Dawson, M.(2011). A strategy for diversity training focusing on empathy in the workplace. *Journal of Hospitality & Tourism Research*, 35(4), 469 – 487.

Magnini, V. P.(2009). An exploratory investigation of the real-time training modes used by hotel expatriates. *International Journal of Hospitality Management*, 28(4), 513 – 518.

Magnini, V. P., & Honeycutt, E. D.(2005). Face Recognition and Name Recall Training Implications for the Hospitality Industry. *Cornell Hotel and Restaurant Administration Quarterly*, 46(1), 69 – 78.

Marco-Lajara, B., & Úbeda-García, M.(2013). Human resource management approaches in Spanish hotels: An introductory analysis. *International Journal of Hospitality Management*, 35, 339 – 347.

Martin, J. E., & Peterson, M. M.(1987). Two-tier wage structures: Implications for equity theory.*Academy of Management Journal*, 30(2), 297 – 315.

Millar, M.(2010). Internet recruiting in the cruise industry. *Journal of Human Resources in Hospitality & Tourism*, 9(1), 17 – 32.

Masterson, S. S., Lewis, K., Goldman, B. M., & Taylor, M. S.(2000). Integrating justice and social exchange: The differing effects of fair procedures and treatment on work relationships. *Academy of Management journal*, 43(4), 738 – 748.

McClelland, D.(1961).*The achieving society*. Van Nostrand.

McClelland, D. C.(1985).*Human motivation*. Glenview, IL: Scott, Foresman

McQuilken, L., McDonald, H., & Vocino, A.(2013). Is guarantee compensation enough? The important role of fix and employee effort in restoring justice. *International Journal of Hospitality Management*, 33, 41 – 50.

Milkovich, G. T., Newman, J. M., & Milkovich, C.(1999). *Compensation*. T. Mirror(Ed.). Burr Ridge, Ill.: Irwin/McGraw-Hill.

Miller, B.(2010). Compensation practices in restaurants and the impact on service quality. *Journal of Foodservice Business Research*, 13(1), 24 – 35.

Muller, D., Judd, C. M., &Yzerbyt, V. Y.(2005). When moderation is mediated and mediation is moderated. *Journal of personality and social psychology*, 89(6), 852.

Moncraz, E., Zhao, J., & Kay, C.(2009). An exploratory study of US lodging properties' organizational practices on employee turnover and retention. International Journal of Contemporary Hospitality Management, 21(4), 437 – 458.

Moorman, R. H. (1991). Relationship between organizational justice and organizational citizenship behaviors: Do fairness perceptions influence employee citizenship? *Journal of applied psychology*, 76(6), 845.

Murphy, K. S., & DiPietro, R. B.(2005). Management compensation as a value-added competitive method for casual theme restaurants. *Hospitality Review*, 23(2), 4.

Murphy, K. S., DiPietro, R. B., Kock, G., & Lee, J. S.(2011). Does mandatory food safety training and certification for restaurant employees improve inspection outcomes? *International Journal of Hospitality Management*, 30(1), 150 – 156.

Namasivayam, K., Miao, L., & Zhao, X. (2007). An investigation of the relationships between compensation practices and firm performance in the US hotel industry. *International Journal of Hospitality Management*, 26(3), 574 – 587.

Nestel, D., Cooper, S., Bryant, M., Higgins, V., Tabak, D., Murtagh, G., & Barraclough, B. (2011). Communication challenges in surgical oncology. *Surgical oncology*, 20(3), 155 – 161.

Newman, B., & Newman, Philip R. (2014). *Development through life: A psychosocial approach*(Twelfth walshed.). Stamford, CT: Cengage Learning.

Noone, B. M.(2008). Customer perceived control and the moderating effect of restaurant type on evaluations of restaurant employee performance. *International Journal of Hospitality Management*, 27(1), 23 – 29.

Oldham, G. R., & Cummings, A. (1996). Employee creativity: Personal and contextual factors at work.*Academy of management journal*, 39(3), 607 – 634.

O'Reilly, C. A., Chatman, J., & Caldwell, D. F.(1991). People and organizational culture: A profile comparison approach to assessing person-organization fit. *Academy of management journal*, 34(3), 487 – 516.

Patiar, A., & Mia, L.(2008). The interactive effect of market competition and use of MAS information on performance: Evidence from the upscale hotels. *Journal of Hospitality & Tourism Research*.

Perron, G. M., Côté, R. P., &Duffy, J. F. (2006). Improving environmental awareness training in business. *Journal of Cleaner Production*, 14(6), 551 – 562.

Pfeffer, J., & Baron, N. (1988). Taking the workers back out. *Research in organizational behavior*, 10, 257 – 303.

Podsakoff, N. P., LePine, J. A., & LePine, M. A.(2007). Differential challenge stressor-hindrance stressor relationships with job attitudes, turnover intentions, turnover, and withdrawal behavior: a meta-analysis. Journal of applied psychology, 92 (2), 438.

Podsakoff, P. M., MacKenzie, S. B., Moorman, R. H., & Fetter, R. (1990). Transformational leader behaviors and their effects on followers' trust in leader, satisfaction, and organizational citizenship behaviors. *The leadership quarterly*, 1(2), 107 – 142.

Revilla, G., Dodd, T. H., & Hoover, L. C.(2001). Environmental tactics used by hotel companies in Mexico. *International Journal of Hospitality & Tourism Administration*, 1(3 – 4), 111 – 127.

Redmond, M. V., & Bunyi, J. M. (1993). The relationship of intercultural communication competence with stress and the handling of stress as reported by international students. *International Journal of Intercultural Relations*, 17 (2), 235 – 254.

Richard E. Boyatzis. (1982). *The competent manager: A model for effective performance*. John Wiley & Sons.

Robbins, S. P.(1974).*Managing organizational conflict: A nontraditional approach*. NJ, Prentice-Hall.

Roberts, K. R., & Barrett, B. B.(2011). Restaurant managers' beliefs about food safety training: An application of the Theory of Planned Behavior.*Journal of Foodservice Business Research*, 14(3), 206 – 225.

Rupp, D. E., & Cropanzano, R.(2002). The mediating effects of social exchange relationships in predicting workplace outcomes from multifoci organizational justice. *Organizational Behavior and Human Decision Processes*, 89(1), 925 – 946.

Schneider, B., Salvaggio, A. N., & Subirats, M.(2002). Climate strength: a new direction for climate research. *Journal of Applied Psychology*, 87(2), 220.

Schwartz, S. H. (1992). Universals in the content and structure of values: Theoretical advances and empirical tests in 20 countries.*Advances in experimental social psychology*, 25(1), 1 – 65.

Schulz-Hardt, S., Jochims, M., & Frey, D. (2002). Productive conflict in group decision making: Genuine and contrived dissent as strategies to counteract biased information seeking. *Organizational Behavior and Human Decision Processes*, 88(2), 563 – 586.

Scott, S. G., & Bruce, R. A.(1994). Determinants of innovative behavior: A path model of individual innovation in the workplace. *Academy of management journal*, 37(3), 580 – 607.

Seibert, S., Crant, J., Kraimer, M., & Murphy, Kevin R.(1999). Proactive Personality and Career Success.*Journal of Applied Psychology*, 84(3), 416 – 427.

Seibert, S. E., Wang, G., & Courtright, S. H.(2011). Antecedents and consequences of psychological and team empowerment in organizations: a meta-analytic review. *Journal of Applied Psychology*, 96(5), 981.

Shalley, C. E., Zhou, J., & Oldham, G. R.(2004). The effects of personal and contextual characteristics on creativity: where should we go from here? *Journal of management*, 30(6), 933 – 958.

Sheldon, K. M., & Elliot, A. J.(1998). Not all personal goals are personal: Comparing autonomous and controlled reasons for goals as predictors of effort and attainment.*Personality and Social Psychology Bulletin*, 24(5), 546 – 557.

Sheldon, K. M., & Elliot, A. J.(1999). Goal striving, need satisfaction, and longitudinal well-being: the self-concordance model.*Journal of personality and social psychology*, 76(3), 482.

Sheldon, K. M., Turban, D. B., Brown, K. G., Barrick, M. R., & Judge, T. A.(2003). Applying self-determination theory to organizational research. *Research in personnel and human resources management*, 22, 357 – 394.

Sheldon, K. M., & Houser-Marko, L.(2001). Self-concordance, goal attainment, and the pursuit of happiness: Can there be an upward spiral? *Journal of personality and social psychology*, 80(1), 152.

Shin, S. J., & Zhou, J.(2007). When is educational specialization heterogeneity related to creativity in research and development teams? Transformational leadership as a moderator.*Journal of applied Psychology*, 92(6), 1709.

Simons, T. L., & Peterson, R. S.(2000). Task conflict and relationship conflict in top management teams: the pivotal role of intragroup trust. *Journal of applied psychology*, 85(1), 102.

Sobaih, A. E. E.(2011). Half Job—Half Training? Management Perceptions of Part-time Employee Training in the Hospitality Industry. *Journal of Human Resources in Hospitality & Tourism*, 10(4), 400 – 420.

Stamper, C. L., & Dyne, L. V.(2001). Work status and organizational citizenship behavior: A field study of restaurant employees.*Journal of Organizational Behavior*, 22(5), 517 – 536.

Stamper, C. L., & Masterson, S. S.(2002). Insider or outsider? How employee perceptions of insider status affect their work behavior. *Journal of Organizational behavior*, 23(8), 875 – 894.

Sharma, A., & Christie, I. T.(2010). Performance assessment using value-chain analysis in Mozambique. *International Journal of Contemporary Hospitality Management*, 22(3), 282 – 299.

Stahl, M. J., &Harrell, A. M.(1982). Evolution and validation of a behavioral decision theory measurement approach to achievement, power, and affiliation. *Journal of Applied Psychology*, 67(6), 744.

Sturman, M.C. and McCabe, D.(2008). Choosing whether to lead, lag, or match the market: developing a competitive pay strategy for a new restaurant. *Journal of Human Resources in Hospitality and Tourism*, 7(1), 85 – 97.

Sturman, M. C., & Sherwyn, D.(2009). The Utility of Integrity Testing for Controlling Workers' Compensation Costs. *Cornell Hospitality Quarterly*.

Srivastava, A., Bartol, K. M., & Locke, E. A.(2006). Empowering leadership in management teams: Effects on knowledge sharing, efficacy, and performance. *Academy of management journal*, 49(6), 1239 – 1251.

Sun, K. A., & Kim, D. Y.(2013). Does customer satisfaction increase firm performance? An application of American Customer Satisfaction Index (ACSI). *International Journal of Hospitality Management*, 35, 68 – 77.

Testa, M. R., & Sipe, L.(2012). Service-leadership competencies for hospitality and tourism management. *International journal of hospitality management*, 31(3), 648 – 658.

Tews, M. J., Stafford, K., & Tracey, J. B.(2011). What matters most? The perceived importance of ability and personality for hiring decisions. *Cornell Hospitality Quarterly*, 52(2), 94 – 101.

Tews, M. J., & Tracey, J. B.(2009). Helping Managers Help Themselves: The Use and Utility of On-the-Job Interventions to Improve the Impact of Interpersonal Skills Training. *Cornell Hospitality Quarterly*, 50(2), 245 – 258.

Tierney, P.(2008). Leadership and Employee Creativity in Handbook of Organizational Creativity. *Leadership and Employee Creativity in Handbook of Organizational Creativity*, J. Zhou and C. Shalley, Eds. United States: Lawrence Erlbaum Associates.

Tierney, P., & Farmer, S. M.(2011). Creative self-efficacy development and creative performance over time. *Journal of Applied Psychology*, 96(2), 277.

Tjosvold, D.(2008). Conflicts in the study of conflict in organizations. In Dreu, C., & Gelfand, Michele J. *The psychology of conflict and conflict management in organizations*(The organizational frontiers series). New York, N.Y: Lawrence Erlbaum Associates.

Toh, S. M., & Denisi, A. S.(2003). Host country national reactions to expatriate pay policies: A model and implications. *Academy of Management Review*, 28(4), 606 – 621.

Toh, S. M., & Denisi, A. S.(2007). Host country nationals as socializing agents: A social identity approach. *Journal of Organizational Behavior*, 28(3), 281.

Torres, E., & Adler, H.(2010). Effects of Management-Development Practices on Hospitality Management Graduates' Job Satisfaction and Intention to Stay. *Hospitality Review*, 28(2), 4.

Torres, E., & Adler, H.(2012). Hotel compensation strategies: Perceptions of top industry executives. *Journal of Human Resources in Hospitality & Tourism*, 11(1), 52 – 71.

Tracey, J. B. (2014). A review of human resources management research. International Journal of Contemporary Hospitality Management, 26(5), 679 – 705.

Tracey, J. B., Sturman, M. C., & Tews, M. J.(2007). Ability versus personality factors that predict employee job performance. *Cornell Hotel and Restaurant Administration Quarterly*, 48(3), 313 – 322.

Triandis, H. C.(1989). A strategy for cross-cultural research in social psychology. *Recent advances in social psychology: An international perspective*, 491 – 499.

Úbeda-García, M., Marco-Lajara, B., García-Lillo, F., & Sabater-Sempere, V. (2013). Universalistic and Contingent perspectives on human resource management: an empirical study of the Spanish hotel industry. *Journal of Human Resources in Hospitality & Tourism*, 12(1), 26 – 51.

Velasquez, M. G.(2002). Business ethics(5th edition). Upper Saddle River, N. J.: Prentice Hall.

Wallach, E.J.(1983). Individuals and Organizations: The Cultural Match.*Training & Development Journal*, 37, 29 – 30.

Wagner, R. K., & Sternberg, R. J.(1991). Tacit knowledge: Its uses in identifying, assessing, and developing managerial talent. *Applying psychology in business: The manager's handbook*, 333 – 344.

Wall, J. A., & Callister, R. R.(1995). Conflict and its management. *Journal of management*, 21(3), 515 – 558.

Walsh, K., & Taylor, M. S.(2007). Developing in-house careers and retaining management talent what hospitality professionals want from their jobs. *Cornell Hotel and Restaurant Administration Quarterly*, 48(2), 163 – 182.

Watkins, J.(2003). Stress-busters.*People Management*, 9, 12 – 13.

Way, S.A., Tracey, J.B., Fay, C.H., Wright, P., Snell, S.A., Chang, S. and Gong, Y.(2015).Validation of a multi-dimensional HR flexibility measure. *Journal of Management*, 41(4), 1098 – 1131.

Wayne, S.J., Shore, L. M., & Liden, R. C.(1997). Perceived organizational support and leader-member exchange: A social exchange perspective. *Academy of Management journal*, 40(1), 82 – 111.

West, M. A., &Farr, J. L.(1989). Innovation at work: Psychological perspectives. *Social Behaviour*, 4, 15 – 30.

Wu, M., Huang, X., Li, C., & Liu, W.(2012). Perceived Interactional Justice and

Trust-in-supervisor as Mediators for Paternalistic Leadership. Management and Organization Review, 8(1), 97 – 121.

Wu, X., Sturman, M. C., & Wang, C.(2013). The motivational effects of pay fairness a longitudinal study in Chinese star-level hotels. *Cornell Hospitality Quarterly*, 54(2), 185 – 198.

Wu, X., & Wang, C.(2008). The impact of organizational justice on employees' pay satisfaction, work attitudes and performance in Chinese hotels. *Journal of Human Resources in Hospitality & Tourism*, 7(2), 181 – 195.

Yang, K. S.(1998). Chinese responses to modernization: A psychological analysis. *Asian Journal of Social Psychology*, 1(1), 75 – 97.

Yang, K. S.(1993).Chinese social orientation: An integrative analysis. In Cheng, L., Cheung, Fanny M, & Chen, Char-nie. *Psychotherapy for the Chinese : Selected papers from the first international conference*, 9 – 11 November, 1992. Hong Kong: Dept. of Psychiatry, Chinese University of Hong Kong.

Yang, K. S., Yu, A. B., & Yeh, M. J.(1991). The individual traditionality and modernity of Chinese people: Concepts and measurements. *The psychology and behavior of Chinese people*, 241 – 306.

Yen, C. L., Murrmann, S. K., & Murrmann, K. F.(2011). The influence of context orientation on job seeker perceptions of recruitment, person-organization fit, and job application intention in the hospitality industry. *Journal of Human Resources in Hospitality & Tourism*, 10(3), 315 – 330.

Zakrzewski, C., Feinstein, A. H., & Sammons, G.(2005). A new approach to CAI: Online applications for procedural based activities. *Journal of Hospitality & Tourism Education*, 17(1), 48 – 55.

Zelenskaya, K., & Singh, N.(2011). Exploring virtual recruiting from employers' perspective using "SL". *Journal of Human Resources in Hospitality and Tourism*, 10, 117 – 128.

Zhang, X., & Bartol, K. M.(2010). Linking empowering leadership and employee creativity: The influence of psychological empowerment, intrinsic motivation, and creative process engagement. *Academy of management journal*, 53(1), 107 – 128.

Zhang, X. G., Zheng, X., & Wang, L.(2003). Comparative research on individual modernity of adolescents between town and countryside in China.*Asian Journal of Social Psychology*, 6(1), 61 – 73.

Zhang, H. Q., & Wu, E.(2004). Human resources issues facing the hotel and travel industry in China. *International Journal of Contemporary Hospitality Management*, 16(7), 424 – 428.

Zhao, X., & Namasivayam, K.(2009). Posttraining self-efficacy, job involvement, and training effectiveness in the hospitality industry. *Journal of Human Resources in Hospitality & Tourism*, 8(2), 137 – 152.

Zhou，J.，& Shalley，C. E.(2008). Expanding the scope and impact of organizational creativity research. In *Handbook of organizational creativity*，edited by J. Zhou and C. E. Shalley，347 - 68. New York：Lawrence Erlbaum.

Zohar，D.，& Luria，G.（2004）. Climate as a social-cognitive construction of supervisory safety practices：scripts as proxy of behavior patterns. *Journal of applied psychology*，89(2)，322 - 333.

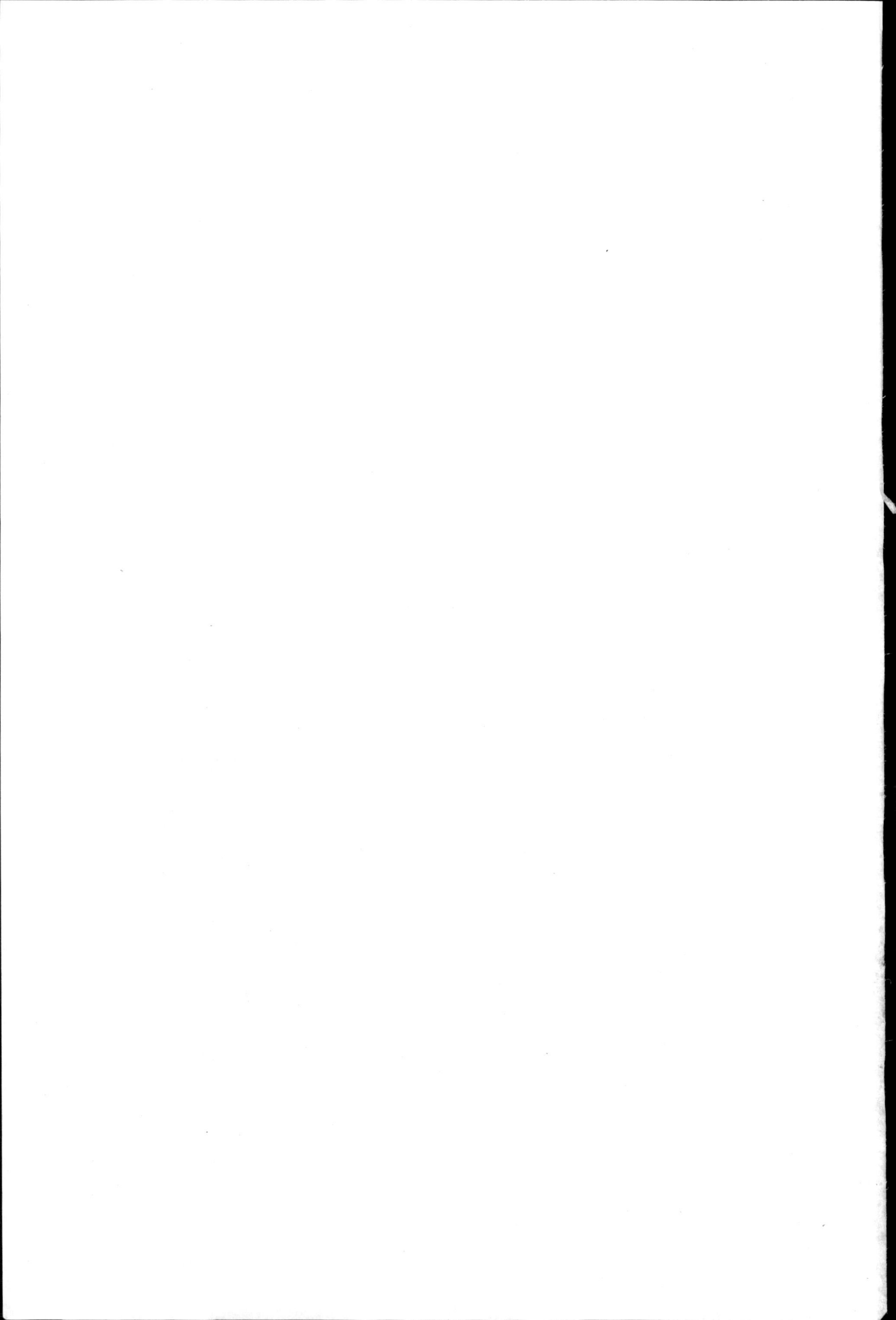